The English Wool Trade in the Middle Ages

The English Wool Trade
in the Middle Ages

T. H. LLOYD

LECTURER IN ECONOMIC HISTORY
UNIVERSITY COLLEGE OF SWANSEA

CAMBRIDGE UNIVERSITY PRESS

CAMBRIDGE

LONDON · NEW YORK · MELBOURNE

CAMBRIDGE UNIVERSITY PRESS
Cambridge, New York, Melbourne, Madrid, Cape Town, Singapore, São Paulo

Cambridge University Press
The Edinburgh Building, Cambridge CB2 2RU, UK

Published in the United States of America by Cambridge University Press, New York

www.cambridge.org
Information on this title: www.cambridge.org/9780521212397

First published 1977
This digitally printed first paperback version 2005

A catalogue record for this publication is available from the British Library

Library of Congress Cataloguing in Publication data
Lloyd, Terence H
The English wool trade in the Middle Ages.
Bibliography: p.
Includes index.
1. Wool trade and industry—England—History.
2. England—Civilization—Medieval period, 1066–1485. I.Title.
HD9901.5.L55   382′.45′677310942   76–11086

ISBN-13 978-0-521-21239-7 hardback
ISBN-10 0-521-21239-1 hardback

ISBN-13 978-0-521-01721-3 paperback
ISBN-10 0-521-01721-1 paperback

TO NESTA
WHO COUNTED MANY SHEEP
AND MUCH WOOL

Contents

Tables

Maps

Preface

The importance of the wool trade in English history was clearly recognised by the first generation of native economic historians in the late nineteenth century. The index of the medieval volume of W. Cunningham's *The Growth of English Industry and Commerce*, for example, lists no fewer than 41 entries under the heading 'wool' and 19 under 'staple'. Despite certain changes in interpretation, Cunningham's work, like that of his great contemporary, J. E. Thorold Rogers, may still be read with far less consciousness of its being 'dated' than is experienced in reading most of the political histories written in that period. With economic history established as a discipline the wool trade did not wait long for researchers who singled it out for special treatment. R. J. Whitwell's 'English Monasteries and the Wool Trade in the Thirteenth Century' (1904) remains a classic, although, like other notable pieces of English scholarship of the early twentieth century, it appeared in a German publication. Some other specialist works of the same period are best passed over in silence, but mention must be made of the study by Adolf Schaube (1908). Although not without its limitations, Schaube's article has been used, or at least acknowledged, by every succeeding generation of historians.

The period of the First World War saw a stream of valuable studies by A. E. Bland, J. C. Davies, D. Hughes, S. B. Terry, T. F. Tout and G. Unwin and his pupils, all of whom, however, were concerned primarily with the role of the wool trade as a mainstay of royal finance. The inter-war years were dominated, of course, by the figure of Eileen Power, who broadened the field of study by dealing with the trade as a commercial activity. Although most of her published work was restricted to the fifteenth century, her Ford Lectures, issued posthumously as *The Wool Trade in English Medieval History*, has remained the only monograph devoted to the wool trade in general.

Immediately after the Second World War E. B. Fryde devoted a doctoral thesis to a re-examination of the wool trade in the early war finance of Edward III, much of which has subsequently been published in various articles. After this, new research into the wool trade tended to flag, although mention must be made of R. L. Baker's work on the early customs and the publication by E. M. Carus-Wilson and O. Coleman of the wool export figures in *England's Export Trade, 1275–1547* (1963). Although most of the figures had already been published in various places they have been utilised far more by historians in their new form.

The present book was originally planned as a comprehensive study of the wool trade, incorporating new research as well as synthesising earlier knowledge. Unfortunately the harsh economic realities of present-day publishing have necessarily restricted its scope and certain topics, including sheep farming and the relationship between the wool trade and the shipping industry, have had to be excluded entirely, while others have been discussed in less detail than might seem desirable. The work of selection was influenced by knowledge of the fact that another scholar had impending a detailed study of the wool trade in the age of the Celys. There appeared to be little need, therefore, for the present writer to attempt to expand the commercial picture of the fifteenth century drawn by Eileen Power, since this enabled more space to be devoted to the marketing of wool in the early middle ages. Two important books, by G. L. Harris and G. Holmes, appeared only after the present work was completed and had been sent to the publisher. The former is particularly important since it proposes a major revision of Bertie Wilkinson's ideas, which have stood unchallenged for forty years, about parliamentary control of the wool subsidy. Although the present writer does not regard the new thesis as beyond dispute no revision of his own text could do justice to the ideas of any parties involved in the dispute and the matter has had to be passed over in silence.

In conclusion I would like to thank Professor R. H. Hilton, who read this book in manuscript, and Mrs J. Davies and Mrs J. Evans, who typed it.

Abbreviations used
in Notes and Bibliography

CCR	*Close Rolls* (1227–72) and *Calendars of Close Rolls.*
CChR	*Calendar of Charter Rolls.*
CFR	*Calendars of Fine Rolls.*
CPMR	*Calendars of Plea and Memoranda Rolls (London).*
CPR	*Patent Rolls* (1216–32) and *Calendars of Patent Rolls.*
EcHR	*Economic History Review.*
EHR	*English Historical Review.*
Foedera	*Foedera, Conventiones, Litterae* (T. Rymer).
Letter Books	*Letter Books of the City of London.*
POPC	*Proceedings and Ordinances of the Privy Council.*
PR	*Pipe Rolls* (Editions of the Pipe Roll Society).
Rev. Belge.	*Revue Belge de Philologie et d'Histoire.*
Rot. Parl.	*Rotuli Parliamentorum.*
Rot. Litt. Claus.	*Rotuli Litterarum Clausarum.*
Rot. Litt. Pat.	*Rotuli Litterarum Patentium.*
Statutes	*Statutes of the Realm.*
TRHS	*Transactions of the Royal Historical Society.*
VJSSWG	*Vierteljahrschrift für Sozial-und-Wirtsschafts-geschichte.*

I

The growth of the Flemish connection

In 1297, at the height of a constitutional crisis, the English barons advanced the claim that nearly half their country's wealth derived from wool.[1] Although in one sense an exaggeration, in another this statement is less than the truth for, although wool cannot have made up anything like half the gross national product, it contributed nearly all the country's export earnings. Yet while the wool trade was then the most important branch of English commerce it was not necessarily the oldest, for woollen cloth was sent abroad long before there is evidence of the export of raw wool. The medieval export trade may be represented, perhaps, as a cycle in which the earliest and latest periods were distinguished by manufactured woollen cloth, the volume in the last being vastly greater than in the first, while intermediate stages in the cycle saw the growth and the decline of the wool trade. During the first half of the eighth century gifts of cloaks were sent to English missionaries on the continent and, although this can hardly be described as commerce, Charlemagne's letter to Offa of Mercia later in the same century, complaining about English cloaks and requesting that they should be made as of old, suggests a trade of some standing. There is a possibility that English cloth went into the famous 'Frisian cloaks' which had wide currency at that time, and by the ninth and tenth centuries the fame of the English product had reached the Arab world.[2] While references of this nature do not prove the existence of an industry geared to an export market they presuppose one able to produce a surplus above purely local needs. Unless the organisation of this industry was so rudimentary that each family merely worked up the fleeces of its own sheep there was of necessity some marketing of wool, although little evidence of such a traffic has survived.[3] A clause in Edgar's Andover code (959–63) apparently sought to fix the price of wool, but it is not clear whether this was intended to be the minimum or the maximum: 'And a wey of wool shall be sold for half a pound (120 pence), and no-one shall sell it for less (or more).'[4]

When raw wool began to be exported is an open question and will always remain so. Many writers have stated their belief that the trade was firmly established before the Norman conquest, but there is no proof of this.[5] The only evidence suggestive of a pre-Conquest export trade does not bear close scrutiny. It is a clause in a list of tolls exacted at Billingsgate, London (991–1002) which apparently grants permission to subjects of the Emperor to buy wool: *Praeter discarcatam lanam et dissutum unctum, et tres porcos vivos licebat eis emere in naves suas.* Besides wool, which had been unloaded, and melted fat, they were also permitted to buy three live pigs for their ships.[6] Robertson glosses *discarcatam lanam* as wool which is offered for sale by retail, but surely the very word *lanam* is suspect? Wool seems a rather unlikely commodity to have been bought by export merchants through retail outlets. More importantly what is wool doing in this place at all? The tenor of the clause appears to be that the merchants have been granted the privilege of buying limited quantities of certain goods for their own immediate use; by implication they are not to engross the market and take these things abroad for this would make life difficult for the citizens. If we reject wool what article which might be bought by retail should we put in its place? In a trinity which includes melted fat and live pigs the obvious choice is pork or bacon and therefore it is suggested that *lanam* may be a corruption of *lardam* or *lardum*, the latter having a known use in the middle ages as a synonym of *bacon* and *porcum salsatum.*[7]

The foundation and growth of an export trade in wool depended directly on the growth of the cloth industry in Flanders and although this was certainly in existence at the beginning of the eleventh century it did not as yet need English wool, for in its early days it was self-sufficient in all manner of raw materials.[8] The classic thesis of the Flemish cloth industry, established by Pirenne and his followers, states that at a comparatively early date local supplies of wool became insufficient both in quality and quantity for the needs of industry, which thus became dependent upon English wool until, in the later middle ages, it turned to Spanish imports. A later generation of scholars, however, reacted strongly against the suggestion that indigenous wool played little or no part in the economy of the matured Flemish cloth industry.[9] They have shown that native wool was by no means despised and neglected by the manufacturers and that English exports were probably insufficient to meet all the needs of the Low Countries. While accepting these revisions one must exercise care to ensure that the pendulum does not swing too far in the opposite direction. It would be dangerous to underrate the importance of the Anglo-Flemish connection forged by the wool trade. For at least two centuries the economy of the two countries was interdependent.

According to the classic thesis the Flemish cloth industry was based initially in the countryside or in the cloister and was inevitably simple in structure and small in scale. It has been argued that in such an environment there was at that time no scope for large-scale industry, for until the mid-twelfth century merchants, suppliers of the essential entrepreneurial element, were illiterate and so incapable of exercising control over a scattered industry.[10] A prerequisite of the 'great industry' of Flanders was an urban society in which industrial production could be concentrated and easily controlled. The urban infrastructure began to be established at an early date and at the very time that the Normans were conquering England the last considerable gap in the network of towns was being filled. This void was in the barren interior of Flanders which, lacking roads and settlements, separated the maritime towns from those of the Scheldt valley and made communication between the two groups difficult. The deficiency was made good by deliberate comital policy from the reign of Baldwin V (1037–67) onwards. Between the middle and the end of the eleventh century this

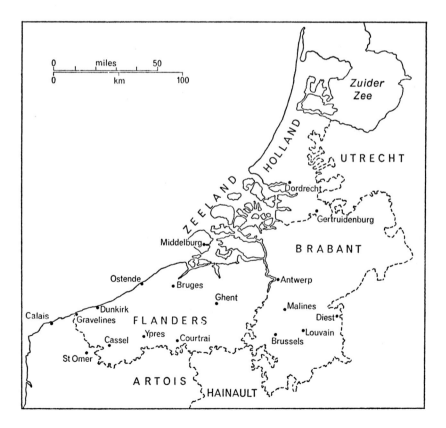

region saw the appearance of the towns of Lille, Messines, Ypres, Thourout, Aire and Cassel. Once established they made rapid economic progress, largely as a result of the favour of successive counts, which was expressed particularly in the granting of fair rights. The fairs of Thourout, Ypres, Messines and Lille, four of the five great *frankes fiestes de Flandre*, were all established by 1127 at the latest.[11] The towns of central Flanders were among the most flourishing centres of the cloth industry in the twelfth and thirteenth centuries.

Pirenne believed that true towns grew up only as merchants established settlements in which they resided and stored their wares between journeys. The towns expanded with the immigration of artisans who found employment both in supplying the personal needs of the merchants and in providing them with trade goods. Ch. Verlinden, however, reverses the sequence of events, saying 'Le commerce y est ne de l'industrie et non le contraire.'[12] For him the town had its point of departure when groups of artisans, above all groups of cloth workers, were to be found plying their crafts in close proximity. The artisans provided the focal point to which the merchants flocked. According to this thesis a cluster of cloth workers might antedate a town and provide a nucleus for urban growth.

Once the Flemish industry came to need English wool it would have had little difficulty in satisfying its demand, for although in the dark ages Flanders had been commercially backward compared with the regions to the north and the south by the beginning of the eleventh century it had established trade links with England.[13] This relationship was not permanently damaged by the Norman conquest of the island; on the contrary it was probably strengthened, for Flemish knights played an important part in the Conquest and afterwards were rewarded with grants of land. At the time of the Domesday Survey Flemings were particularly well-established, both as tenants in chief and as mesne tenants, in the eastern counties, including the important wool-producing areas of Holderness, Lincolnshire and Northamptonshire.[14] In the absence of direct evidence it would be unwise to suggest that Flemish ownership of English manors necessarily stimulated the export of wool, but it would be equally foolish to deny that such connections might be valuable to any Flemish merchant disposed to venture here in search of wool.

The location or relocation of the Flemish cloth industry in an urban setting did not necessarily bring about an immediate dependence upon English wool, for at first local supplies may have continued to suffice. The stage at which it became desirable to supplement these with imports was reached when the cloth industry became geared to an export market. It was not merely that more wool was needed, it had also to be of a higher quality, for if merchants were to go to the trouble of exporting cloth over a great distance then they had to have a high quality product. Poor and middling cloth could not have borne the costs of transportation and still have competed in price with a similar cloth or with a substitute made nearer at hand. Since English wool was superior to the home-grown variety it came to be preferred in the manufacture of fine cloth. But when did this happen? A sure sign of confidence in the quality of one's wares is the decision to market them under a brand name so that the customer may place a repeat order if he is satisfied. In the case of medieval cloth this meant selling it as the product of a given town, 'cloth of Ypres', 'cloth of Arras' and so forth. This stage had been reached by the 1180s at latest for from that time onwards we find named cloths from Flanders and northern France being sold throughout the Mediterranean and the Levant. The export trade itself was undoubtedly older than this for Italian merchants were in northern France and the Low Countries by the end of the eleventh century, while northern merchants were themselves frequenting the Champagne fairs before the middle of the twelfth century and shortly afterwards they advanced as far as Genoa.[15]

Although the Flemings may have been attracted to England in the first instance by the quality of the wool its very abundance soon became a virtue. Nor must one overlook the wools of Wales, Ireland and Scotland which although poorer than those of England were also exported at an early date. From sometime in the late eleventh or early twelfth century to the early fourteenth century Flemish clothiers had an apparently insatiable demand for wool and it is likely that throughout the greater part of this period exports from the British Isles were growing continuously. A number of developments favoured the expansion of the cloth industry in the Low Countries at this time, prominent among which was the rapid growth of population. The increase in population throughout Europe meant that there were many more people to be clothed as well as fed, a task which Flanders was only too ready to undertake as its own population grew beyond the capacity of the countryside and turned increasingly from agricultural to industrial pursuits. The transition was helped by the early maturing of an entrepreneurial class which organised the workers into more efficient industrial units and provided the capital necessary for the import of raw materials. Finally one must not overlook the technological innovations which were made during the twelfth and thirteenth centuries, notably the fulling mill, the horizontal loom and the spinning wheel, all of which increased the productivity of manpower and consequently helped to increase the demand for raw materials, including English wool.[16]

Although it is fairly easy to explain the causes which led to the beginning of the export of wool from England it will probably never be possible to say exactly when the trade began. It would be rash to say that wool was never exported before the Norman conquest but, as already stated, it is unlikely that a regular trade existed at such an early date. On the other hand by the reign of Henry I there was probably a thriving trade between Flanders and England which included the export of wool. Traffic between the two countries was apparently frequent and speedy, for in 1127 the news of the murder of Charles the Good of Flanders reached London within two days. The earliest important reference to the export of wool can be dated to the year 1113 – the often told story of the canons of Laon.[17] During the reign of Stephen overseas trade may have suffered a setback, but the strong government instituted by Henry II made it possible for foreign merchants to resume their business. Moreover the king's willingness to concede commercial privileges, such as that granted to the men of St Omer (1155–8), was an even greater stimulus to trade. There can be no doubt that during the reigns of Henry II and his sons the wool export trade underwent a considerable expansion. Unfortunately there is no evidence as to the volume of trade during this period and paradoxically the best indications of its extent and importance are to be found during the periodic disputes between England and Flanders which brought trade to a halt. It has been suggested that one indication of an increase in commercial activity is provided by the greater precision which appears in descriptions of alien merchants in England at the beginning of the thirteenth century, brought about by greater familiarity.[18] Whereas formerly they were described bluntly as *extranei mercatores* or *Flandrenses*, now they are stated to be burgesses or merchants of St Omer, Ypres, Ghent and so forth.

By the end of the twelfth century English wool was essential to the economy of the Low Countries and by threatening to cut off supplies the King of England could influence the allegiances of those provinces. It was Richard and John who first learned to use the wool trade as a diplomatic lever, not Edward I nor Edward III. The lesson had been fully grasped by 1208 when John was able to force the Flemish towns to remain loyal at a time when the Flemish nobles were breaking away from him and going over to the King of France. The history of Anglo-Flemish relations over the previous thirty years or so forms a prologue to that event. When Henry II's sons rose in revolt in 1173 some of those who aided them seem to have been lured by the prospect of obtaining English wool on easy terms. The main figure behind the young king Henry was Louis of France, but the Count of Flanders was drawn into the conspiracy and in the summer of 1173 the Earl of Leicester led an army of Flemings into eastern England. Jordan Fantosme wrote of them:[19]

> 'We have not come into this country to sojourn,
> But to destroy King Henry the old warrior
> And to have his wool, which we long for'.
> Lords that is the truth: the greater part of them were weavers,
> They did not know how to bear arms like knights.
> But they had come for this – to have gain and fighting.

A little later Fantosme remarks sarcastically,

> They gathered the wool of England very late.
> Upon their bodies crows and buzzards descend.

Their aggression rebounded, however, not only upon themselves but upon Flemish merchants who were trading in every quarter of England and in Ireland. The pipe roll of 1173 and those of the next two or three years contain numerous references to the seizure and sale of Flemish goods, including wool in Essex, Sussex and Yorkshire, and woad belonging to 'fugitives' who had taken refuge in Leicester castle. Englishmen who had harboured the goods of Flemings were also punished for their misdemeanours.

Following the restoration of peace Flemish merchants appear to have traded freely in England until 1193 or 1194. It is well known that in order to raise money for the king's ransom the entire wool clip of the Cistercian, Gilbertine and Premonstratensian orders was confiscated. Since the wool had to be converted to cash the government would not lightly have closed the door to the rich Flemish market. On the other hand in order to ensure that no wool escaped its clutches it would have been perfectly natural to place a temporary ban upon the sale of wool or upon its export. Although such a ban would seriously have inconvenienced the Flemings the very fact that they were the major customers of many monasteries made it necessary. If the government offered to sell any part of the confiscated wool to the Flemings insult was added to injury since the latter had probably paid the monasteries in advance for much of it. Evidence for the ban is slight but conclusive. In the pipe roll of 1194 Humfrey *filius* Stanhard and Alan, priest of Louth, made fine of $3\frac{1}{2}$ marks to have the king's peace for selling wool to Flemings, while Alan Saterdai and Humfrey *filius* Siward gave 3 marks in a similar cause.[20] Disobedience by the Flemings of a ban upon the buying and selling of wool would in itself have led to a restriction of their activities, but the seeds of further discord were probably sown by the levying of a tax of one tenth upon overseas trade, presumably as a contribution to the ransom. This tenth has been strangely overlooked by historians, who have taken the fifteenth levied by John in 1203 as the first national customs duty. The oversight is the more remarkable in that although most of the receipts were probably accounted for at the special ransom Exchequer, records of which have not survived, there are sufficient indications in the pipe rolls to show what was going on. In the pipe roll of 1195 William of Yarmouth accounted for £573 14s 2d from the tenth of merchandise levied in the ports of Norfolk and Lincolnshire. It is possible that this tenth was not a once and for all levy but a regular impost, creating a precedent for John's fifteenth. At any rate Hugo and Adam Oisel of Ypres were willing to give 50 marks to be quit of the tenth for a period of two years commencing at Easter 1195, while in an account covering the period May 1197 to May 1199 Gervase of Aldermanbury, chamberlain of London, included £18 6s 6d received as a tenth of the goods of various merchants paid on 10 days in the 'first year'. In addition to the tenth, or possibly in place of it, Richard exacted fines for licences to trade in particular commodities. Gervase of Aldermanbury accounted for £96 6s 8d for import licences for woad in the two years from Whitsun 1195 and £71 14s 9d for similar licences in the following two years, together with £23 12s 0d for licences to export wool and hides.[21] Fines for permission to import woad continued to be exacted in the early years of John's reign.

Whatever the cause Anglo-Flemish trade relations suffered a setback in this period. It is difficult to doubt that Flemish goods were among the 'chattels of the king's enemies' sold for £513 5s 9d in Norfolk and Lincolnshire in 1193–4, while similar sales were made in other parts of the country in succeeding years. Some merchants managed to evade the net and Simon Kime was fined 1000 marks for allowing alien merchants to depart with their goods and ships from Boston fair. Less fortunate were those who returned to England in 1195 when Richard appeared to be settling his differences with Baldwin IX, Count of Flanders. In 1196 Baldwin made an alliance with the King of France and Richard wreaked vengeance upon the merchants. Flemish merchants were seized at Lynn Fair and taken as prisoners to Hertford castle while in the same year 45 sacks of Flemish-owned wool, valued at 225 marks, were seized at Hull. Trade did not cease altogether for apart from a large-scale, though illicit, export of grain to Flanders some merchants probably continued to operate under licence. Hugo Oisel, for example, gave 400 marks in 1196 for permission to trade in

England and in Richard's other lands in time of war as well as in time of peace. Nevertheless the interruption of trade must have had a serious effect on the Flemish economy and the prospect of its restoration was probably as important a factor as the promise of subsidies of silver in deciding Baldwin IX to abandon France and to form an alliance with Richard in September 1197.[22]

Although anxious to retain the friendship of Flanders John seems to have visualised circumstances in which it might be expedient to present a show of force towards Flemish merchants in England. This, at any rate, appears to be the implication of his agreement with Nicholas Morel. In 1195 Morel had offered Richard £60 to distrain the Count of Flanders for £343 stolen from him, as was later alleged, by men of Ghent in the service of the widow of Philip of Alsace, the late count. Since Richard found it more profitable to sell arrested Flemish goods on his own account Morel saw none of his money and when John came to the throne he increased the offer to half of the sum recovered. Moreover in respect of 2000 marks stolen by the men of Lille, also in the service of the countess, Morel offered the king two thirds of the sum recovered. It was agreed that goods belonging to Lille and Ghent should be seized wherever Morel might identify them. It is unlikely, however, that any action was taken on his behalf for John soon showed himself favourable to freedom of trade in general and to the Flemings in particular. In March 1200 orders were sent to London and to the coastal shires of the south and east that merchants of all nationalities might freely enter and leave the realm for purpose of trade. At the same time certain Flemish merchants were given personal safe conducts protecting them and their goods from arrest. The following May a general safe conduct was issued in favour of all Flemings which accorded them the same protection as that enjoyed by merchants of the king's own dominions.[23]

Freedom of trade did not long survive the outbreak of war between John and Philip of France and restrictions were placed upon the movement of goods and merchants. The most outstanding feature of these was the imposition of a tax of one fifteenth upon imports and exports. The circumstances of the fifteenth are obscure; in particular the dates between which it was levied are agreed upon by hardly any two historians. The earliest record of the fifteenth appears to be a letter patent of 13 July 1202 directed to the justiciar, Geoffrey fitz Peter, exempting Henry Costein and John de Espaygni, merchants of the Earl of Leicester, from payment of the fifteenth levied upon merchants of France and Flanders, from 11 July to Michaelmas 1202. The next reference is a further exemption granted to John de Spanny on 7 June

1203.[24] Although it is clear that an extraordinary tax was levied upon merchandise from the summer of 1202 it is not certain who paid it nor how it was collected. The only extant account of the fifteenth is entered in the pipe roll of 6 John, made up in Michaelmas term 1204. This offers the historian three choices of dates, for its rubric reads that William de Wrotham, Reginald de Cornhill and William Furnell, keepers of the fifteenth, accounted *a festo sancte Margarete anni quarti usque ad festum sancti Andree anni vi^{ti} sicut ipsi dicunt. quod tempus secundum annotationem scaccario. incepit in festo sancte Margarete. anni v^{ti} (durans) usque ad festum sancti Andree anni septimi.* The account also includes the issues of the fairs of Lynn and Boston for year 7. The editor of the pipe roll made no comment on the discrepancy in the dating of the account but noted than it covered the period 20 July 1202 to 30 November 1204,[25] apparently accepting the dates given by Wrotham and his colleagues and using the Chancery dating of John's regnal year, beginning on Sunday following the feast of the Ascension. If we use Chancery reckoning the alternative dates merely postpone the account by twelve months, 20 July 1203 to 30 November 1205.[26] However, the reference to Exchequer annotation suggests Michaelmas (28 September) as the terminal date of the regnal year and this usage reduces the period of account by a full year, 20 July 1203 to 30 November 1204.[27] The evidence of a fifteenth having been levied as early as 1202 does not necessarily conflict with the acceptance of 20 July 1203 as beginning the period of account recorded in the pipe roll, for it is likely that for the first twelve months or so of its existence the fifteenth was not the responsibility of the Exchequer. During this first period Wrotham and Cornhill were associated with the collection of the tax but the justiciar was probably the minister ultimately responsible for it. The first attempt to alter the method of administering the fifteenth was a proposal to assign it to Hugo Oisel in return for an advance of 1000 marks, but this arrangement was not carried out.[28] Instead Wrotham and Cornhill, with the addition of William Furnell, were confirmed in their responsibility but apparently made accountable at the Exchequer. The change was probably associated with the thorough overhaul of royal naval forces which was effected about this time, since the loss of Normandy had exposed the south east of England to a hostile power for the first time since the Conquest.[29] Wrotham, Cornhill and Furnell were made responsible for the navy as well as for the collection of customs, writs being directed to them, apparently indiscriminately, as *custodibus quindene* and as *custodibus longarum navium et portuum maris Anglie.*

Details of the new custom were incorporated in an assise which was

entered on the patent roll as the first entry for the sixth year, 3 June
1204. Wrotham, Cornhill and Furnell were at the head of the administration and at each port six or seven worthy men, elected by the community but assisted by a clerk and a knight, were charged with the
task of valuing goods and levying a duty of one fifteenth. Where the
labour was heavy the local officials received some remuneration, those
in Lincolnshire being excused a tallage levied on the royal demesne, in
one instance the quittance being as great as thirty marks. The earliest
reference to the fifteenth suggests that it was then confined to French
and Flemish merchants, but it was later extended to all, including
denizens. It is impossible to say when the new custom ceased to be
levied, but it may be significant that in the spring of 1206 writs directed
to the custodians of the ports, instructing them to allow merchants to
export, make no reference to it, merely specifying that *rectas et antiques
consuetudines* should be paid. A mandate to Wrotham in July 1207
ordering him to hear the accounts of the keepers of the fifteenth in
Norfolk and Suffolk probably reflects the slowness of the audit rather
than the continuance of the duty. In 1206 the merchants of London
proffered two hundred marks to be quit of the fifteenth and the fact
that it remained outstanding for many years may indicate reluctance
to pay once the tax had been abandoned for all merchants. Some
years later John again turned to overseas trade for fiscal purposes but
this time the duty was confined to imported woad. Various officials
accounted for £979 9s 2d from this source between Michaelmas 1210
and 20 December 1211, although the total receipts may have been
greater. The figure suggests that duty on woad made up no small part
of the sum of £4958 6s 3½d levied on imports and exports in 1203–4.
On the other hand it cannot be doubted that duty on exported wool
figures very largely in the latter sum. Wool and woad together account
for the preponderance of the east coast ports in table 1.[30]

The assise of 1204 was more than a fiscal measure, for it was also
concerned to prevent munitions of war from falling into the hands of
the king's enemies and to this end banned the export of weapons and
of virtually all foodstuffs. Wool was not among the prohibited goods
but the trade was strictly regulated to prevent evasion of customs duty.
Merchants were forbidden to remove wool from abbeys to any place
whatsoever without a licence issued by the chief custodians of the
fifteenth. Local officials were instructed to prevent the export of wool
except on the production of such a licence, which had to contain particulars of the amount and the value of the wool. Wool was the only
commodity treated in this way, a fact which attests to the importance
of the trade at this time. Although banning the export of certain goods

TABLE 1   *The fifteenth of 1203-4*

	£	s	d
Newcastle	158	5	11
Yarm	42	17	10
Coatham		11	11
Whitby		4	0
Scarborough	22	0	4½
Hedon	60	8	4
Hull	344	14	4½
York	175	8	10
Selby	17	11	8
Lincoln	656	12	2
Barton-on-Humber	33	11	9
Immingham	18	15	10½
Grimsby	91	15	0½
Boston	780	15	3
Lynn	651	11	11
Yarmouth	54	15	6
Norwich	6	19	10
Dunwich	5	4	9
Orford	11	7	0
Ipswich	7	11	7½
Colchester	16	12	8
Sandwich	16	0	0
Dover	32	6	1
Rye	10	13	5½
Winchelsea	62	2	4½
Pevensey	1	1	11½
Seaford	12	12	2
Shoreham	20	4	9
Chichester	23	6	7
Southampton	712	3	7½
Exmouth	14	6	3
Dartmouth	3	0	0
Saltash	7	4	8
Fowey	48	15	11
London	836	12	10
	£4958	7	3½

the assise affirmed the right of subjects of the King of France, among whom Flemings were specifically included, to come to England for purposes of trade. Three days later John issued more explicit letters of protection granting them safe conduct and promising that should this be withdrawn they would be allowed forty days to remove themselves and their goods from the realm. This promise seems to have been honoured, for although Flemish ships were among those arrested in February 1205 in face of an expected French invasion, on 1 March instructions were given to allow Flemings to leave London with their ships and goods provided that they gave security not to take messages out of the country.[31] For a considerable period following this emergency it seems to have been necessary, or at least advisable, for merchants wishing to export any goods to obtain licences from the keepers of the ports.

The position of Flemish merchants in England remained precarious after 1205 as a result of the political revolution which was being carried out in Flanders. English influence there was weakened in 1203 by the departure of Baldwin IX to take up the crown of Jerusalem. Gerard d'Alsace, chief of the *bailis* left to govern Flanders, although personally pro-English, was not strong enough to resist the overtures which were being made to the Flemish nobles by Philip Augustus. The English party probably remained the stronger until the death of Baldwin IX in 1205, when Philip of Namur, governor of Hainault since 1202, became regent of Flanders on behalf of his two nieces, the daughters of Baldwin. Philip's francophilia was openly displayed in 1206 when he sent the sisters to be educated at the French court. The support of the Flemish nobility for a pro-French policy was secured both by grants of money fiefs and by encouraging them to appeal to their overlord, the King of France, against adverse judgments awarded in the feudal court of Flanders. With the government and the nobility of Flanders gone over to France the trade of the Flemish merchants with England was a hostage to their own support for John. The situation crystallised in 1208 when John mounted a campaign to recover Normandy. From February onwards orders were repeatedly issued for the arrest of shipping and the export of weapons, horses and victuals was banned. There is no suggestion that the ban extended to wool, but shortage of shipping must have brought trade to a standstill. On 26 July 1208 John directed the bailiffs of all ports to dispose of the goods of Flemings according to instructions which would be sent to them by the justiciar and other officials. This cannot necessarily be interpreted as a hostile act, for in May orders had been issued for the arrest of ships and chattels of all nations, except those of Scandinavia.[32] It is possible that the instructions of the justiciar, which have not survived, were for the release of Flemish goods, since the main concern of the government was to mobilise ships. The events of 1208, however, showed the Flemish bourgeoisie where their best interests lay and by 13 September of that year the towns of St Omer, Ghent, Bruges, Lille, Douai and Ypres had sworn allegiance to John, *salvo tamen heredum Flandriae et honore nostro*.[33] In return they were awarded trade privileges.

Notwithstanding this grant of privileges the position of Flemish merchants in England may have remained somewhat precarious unless, like Simon Saphir of Ghent, they were able to obtain the status of demesne merchant of the king, which carried the guarantee of royal protection even if the general safe conduct of Flemish merchants should be withdrawn. There is, however, no evidence of overt royal hostility to the Flemings in the years immediately following. In the summer of 1212 an order was given to release wine belonging to merchants of Douai, Ypres and Ghent which had been seized by the king's galleys, but there is nothing to suggest that the act had been perpetrated at his command. In the following year a more positive attitude towards the Flemings began to emerge as John sought to restore English influence in the Low Countries. The chance came when Ferrand of Portugal, a protege of France who had become Count of Flanders by marriage to Joan, elder daughter of Baldwin IX, began to find the French bridle somewhat oppressive. John obtained the support of Ferrand by means of subsidies and he made sure of the Flemish towns by confirming their trade privileges. In April 1213 merchants of Ypres, Ghent, Bruges and Lille were taken into the king's protection provided that they carried credentials from their échevins, and avowed no merchandise but their own. On various occasions during 1213 and 1214 goods belonging to merchants of St Omer, Douai and Arras were arrested in England, but these may have been reprisals for particular indiscretions, since there is no evidence of general hostility towards the Flemings until after the battle of Bouvines in July 1214. Following this battle French and Flemish merchants were probably given a period of grace in which to quit the realm, for on 5 August the custodians of Lynn fair were ordered to allow Flemish merchants, except those of St Omer and Arras, to depart in ships not large enough to carry horses. On 24 August the bailiffs of Lynn and Southampton were instructed to detain all Flemings and their goods, while an order sent to the sheriff of Kent at the beginning of September refers to a general arrest of Flemings. This interference with trade was short-lived for on 13 September 1214 John wrote to the King of France stating that his merchants were free to trade in England and promising that he would not levy a maltote on their goods. The following summer, however, they were apparently expelled, for on 21 July John wrote to Philip Augustus that French merchants would be permitted to leave London peaceably and requested that he would not molest London merchants then in France. On this occasion they were probably not allowed to take their goods with them, for in March 1216 John issued letters of safe conduct to French merchants allowing them to travel throughout the country to enquire about goods which had been arrested. Time, however, was perilously short, for in May Prince Louis of France invaded England in support of the rebellious barons and the country was plunged into civil war. The unsettled state of the countryside in the summer of 1216 may have made it dangerous for merchants to travel.[34]

After the defeat of Eustace the Monk off Winchelsea on St Bartholomew's day (24 August) 1217 Louis' position in England became untenable and on 12 September he made peace with the supporters of the young Henry III at Kingston on Thames. In return for his withdrawal Louis was promised a large cash indemnity, to which English wool merchants made a substantial, though involuntary, contribution. The first 6000 marks of the indemnity was paid to Louis by Florence Dives, burgess of St Omer, a merchant who for many years had enjoyed a privileged position in England.[35] Although Dives owed the crown a service he had to be repaid and on 21 September 1217 terms were agreed. The king undertook to deliver to him at Bristol 100 lasts of Irish hides valued at 15 marks each and 100 sacks of Irish wool worth 5 marks each, while half of the outstanding debt was to be repaid in cash at All Saints (1 November) and the remainder at Purification (2 February 1218). Should Florence not receive the goods he was to be paid an additional 500 marks in compensation for loss of profit. In the event the hides and wool, taken as a forced loan from English merchants, were not given to Florence, probably because a better price was obtained. All the hides arrested at Bristol were sold in January 1218 to William fitz Benedict for 20 marks per last, and in February the wool merchants, following the example of those whose wool had been seized at London, redeemed their property for 6 marks per sack. Officials responsible for the prest sent 521 marks and 10 shillings to London, but this was not the entire sum raised from the Bristol seizures; William de Ely, citizen of London, gave 57 marks to redeem goods taken from John Toni of Waterford, while there may have been similar cases. Following further payments in August 1218 there remained due to Florence Dives the sum of 2150 marks and to meet this debt there was a further prest of wool. Henry de Ponte Audomari and Ralph de Norwich arrested all wool found at Northampton fair and on 29 November the mayor of Northampton was ordered to have this valued and to offer it to its owners or to any other merchant willing to take it at that price. All wool not redeemed was to be delivered to Dives in part satisfaction of the king's debt, while the owners were promised repayment in the Exchequer in the following Easter. Among those from whom wool was taken were Roger Brun of Chester (£13 14s), Baldwin de Leges and his partners, Philip and Adam (50 marks) and Ralph fitz Lefwin, bailiff of Lincoln (£27 for

4 sacks).[36] The re-establishment of the machinery of government gradually made such extraordinary methods of finance unnecessary and the return to conditions of peace allowed merchants to resume their business.

After the death of Philip Augustus on 12 July 1223 Henry III ordered the Norman barons to return to their allegiance and mustered a fleet at Portsmouth, but this was stood down three weeks later. However the threatened disruption of trade was not averted, merely postponed. The Truce of Chinon expired at Easter (14 April) 1224, but since its renewal was already being negotiated Henry gave a safe conduct to all French merchants to trade in his dominions until 8 July. On 5 May Louis broke off the talks and ten days later Henry notified the bailiffs of his ports that the truce was at an end. On 26 May he instructed them to arrest all ships capable of carrying troops, although merchants remained free to enter the country. Some bailiffs probably exceeded their orders and seized property belonging to Frenchmen for on 5 June the bailiffs of Lynn were ordered to release goods which they had arrested. There is no evidence of any move to molest the French after the breakdown of the truce and on 17 July Henry ruled that all foreign merchants who had been in the country on St Benedict's day (11 July) were to enjoy his protection while coming to, trading at and departing from Lynn fair, the safe conduct to last until 23 August. Not until 6–8 September were orders issued for the arrest of the persons and goods of merchants subject to the King of France, and among those seized were Flemings and Brabanters. The arrest of the Flemings gave rise to concern for the safety of English merchants in Flanders and in order to prevent reprisals merchants of Ghent, Bruges, Ypres, Aardenburg and Damme, detained at Winchester fair, were offered their freedom provided they guaranteed the safety of the English in Flanders. During September Flemings, Brabanters and merchants of Toulouse were allowed to depart but the French remained in custody until 11 May 1225. They were then given two weeks to remove themselves and their goods from the realm, although two days before the deadline the period of grace was extended until St John the Baptist (24 June).[37]

Throughout the autumn and winter a limited amount of Anglo-French trade had continued under licence. The most privileged, in that they obtained a general licence for all their citizens, were the merchants of Dieppe, who as early as July 1224 had received a safe conduct to trade in England until Purification (2 February) 1225. The licence was renewed in April and enlarged to include all Henry's dominions. The men of Rouen were probably as active and although there is no evidence of a collective safe conduct many licences were granted to individual merchants. Comparatively few licences are recorded in favour of other French merchants. Since all trade, including that of Englishmen and non-French aliens, was strictly controlled the small number of licences granted to Flemings suggests that they were not very active during this period. However, Flanders was not without English wool and there is no reason to suppose that the crown was particularly disposed to deny wool at this time. The licensing system was not intended to stop trade but to control the movement of ships, which might be needed at any time to transport troops. The Flemings overcame the difficulty of access by arranging that the English monasteries from whom they bought wool should themselves export it. Between June 1224 and July 1225 licences for shipping space to export wool were granted to the abbeys of Fountains, Furness, Kirkstall, Kirkstead, Holmcultram, St Mary's York, Roche, Thame, Bordesley, Meaux, Byland, Jervaulx, Melrose, Coupar, Garendon, Newminster and to the archbishops of Canterbury and York. English merchants also continued to trade with Flanders and wool was specifically mentioned in the licences to James Baer, James le Flemeng and Edward Serjeant of Southampton, Adam Flur of York, Richard Crassus of London and Hemery of Chichester.[38]

In the late summer of 1225 hostility towards the French declined somewhat or alternatively the need of the English cloth industry for the woad of Picardy became urgent, for in August the king granted a safe conduct until 1 November to the merchants of Arras, Abbeville, Amiens, Corbie, St Omer, Beauvais and Ponthieu. During the winter there seems to have been a general, and perhaps unauthorised, return of Frenchmen, for in March 1226 an order was issued for the arrest of all French merchants in East Anglia except for those bearing a royal licence to quit the realm. In July the officials of London were ordered to seize goods belonging to merchants of Arras and Bapaume, while in September the bailiffs of Dover, Portsmouth and Southampton and the sheriff of Hampshire were instructed to arrest the goods and persons of those merchants and of St Omer. There was probably some special reason for detaining these parties, for despite a renewal of hostilities other French citizens were given a period of grace to leave the country. On 26 September 1226 all sheriffs were ordered to proclaim that French knights and merchants must withdraw themselves within five weeks after Michaelmas. Because of the failure of the harvest of 1226 a self-imposed blockade would have caused more harm to England than to France. Consequently on 5 November the government announced that notwithstanding its recent order French ships bringing grain, victuals and wine would be allowed to come and go in peace. However, French merchants remaining in the country were gradually rounded up. On 12 November orders were issued for their arrest at London, Southampton and Sandwich and in January 1227 similar orders were sent to Boston, St Ives, Stamford and Yorkshire.[39]

Hostilities between England and France were terminated in the spring of 1227 and in April orders were given for the immediate release of goods belonging to Flemish and French merchants. The truce now arranged was to last until St Mary Magdalene (22 July) 1229. Shortly before that date all merchants not subject to Henry III were ordered to quit the realm before the truce expired. On 17 July the king informed all ports on the south and east coasts that he had received reports of French ships gathering to prey upon English trade the moment the truce came to an end. He ordered that all English ships in their own ports and all foreign ships, including those of Gascony, were to be arrested forthwith, while other English ships might depart only to their home ports. This move prevented the remaining aliens from leaving the country and all were arrested. On 25 July the order was given to release those not subject to the King of France and in this category were included the Flemings. The latter were given a safe conduct until Michaelmas 1230 which was renewed periodically throughout the period of the hostilities.[40]

There was probably no impediment to Anglo-Flemish trade during this period apart from shortage of shipping space, for the movement of ships was once again governed by the king's military need. Henry proposed to invade Normandy and his passage was arranged for October 1229 but subsequently deferred until the following Easter. Having secured the homage of the Duke of Britanny he landed at St Malo on 3 May, marched south into Poitou, returned to Nantes in September and crossed to England in the following month. These operations inevitably had a harmful effect upon trade. Although the king actually used only the larger ships, those capable of carrying 16 horses on the outward voyage and 20 on the return, the authorities acted so thoroughly that in May 1230 there were assembled at Portsmouth several hundred ships, both English and alien, in excess of requirements. The master of each of these was issued with a certificate stating that he had obeyed the summons to come to Portsmouth but that he was not needed and was therefore to go about his lawful business. Unfortunately the order for the arrest of ships does not seem to have been withdrawn, for whenever a ship, English or alien, not provided with a certificate of discharge, touched upon an English port it was detained and only released at the specific command of the government. During

June and July 1230 there were many such orders relating to ships laden with wool for Flanders.

In June 1231 England and France renewed the truce until 24 June 1234. Although Henry III was inclined to favour hostilities he was reluctant to take stern measures against French merchants in England and on 17 June 1234 conceded that if the truce was not extended they might have until 1 August to settle their affairs and depart in peace. Four days later the concession was extended to Whitsun 1235. Although the king stayed his hand his subjects did not and even before the truce expired the men of the Cinque Ports and elsewhere seized goods belonging to French merchants. These actions were disavowed by the king who ordered that restitution be made and that there should be no arrests until he gave instructions. In December 1234 and January 1235 all French merchants in England and Ireland, except those bearing personal letters of safe conduct, were detained in reprisal for the imprisonment of William, the king's tailor, and other English merchants in France. Flemings were specifically excluded from this action. Since commissioners of England and France were at that moment discussing terms for a renewal of the truce they presumably took this new development into consideration. On 28 February the order was given to release all French merchants and this news was immediately communicated to the King of France, together with a safe conduct for Frenchmen to come to England. The merchants of Amiens had been freed earlier that month at the request of the men of the Cinque Ports, with whom they may have had a special relationship, for the latter gave £300 surety that the Amiens merchants would obtain the release of the king's tailor.[41]

Within a very short time the prospect of peace was again threatened by alleged wrongs done to English traders in France. In May 1235 East Anglian merchants complained that they and their goods had been detained at various places in Normandy and that some of their compatriots still languished in French prisons. About the same time Hugh Selby, mayor of York, alleged the seizure of merchandise in Poitou. It is likely that the king did not wish to prejudice negotiations by wholesale reprisals, for the action he took was limited to safeguarding the interests of the aggrieved merchants while their complaints were investigated. French goods were arrested and placed in safe custody in Lynn, Yarmouth, St Ives, Beverley, Hedon, Lincoln, Newcastle and York, but French merchants themselves were not molested. The episode was punctuated on 30 July by agreement on terms of a truce and on 16 August the release of French goods in East Anglia was ordered. Hugh Selby, meanwhile, had seized and sold

French property to the value of £94 13s 4d or more; this he was allowed to keep provided that he gave surety to repay should the French claim against the king.[42]

The mid-1230s were marked also by negotiations to settle long-standing disputes between England and Flanders, resulting finally in a treaty which initiated a new era in commercial relations between the two countries. The discussions covered disagreements between merchants of either country and also between the English Crown and Flemish merchants. Towards the end of 1231 there had occurred a series of arrests of English merchants in Flanders and of Flemish merchants in England. Although it is difficult to apportion blame the seizures may have begun with the arrest of Flemish merchants and goods in England during the war with France. Although the Flemings had been granted safe conduct by the Crown the authorities could not always determine the ownership of merchandise without a lengthy investigation, during which time it was necessary to impound the property to prevent its being spirited away. Even Englishmen were in the habit of avowing the goods of enemy aliens in return for a consideration. In November 1231 Henry III wrote to the Count of Flanders requesting that he give credentials to his merchants who had suffered damage in England so that they might come to the king to have their claims settled. The Flemings apparently preferred more direct action and seized English goods in Flanders, belonging mainly to men of Winchester. In reprisal Flemish ships and merchandise were arrested at Portsmouth and Southampton in December and although the ships were released in January the other property remained in custody. The dispute dragged on for years and although the injured Flemings were given a safe conduct to press their claims in October 1233 a settlement was not reached until May 1235. Anglo-Flemish trade was not at a standstill throughout this period for from December 1233 safe conducts were periodically granted to Flemish merchants.[43]

The dispute between the English Crown and the merchants of Flanders was of much longer standing, dating back in fact to the previous reign. Ever since November 1214 John and his successor had been trying unsuccessfully to obtain repayment of loans made to the burgesses of Ghent and Ypres in 1213 and 1214.[44] The Flemings countered with claims for damage inflicted illegally by the king's ships on their own vessels. In June 1236 it was agreed to submit all claims to the arbitration of a mixed commission. Before the end of that year it was found that the king should pay 897 marks plus the cost of 826 tuns of wine, against which was to be set 500 marks and £900 still owed by Ghent and Ypres and 400 marks to be paid collectively by the merchants of Flanders in return for a perpetual safe conduct to trade in England.[45]

The truce between England and France lasted until June 1242 when it was denounced by Henry on the grounds that it had been broken by the French. In fact he had determined upon this course of action as early as December 1241 when he decided to invade Poitou in support of the rebellious counts of le Marche. As soon as the truce was formally ended the barons of the Cinque Ports were ordered to make war upon France by land and sea and their actions included the detention of Frenchmen and their property in Kent. Elsewhere arrests were apparently piece-meal and were represented as reprisals for the arrest of English merchants in France. At the end of July some merchants were arrested in London, but wholesale arrests throughout the kingdom were delayed until 20 September.[46]

Despite the perpetual safe conduct a great deal of Flemish-owned property was inevitably seized during the confusion. In the case of goods detained in England the situation was easily remedied and immediately a Flemish merchant was able to prove his title to arrested property its restoration was ordered. It was otherwise with merchandise taken at sea, for not only were the facts more difficult to establish but the king refused to accept responsibility for Flemish ships and goods seized in French waters by English sailors. Hundreds of sacks of wool were soon in English ports as a result of successful actions, the king taking half as spoils of war. The fact that any English-owned property found in captured Flemish ships was restored to its owners made the situation the more galling for the Flemings. The king refused to remedy matters when appealed to by the Count of Flanders and accordingly in January 1243 the count wrote to say that he would be unable to guarantee the safety of English merchants in Flanders beyond Purification (2 February). This threat was immediately proclaimed in England together with instructions that should any of the king's merchants be harmed by any people of the King of France, by implication the Flemings, such people were to be attacked by all the king's subjects by land and by sea. Privately England was less belligerent and a royal official, Mathew Besill, was immediately dispatched to Flanders with plenipotentiary powers to settle the business of the merchants. There is no record of the result of this mission but it seems to have been successful and fortunately the hostilities between England and France were concluded soon afterwards.[47]

Although peace was not formally declared until the Treaty of Paris in 1259 the truce made in April 1243 effectively ended the series of Anglo-French wars which had begun with the forfeiture of Normandy.

Half a century was to elapse before a clash between the two Crowns once again dislocated trade between England and the continent. Despite a lack of detailed evidence it is safe to conclude that Henry III's wars had no permanently inhibiting effect on trade. Some of the stoppages may have been serious, but they were of very limited duration. Unlike Richard and John, Henry had levied no tax on overseas trade and after the prest of wool at the beginning of the reign there is no evidence that he again forcibly borrowed the property of native merchants, although that of enemy aliens was confiscated during hostilities.

Among the indications of an expansion of overseas trade during this period one of the most interesting is the change in the English attitude towards Flanders during the successive conflicts with France. Henry III, unlike his father and uncle, seems to have had no plan to unite the princes of the Low Countries against the northern flank of the King of France. Consequently he probably began his wars without a positive policy towards Flanders. During the first period of hostilities, 1224–7, Flemish merchants were rounded up along with Frenchmen. Consideration for the safety of English merchants in Flanders, in itself an indication of the direction of English trade, counselled the release of the Flemings, but they were expelled from England, except for a few who received personal safe conducts, and some Flemish goods remained in detention. In 1229 Flemish merchants were arrested on the expiration of the order for all aliens to leave the country, but they were released immediately and provided with safe conducts to remain. In 1234 the warrants issued for the general arrest of French merchants specifically excluded Flemings. Clearly by this date the government was anxious to observe the distinction between Flemings and Frenchmen.

The settlement made between England and Flanders in 1236 marked the beginning of a new era in trade relations between the two countries. During this period there was probably a major expansion of trade and a large part of it was handled by the Flemings. The cornerstone of the Flemish ascendancy was the perpetual safe conduct granted to their merchants to trade by land and sea throughout the dominions of Henry III. Provided that certain formalities had been observed this safe conduct was not to be abrogated even on account of the arrest of English merchandise in Flanders. If any Flemings were injured in England they were to apply to the king for justice and if this was denied to them they could procure the arrest of English goods in Flanders. Such action, however, was not to provoke a breach of the treaty. Reciprocal arrangements were made for the protection of English merchants in Flanders. Even more significant was the clause which provided that conflict between rulers should not automatically involve their subjects. The treaty was not to be broken if the Count of Flanders, in observance of his feudal allegiance to the King of France, took up arms against Henry III in a cause which did not directly involve the realm of England. A direct attack on England, however, was a breach of the treaty. Similarly English merchants in Flanders were not to be molested except in the event of a direct attack by England against Flanders and Hainault.[48]

In the years which followed the Flemings gained additional security as individual towns obtained charters of privileges from the king. The first of these had been granted to Ypres as early as 1232. It stated that neither the merchants of Ypres nor their goods should be arrested in retaliation for any action taken against English merchants abroad to which the men of Ypres were not a party. Further their goods were not to be distrained for any debts except those in which they were themselves the principal debtors or sureties. The charter was confirmed in 1259 and the privileges extended. The conviction of a servant or agent for a crime was not to result in the forfeiture of his master's goods, while the property of a merchant dying in England was assured to his heirs. All these privileges were also granted to St Omer in 1255, Ghent in 1259, Douai in 1260.[49]

The period in which the Flemings dominated the English wool trade is believed by some Belgian scholars to have seen the emergence of an important trade organisation, the so-called Hanse of London. However, there is so little evidence about this body that its very existence may be called into question. The principal Flemish sources are two sets of ordinances, a Latin version from Ypres and a French version from Bruges. Pirenne saw the Hanse as a confederation of Flemish urban hanses or gilds merchant, chiefly those of the maritime towns under the leadership of Bruges, its main concern being the import of wool. He dated the Latin ordinances to about 1187 and claimed that they show that the Hanse was already a well-established and flourishing body. He thought that the French ordinances belong to the period after 1241 and show signs that the institution was beginning to decay. H. van Werveke believed that both sets of ordinances date from roughly the third quarter of the thirteenth century, although he conceded that some form of organisation may have existed since the beginning of the century. He regarded the Hanse as being a very loose-knit organisation without permanent leadership and administration. E. Perroy, in an article which was published posthumously, cast doubt on the existence of the Hanse before the Anglo-Flemish war of 1270–4 and dated both sets of ordinances to 1275 or later. He saw them as proposals for the setting up of such a Hanse, the main sponsor being Bruges which was anxious to increase its share of the trade. The complete silence of English records about the Hanse of London does not in itself prove that it never existed but it lends support to the view that it can have been at best a loose-knit organisation. There is no evidence that England ever recognised the Hanse and the king dealt almost invariably with the Count of Flanders or with individual towns. However, whether the Hanse ever existed or not there can be little doubt that before 1270 Flemish merchants handled the bulk of wool exports. English merchants had held a share of the trade since the early years of the thirteenth century, or even earlier, but they must still have had a minority interest.[50]

2

The end of the Flemish ascendancy

During the later years of the thirteenth century Flemish merchants in large measure withdrew from active participation in international trade. This withdrawal was caused partly by a concentration of energies and capital in the cloth manufacturing industry and partly by growing competition, particularly that presented by German merchants. In the case of the English wool trade, however, the chief factor was the protracted disputes between England and Flanders which occupied much of the last third of the century. During these periods the Flemings lost valuable contracts which could not be recovered when peace was restored. Flanders remained the principal market for English wool but the conduct of the trade passed largely into the hands of merchants of other nationalities. The major dispute began in 1270, but the Flemings began to experience difficulties as early as 1264 and it is likely that during the intervening years they never fully recovered the ascendancy which undoubtedly they had enjoyed at an earlier date. The occasion of the 1264 troubles was the outbreak of war between the king and the adherents of Simon de Montfort. The cause of the troubles was simply the breakdown of good government and there is small reason to accept the idea that from motives of 'political economy' the Montfortians adopted an attitude hostile to Flanders. The basis of such a belief is the statement of Walter of Guisborough[1] that as early as 1258 the baronial party formulated certain 'statutes', including one which ordered that all wool should be made into cloth in England and that none should be sold to aliens. R. F. Treharne has pointed out that Walter's statement, wrongly dated, was probably based on the chronicle of Thomas Wykes.[2] Wykes, however, says nothing about a plan to promote the manufacture of cloth in England. He merely states that in 1264 trade was at a standstill and that Henry de Montfort, son of Simon, spoiled merchants of their wool, and not only that of Flemings, but also of other aliens and Englishmen. Although this may be a fair gloss on the behaviour of Henry de Montfort the edicts of the barons suggest that on the whole they were trying to steer a difficult course between not offending Flanders and preventing that country from providing a base for a royalist attack on England. It must, of course, be admitted that among the popular supporters of Simon de Montfort anti-alien sentiment was not absent.

The violence of 1264 culminated in the battle of Lewes, fought in May shortly before the opening of the wool season. News of the war must undoubtedly have acted as a disincentive to merchants from overseas and on 2 June the barons issued a proclamation stating that peace had been restored and that it was safe for all merchants to enter the country to trade as they were wont to do. Copies were sent to the échevins of St Omer, Ghent, Ypres, Brussels, Malines, Louvain and Liege. Within a few weeks the barons closed the ports, a move which bottled up all merchants, both alien and denizen, who were then in England. This, however, was a side-effect and not the desired end, for the aim was to halt ships which might soon be needed to meet the invasion threatened by the supporters of Henry III. The absence of hostility to alien merchants is indicated by orders issued in late July 1264. Three ships of Ypres had been detained at Harwich; orders were now given to release one of them to take Flemish merchants and their goods to Flanders, with permission to return for the rest of their property. At the same time permission was given for Flemish merchants to embark with their goods in a ship assigned to take an emissary of the barons from Sandwich to Flanders. In September it was ruled that since no shipping could be allowed to depart any Flemish merchant who so desired might take his wool, hides and other merchandise away from the ports and sell them within the realm. At the end of August, and again in November, the Countess of Flanders wrote to England demanding the release of her subjects and giving assurances that all the English merchants then in Flanders were receiving her full protection. These demands merely elicited proclamations that Flemish merchants were under the protection of the government and might if they wished lay up their goods in churches, monasteries and other safe places. While these diplomatic exchanges were taking place Flemish ships found in English waters continued to be arrested, although any merchants aboard were allowed their freedom in England.[3]

Before the end of 1264 Henry de Montfort, who had been made warden of the Cinque Ports, began to seize wool. It was claimed that the wool was being taken into protective custody since 'by reason of the late disturbance in the realm many persons despoiled wool and merchandise of merchants from beyond the seas'. The wool of the men of St Omer found at Ipswich was afterwards declared forfeit on the grounds that their lord, the Count of St Pol, was the king's enemy. Doubtless, other wool was misappropriated without formality. Nevertheless from time to time instructions were given for the release of alien-owned wool together with permission for its owners to trade with it in the realm. In January 1265 the government wrote to a large number of Cistercian monasteries pointing out that many Flemings who had contracted to buy wool of 1264 were unable to travel because of the disturbances. The houses were ordered to keep the wool for them until the following Easter and were forbidden to exact any penalty for late completion of a contract.[4]

The Countess of Flanders seems to have been the first to resort to more severe measures. In April 1264 the barons wrote to her begging her to believe that the goods of her countrymen were in safe custody and would come to no harm, provided that the owners were guiltless of any crime. They were therefore indignant to hear that not merely was she keeping English goods in restraint but the persons of the merchants as well. Nevertheless there was little retaliatory action, although in June the bailiffs of Bristol, Southampton, Boston and Lynn were instructed that while Flemish merchants and their servants were to have their liberty their goods were to be held in custody. After the battle of Evesham in August 1265 the king quickly took steps to reverse the measures taken by the barons. A proclamation was issued guaranteeing the safety of all alien merchants in the realm, general and particular safe conducts were issued in favour of Flemings, orders were given to release Flemish goods and justices were appointed to hear complaints of injuries done to Flemish merchants during the recent disturbances. All Cistercian monasteries were again ordered to deliver any wool due to Flemish merchants without exaction of penalties. Henry III agreed readily to the demand of the countess that the property of her subjects in England should be restored before she released English goods held in Flanders. This suited his plans since many English merchants had supported the rebels and their goods arrested in Flanders could provide security for the fines which inevitably would be exacted to enter the king's peace. At the end of November the king informed the countess that the citizens of London had submitted to his will and requested her to deliver their goods to agents of his son, Prince Edward. He asked her to detain all other goods until it was determined whether their owners had resisted the king. On her part the countess was in no hurry to release any property. Her subjects were still menaced by the sailors of the Cinque Ports who remained in rebellion beyond the end of 1265. Furthermore there was the matter of the pension due to her from the English Crown, which had fallen into arrears during the disturbances. In November 1265 Henry promised that this would be the first charge against the fines inflicted on the rebels of the Cinque Ports, but these had yet to be defeated.[5] Using the excuse that the king was sending contradictory orders about the disposal of the goods the countess managed to delay the release of many of them until at least midsummer 1266.[6]

Following the restoration of royal government Anglo-Flemish trade was resumed until the prolonged break in relations which commenced in 1270. Bearing in mind the fact that this incident was probably the most important in the history of the wool trade down to the outbreak of the Hundred Years War it may occasion surprise that although studied by a number of continental scholars the dispute has not been investigated by a single British historian.[7] Furthermore general histories published in this country have relied exclusively on the oldest study of the conflict, that of the German historian, Adolf Schaube. Schaube was interested primarily in the licences granted in the year 1273 as evidence for the composition of the export trade, and he has comparatively little to say about other aspects of the dispute. In particular he does not exhaust the causes of the quarrel, being content to blame it upon the action of the Countess Margaret of Flanders in seizing English goods to supply arrears of her pension. English historians have been pleased to accept Schaube's explanation, Powicke, for example, describing Margaret's action as 'flagrant'.[8] Since this does less than justice to the Flemish case it is necessary to rehearse all the factors contributing to the quarrel. Although arrears of the pension were not the sole cause of the dispute they were undoubtedly an irritant to the countess and must therefore be considered first. Ever since the time of the Norman kings successive counts of Flanders had received a *fief de bourse* from the ruler of England, an annual payment of 500 marks. During periods of tension between England and Flanders the pension was not paid and it once more fell into arrears during the period of baronial government. Despite assurances that these would be paid there is no evidence that they had been cleared by 1270 when the countess arrested all English goods in her dominions.[9]

Although Margaret's personal grievance against the king may well have provided the trigger for her attack upon his subjects it must be seen against a catalogue of complaints which her own merchants had about treatment at the hands of the English. One source of friction was provided by the assise of cloth. In the first half of the century imported cloth had generally been exempted from the assise, but of recent years the government had been attempting to bring imports within its view. A new edict to this effect was issued in 1269, and although in April 1270 the merchants of Ypres and Douai were given a safe conduct to sell cloth not of the assise, the licence only covered the instant fair of St Ives. Many of those who attended the fair had cause to regret their coming. On the complaint of a German burgess of Lynn that he had not yet recovered wool arrested in Bruges in 1265 all Flemish goods at St Ives were arrested, with the exception of those belonging to merchants who had personal letters of protection. The seizure was a gross breach of the long established privilege that goods of Flemish merchants could be arrested only for their own debts and the debts of those for whom they stood surety, as was pointed out in an angry letter which the countess sent to the king in June 1270. It is impossible to doubt the connection between the St Ives arrests and her own subsequent action. Among the other grievances of the Flemings were acts of piracy and robbery committed against them by Englishmen, redress for which was not always immediately forthcoming. In August 1268, Hugh de Boinebroke and other merchants of Douai had been robbed off Whitby, during the course of a voyage to Scotland, while similar incidents, although not precisely dateable, probably belong to this period. A number of prominent Flemish merchants were also experiencing difficulty in effecting payment for cloth supplied to the Wardrobe. However, given the usual delay in meeting royal debts in the middle ages, it is not possible to judge how serious an irritant this was.[10]

The exact date on which the countess issued the order for the seizure of English goods is not known, but well before the end of September 1270, all Flemish merchants and their goods had been arrested in England in retaliation. The arrests were presumably accompanied by a formal ban on trading with Flanders and with Flemish merchants. So far there is nothing particularly unusual about the sequence of events; the uniqueness of the situation lies in the length of the disruption of trade which followed. This resulted largely from the failure of attempts to settle the dispute by diplomacy. Unfortunately no details of the talks have survived, the only evidence consisting of letters of safe conduct to Flemish envoys to come to England. Between January and May 1271 letters were issued on at least three occasions to representatives of the countess. It seems likely that following a breakdown in these discussions the king attempted to open negotiations directly with the Flemish towns. In September 1271 he issued a safe conduct to Nicholas de Lyons of Douai and John de Lo of Ypres, to bring eight other burgesses representing Ypres, Douai, Ghent, Bruges and Lille. Since Lyons and Lo were unable to be in the delegation three weeks later a new safe conduct was issued for it to be led by John Bardun of Ypres. The following spring further negotiations were held with envoys of the countess, but by Whitsun all hopes of a diplomatic settlement had disappeared.[11]

The bargaining power of the English was weakened by the facts that their goods seized in Flanders were worth much more than those of Flemings held in England and that they were unable to impose effective sanctions on Flanders. The main burden of sanctions lay on the well-tried expedients of denying English wool to the Flemish cloth manu-facturers and of preventing their wares from finding a market in England. The embargo proved a total failure, both because the king himself licensed breaches of it and because it was widely ignored by his own subjects and by alien merchants. At the request of various mem-bers of the royal families of England and France a number of Flemish merchants were, throughout the dispute, allowed to trade within the realm and to export wool and import cloth. Some of these were merely household merchants, but others claimed citizenship of English towns, such as London and Dover, and were 'reputed' denizens. In addition a number of English and German merchants were allowed to import Flemish cloth, even that which did not conform to the assise.[12]

It was not officially sanctioned breaches which most weakened the bargaining strength of the English, but the wholesale and illegal evasion of the trade embargo. This took two forms, illicit dealings with Flemish merchants in England, and the equally illegal export of wool to Flanders. The comparatively low value of Flemish goods seized by the Crown may be explained in part by the fact that there was much collusion about the ownership of merchandise. Englishmen avowed goods as their own, or actually bought them from Flemings, presum-ably at a favourable price. Stephen de Cornhull, alderman of London, was disclosed as having bought $8\frac{1}{2}$ sacks of wool in this manner. Furthermore Flemish merchants continued to come to England even after the initial seizures. Although any Flemish ship found carrying wool in English waters was liable to be arrested the whole of the east coast was wide open to blockade runners. Later enquiries in Lincoln-shire revealed wholesale connivance by local officials at the smuggling of wool through small fishing villages. Evasion was no doubt made easier by the fact that some Flemish vessels had legitimate business in English waters. When it was complained that the Yarmouth herring fairs would suffer if Flemish fishermen were prevented from coming there the ban on their attendance was replaced by an additional duty of 2s on every last of herrings they landed.[13] The greatest harm to the English cause, however, was done not by illegal dealings with Flemings in England, but by the export of wool by Englishmen and alien mer-chants, either directly to Flanders, or through other parts of the Low Countries or northern France. This was simplicity itself, for although all exporters of wool were required to subscribe to an oath they would have no dealings with the Flemings, there appears to have been no check on their activities once the cargoes had left an English port. With no greater safeguard than this the licensing which was established was farcical, and should have been seen to be so by the government. On the other hand it is difficult to imagine how wool could have been prevented from reaching Flanders, except by imposing a total ban on exports.

There was, in fact, a total ban from September 1270 to 14 March 1271. On the latter date the government issued a total of 42 licences, valid until Whitsun (24 May), authorising the export of wool to any place not within the dominion of the Countess of Flanders. Subsequently 11 licences were issued on five occasions down to 10 May. All were made out to individual merchants or small partnerships, with the exceptions of one to the bailiffs and burgesses of Southampton, a similar more or less collective licence to the commonalty of Amiens, one to the Knights Templar of England and one to the proctor of the abbey of Bec. Only in six cases was the amount of wool to be exported not specified in the licence, while the total of the remaining 47 was 2206 sacks of wool and 2 sacks of fells. Although the figures given in many of the licences were very rounded, there is no reason to doubt the general reliability of the total. The wool in question was the residue of the 1270 clip, the export of which had been delayed by an arrest on the movement of wool. This was stated explicitly in the case of a group of London merchants, and there can be little doubt that in most cases the wool was already the property of the licensees. The licence for 24 sacks issued to James de Sevenaunt of Douai clearly refers to the 24 sacks of Margam Abbey wool which had been taken from him in the autumn at Portsmouth.[14]

The first licences for the export of wool of the new season were enrolled on 29 July 1271 and were valid until All Saints (1 November), while additional licences were enrolled on 19 occasions down to 20 October.[15] Whereas in the spring there had been little distinction between the licences a clear distinction was now made between those issued to Englishmen, Gascons and a few resident aliens on the one hand and all other aliens on the other. Licences issued to the first group were for unlimited amounts of wool while those going to the second group specified the amount of wool which might be exported. The first group received a total of 95 licences up to 22 August and a further 5 after that date, most of them going to individual merchants, although a few went to partnerships. Since there was no restriction upon the amount of wool which might be exported very few parties took more than one licence. Six licences went to Italians, 5 to Gascons,

3 to Cahorsins, 2 to Frenchmen and 2 to Germans. The remaining 82 went mostly to natives, although the number possibly includes a few denizened foreigners. The less 'privileged' group received a total of 249 licences, most of them going to different individuals or partnerships. The considerable range in the number of sacks specified in each licence suggests that the figure was nominated by the merchants themselves and may have corresponded to the amount of wool which each held at the time the licence was issued. The grand total was 14 589½ sacks 26 pokes of wool and 89 sacks of fells.

Following a further ban on the export of wool during the winter months licences began to be issued once more on 21 January 1272, the last batch being enrolled on 12 April. In all, 59 licences were issued for the export of the residue of the 1271 clip, 35 of them being for unspecified amounts. The total of the wool in the remaining 24 licences was 1031½ sacks, 3 sacks of fells and 1400 fells. There was, however, no obvious discrimination between denizens and aliens in the type of licence which was issued. The first licences for wool of the 1272 clip were enrolled on 29 May, and down to 18 September a total of 375 were entered. Many of these were collective licences, issued to large groups, so that total number of merchants was considerably greater than the number of licences. There was again no discrimination between denizens and aliens and all licences were for unlimited amounts of wool. On 2 and 5 November 1272, 41 licences were issued to aliens and denizens, in all of which the amount of wool was specified, the total being 2287 sacks. The export of the residue of the 1272 clip was authorised in 71 enrolments of licences made between 17 January and 4 April 1273, all valid until Easter (9 April).[16] In the new reign it is necessary to refer to totals of enrolments rather than to totals of licences actually issued, since frequently a single enrolment records the issue of a number of licences to an individual or partnership.

In the year 1273 there was probably no period in which there was a real stoppage of exports, for licences were issued more or less continuously from 30 April to 8 January, 1274.[17] The longest interval in which no licences were enrolled lasted from 24 September to 3 November. The total enrolments in this season was 920, although the number of merchants was considerably smaller and the total of licences issued somewhat larger. In order to appreciate the reason for the great increase in the number of licences issued it is necessary to understand the change in the method of administering them which was made after the accession of Edward I. For the greater part of 1272 all licences had permitted an unlimited amount of wool to be exported. Therefore, although a merchant may have obtained more than one official copy of his licence he did not need to renew it, unless its period of validity expired before he had completed his business for the season. From the beginning of 1273 a licence consisted of a pair of letters patent, presumably one for retention by the merchant and one to be surrendered at the port of export. With rare exceptions each licence now authorised the export of 20 sacks of wool. This meant that a merchant exporting anything up to 20 sacks from a single port needed only to obtain one pair of letters patent. However, one exporting the same amount of wool, but divided between more than one port, would probably need to obtain more than one pair of letters. Similarly anyone exporting more than 20 sacks would also need more than one pair of letters. Hence an enrolment stating '60 by 3 pairs of letters' may conceal either a shipment of anything from 41 to 60 sacks from a single port or alternatively shipments of, for example, 8, 13 and 15 sacks from 3 different ports. Because of this it is quite impossible to use the licences granted in 1273 as evidence of the amount of wool which was exported. Although they indicate the maximum amount which was officially authorised to leave the country the actual size of the legal export was probably smaller. On the other hand the official exports were supplemented by smuggled wool These facts were not understood by Adolf Schaube who assumed that each merchant probably exported the full quota of wool contained in his licences.[18] Schaube's figures for the wool exports of the year 1273 are therefore merely the sum of a series of multiples of 20 sacks. Neither his total, nor its division among merchants of different nationalities necessarily correspond with reality.

The English government was well aware that its orders forbidding intercourse with the Flemings were widely disregarded but its efforts to enforce the law can only be described as half-hearted. In October 1270 a commission had been set up, consisting of the wool merchants Nicholas Adele de la Pole and Alexander le Riche, of Andover, and Roger de Dunstable, of Winchester, together with the royal clerks, William de Hibernia and John de Yarmouth. This body was charged firstly with enumerating all Flemish-owned goods which had been arrested in England and subsequently with enquiring about illegal dealings with Flemings and illegal exports of wool to Flanders. The progress of the commission was so slow that by August 1271 they had not completed a circuit of the country. Therefore Poncius de Mora, merchant of Cahors, was ordered to conduct enquiries in the parts around Boston and Hull. In February 1272 the continuing task of tracing Flemish assets was transferred to a new commission, while the original body was appointed as receivers. By May, when it was clear that the diplomatic negotiations had failed, it was decided to distribute the assets among the English merchants who had suffered losses in Flanders. The following month the government attempted to clamp down on the export of wool to Flanders and a new commission was issued to Poncius de Mora and others, instructing them to enquire about offences. During the autumn this commission was responsible for the arrest of a number of alleged offenders at Boston, but the illegal traffic was not contained.[19]

By the early part of 1274 it was obvious that short of a total ban there was no way in which wool could be prevented from reaching Flanders and on 28 February the government issued instructions that writs should be made out as quickly as possible forbidding all export. On 10 April writs were sent to sheriffs ordering them to proclaim that no-one, on pain of life and limb, might take any wool out of the realm, neither beyond the seas, nor to Wales, Scotland or Ireland. This time a determined effort was made to enforce the ban, both by land and by sea. In a commission enrolled on 18 April all the coastal counties from Northumberland to Cornwall were divided into seven groups, and in each a royal official was charged with the duty of preventing the export of wool. As a result of this action all ships caught carrying wool during the spring and summer were arrested. The further decision to control the movement of wool within the realm may have developed from the high-handed action of local officials. Early in April Roger Pride of Shrewsbury and other merchants complained that under the pretext of stopping exports sheriffs and other officials were preventing them from bringing wool to London and other centres. On this occasion the merchants were issued with letters forbidding sheriffs from interfering with the movement of wool. By the end of May, however, a regular licensing system had been established and only merchants holding a licence could transport wool about the country. On 7 June 1274 Edward I, returning from the Holy Land, wrote from Limoges to Robert Burnell, the Chancellor, complaining that the ban on exports was not being enforced. He alleged that there was no shortage of wool in Flanders and that consequently the men of those parts were mocking him. As a result of this letter a commission was issued on 28 June, followed by further commissions in November and in January 1275 calling for the apprehension of all who had exported wool during the period of prohibition. Meanwhile, despite the king's fears, the prospects of a wool famine seems to have brought Flanders to the conference table. By 28 July 1274 Guy Dampierre, son of the Countess Margaret, and English envoys, meeting at Montreuil had arranged a truce and agreed upon terms for settling the dispute.[20]

Since both rulers had already disposed of much of the arrested merchandise a mutal restoration of property was out of the question. Therefore to simplify matters, and to hasten a final settlement, it was agreed that each ruler should satisfy the claims of his own subjects out of enemy assets already seized or yet to be identified. Any balance due to the merchants beyond the value of these was to be paid by their own ruler, subject to his being reimbursed by the other side. This removed the need for each merchant to sue for his property in the courts of the other country. The verification of claims, which corresponded, of course, to the identification of assets in the other country, was vested in mixed commissions. The English commission was issued on 16 October 1274 to the royal clerks Fulk Lovel and John Bek, assisted by 4 English merchants chosen by the merchants of Flanders, and 4 Flemings chosen by the English. By July 1275 the commission had accepted claims by English merchants totalling £10 627 10s 2½d, while established Flemish claims amounted to £5871 13s 2½d. The English losses had consisted almost entirely of merchandise arrested in Flanders at the beginning of the dispute, principally 1389½ sacks of wool, valued at £7810 18s 3d. Since Flemish claims included compensation for ships seized as late as 1273 some of their other items may also refer to losses in later stages of the conflict. The admitted losses of the Flemings totalled about 320 sacks, valued at £2124 16s 3d. The remainder of the claim included cloth and other merchandise, but was made up principally of money debts owed to Flemings and some earnest money which had been paid to monasteries for wool. Many of the debts represented cloth which had been sold on credit. It is difficult to escape the conclusion that in September 1270 the Flemings held fewer assets in England than the English did in Flanders. It was claimed that this was because the countess had forewarned her subjects of her intention of arresting English goods. It is not necessary to accept that she was thus obliging. The situation in England throughout the year had been such that any prudent Flemish merchant would conduct his business and return home as quickly as possible. The same transports which took much of the English merchants' new wool to Flanders had probably also brought home many Flemings with their wool. Nevertheless it is possible that the comparatively low level of the Flemish assets resulted in part from their inability to establish some claims to the satisfaction of the English commissioners.[21]

Edward I called upon Guy de Dampierre, co-ruler of Flanders with his mother the countess, to pay the balance of £4755 17s between the claims of the English and Flemish merchants at the Octave of St Mary (22 August) 1275. In addition the count was required to pay 730 marks to Gilbert de Cur of Ghent, which was owed to the latter by the City of London. This money had been paid to the account of the English merchants, but was not included in the calculations already mentioned. The failure of the count to respond to the English request for payment was probably caused by the demands made upon him by his own subjects to settle their claim. In at least one instance a Flemish merchant claimed a far higher amount of compensation than had been admitted in England. If there were numbers of such claims, and if the count had settled them without dispute, he would have been heavily out of pocket. The merchant in question was Jean Boinebroke of Douai, whose claim for compensation against the count may be compared with assets allowed to him in an account in the English Exchequer. The English account records that Boinebroke had lost 40 marks earnest money which he had paid to Newminster Abbey and that 92 sacks 10 stone of abbey wool had been taken from his agent, Gerard Poinmoilliés, at Newcastle. The value of the wool amounts to £646 10s 9d, although because of faulty addition Boinebroke is given a total credit of only £639 11s 2d instead of £673 4s 1d. Boinebroke's claims against his own ruler totalled £1086 16s 6d sterling (£1086 19s 8d corrected); how did this discrepancy arise? In addition to the earnest money Boinebroke claimed money debts totalling £86 6s 10d. Most of the difference, however, is accounted for by discrepancies in the valuation of the wool. Boinebroke alleged that the English appraised his Newminster wool at only £534 13s 4d, while he also claimed that he lost 27 sacks of wool at Tynemouth, which the English valued at £87. This latter item does not appear in the English account at all. Against the alleged English appraisal of £621 13s 4d Boinebroke claimed that the wool had cost him £857 5s 0d to buy. He claimed the difference between the two sums from the count, together with £100 13s 4d expenses incurred in procuring the wool and £9 8s custom paid for the Newcastle wool. While some of the discrepancies between the English account and that of Jean Boinebroke cannot now be explained it is easy to understand why wool might be appraised at lesser sums than Flemish merchants had paid for it in the first place. The English figures represented the prices at which arrested goods were sold to English merchants and since there was often a considerable delay between arrest and sale the wool probably deteriorated in quality. Boinebroke's Newminster wool was sold to Thomas de Basing, of London, and a group of Newcastle merchants. The Englishmen took the wool to Abbeville, whose lord had requested Henry III to proclaim a staple in that town. There, however, some of it was arrested for a time by the échevins at the behest of Jean Boinebroke and others.[22]

While the commission of 1274 was doing its work there was a military truce between England and Flanders, although normal trade rela-tions were not restored. The formal ban on the export of wool remained in force, and at first certificates of exemption were probably granted with discretion. On 14 July 1274, the merchants of Amiens were authorised to export wool acquired before 29 June, but were expressly forbidden to traffic with the Flemings. On 28 July the men of Paris and of Auge, in Normandy, were allowed to export new wool, and on 7 August John de Brilond, a Lübecker domiciled in London, was given similar authority. The customs records prove that by the time of the 1275 clip, exports were in full swing once more. However, despite the fact that there are no surviving enrolments of licences for this period restrictions of some sort or other undoubtedly remained in force throughout 1275.[23]

By the spring of 1275 Flemish merchants were beginning to return to England and on 19 April they were authorised to deal in wool within the realm and even to export it wherever they wished until Sunday after the Holy Cross (5 May). At first they came under indivi-dual letters of protection, but on 28 July the king granted a collective safe conduct to the men of Ypres for five years, on condition that the peace continued. However in the early part of 1276 the king grew impatient with Guy's reluctance to deliver the money owed to the English merchants and reimposed sanctions on Flanders. On 23 May he issued instructions that no wool was to be exported anywhere except under special licence, and that no-one should traffic with or on behalf of Flemish merchants now in England. This order fell short of seizing Flemish goods, although care was to be taken that none were removed from the country. Later in the summer the government prepared to seize all the Flemish goods which it could lay hold of, but the plan seems to have misfired. Orders were given to arrest all Flemish goods at Boston, Lynn and Lincoln, but probably only those of Douai were stopped. Even these had to be released but it was recalled that all Flemings were covered by a safe conduct which was valid until 1 August. In the middle of August orders were sent to the authorities of Bristol, Portsmouth and Southampton, ordering them to arrest 'warily and secretly' all the wool and other goods belonging to Flem-ings. However although most or all Flemish-owned property appears to have been under restraint by this time, the government did not wish to cause unnecessary hardship to the merchants. It therefore allowed goods to be disposed of, provided that the buyers answered to the king for the price. By 20 October 1276 there had been some sort of settle-ment and all merchants of Bruges, Ypres, Douai and Ghent were given a safe conduct until the following Whitsun. Shortly afterwards Nicholas de Ludlow and Thomas de Basing, two leading wool merchants, were sent to Flanders to demand immediate payment from Count Guy.[24]

From Whitsun 1277 the Flemings were once again forbidden to trade in England, while all native and alien merchants were required to subscribe to an oath they would not deal with or on behalf of Flemish merchants in this country. The oath also compelled them to reveal any debts which they, or anyone known to them, owed to Flemings. This applied, apparently, to debts incurred since the settlement of Montreuil, as well as to those outstanding from the period before the dispute. On the other hand, although wool might be exported only by licence, it was specifically stated that it could be sold to Flemings once it had passed overseas. It could even be exported in Flemish ships. The explanation of this is provided by the fact that since the imposition of a regular export duty the king was not prepared to make the personal sacrifice involved in preventing wool from reaching Flanders. Before the end of 1277 it had become clear that until the losses of the English merchants had been settled, whether by the count or some other party, his subjects would be unable to trade freely in England. Accordingly the burgesses of Ypres, Douai, Dikemue and Poperinghe agreed with the English government that they would pay £2022 of the sum outstanding. This had apparently been paid by the beginning of February 1278 and the merchants of these towns were given a safe conduct to trade in England, which guaranteed that they could not be molested for any part of the remaining debt.[25]

In May 1278 at another conference held at Montreuil the English envoys reported that with the greatest difficulty the king had persuaded his subjects to respite their claim until the following Easter. The count and his pledges were required to give new guarantees that if the money was not paid in full on that occasion they would all surrender themselves and submit to imprisonment. At Easter 1279 the English promptly claimed the money and somewhat tardily the count paid £1316 18s 6d via the hands of the Italian firm of Riccardi. In November 1280 payment of another £1000 was ordered, although it seems likely that little of this was paid. In 1282 John Bek was appointed to review the case in Boston at Michaelmas, but the count requested a delay and called upon the king to preside in person. This the king was unable to because of the war in Wales, but he deputed Edmund of Cornwall to determine the matter in his place on the morrow of Hilary (14 January) 1283. In June 1285, with the debt still unpaid, the English called upon the Flemish hostages to surrender themselves in 6 months time. This threat seems to have brought matters to a head, for in February 1286 it was arranged that the count should pay the outstanding balance of £1131 11s 6½d in quarterly instalments. On 18 November 1287 proctors of the English merchants gave quittances for the final payment of £282 and on the same day the Flemish proctors requested the cancellation and return of the instruments given by their hostages and all other documents relating to the case. The long dispute seemed finally to be at an end.[26]

Although some Flemish merchants returned to England in 1275 and later years and began once more to engage in the wool trade they were unable to recover the ascendancy which they had formerly enjoyed. In particular they lost for ever most of the valuable Cistercian contracts. Although there are instances of clandestine dealings between Cistercians and Flemings during the period of prohibition there was no real need for the monks to incur the king's displeasure in this manner. They had no trouble whatsoever in finding new customers who were only too eager to shoulder the risk of exporting wool to Flanders. Early in 1275 the government wrote to all monasteries enquiring about earnest money which had been paid for wool and about all other debts owed to alien merchants. Among the few surviving returns is that from Meaux stating that the wool of the next two years was contracted to the Scotti of Piacenza, who had paid 400 marks in earnest, while that of the following ten years was contracted to the Cerchi of Florence, who had advanced 1600 marks. In 1270 Bernard Pilate of Douai had bought 16 sacks of wool worth £140 from Meaux. Newminster Abbey replied that the wool of the years 1274–6 was contracted to the Bardi of Florence, who had given £100 in earnest, while that of the following four years was to go to another company, probably the Cerchi, who had also advanced £100. In 1270 Jean Boinebroke had bought 72 sacks of abbey wool and 20 sacks of *collecta* from Newminster as well as giving 40 marks in earnest of future payments. Shelford Priory answered that in 1271 they sold their wool to a stranger at Boston fair, in 1272 to John atte Cemetary of Grantham, in 1273 to the Cerchi and in 1274 to the Bardi, who had also given 90 marks in earnest for the clip of 1275. Welbeck Priory in 1273 sold their wool of that year and the next two years to the Bardi, while in 1274 they received 100 marks from the Frescobaldi in earnest of four years wool from 1276. Fountains Abbey as late as 1273 sold its wool for two years to Baldwin fitz Jeremiah of Flanders and received some 500 marks in earnest. The buyer was unable to collect the clip of 1274 and in 1275 the king ordered the abbey to let him have the current year's clip in recompense. The monks replied that they had already promised it to the Riccardi of Lucca, while in 1276 they contracted to sell their wool of the next four years to Florentines.[27]

It is no coincidence that in each of the examples cited above Flemish purchasers were replaced by Italians. The Italian merchants had greater liquidity than any other group and were able to meet the Cistercian demand for cash in advance. Moreover some of the houses were already indebted to Italian companies, who were therefore the natural successors of the Flemings. Within a very few years the Italians were able to acquire a near monopoly of Cistercian wool. However the Italians were not the only group to benefit from the misfortunes of the Flemings, for there can be little doubt that merchants of other nationalities were able to increase their exports during this period. It is essential, therefore, to appreciate that the licences of the 1270s, even if they can be used to indicate very roughly the share-out of the legal export trade, reflect a situation which was fundamentally new. The Flemings, probably the largest and oldest group of exporters, had been rudely thrust aside and others were rushing in to fill the vacuum. Any attempt to assess the degree of novelty must include a study not only of the licences but also of the earlier participation of each nationality engaged in the wool trade.

After native Englishmen the group with the largest share of the licences issued in 1273 was the Italian, whom Schaube showed as receiving licences to export 8000 sacks, 24.4 per cent of the total. It is by no means impossible that the Italian share of exports was proportionately larger than this. Given that each licence authorised the export of up to 20 sacks a small number of merchants who found it necessary to obtain many licences are likely to have successfully exported more wool than a larger number of merchants, nominally licensed to export an equal amount, but for many of whom a single licence was sufficient warrant. In Schaube's calculations the average quota for each Italian licence was 182 sacks compared, for instance, with 78 sacks for the southern French and 40.2 sacks for Englishmen. All the Italians who received licences were natives of Florence, Lucca or Piacenza. Although it would be incorrect to say that no other cities shared in the English wool trade in the thirteenth century, the role of the others, with the possible exception of Pistoia, was minimal. In 1251 the king confirmed the sale of the Cotswold wool of Westminster Abbey to a Siennese company for six years. Even if the abbot died in this period and the abbey came into the king's hands the merchants were to have the wool.[28] The Siennese, however, were primarily usurers and from an early date their concern with trade was very limited.

Difficult though it may be to credit that the Italians acquired a 25 per cent share of the wool trade almost overnight this is probably not very far from the truth. Jordan Fantosme[29] put Lombards in the company of the Flemish mercenaries who came to rob England of her wool in 1173, but it is impossible to believe that at this date, or for many years to come, Italians played any regular part in the wool trade. This claim is based on the belief that not until the middle of the thirteenth century was the Italian presence in England strong enough and continuous enough for them to have built up a large stake in this enterprise. Until they were firmly established their principal export was probably cloth. In the first half of the thirteenth century Florentines seem to have constituted the most numerous group of Italians in England. They were first mentioned in 1224[30] and thereafter were given letters of safe conduct during periods of hostility with France. The fact that there appear to be no similar letters enrolled during the troubled years of John's reign suggests the possibility that they began to trade regularly in England after the restoration of peace early in the reign of Henry III. To begin with they were not domiciled here and safe conducts were issued to an individual or individuals for a limited period, providing security in coming and going and in trading in the realm. The earliest surviving record of a general safe conduct was that issued on 9 October 1234, which promised to protect all the merchants of Florence and their goods for a period of two years from All Saints (1 November). Dr von Roon-Basserman has shown that these Florentines were not petty merchants adventuring on their own account; they represented companies which, albeit the membership changed over a period of time, had a continuous existence for many decades. She has identified five companies which were active in England in the 1220s, only one of which dropped out of the picture in the 1230s, the remainder continuing to operate until the 1260s when the internal politics of Florence adversely affected the overseas interests of some of the companies. Throughout this period each company was normally represented by two partners or principal factors, although occasionally by only one and rarely by three. It may be presumed that they were always accompanied by servants, the numbers of whom are indeterminable.[31]

During the middle years of the thirteenth century one group of Florentines became established particularly firmly in England – that centred on the family of Willelmi. Felinus Willelmi was dead by April 1250 and his place as head of the family was taken by his brother, Deutayutus, although another brother, Beneventus, was in England in 1249 and 1250. In November 1252 the king granted extremely valuable privileges to Deutayutus and his heirs, as citizens of London and members of its gild merchant. Deutayutus also bought a house in the city for the large sum of 400 marks. The Willelmi were not excused an expulsion of 1253, but they served the king loyally in Gascony in 1254 and 1255 and Deutayutus returned to England in November 1255. In February 1256 the king gave him a present of 100 marks *pro laudabili servitio nostro* and thereafter he was probably never out of royal favour, serving the crown as demesne merchant. Members of the Willelmi family seem to have acquired the status of denizens and established a company which was based not on Florence but on London.[32]

Although the Florentines were principally merchants they increasingly engaged in usury and on these grounds they were periodically expelled from the country, as were the Siennese and some other Italians. Expulsions are recorded in 1240, 1245, 1251, and 1253. In 1256, however, Henry III, deeply in debt to the papacy in the vain pursuit of the crown of Sicily for his son Edmund, was allowed to relieve his difficulties by taxing the English church. The proceeds were transmitted to Rome by merchant bankers, the first occasion on which this was done on any large scale.[33] Among those who returned to England in this business were the Florentine companies of Scala, Gualfredi and Ghiberti-Bellindoti. A representative of the Pulci-Rimbertini was in England in 1258 trying to collect debts owed to this company, but it was not employed to transfer cash to Rome, probably because it was temporarily short of funds.[34] In 1262 the Florentines again incurred the king's displeasure on account of injuries allegedly done to his kinsman, Peter of Savoy, and it is likely that many of them were expelled. In September 1263 letters of protection were issued to representatives of the Pulci-Rimbertini, Scala and Gualfredi. Since this coincided with the resumption of power by the baronial party it provides yet one more hint that the Montfortians should not too readily be charged with hostility to alien merchants.[35]

The repeated expulsions which were the lot of Florentine merchants down to the 1260s must surely have hindered the growth of their trade in England. In particular it must have made it difficult for them to entice the leading monastic producers away from their contracts with the Flemings. In the late 1260s, however, the Florentine presence in England was greatly strengthened. Although there was an increase in money lending large advances to the Crown ensured that there was a respite until 1275 in prosecutions for usury. The Willelmi, Gualfredi, Scala and Pulci-Rimbertini were all active in these years and a number of new companies were established. A representative of the Bardi was in England by January 1267 at the latest, while the Cerchi were here before the end of 1268. When the breach occurred between England and Flanders it was, by and large, the new companies, not those long established, which took advantage of the situation to take over a large share of the wool trade.

The leading wool-exporting company during the early 1270s was probably that of the Cerchi. This position was achieved as much by the inflow of personnel as of capital. No fewer than eleven partners or factors were named among the recipients of export licences, while at least two others are known to have been in the country by 1277. The earliest member of the company whose presence is recorded in England was Rustikellus Thedaldi, who had dealings with the queen in 1268. In 1271 Rustikellus, described as citizen and merchant of London, was granted two unlimited licences. In the same period another member of the company, Paganel Walbon, was issued with a licence to export 425 sacks. In the 1273 season members of the company received licences to a total of 1020 sacks. In May 1275 they admitted to offences relating to 3626½ sacks of wool, a figure which possibly represents their total exports, authorised and unauthorised, over the previous three or four seasons. Since profits from the sale of wool must have more than covered the fine of 10s per sack the company stood to lose more by any attempt at concealment than by disclosing all their dealings and buying a full pardon. The Frescobaldi, who admitted the offences relating to 1059 sacks, were probably attracted to England by the openings created in the wool trade after 1270. There is no trace of any member of the company in this country before May 1272 when they received licences to export wool. In the 1273 season four members of the company obtained licences authorising the export of up to 880 sacks. This is true also of the company of Falconieri which is first met with in 1272. The following season three members of the company received licences for up to 620 sacks, and they later paid a fine for a total of 1068 sacks. The company of Bardi received licences to export wool throughout the period of the troubles, including one of 100 sacks at the tail-end of the 1270 season, but no member of the company was among the group of Italians who were treated like denizens. In the 1273 season the company's licences authorised the export of up to 660 sacks. There is no record of any fine which may have been paid.[36]

Among the long-established firms the only ones who sought wool licences were the Willelmi and the Pulci-Rimbertini. Dr von Roon-Basserman has written about a 'consortium' composed of the families of Willelmi and del Papa and the relationship between the two is indisputable. On the other hand there seems no reason to doubt that now, as later, Hugo del Papa was the chief representative in England of the company of Pulci-Rimbertini. Hugo del Papa was in England by the beginning of 1269 at the latest and in 1271 was described, like Deutayutus Willelmi, as king's merchant and citizen of London, and numbered among the privileged Italians. The group, consisting of at least six members of the del Papa family, three or four Willelmi and half a dozen others, exported wool throughout the early period of the licences and in 1273 were authorised to export up to 640 sacks. The link between the Pulci-Rimbertini and the Willelmi was probably forged to farm the new aid on merchandise which had been granted to Prince Edward and may not have survived much beyond 1273. In 1276 the Willelmi were associated with the Cerchi in a contract to buy wool from Fountains Abbey, but on the whole the family seems to have traded independently. In addition to the Willelmi there were probably a few smaller independent firms having a minor stake in the wool trade in the early 1270s. Nutus Fulberti, who married an English-woman and with his brothers was active in England throughout the 1270s and 1280s, obtained privileged licences as the king's merchant in 1271 and 1272. Lottus Bonpare, probably identical with Ottoman Beaupar, was authorised to export 40 sacks at the end of the 1270 season, 140 sacks in 1271, an unlimited amount in 1272 and 40 sacks at the end of that season. But was he an independent, or should he perhaps be identified with Loterius Bonaguyde of the Scala, a company otherwise not represented in the enrolments of wool licences? This Loterius was involved in proceedings in the Exchequer in 1276 where it was admitted that Kirkstall Abbey owed 2 sacks 3 stones of wool to the Scala. However in actions against other monasteries in the same year only cash debts are acknowledged. Similarly who was Osbert Galigi who was licensed to export 60 sacks in 1273? The biggest mystery, however, surrounds nine individuals authorised to export wool in 1272. Although these nine were grouped with Hugh Post, later one of the leaders of the Pulci-Rimbertini, the fact that their names do not appear again in English sources makes one reluctant to assign them to this or to any other of the main companies.[37]

Like the merchants of Florence those of Piacenza were trading in England by the 1220s at the latest, when they were licensed to freight ships during the Anglo-French wars. Like the former, the Piacenzans were expelled from the country from time to time, as in 1256 when they incurred the displeasure of the king's kinsman, Peter of Savoy.[38] Nevertheless in the 1273 season Piacenzans were issued with licences authorising the export of up to 2320 sacks of wool, double the number obtained by any other company. Of the twelve Piacenzan merchants who received licences between 1271 and 1273 at least nine, and prob-ably all, were members of the company of Scotti, who took all the 1273 licences.

The merchants of Lucca may have been comparatively late in com-ing to England, for not until the mid 1240s is there conclusive evidence of their presence, at which time they were supplying silks, cloth of gold and other luxury fabrics to the royal household. By 1251 they were established in force and in that year no fewer than six members of the company, or future company, of Riccardi were issued with letters of protection for periods of two and three years.[39] Members of the company of Bettri were in England during the same period. In the late 1260s the Riccardi built up a very strong position in England through the service to the king and to Prince Edward and by 1270 their leaders were citizens of London and crown merchants. The company was issued with licences throughout the period of the ban on trade with Flanders, those of the 1273 season authorising the export of up to 1140 sacks. Later the company was pardoned a fine of £1498 5s for offences relating to the export of 2996½ sacks of wool. The Riccardi, however, was not the only Lucca firm engaged in the wool trade, for the Bettri received licences in 1272 and 1273. In the latter season the company was authorised to export up to 560 sacks. Finally licences were issued to two Lucchese who cannot positively be identified with either company.

Despite the ascendancy which they enjoyed during the last three decades of the thirteenth century the Italians were not the first southern capitalists to secure a firm foothold in English economic life, for there can be little doubt that the merchants of Cahors and Montpellier were here before them. It is not always possible to distinguish between these two groups, since occasionally southern French merchants are described merely as subjects of the Count of Toulouse. However the merchants of Cahors were the more numerous and more important.[40] N. Denholm-Young has suggested that the link between England and Cahors may have been established as a result of the marriage of Henry II to Eleanor of Aquitaine. This proposal has much to recommend it, although care should be taken not to antedate the connection. The first positive date which can be given to Cahorsin merchants in England is 1205 and their presence even in the Atlantic and Mediterranean ports of France can be proved no earlier than the last quarter of the twelfth century.[41] Once they discovered England the Cahorsins quickly built up a strong presence. More than a score of merchants are known to have visited it before 1230 and many of these were in the country at the same time. Family partnerships formed the basis of their organisation, but there seem also to have been associations which transcended the family. On one occasion representatives of a number of families were described as *mercatores de Tabula Gaillard*. Long before Edward I became dependent on the Italians these men of Cahors were serving the crown in a financial capacity. During the Gascon campaign of

1225 they were entrusted with the transfer of funds from England, while at various times they loaned money in Gascony, Flanders and Champagne for purveyances for the royal household. At Christmas 1243 Ernald Beraud and Ernald Geraudon were presented with royal liveries, an action indicative of service to the Crown. In 1246 Ernald Geraudon was appointed chamberlain of London and Sandwich, a post he held until his death in 1253. In this capacity he was one of the chief buyers of the king's wine, a service performed from 1269 by another Cahorsin, Poncius de Mora. In 1263 Peter and William Beraud and their fellows lent money to Prince Edward, taking as security the issues of the Jewish Exchequer, which they were to hold for three years. After the barons' war this same group farmed the new aid of merchandise, while another group farmed the great custom of Bordeaux.[42]

The Cahorsins evidently obtained a share of the wool trade at a relatively early date, for shortly before the death of King John Reginald Willelmi and Hubert of Cahors were given royal protection while moving 51 sacks of wool which they had bought from the Archbishop of Dublin.[43] Their activities soon extended to all parts of the country and during the 1230s and 1240s Cahorsins may be found shipping wool from Southampton, London, Yarmouth, Orwell and Hull. This wool may have been directed towards any one or more of a number of destinations. In the early middle ages Cahors itself had a cloth industry, based in the first instance on the sheep which were the mainstay of the chalk uplands of the region. By the beginning of the fourteenth century, although how much earlier is unknown, wool was transported from England to Italy via Gascony and Montpellier.[44] On the other hand the Cahorsins were not restricted to a simple bilateral trade between England and Gascony. In the early thirteenth century they engaged in trade between England and Flanders and England and the Champagne fairs, and they may have taken wool to either of these regions.

In the first half of the thirteenth century the Cahorsins probably enjoyed a greater share in the English wool trade than the Italians did, but during the 1270s, or even before that date, they lost the advantage. In the 1271 season merchants of Cahors and Montpellier received licences to export a total of 1528 sacks, apart from licences issued to Poncius de Mora, buyer of the king's wine, who was 'reputed' a denizen. Merchants of Toulouse and elsewhere in the south of France outside of Gascony received licences for 379 sacks. In the 1273 season the merchants of Cahors and Montpellier were authorised to export up to 1725 sacks.[45] In the 1280s there were four or five companies of

Cahors and Montpellier merchants who were wealthy enough to be a frequent target for royal demands for loans and the number was probably about the same a decade earlier. Relations within the companies may have been less formal than in contemporary Italian practice, at any rate it is more difficult to assign individuals to a particular society.

The most influential, and possibly the largest, group was that centred on Poncius de Mora. Apart from the unlimited licences which were issued to Poncius himself he was named in licences, both limited and unlimited, with six other men. The limited licences authorised the export of 500 sacks, but this may be an understatement of the group's activities, for possibly one should add to this the exports of John Donedeu and Peter Beraud. The former had licences for 220 sacks in 1271 and 580 sacks in 1273 and the latter 490 sacks in 1271. Although the licences neither associate John Donedeu and Peter Beraud with one another, nor either with Poncius de Mora, it is possible to provide the connecting links. Poncius was named in a licence for 60 sacks with William Beraud and Benedict Johannis. William was the brother of Peter, while the Beraud family had connections with England from the earliest appearance of the Cahorsins to at least the end of the thirteenth century. Benedict Johannis was named as the partner of John Donedeu, when they and their associates were pardoned a £200 fine imposed for wool offences. Moreover by the 1280s, when Poncius de Mora was no longer active in commercial life, John Donedeu and William Johannis appear to have been the leading members of the group formerly headed by Poncius. The second most prominent group was that headed by Arnold Griffin, citizen of London, who in 1271 was licensed to export wool without limit. Griffin first appears in English sources in 1259. In that year, besides importing wine, he made a contract to buy from Robert de Tateshall in 1260 70 sacks of the *collecta* of Deeping, Spalding and Holland in Lincolnshire. The associates of Griffin in the period of the licences were William Servat, Gaubert of Navarre and John de Soliz. The last two were pardoned £40 of a fine imposed for wool offences. Thirteen other Cahorsin merchants, who cannot positively be attached to any particular group received export licences in the years 1271 to 1273. Among them was at least one distinct company, possibly headed now, as later, by Aumfrey Mauryn. The Montpellier society of Chapdemaill was headed by James Chapdemaill and Bertrand de Croyses, but John and Bertrand Squier were named as associates of the former in 1271.[46]

Southern French participation in the English wool trade was greatly surpassed by that of the northern French merchants from the country lying between Paris and the Channel coast. Within this region the overwhelming bulk of the trade was handled from five centres, Amiens with Corbie and Nesle, Rouen, St Omer, Paris and Cambrai. In the first two centres the trade was distributed between a comparatively large number of merchants, while in the remaining places the participants were far fewer. The tendency towards concentration was most pronounced in the case of Cambrai, where only eight merchants shared in the export of 1022 sacks in the 1271 season and only six in the licences for up to 680 sacks in 1273. Schaube credited northern French merchants with an export of 5280 sacks in 1273, 16.1 per cent of the total for the year.[47] Dr von Roon-Basserman has urged caution in accepting these figures, on the grounds that the total, as also that for Brabant, includes many single licences for 20 sacks.[48] She points out that in many cases the merchants concerned had licences for fewer than 20 sacks in 1271 and she regards it as unlikely that all were able in the meantime to raise sufficient capital to increase their export to that figure. In the case of Amiens, the most important centre of the trade, we find that in the period of 1270–4 a total of about 128 merchants were named in licences, including a few Yorkshiremen who apparently enjoyed burgess rights in the French town and are sometimes enrolled among the merchants of the King of France. In 1273 25 out of 51 Amiens licensees took single licences, and of these seven can be identified as having been exporters in 1271. In 1271 exports of five of the seven totalled 45 sacks while the other two had participated in partnerships which had each exported over 100 sacks. A further ten of the 1273 licensees, authorised to export up to 480 sacks, can be identified as having exported a total of 462 sacks in 1271. The total Amiens export for the 1271 season was 1474 sacks, enumerated in 50 licences, plus 4 unlimited licences, compared with an export of up to 1660 sacks from Easter to December 1273 (Schaube 1800). Outside Amiens and Rouen small exporters were less important and there is correspondingly less danger of their exaggerating the total. In fact Schaube's total of 5280 sacks for the whole of northern France in 1273 is less than that for the 1271 season, which amounted to over 5222 for the 5 centres already mentioned, 517 for other northern towns and 359 for merchants described merely as subjects of the King of France.

Beyond the boundaries of France classification of exporting merchants becomes increasingly difficult, for even in the thirteenth century the English were puzzled by the question of allegiance within the Empire. When in doubt they described a merchant merely as subject to the King of Almain, including in this category those of Friesland, Liege and even those from the Duchy of Brabant. In 1273 the Brabanters were the most important group of imperial merchants, Schaube crediting them with an export of 3678 sacks, 11.2 per cent of the total. If this figure is reliable it suggests that the Brabanters greatly increased their export during the period of crisis, for in the 1271 season they had acquired licences to export only 1239 sacks.[49] The trade was centred on Malines and Louvain, with Brussels and Antwerp handling a much smaller share. Schaube's figure of 820 sacks, 2.5 per cent, for the province of Liege is again much larger than the corresponding figure for 1271, which totalled only 341 sacks. However, a number of Liegois and Brabanters may be concealed among those described as 'merchants of Almain', who exported 353 sacks in 1271.

The remaining imperial merchants were classified by Schaube as German and credited with an export of 1440 sacks, 4.4 per cent of the total. This figure is surprisingly low considering that in 1271 the corresponding sum, even without the exports of the 'merchants of Almain', had been over 2325 sacks. The 1273 figure may be increased slightly by the addition of the licences for 240 sacks granted to the Lübeck merchant John de Brilond. These were omitted by Schaube on the grounds that Brilond, a citizen of London, was treated by the English as a denizen. Nevertheless the possibility remains that the total German export of 1273 was considerably lower than that of two years earlier. This must not be allowed to obscure the fact that in the slightly longer term the Germans benefited greatly from the withdrawal of the Flemings from the wool trade and within a few years were able to increase their share enormously. The leading German wool merchants were those of Lübeck, a city whose links with England were comparatively recent, having their seeds in the decline of the activities of the Gottland community in the middle of the thirteenth century. In the 1271 season 9 Lübeckers took 8 licences for 709 sacks and another 2 unlimited licences. Besides John de Brilond their number included Gerard Merbode, denizened by virtue of burgess rights in London, who was a kinsman of the famous Clipping family of Lübeck. Both men were in partnership with brothers or cousins in their home city. Cologne, whose commercial ties with England dated back to pre-Conquest times, contributed 15 merchants and 350 sacks. From Westphalia came 15 merchants of Soest with 480 sacks, 7 merchants from Dortmund with 310 sacks and one from Münster with 100 sacks. The remaining German quota was made up of 376½ sacks contributed by nine towns lying between the Rhine and the Zuider Zee, most of them now in the Netherlands. The merchants of the counties of Holland and Zeeland took no part in the wool trade at this period since, by an unfortunate coincidence, their ruler was at odds with the King of England.

Apart from a negligible amount taken by Spaniards, Schaube assigned all the remaining licences of 1273 to Englishmen, giving them 11 415 sacks, 34.9 per cent of the total. This undoubtedly exaggerates the English share, since Schaube has counted with them all of those whose nationality cannot be established and many denizened foreigners, including Flemings. If these groups are removed there remains 8651 sacks, 925 in the early part of 1273 and 7726 after Easter, with a further 380 in January 1274. Although Englishmen probably constituted the largest single group of exporters their lead was probably less than that proposed by Schaube. Moreover it is highly likely that before the troubles Englishmen had taken second place to Flemish exporters. This is not to deny that there had been a long-standing English participation in the export trade, for during the emergency of 1224–5 many natives had been granted licences for shipping space to take wool to Flanders. On the other hand it is significant that during the absence of Flemish merchants many of the leading wool-producing monasteries had at that time handled their own exports. It may seem reasonable to suppose that the disgrace of the Flemings in the 1270s presented the chance for many Englishmen to enter the ranks of the exporters for the first time. Two groups in particular might have been induced to step into the breach; firstly, middlemen in the wool trade whose dealings had been chiefly with the Flemings; secondly, Englishmen who had acted as hosts for Flemings. There must have been a strong temptation for men of both sorts to act in collusion with Flemings who could no longer trade openly in England. Collusion there undoubtedly was, but it took the form of clandestine trade and smuggling; the Englishmen did not rush to acquire licences to export wool in their own names. This conclusion is suggested by an analysis of the geographical distribution of export licences granted in the years 1271–4, supplemented by two other pieces of evidence.[50] Besides indicating the regions from which English merchants drew their wool the latter documents prove conclusively that the leading licensees were not newcomers to the export trade.

In the years 1271–4 at least 327 Englishmen obtained licences to export wool. Leaving aside London the principal region in which natives were actively engaged in the export trade was the south-east, from Kent to Hampshire. Although a large number of towns could claim at least one wool merchant the chief centres of the trade were the ports of Southampton and Sandwich and the inland towns of Winchester and Andover. Seventeen merchants of this region owned 348 out of 1389½ sacks of English wool confiscated in Flanders in 1270. One hundred and twelve were licensed to export wool in the years

TABLE 2 *Licensed merchants, 1271–4*

Locality	Licensed merchants March 1271 to Jan. 1274	Licences, May 1273 to Jan. 1274		Exports via London, 1273 season	
		Merchants	Authorised wool (sacks)	Merchants	Wool (sacks)
South of England	3	3	60		
Dorchester	1	1	20		
Winchester	40	21	945	1	10½
Newbury	1				
Southampton	19	11	260		
Portsmouth	1				
Alresford	3	1	20		
Stockbridge	3	1	20		
Basingstoke	2	1	20		
Andover	15	10	312		
Chichester	1				
Steyning	1				
Winchelsea	2	2	20		
Dover	1	1	60		
Sandwich	9	7	240		
Canterbury	5	3	100	1	45
Faversham	1				
Rochester	3	2	20		
Maidstone	1	1	80		
London	96	57	2688	Incomplete	
Bristol	9	6	280		
Gloucester	4	1	20		
Burford	1	1	20		
Chipping Norton	1				
Oxford	4	1	20		
Dunstable	10	6	960	6	892
Brackley	1			1[a]	30
Buckingham	1	1	60	1	14
Watford	1			1[a]	20
Baldock	2	1	80	2[a]	92½
Stanstead	1				
Maldon	1	1	60		
Ipswich	1				
Bury St Edmunds	1				
Dunwich	4	3	80		
Yarmouth	4	2	80		
Swaffham	1				
Lynn	10	6	240		
Fakenham	1	1	20		
Shrewsbury	12	6	620	7	493½
Ludlow	6	4	120	5	113
Hereford	1				
Abergavenny	2	2	40		
Chester	1				
Coventry	1	1	20	1	40
Leicester	3	1	20	3[a]	46
Stamford	1				
Lincoln	3	2	40		
Newcastle	15	9	281		
Scarborough	1				
Hedon	1	1	20		
Beverley	1				
York	7	1	20		
Pontefract	6	5	140		
Totals	327	184	8106		

[a] Includes recipients of licences before Easter, 1273.

1271–4, of whom 65 acquired licences for a total of up to 2177 sacks from the beginning of the 1273 season to the following January. Most of these operated on a limited scale, exporting comparatively small amounts of wool drawn from a restricted area. The wool seized from two Winchester merchants in 1270 was described as *collecta* of Winchester, while the 112 sacks taken from six Sandwich merchants were all made up of lambs wool from Kent. On the other hand there were a few men whose operations were larger. Alexander le Riche and Nicholas Adele de la Pole, both of Andover, were sufficiently prominent to be chosen to act for the community of English merchants in the protracted negotiations with Flanders. In 1270 Alexander bought his wool from around Cricklade and Somerset, while Nicholas, in partnership with Thomas de Anne of Dorchester, had 100 sacks drawn from places as far apart as Tewkesbury, Burford, Faringdon, Silchester, Salisbury, Lacock, Trent and Monkton. Simon Draper, mayor of Winchester, whose licences in the 1273 season totalled 60 sacks, bought extensively from the Bishops of Winchester in the seasons 1271–3. The comparatively large number of native wool merchants in the southern counties is not to be explained by a sudden influx into the trade brought about by a Flemish withdrawal, for it is unlikely that Flemish competition had previously been very great. The chief competitors to English merchants were those of Normandy and these remained as active in the 1270s as before. The strength of the English merchants is to be explained by the precocious commercial development of the south-east and the paradox that the wool of the region was mediocre in quality. This fortuitous combination must have made the southern counties relatively unattractive to Flemish adventurers. They could obtain better wool in areas which not only were more accessible to their homeland but in which a native commercial class was less developed.

One of the most profitable areas for Flemish wool exporters had undoubtedly been the lowlands of the Midlands and eastern England north of the Wash. In the years 1271–4 this region produced only eight licensees, from the towns of Coventry, Leicester, Stamford and Lincoln. It is suggested that this mirrors a dearth of native exporters during the previous period. If this view is correct the deficiency is probably to be explained by the strength of Flemish competition in the export field coupled with the fact that native economic enterprise was still devoted largely to the cloth manufacturing industry, although the latter was already beginning to experience hard times.[51] The wool export trade had probably engaged the energies of large numbers of Englishmen acting as middlemen, but the Hundred Rolls make it abundantly clear that when the crisis came many of these continued to deal clandestinely with Flemings rather than acquire export licences in their own names. Yorkshire, like the region to the south of the Humber, and probably for much the same reasons, seems to have had comparatively few native wool exporters, although even in the early part of the century they were by no means an unknown breed. It seems very likely that those who did export plied their trade with Picardy rather than with Flanders. Here they found return cargoes of woad for the Yorkshire cloth industry. The evidence for this relationship is greater at a slightly later date, but already in the 1270s the Wiles family of Pontefract and their partner John de Seterinton of York had burgess rights in Amiens. North of Yorkshire there seems to have been quite a strong pocket of native exporters in Newcastle. This may possibly be explained by the fact that we are now beyond the region most attractive to the Flemings. However, as already mentioned, even Jean Boinebroke of Douai did not disdain to buy the wool of Northumberland.

In East Anglia there was a native export trade based on the ports which, although uninspiring in volume, was not a novelty of the 1270s. The seizures in Flanders in 1270 suggest that these merchants dealt mainly in local *collecta*, although the wool of Gilbert de Multone of Lynn included some from Westmorland. More interesting than that of East Anglia is the trade of three inland areas, which again antedated the 1270s. In each case the basis of the trade was a local supply of wool of good quality exploited by local men of great enterprise. The first area was centred on Dunstable in Bedfordshire, but extended to Brackley in Northamptonshire and to Baldock in Hertfordshire. The merchants of this region probably acted as collecting agents for the wool of the Chiltern downlands as well as for the surrounding clay vales. Sixteen received export licences in the period 1271–4, nine of them taking licences for 1100 sacks in 1273. These figures tend to obscure the fact that three names dominate the scene, those of William Fisher, John Duraunt and Henry Chadde, all of Dunstable. These three lost wool valued at £456 14s 2d in 1265 and 138 sacks, worth £800 1s 8d in 1270. In 1273 Fisher received a licence to export 320 sacks and Durant one for 360 sacks, while together they had a licence for 40 sacks. Henry Chadde and John Chadde took licences for 160 sacks. In 1270 all three exported wool of the *collecta* of Dunstable, while Chadde also exported wool of St Alban's Abbey and the Knights Templar. The natural outlet for the wool of this region was clearly the port of London, although it is interesting to note that one of the leading wool families of Winchester bore the surname Dunstable.

The centre of the wool trade along the western border of England

and in the marches of Wales was undoubtedly Shrewsbury. This town supplied twelve of the 22 merchants between Chester and Abergavenny who received export licences in the period 1271–4. Ludlow supplied six of the remainder. Shrewsbury was the base of Nicholas de Ludlow, founder of the greatest dynasty of English wool merchants before the days of William de la Pole of Hull. In 1265 Nicholas lost wool worth £158 13s 9d while in 1270 he lost 330 sacks valued at £1828 11s 5d. In 1273 he was licensed to export up to 300 sacks. Another prominent Shrewsbury merchant was Roger Pride, kinsman of the aristocratic Burnell family, who lost 32 sacks of wool worth £203 8s 4d in 1270 and received a licence to export 120 sacks in 1273. The wool of the southern marches, together with that of South Wales and some Cotswold wool came to Bristol. Despite the quality of the wool of Cotswold, exporting merchants in this region were few in number and of limited importance. Bristol produced nine licensees and Gloucester four in the period 1271–4, but the six Oxfordshire men probably directed their exports towards London. The absence of local exporters is probably to be explained in large measure by the ease with which Londoners and aliens could reach the north Cotswolds via the Thames, while southern merchants could easily reach the south Cotswolds. Bristol merchants took their wool overland to Southampton for export and the most prominent of them, John de Kaerdif, is often described as 'of Southampton'.

Finally we are left with the citizens and merchants of London. Excluding all those who can safely be identified as alien by birth there remain ninety-six who acquired export licences in the years 1271–4. The majority of these were undoubtedly English by birth, although very many of them were Londoners only by adoption. The aldermanic class had a large stake in the city's wool trade but was far from monopolising it. In London the wholesale trade in wool, as in other commodities, was open to members of all the crafts and many occasional speculations were made by men whose chief economic interest lay elsewhere. There were a few, however, whose fortunes were heavily committed to the wool trade. London was not the centre of a wool-producing region and few exporting Londoners can have had direct contacts with the growers. Probably most of them bought wool which other English middlemen brought to the city. However some were already overcoming the geographical limitation by sending agents to deal directly with the growers or to buy at up-country fairs. Wool seized in Flanders in 1270 from Thomas de Basing was named as the product of the abbeys of Flaxley and Netley. The Basings were a family long established in the wool trade; in 1244 Thomas' uncle, Adam de

Basing, had bought from the king all the wool of the see of Winchester, while in 1251 he bought March wool from the king.[52]

As well as the enrolled licences a certain amount of evidence about the volume of exports in the 1273 season is provided by three other lists of merchants. All are fragmentary and lack titles and dates but internal evidence establishes beyond doubt that they represent the findings of an inquest about the export of wool through the port of London in 1273, either for the whole year or, what seems more likely, only for the period after Easter. They are probably parts of the return of a commission issued on 28 June 1274.[53] We have firstly a document beginning with a list of French merchants, the greater part of which has been torn away.[54] It then lists 29 English merchants with a total of 1795 sacks of wool, which undoubtedly represents the total of known exports by provincial merchants through London during the period in question. This is made clear by a consideration of the exports of the Dunstable merchants. Six merchants received licences authorising the export of up to 960 sacks between 30 April 1273 and January 1274, while the same six actually exported a total of 892 sacks. In each case there is a correspondence between licences and exports. Richard Cook and Stephen Angevin each received a single licence and exported $13\frac{1}{2}$ and 20 sacks respectively; John and Henry Chadde had licences for 40 and 120 sacks and exported 36 and $88\frac{1}{2}$ sacks; William Fisher and John Duraunt, jointly and severally, had licences for up to 760 sacks and exported 340 and 394 sacks. The correspondence between licences and exports is not always as close, but this may be accounted for by the fact that merchants from the more distant provinces did not necessarily send all their wool through London. Nicholas de Ludlow of Shrewsbury had licences for 300 sacks and exported 196 via London, while three fellow townsmen with licences for 260 sacks sent a total of $205\frac{1}{2}$ sacks. The names of three more Shrewsbury men, with a total export of 92 sacks, are not to be found among the licences either of 1273 or earlier years, but there is no suggestion that the export had been unauthorised. As well as the provincial English merchants the list contains the names of two aliens, Wambert Baudan of Douai, merchant of Dover, with 29 sacks and Robert de Accon, 'who now lives in London', with 20 sacks. The inquest recorded the fact that all the English merchants sent their wool to St Omer and knowingly traded with Flemings, while Wambert Baudan and Gamelin of Dover exported direct to Flanders.

Following the English merchants are the names of forty-eight individuals or partnerships of Brabant, each exporting between three and 60 sacks. None of these traded with Flemings, but took the wool to their own country to be made into cloth. Then follows a short list of seven merchants of Cahors with a total of 335 sacks. Individually and collectively their exports are much smaller than the total enumerated in the licences issued to them in 1273. This is probably to be explained by the fact that much of their trade was done through Boston and Hull. All the Cahorsins exported to Flanders 'except Humfrey Moryn' whose name does not actually figure in the list of exporters. He 'frequently took wool to Provence'.

The second document[55] is part of a list of exports by citizens of London and a comparison of the amounts with the licences granted after Easter 1273 suggests that it relates to this period. From the beginning of the 1273 season to the end of December 57 Londoners acquired licences for the export of up to 2508 sacks, while in a last issue in January 1274 a further 180 sacks were licensed. Twenty-nine of the fifty-seven are to be found among the 34 names of Londoners whose exports are enumerated in the surviving fragment of the inquest. The remaining five mentioned in the inquest did not acquire licences in 1273, although some of them had done so earlier; these were all among the less important merchants, their exports known to the jurors totalling $79\frac{1}{2}$ sacks. Reverting to the 29 names common to both lists we find that eleven acquired only one licence, authorising them to export up to 20 sacks each; in ten instances the jurors recorded 20 sacks or fewer, the total being $133\frac{1}{2}$ sacks, but the eleventh exported 54 sacks. Among five who were authorised to export 40 sacks each four exported fewer, the total being 134, while the fifth exported 65 sacks. Of three with licences for 60 sacks two took $46\frac{1}{2}$ and 36 respectively, while the third took 94. Among five with licences for 80 sacks three took a total of $177\frac{1}{2}$ sacks, while Robert de Araz took 96 and Alexander de Wattleye took $124\frac{1}{2}$ sacks. Finally Robert de Basing, Nicholas de Winton and Thomas de Basing, with licences for 100, 184 and 224 sacks respectively exported 80, 99 and 124 sacks, whereas Wolmar de Essex and William Box, authorised to export 140 and 200 sacks, took $151\frac{1}{2}$ and 303 sacks respectively. Among the remaining 28 licensees of 1273, whose names no doubt appeared in the missing fragment of the inquest return, two shared a single licence, fifteen had one licence each, two shared a 40 sack licence, six had 2 licences each, two had licences for 80 sacks, while Stephen de Cornhull had licences for 100 sacks. The return alleges that during the period in question all the Londoners took their wool to St Omer, where they sold it to Flemings. Only John de Brilond and two other alien citizens dared take wool directly to Flanders. Stephen de Cornhull, William Bokerel and Richard de Abyndon were charged with buying cloth from the Flemings at St

Omer, while Thomas de Basing and William de Bosco were said to have sent to Flanders for cloth.

The third document[56] is in a very poor state of preservation but there can be little doubt that it belongs to the same series as the other two and is concerned only with exports through London. It begins with Italian merchants, among whom the most prominent were the Riccardi with 260 sacks. The generally low level of Italian exports compared with licences issued is again to be explained by the fact that the bulk of their wool went through Boston and Hull. In second place is the Hanse of Almain, a list of about forty-two individuals or partnerships which is virtually indecipherable. A third group of about twenty merchants is in an even worse condition. Then follow the names of three Gascons and seven Spaniards, all of whom are said to have exported directly to Flanders. Although most of the preceding merchants had offended by trading with Flemings their offence did not actually lie in the export of wool. Only about four individuals, including two Londoners, are named in this document as having exported without warrant, smuggling wool in barrels and bundles.

The concluding part of the last document consists of a statement which must be left in its original Latin since its exact meaning is uncertain. It seems to imply, however, that those exporting wool direct to Flanders were exacting a commission or making an excess profit of one mark for every sack exported.

> *Omnes isti adiverunt Flandriam per se et suos et miserunt lanas ibidem quas in Anglia emerunt ad opus eorum, capiendo ab eis pro quolibet sacco lucrum videlicet pro aliquo sacco XX saccis pro aliquo 1 marc. Et hoc didicerunt per relatum Flandrensium qui hoc dicunt modo. Et aliqui ipsorum mercatorum pannos Flandrensos reduxerunt, communicantes cum eisdem scienter et prudenter arte et ingenio et quoquo modo poterunt. Et alii similiter de partis illis qui non transfetaverunt London set alibi in regno.*

The statements of the London jury or juries make it reasonably certain that while aliens could safely export wool to Flanders throughout the period of the dispute it was unwise for most English merchants to do so. They side-stepped this difficulty by creating a staple where they could trade with the Flemings on neutral ground. This may have been originally at Abbeville but by 1273 it had been transferred to St Omer, on the border of Flanders. Because of the ease with which licences could be obtained there was little need for merchants trading from London, and probably from the other major ports, to export without warrant. Once the wool had left the country, however, the merchants blatantly disregarded their oath that they would not trade with Flemings. It is likely that most of the wool exported even by

Englishmen was sold directly to Flemings and cloth bought in exchange.

In concluding this survey of the export trade in the early 1270s one must note that the role of the English merchant community was strictly limited. It is necessary to emphasise this as a corrective to Schaube's work which tended to exaggerate the importance of the English. Moreover since Schaube's conclusions are known to many only at second hand the picture has become even more distorted. Although English merchants won a share in the export trade at an early date it is difficult to doubt that on the eve of the great conflict with Flanders the volume of their exports was inferior, possibly considerably inferior, to that of the Flemings. The English were probably slow to respond to the eclipse of the Flemings. In mitigation it must, of course, be pointed out that it was as dangerous for English merchants to export directly to Flanders as it was for Flemish merchants to resort to England. The immediate beneficiaries were undoubtedly the Italians. In the somewhat longer term the Germans benefited. It probably needed another war and a general reapportionment of the export trade to make any substantial addition to the share enjoyed by English merchants.

3

The Italian hegemony

The most long-lasting outcome of the dispute with Flanders was the imposition of a permanent customs duty on exported wool, that which in the course of time became known as the *magna et antiqua custuma.* For the economic historian this is an event of the utmost significance since it has provided him with one of the most valuable of all his medieval records. Constitutional historians, of course, have been more interested in the origins of the tax, which has provided fuel for debate. It is clear that the magnates were party to the formal approval, which was given in an assembly in spring 1275. But what was the form of the all-important consent of the Commons? Was it given by a body representative of the entire commonalty, or by one representing the merchants alone? Gras found no difficulty in accepting Stubbs' doctrine that the custom was granted by a true parliament, but Wilkinson, whose opinion has found more general acceptance, taught that the merchants alone provided the vital constitutional consent.[1]

Gras' confidence in the parliamentary nature of the 1275 grant was strengthened by his conviction of the complete novelty of the custom. He rejected the possibility that it might have any connection with any earlier impost. There are, however, antecedents which, insofar as they involved only the king and the merchants, lend support to Wilkinson's case. The antecedents take us back to February 1266 when, in the aftermath of the civil war, Henry III commended all alien merchants to the 'protection' of his eldest son. Only by Edward's licence might they stay in the realm. The outcome was predictable and in April 1266 the king confirmed a pact which the prince had made with the merchants. In return for his protection Edward was to levy 'a reasonable portion on imports and exports whereby merchants will not be grieved immoderately'. By this time denizen merchants had also been taken into the prince's protection and were therefore required to pay the tax. The degree of consent may be gathered from the fact that in October 1266 the sheriffs were ordered to assist the collectors to levy the tax from merchants who refused to pay. The following year the king of France made representations on behalf of his subjects and it was conceded that they should be temporarily absolved from the levy while they sent proctors to discuss the matter. Later, the merchants of Rouen at least were permanently exempted from payment.[2]

At first the collectors of the new aid were required to account for the proceeds to the prince's officers, but later a system of farming was adopted. The farm, which yielded some 6000 marks a year, passed backwards and forwards between the Beraud brothers of Cahors and various groups of Italian merchants.[3] Although there is no record of the way in which contributions to the new aid were assessed wool must have figured prominently among dutiable goods. Reference has already been made to Jean Boinebroke's claim that the 92 sacks of wool seized at Newcastle in 1270 had paid a duty of £9 8s. Since this was described as *le maltote le Roi* it is difficult to avoid the conclusion that this was payment of the new aid at the rate of about 2s per sack. The new aid was being collected in London and Southampton in October 1273 and the presumption must be that it remained in being during the period of the embargo on trade with Flanders. On 27 March 1275 the Lucchese firm of Riccardi was appointed to collect the new aid on all imports until a week after Easter (21 April).[4] What significance should be attached to the omission of any reference to exports is difficult to say. A possible explanation is that the Crown and the merchants were already renegotiating the terms of a customs duty and that the collection of the new aid on imports was continued as an interim measure. In the final event the duty on imports was abolished, as was that on all exports save wool, fells and hides. The latter was fixed at a rate of half a mark for each sack of wool or 300 fells and one mark for each last of hides.

The decision to narrow customs duty to wool and hides may have been not unconnected with the results of the enquiries into contraventions of the embargo on trade with Flemings. The guilty parties were amerced and although some were subsequently pardoned others paid the penalties. The merchants of Bristol paid £36 13s 4d, those of Southampton paid £27 10s, while the Italian merchants paid a fine of 10s for every sack of wool which they had exported. The total amount collected in fines and amercements appears to have been at least £13 321. This was in effect a retrospective duty and the observation that exporters could sustain such a charge without being ruined may have suggested that the custom be concentrated on wool. Increasing the duty on wool and abolishing it on all other commodities greatly simplified the work of collection and may incidentally have enhanced the yield. To sum up, the new aid was collected on imports until at least 21 April 1275, the English merchants had granted the new custom by 10 May at the latest, while writs of aid for its collection were made out on 19 May. A Florentine, Falco Masner, who had been farming the new aid 'on wool and other wares' in Ireland later complained that he lost 20 marks when it was brought to a premature end. Who, then, can share Gras' confidence that the new custom of 1275 was totally unconnected with anything that preceded it?[5]

The new custom provided a most welcome addition to the king's revenue, the gross yield of the first 4 years amounting to £43 802. Compared with existing forms of taxation collection was simple and economical. All that was required was to station officials at appointed ports to receive payment before the wool was put aboard ship. More than this, because of its regularity the custom provided ideal security for the loans with which Edward I anticipated his income. Any and all sources of royal revenue were used to repay loans but the customs was the chief provider. The main lender was the Riccardi of Lucca, and this firm apparently had an unbroken assignment of the custom from its beginning in May 1275 to July 1294.[6] In England the Riccardi stationed an attorney at every customs port to receive payment from the collectors of customs. The latter, two in number, were Englishmen elected by the local community under instructions from the king. Each of the parties was entrusted with one leaf of the double-faced cocket seal which authenticated customs documents. The master of every ship leaving an English port laden with wool had to carry letters, sealed with the cocket, showing that his cargo had been duly customed. The division of the seal was designed to prevent fraud, for it could not be used without the knowledge of both sets of officials. The attorney used his knowledge to ensure that he received all the money which was paid to the collectors. The latter, who accounted at the Exchequer, ensured that the king's bankers acknowledged all the sums which they had received from the customs towards the liquidation of the royal debt. Only by collusion between attorney and collectors could the king be cheated. In order to minimise this risk the collectors, whenever they came to account at the Exchequer, were required to produce rolls giving particulars of all wool dispatched through their port. If there was any suspicion of fraud these rolls could be submitted to a local inquest for verification.

The creation of a permanent customs service resulted in an enlargement of the royal archives and this has provided the historian, for the first time, with a reliable statistical framework for the study of the wool trade. The surviving documents are divided into two main classes, enrolled accounts and particular accounts. The former, entered at first on the pipe rolls and later on special customs rolls, are concerned only with the total charge of each accountant. They show the total custom which should have been collected. They also record all allowances and expenses, together with the deliveries of cash made by the collectors, so providing the Exchequer with a permanent record of any balance due. This series of accounts is almost complete. The second series, the particulars, are the rolls containing details of the exports, which were brought up by the collectors when called to account. Although potentially the more valuable type of evidence the particulars have suffered badly from the ravages of time. Only a small fraction of those submitted have survived and many of these are in poor condition.

The enrolled accounts enable the historian to determine England's total wool export year by year, besides showing how the trade was divided between individual ports. The average annual export for the years 1279–90 was about 26 750 sacks, the actual amounts varying from 24 000 sacks to 31 000 sacks.[7] During the preceding 4 years the total customs revenue, including that on hides, was £43 801 18s 9d, while in the years 1290–4 total revenue was £46 256 19s. These figures suggest that the period was one of general stability in the export trade, but there were a number of complicating factors, the possible effects of which are not easy to determine. It is difficult, also, to suggest how the export totals of the 1280s may have compared with those of the middle years of the thirteenth century. The possibility must be considered, although proof cannot be adduced, that in the later period exports were at a lower level than formerly. There is little reason to suppose that the modest duty of half a mark had an inhibiting effect on the export market. On the other hand during the 1270s the price of wool rose rapidly as a consequence of internal inflation and the outbreak of a severe epidemic of scab among sheep flocks.[8] In the 1280s the level of wool prices seems to have fallen somewhat, following the recoinage of 1279, which induced a general fall in prices. Nevertheless, with the exception of the year 1283–4 exports tended to stick at around the 25 000 sack mark. This suggests that the cost of wool was not the most critical factor. It is likely that the main difficulty confronting wool merchants in this period was a shortage of wool of a sufficiently high quality to satisfy the standards of the Flemish cloth industry. Scab continued unabated in the 1280s and besides killing sheep ruined the fleeces of the survivors. Poor wool may have been difficult to sell while good wool rose in price. The latter effect is not observable in the averages of the surviving price data of the 1280s, which are heavily weighted with prices paid to the Bishop of Winchester. Winchester wool was middling in quality to begin with and the flocks were badly hit by scab. By the late 1280s the worst effects of the epidemic may have been over, allowing the recovery of exports which the customs figures appear to indicate.

Although 13 customs ports were established in 1275, and a few more were added later, well over half of all wool exported was handled by 2 ports, most of the rest being divided between the 4 ports next in importance. In this period the passage of wool through a customs port was not obligatory and a merchant could export from any place provided that he had first paid his custom at the nearest port. However, there can be no doubt that the great bulk of all wool actually passed through the appointed ports. The leading port was Boston, with an annual average of 9623 sacks, but London, average 7020 sacks, also deserves to be regarded as a port of the first class. In the second class stand Hull and Southampton with averages of 3415 and 2883, while Lynn, average 1350 sacks, stands alone in the third class. Newcastle, average 873 sacks, should probably be consigned to a fourth class together with Chichester, Ipswich and Sandwich, with averages of 536, 376 and 320 respectively. The remaining ports exported only a hundred sacks a year or less.

Each of the ports named above, with the exception of London, has left at least one example of a particular customs account dating from the period before 1294. These, even though damaged, provide valuable evidence about conditions in the export trade in the late thirteenth century. The most useful accounts are those for Hull covering the periods 27 June 1275 to 27 April 1276[9] and 22 April 1291 to April 1292.[10] In each of these years the amount of wool exported from Hull was substantially higher than the average annual export for the intermediate period. In the earlier year the total was about 4383 sacks of wool and a few thousand fells, equivalent to 14 sacks of wool, while in the later year the total sum was 4270 sacks and 11 384 fells, the equivalent of 38 sacks of wool.

The account of 1275–6 is, from the historian's point of view, an ideal one, since it records not only the home port of every ship freighting wool but also the place of origin of nearly every merchant. The later account is less accommodating and despite the fact that some of the deficiency can be supplied from other sources the nationality of a number of ships and of merchants owning about 15 per cent of the wool remains unidentified. Table 3 provides a comparison of the operations of the merchants in the respective years.

Although no final conclusions can be made from the evidence of 2 accounts attention must be drawn to the increase in the amount of wool exported by Englishmen in the respective years, and the decline in that exported by Italians and Cahorsins. None of the unidentified merchants were Italian and few, if any, were Cahorsins. The fall in the figures attributed to Germans, Flemings and Frenchmen is not signi-

ficant since any of these groups, together with the English and Brabanters, may have owned a share of the unidentified wool. No fewer than
331 sacks of this were the property of just 3 merchants.

TABLE 3   *Division of exports at Hull (late thirteenth century)*

	1275–6		1291–2	
Nationality	No. of exporters	Wool (sacks)	No. of exporters	Wool (sacks)
Italy		2318		1715
Germany	27	729	11	601
Flanders	14–15[a]	451[a]	16	389
S. France	12	397	2	24
N. France	24	319	21	268
England	15	158	38	546
Liege	1	24	1	10
Brabant	–	–	4	71
Unidentified	–	–	53[b]	664[b]
Totals		4397		4288[c]

[a] In addition a few sailors took small quantities totalling slightly more than 1 sack.
[b] Including sailors taking a few stones or fleeces.
[c] There is a deficiency of 20 sacks compared with the accountants' totals. A few
entries are now illegible.

The amount of wool owned by Englishmen in 1275 may actually
have been smaller than that shown in the above table, since it includes
47 sacks belonging to Peter Lengleis of Rochester, who may have been
of alien origin. One Londoner took 18 sacks, 4 Berwick merchants took
14 sacks between them, while the rest were shared by 9 local merchants
from Beverley, Pontefract, York and Hedon. The increase in the
amount of wool exported in 1291 was supplied entirely by local merchants. The Yorkshire centres of the trade were, in order of importance,
Pontefract, York, Doncaster, Beverley, Bawtry, Yarm, Hedon and
Whitby, and in Lincolnshire Grimsby and Lincoln. Yarmouth contributed one merchant and London four, three of whom were members
of the well-known Box family. It appears that as far as English merchants were concerned the port of Hull still had only local significance.
From this one may probably infer that with the exception of local
merchants Englishmen played little part in the wool trade within the
region served by this port. In 1275 the Yorkshiremen were exporting
almost exclusively to Picardy and in the later year the main ties were
probably still with that region.

After the Italians the largest group of exporters in each of the years under consideration was German. The figures given in the table probably understate their exports in 1291 by a considerable amount, since there is some reason to suppose that a majority of the wool classified as unidentified was the property of German merchants. In 1275 15 merchants from the Baltic towns of Lübeck, Stralsund and Wismar took 490 sacks, 8 from the Westphalian towns of Kapellen, Dortmund and Minden took 184, one merchant from Brunswick in Lower Saxony took 13 sacks, while the remaining three, with 41 sacks, came from Asseburg, location uncertain. In 1291 few Germans can be ascribed to particular towns and the total includes some Low Germans or Dutchmen. The largest non-Italian exporter this year, with 228 sacks, was Tidemann of Doesburg, county of Zutphen, now in the Netherlands. The next most important group of alien merchants in both years were Flemings, who were few in number but owned a high average amount of wool. Most of the export was supplied by merchants of Ghent and Bruges; Ypres made a very small contribution in both years, while Douai was represented in the earlier year and Arras and Lille in the later. The 1291 figures include 14 sacks taken by five ships' captains from Biervliet and Monikerede, while the unidentified wool includes small amounts taken by Flemish sailors. In 1275 there were no exporters from Brabant, but in 1291 three merchants from Louvain took 66 sacks of wool and a Brussels merchant took 1372 fells. One merchant from Dinant in the bishopric of Liege was present in each year. The northern French merchants were drawn overwhelmingly from the towns of Amiens, Corbie and Abbeville in Picardy, who brought wool to Yorkshire in exchange for wool for their own cloth industry. St Omer, in Artois, took a small amount of wool in both years, Dieppe and Poreville took fells in 1275 and a merchant of Waban in Ponthieu exported 19 sacks of wool in 1291.

It is unfortunate that the only surviving particulars for Boston before 1294 are both damaged, one quite seriously. The account of 1287–8[11] provides evidence as to the ownership of some 8600 sacks out of a total of 9373 sacks exported that year, but that of 1290–1[12] for only about 6350 sacks out of a total export of 10 280 sacks of wool and 24 687 fells. Neither account records the places of origin of merchants, except in those instances where they took their surname from a town. Although it is possible to establish the nationality of some of the more important merchants it is not possible to allocate all the wool between the different nationalities.

In 1287–8 Italian merchants exported at least 2828 sacks, but probably not much more, since Italians are easily identified in the customs accounts. In 1290 they exported a minimum of 1756 sacks, although the figure has no great significance since a large part of the account is illegible. Among non-Italian exporters it is safe to say that Germans, Flemings and Brabanters played a significantly greater role than Englishmen and Frenchmen. The largest of these in 1287 was Peter Brun, nationality unknown, with an export of 110 sacks. Collectively, however, the Lo family of Ypres had a larger total, Nicholas having 104 sacks, John, senior, 35 sacks, and John, junior, 73 sacks. In 1290 John, Henry and Clays de Lo had at least 224 sacks between them. This family, which had represented Ypres in the diplomatic negotiations with the English crown in the 1270s were major cloth importers. In 1287 only one other merchant can be shown as having exported more than 100 sacks. William de Wagenare, a German, who had 104 sacks. Only three Englishmen can be readily identified among the larger merchants of 1287, that is those who exported more than 30 sacks. Thomas de Ludlow had 32 sacks, Robert de Basing of London 76 sacks, and Gilbert de Chesterton of Grantham 87 sacks. In 1290 Gilbert exported at least 100 sacks, while Laurence de Giselingham, with at least 107 sacks, sounds like an Englishmen.

TABLE 4 *Division of exports at Boston and Hull (excluding Italian wool)*

Range (in sacks)	Merchants	Total (sacks)	Average (sacks)	% of non-Italian total
Boston, 1287–8				
30 and over	64	3369	52.6	58
10–30	109	1845	17	32
Under 10	134	571	4.3	10
Hull, 1275–6				
30 and over	23	1320	57.4	64
10–30	34	591	17.4	28
Under 10	36	168	4.7	8
Hull, 1291–2				
30 and over	18	1458	81	57
10–30	49	813	16.6	32
Under 10	79	302	3.8	11

In 1287–8 at least 307 merchants and sailors, apart from the Italian firms, paid custom on wool exported through Boston. About one fifth of their number took nearly 60 per cent of the total wool and a comparison with the situation at Hull suggests that a similar division between large and small exporters may have been typical of the non-Italian interest at the two ports.

Although the clerk who kept the Lynn account for 1287–8[13] was not much concerned to record the nationality of exporting merchants it is quite clear that the most important group in this port was German. Twenty-three Germans exported 543 sacks out of the 1407 sacks of wool and there is little room to doubt that much of the remainder was also taken by Germans. Many of these were also exporting through Boston in this same year. From other sources it is known that Germans were burgesses of Lynn and it seems likely that many of them made the town their headquarters in England. Among the other exporters can be recognised a couple of Amiens merchants and an Ypres merchant, the latter also being one of the bigger exporters from Boston. The biggest exporter, with 134 sacks, was one John de Spalding. The 15 exporters who each had more than 30 sacks owned a total of 756 sacks, leaving the remaining 651 sacks to be shared between 67 merchants. Two of the latter also exported a few fells, but the bulk of the 29 062 fells[14] were handled by 22 men who had no fleece wool. The number of fells is noteworthy in light of the fact that virtually no fells were exported through Boston this year.

Newcastle has left three accounts[15] before 1294, although that for 1287–8 is missing after the end of July, by which time less than half the season's wool had been exported. The accounts for 1292–3 and 1293–4 are complete and only slightly damaged. It is quite clear that the wool trade of Newcastle was sustained very largely by local merchants and that the families who had obtained export licences in the 1270s still led the field 20 years later. As in the case of Yorkshire there may have been close links with Picardy, based on the exchange of wool and woad. One of the leading Newcastle families bore the surname de Abbeville, while Sampson le Cuteller of Newcastle must be compared with John le Cuteller of Amiens. In 1292 four Newcastle men exported more than 30 sacks each, total 194 sacks, a fifth man, with 54 sacks, was probably English, leaving an Amiens merchant with 51 sacks and a Bruges merchant with 88 sacks. In the intermediate group seven merchants of Newcastle and Barnard Castle took a total of 131 sacks, while half of the remaining eight merchants may also have been English.

Italian merchants customed 84 sacks of wool at Newcastle in 1293 and 227 sacks the following year. The total amount of non-Italian wool, on the other hand, was more than halved in the same period. Table 5 shows that this fall resulted largely from a decline in the amount of wool exported by the leading merchants, the aliens being largely eliminated and the quotas of natives drastically reduced. On the other hand Walter de Cugat, who had 14 sacks in 1292, was the only man to export more than 30 sacks in 1293.

Of the two surviving accounts for Ipswich the first, 1287–8,[16] covers a poor year, when only 161 sacks of wool and 10 399 fells were exported, including small amounts from Dunwich and Orford. The second, 1292–3,[17] is remarkable for the very large number of fells exported, 45 654, in addition to 231 sacks of wool. The port does not

TABLE 5 *Division of exports at Newcastle (excluding Italian wool)*

Range (in sacks)	Merchants	Total (sacks)	Average (sacks)	% of non-Italian total
		1292–3		
30 and over	7	388	55.5	51
10–30	15	238	15.9	31
Under 10	57	141	2.4	18
		1293–4		
30 and over	1	37	37	11
10–30	10	164	16.4	47
Under 10	55	149	2.7	42

seem to have been patronised very much by merchants of consequence and in each year only two men exported more than 30 sacks. The Clement of Stamford who exported 39 sacks in 1287 may have been English, but Walter Daundeleye, with 30 sacks, was from Amiens. Walter exported 43 sacks in 1292. The le Mouner family of Amiens also used this port, Fermin taking 21 sacks in 1287 and John 33 sacks in 1292. The Riccardi of Lucca shipped 16 sacks from the port in 1287, while the Bettri of Lucca sent 19 sacks in 1292.

The three surviving accounts for Yarmouth[18] show that this port was used regularly by the same group of a dozen or so merchants, most of them probably alien. Both individually and collectively their investment in the wool trade was small. Not one of them exported as many as 30 sacks and their total exports in the years 1287–8, 1288–9 and 1291–2 amounted to only 103, 90 and 125 sacks.

Moving to the south coast we have three complete accounts[19] for Southampton for the years 1286–7, 1288–9 and 1290–1. This port was still dominated by the same group of English merchants which had figured prominently in the licences of the 1270s. The second most important group was made up of northern French merchants, while

Flemings and other merchants from the Low Countries were comparatively unimportant. Germans were completely absent, while Italians
exported 111 sacks, 121 sacks and 122 sacks in the respective years.
The distribution of non-Italian wool is shown in table 6.

TABLE 6   *Division of exports at Southampton (excluding Italian wool)*

Range (in sacks)	Merchants	Total (sacks)	Average (sacks)	% of non-Italian total
		1286–7		
30 and over	18	1014	56.3	51
10–30	42	737	17.5	37
Under 10	66	233	3.5	12
		1287–8		
30 and over	18	896	49.4	53
10–30	36	576	16	34
Under 10	55	218	4	13
		1290–1		
30 and over	23	1237	53.8	55
10–30	41	722	17.6	32
Under 10	79	292	3.7	13

Excluding the Italian companies, about 260 merchants were involved in the shipment of wool from Southampton during the periods
under consideration, of whom 38 exported in all 3 years, while
another 38 exported in 2 years out of 3. Those who exported every
year handled 3200 sacks out of the total of 5925 sacks and of these at
least 13, with an export of 1692 sacks, came from Winchester, Andover
and Southampton. This by no means completes the roll-call of English
merchants exporting in all years and they were equally prominent
among those exporting in only one or two years.

Moving along the coast from Southampton we find that a handful
of particulars have survived for the minor ports of the south-east. At
Chichester[20] the trade seems to have been entirely in the hands of
local men, 5 of them exporting a total of 104 sacks of wool and 7272
fells in 1287–8, while 7 exported 150 sacks and 5074 fells two years
later. The only name common to both lists is that of Ralph Polle of
Chichester, who exported 68 sacks and 5194 fells in the earlier year
and 58 sacks and 706 fells in the later. In contrast local men played
an insignificant role in the wool exports of Shoreham,[21] where Norman
merchants dominated the trade. Six Rouen men exported a total of at

least 153 sacks in 1287–8, while 11 took 183 sacks 2 years later; one Fécamp merchant took 7 sacks in the earlier year and 5 took 66 sacks in the later. Small amounts were taken by merchants of Abbeville, Dieppe and Calais and by Flemish sailors, while the list of alien exporters is completed by the Riccardi, who took 17 sacks in 1287 and 31 sacks in 1289. The most important English exporter was John Brech of Sandwich with 51 sacks and 1825 fells and 35 sacks and 225 fells in the respective years; only 2 merchants are positively identified as Shoreham men. At Seaford[22] the trade was handled by a comparatively large number of local men, each exporting trifling amounts. Most of them lived at Seaford, but there was also a significant concentration of exporters at Lewes. The only aliens using the port were merchants of St Omer. At Sandwich[23] we have the interesting spectacle of an Englishman, Thomas Shelfing, trying to monopolise the trade. In 1287–8 out of a total export of 207 sacks, Thomas was credited with 75 sacks, he and his 'associates' with 23 and John Shelfing with 28 sacks. Two years later Thomas and associates handled 164 sacks out of a total of 214. A few merchants remained outside the syndicate, including Walter Draper of Sandwich and William de Wendlesworth of London, who exported not insignificant amounts in either year. In 1287 the Cerchi of Florence sent 6 sacks through Sandwich, while 22 sacks were put into a Genoese galley, probably being the property of a Genoese merchant. The Sandwich accounts also record the small amounts of wool exported through Rochester and Dover. These show that Walter Dirie of London used the former port, while Dover was used by 2 local merchants and one from Canterbury.

In the foregoing analysis of customs accounts Italian-owned wool was deliberately omitted since these stocks cannot be represented as the property of individuals. Although, as a general rule, wool was exported in the name of a single merchant it usually belonged to the company in which he was either a partner or an agent. It is the company, therefore, not the individual which must be the object of study, although, unfortunately, individual exporters cannot always be identified with a known company. The reservation of Italian-owned wool for separate treatment is further justified by the prominent position occupied by the companies in the wool trade of the late thirteenth century. In the absence of particulars for the port of London it is hazardous to attempt to quantify the Italian export since there is no means of telling how much wool they dispatched by this route. In 1294–5 less than one sixth of the total Italian export went through London but, as will be seen later, this was a somewhat unusual year. There can be little doubt that most of the Italian export was normally dispatched through Boston and

Hull, although it is likely that small consignments regularly went through Newcastle and Southampton and occasional use was made of other ports.

It seems more than probable that during the 1280s Italian exports came increasingly under the control of a number of prominent Florentine companies, to the detriment of most other Italians, with the significant exception of the Riccardi, and also to the detriment of the merchants of Cahors. Table 7 gives details of some of the wool which

TABLE 7 *Italian wool, 1294–5*

	Contracts	Exports
Frescobaldi Bianchi	360	721
Frescobaldi Neri	154	164
Cerchi Bianchi	301	396
Cerchi Neri	350	466
Bardi	99	313
Pulci-Rimbertini	258	215
Mozzi	261	231
Spini	154	145
Riccardi	413	–
Bettri	35	–

these companies, and the Bettri of Lucca, had contracted to buy in 1294,[24] together with the amount which they exported by licence in 1294–5. The table undoubtedly understates the normal volume of exports to a large degree. Except in the case of the Riccardi the Exchequer documents on which the table is based list only monastic contracts and in some instances the amount of wool to be delivered was not yet known. Furthermore many of the companies had other contracts with lay wool producers or with English middlemen, while all might expect to buy additional wool on the open market.

The first six companies listed in table 7 were direct successors of Florentine groups which had exported wool under licence during the early 1270s, although both the Frescobaldi and the Cerchi had divided into black and white factions by 1288 at latest. A division in the ranks of the Cerchi had apparently taken place by 1282 or earlier. Previously members of the partnership were described in English sources as the society of Durand le Bon. In that year, however, the partners of Durand le Bon were clearly a separate group from the company of the Cerchi. The division of the Cerchi in the early 1280s may have resulted from or, alternatively, may have given rise to, a financial crisis which seems to have provided the opportunity for another company, the

Mozzi, to enter the wool trade. The Mozzi were in England in the late 1270s as one of the firms engaged in the collection of the crusading tenth, but there is no evidence of their involvement in the wool trade at that date. In 1284 the Mozzi took over from the Cerchi contracts with no fewer than 24 monasteries, to whom the latter group had advanced considerable sums of earnest money, although in some cases no wool was to be delivered until 1288.[25] The Spini does not appear as a separate company until 1294, at which date its leading figure was Ristorio Bonaventure, who until two years previously had been one of the leaders of the Mozzi. Simon Gerard of the Mozzi also went over to the Spini.

In 1275–6 the Italian export from Hull, 2317 sacks, was shared between 7 companies. For Florence there were the Bardi, 386 sacks, Cerchi, 240 sacks, Frescobaldi, 191 sacks and Falconieri, 81 sacks; for Lucca the Riccardi, 381 sacks, and Bettri, 183 sacks; for Piacenza the Scotti, 676 sacks. In 1291–2 Florentines owned 1280 sacks out of a total Italian export of 1715 sacks from Hull. The Frescobaldi Bianchi had 374 sacks, the Cerchi Bianchi 153 sacks and the Falconieri 13 sacks; Brace Gerard of the Pulci-Rimbertini took 117 sacks, while John Pouce, 95 sacks, may have been another member of the firm; Simon Gerard of the Mozzi had 100 sacks, while Simon Grange, 95 sacks, may have been an eccentric spelling of the same name. Manninus of Florence, 180 sacks, may perhaps have been one of the Bardi or another member of the Cerchi Bianchi, but there are no suggestions as to the affiliations of Deutaitus Donede, 137 sacks, Artemise of Florence, 14 sacks and Ducheus Faon, 2 sacks. Among the Lucca merchants we find Barencino Gualteri, Riccardi, 71 sacks, and Bettinus Malagalus, Bettri with 46 sacks, but the affiliations of Wan' Tadelin, 226 sacks and John Lomberd, 30 sacks, are not known. Pascalinus of Piacenza, 61 sacks and 1685 fells, was probably a member of a society known as the Rusticacchi.

In the case of the Boston accounts of 1287–8 and 1291–2 only a minimum figure can be set upon Italian exports. The 2828 sacks of the earlier year is tolerably complete but the 1756 sacks of the later year is very much incomplete. Once again the Florentines outstripped all their competitors. The Bardi exported 559 sacks in 1287 and either 121 or 256 sacks in 1291; the Frescobaldi Bianchi had 656 sacks and 649 sacks; the Frescobaldi Neri 193 sacks and 137 sacks; the Pulci-Rimbertini 253 sacks and 183 sacks; the Mozzi 210 sacks and 255 sacks; the Cerchi Neri had 125 sacks in the earlier year, while they or the other branch had 87 sacks in the later year; the Falconieri had 41 sacks in 1287. Guy de Bonaventure, formerly a partner of the Willelmi, had 19 sacks in 1287 and another independent exporter 10 sacks in the same year. Outside the ranks of the Florentines we find the Riccardi with 340 sacks and 94 sacks, the Bettri with 97 sacks and 133 sacks, Tholomeus of Pistoia with 17 sacks in 1287 and Pascalinus of Piacenza with 14 sacks in 1291. There was also a handful of exporters whose affiliations are not known; Ardinis Ardingel, 94 sacks, Bartholomew Usebard, 72 sacks, Bartholomew Barbedeor, 106 sacks, in 1287 and James Ugolinus, 33 sacks in 1291. The recorded exports through Southampton, Newcastle and Ipswich, were all made by the companies of Florence and Lucca.

In the year 1290, for reasons which cannot now be determined, hostilities once more broke out between the subjects of England and Flanders. Despite the fact that their claims had apparently been settled in 1286 the English merchant community took this opportunity to renew their demands against the Count of Flanders. In the parliament which was held that summer they claimed £2000 for damages sustained as a result of the detention of their goods 20 years before. The king replied that he could only remind the count of his promise to satisfy the English merchants, but pointed out that there was no mention in the Treaty of Montreuil of damages. If they were now to submit a claim for compensation on these grounds the count might advance a counter claim. The merchants then presented a second petition asking for payment of £500 out of goods which the men of the Cinque Ports had already seized from Flemings. The King's reply to this was that they should be issued with a writ of *contra Detentores*. Despite, or possibly even because of, these signs of hostility on 25 September 1290 the Count of Flanders issued a charter of privileges to the English merchant community in Flanders, confirming, among other matters, their right to trade freely in wool.[26]

Friction between the two countries lasted into the following year, but in February 1291 the warden of the Cinque Ports was empowered to make a truce with the Flemings, which was operative between Easter and All Saints (22 April to 1 November). During the period of the truce orders were issued for the restoration of Flemish goods in Ireland, although there is no record of a similar order concerning England. A definitive peace was not made until Spring 1292. Letters were issued on 6 April granting a safe conduct to the count to come to England and the peace treaty was enrolled on 6 May. This treaty established that all claims were to be dropped on either side, except for depredations committed by the English during the period of truce. Shortly before the arrival of the count in England a ban was placed upon the export of wool to Flanders, possibly as a salutary reminder of the power which England could exert on the county. This ban was lifted as part of the settlement, while ships and merchandise held in England were also restored to the Flemings.[27]

Normal relations between England and Flanders were fated to last for only a short period, for in the following year England began to drift into war with France; Flanders, as a fief of the French Crown, was drawn helplessly into the dispute. In May 1294, having failed to bring the count into his system of alliances, Edward I revoked his safe conduct to Flemish merchants.[28] The break with Flanders was the prelude to an acute dislocation of the wool trade which lasted throughout the war. Severe hardship was caused to the growers and no doubt to many merchants, since for much of the time opportunities to export were limited. Moreover during this time the taxation of wool became a major issue in the constitutional conflict which developed between the Crown and its subjects. For much of the time the king was desperate for money and was forced to look to the wool trade to supply part of his needs both at home and abroad. The government, in the form of the Exchequer, poured forth writs and ordinances in an attempt to use the country's greatest trade to finance the war.

The first plan which emerged was one to seize all the wool in the country as a forced loan and to sell it in the name of the Crown. On 12 June 1294 writs were dispatched to all sheriffs ordering them to engage the assistance of two knights and to arrest all wool, wool-fells and hides found in 'cities, boroughs, market towns and other places'.[29] These were to be sealed with the seals of the knights and details of the stocks arrested were to be sent to the Exchequer. At this stage no mention was made of a prise, the ostensible reason for the arrest being fear that wool might find its way into the hands of the French. This was palpably an excuse and the speed of subsequent events indicates that the government already had a prise in mind.

It is possible that action was taken rather too early in the shearing season to obtain the maximum results from a prise, although the amount of wool uncovered in each county varied, no doubt, according to the degree of zeal shown by the searchers. Only for Bedfordshire and Buckinghamshire has a complete return survived and here they do not seem to have been over-active.[30] In Bedfordshire they found 69 sacks of wool in five religious houses and a further $140\frac{1}{2}$ sacks and 1598 fells in eight market towns. Outside of Dunstable, Bedford and Potton there was no place where wool was stopped in more than three houses and only two considerable hauls were found in lay hands in the entire county – 28 sacks belonging to John Duraunt, a leading wool merchant of Dunstable, and 31 sacks belonging to two merchants of Brabant, found in the house of their Dunstable host. Buckinghamshire, ostensibly, was even more bare of wool, only 41 sacks being found, mostly belonging to Brabanters. In Gloucestershire the searchers visited not only towns but rural areas including, among other places, the manor of Hawkesbury.[31] Moreover they did not merely stop wool in the hands of merchants, for the hundreds of small amounts recorded show that they arrested wool in the hands of husbandmen or, more probably since this was a cloth producing area, stocks held by domestic cloth workers.[32]

On 18 June letters patent were drawn up authorising royal agents to seize all stocks of wool greater than half a sack. These agents were mostly wool merchants of London and the home counties, men accustomed to the business of valuing and transporting wool, the task with which they were now charged. As late as 6 July the plan was still to seize the wool and arrangements were made to handle it at specified ports. By 26 July, however, this plan had been abandoned and the sheriffs were ordered to release all arrested wool except that belonging to Frenchmen. At the same time they were to proclaim that all might freely trade in wool.[33]

Little is known about the background to the events so far described. The prise was stated to have been authorised by *les graunz seigneurs de nostre terre, prelaz, countes, barouns e par nostre conseil*, nothing being said about the consent of the Commons or of the merchants.[34] Subsequently the merchants became a party to the negotiations and the writs of 26 July state that the prise was abandoned at their request. In its place was substituted an additional tax on exported wool, the notorious *maltote*. The merchants cannot have been so sanguine as to imagine that the king would abandon the prise without something in return, but it is not certain from which quarter the idea of the *maltote* emerged. The Dunstable annalist[35] said that Laurence de Ludlow persuaded the merchants to concede the *maltote*, and it is possible that he was used to convey such a proposal when it became apparent that, because of delays or difficulties in disposing of the wool, no instant supply of cash would be forthcoming from this source. At this point mention must be made of a document found in the French national archives, which is more or less contemporary with the events under discussion. It contains suggestions as to various ways in which the King of England might raise money, one of them being a proposal that Italians and other aliens exporting from England to Holland and Brabant should pay a tax of five marks on each sack of wool and each last of hides. M. Langlois' conclusion that the proposals never reached England, rests solely on the fact that the document in question lies in a French archive. There is nothing to prove that another copy did not reach its destination. However, it must be confessed that an increased export tax was such an obvious way to raise money that the idea might have emanated from any source, or several.

Initially the *maltote* was a differential tax, the rate being five marks for each last of hides and each sack of *melioris lane fracte* and three marks for other wool, *alterius lane*. The former wool was carefully prepared and graded, while the latter consisted of fleeces which had received less attention from the winders and packers. Early in November 1294, however, it was ordered that as from 15 November custom was to be levied on each type of wool at the rate of three marks.[37] The enrolled customs accounts show that from that date until the *maltote* was abolished on 23 November 1297 the single rate of duty was charged. The situation seems to have been rather more complicated than this, however, and two anomalies must be mentioned.

On the King's Remembrancer Memoranda Roll of 1295 are drafts of writs directed to the customers of London, dated 16 September, and to Boston and Hull, dated 21 September, declaring that all merchants, except those of France and of certain Italian companies, might export wool on payment of custom of three marks for each type of wool, *de quolibet sacco tam lane fracte quam alterius*.[38] These writs were not sent, the drafts having been cancelled in favour of other writs, all dated 20 September and directed to the above-named ports and to Newcastle, Sandwich, Southampton, Yarmouth and Ipswich; *Ista brevia non fuerunt directa collectoribus, viz, cancellata quia sub alia forma demandatur eisdem ut infra continetur*. The new writs extended the list of banned Italian companies, but more importantly they designated a dual rate of duty, viz, five marks and three marks for each type of wool. The second observation relates to the constitutional crisis of 1297. Among the grievances of the dissident barons, the so-called *monstraunces*, was one concerning *la maltolt de laynes qe est si grevouse a chescun sake de la layn entire xls, et de la layn brisee a chescun sake v marcs*.[39] Unless we are to accuse the barons of getting their facts wrong we are obliged to conclude that the dual rate of duty was still chargeable. How then are we to explain the complete absence from the customs accounts of wool rated at five marks? A possible explanation is that no wool of this quality came to the ports during this period. *Layn brisee* came almost exclusively from the wool-houses of Cistercian monks and it is possible that with the fall in prices it no longer paid them to incur trouble and expense in carefully preparing wool. Alternatively the king may have consolidated the rates of duty for a second time, but the barons, for safety's sake, quoted the terms of the original grant.

Returning to the events of 1294 we find that the writs of 26 July, which ordered the sheriffs to proclaim the resumption of free trade in wool, qualified that freedom by commanding that merchants who wished to export must deliver their wool to the ports of Newcastle, Hull, Boston, Ipswich, London, Sandwich or Southampton before the Nativity of the Virgin (8 September), under pain of forfeiture. Safe passage was guaranteed by the Crown and three days later, on 29 July, the customs were removed from the control of the Italian firm of Riccardi and Englishmen were appointed as keepers at each of the above-named ports. The haste was dictated by the king's need for money, and having abandoned the prise in favour of the *maltote* he wished to realise the proceeds as quickly as possible. However there seems once more to have been a change of plan, for wool delivered to the ports, whether before or after 8 September, was arrested there until late in the autumn. The customers at Ipswich began to tron and custom wool on 13 November, those at Boston on 19 November, Sandwich on 27 November, Yarmouth on 7 December, Hull on 8 December and Newcastle not until 27 February 1295. It can only be assumed that this delay was part of an agreement made between the king and a consortium of the country's leading wool merchants headed by Laurence de Ludlow.[40] In order to provide money to subsidise the king's allies in the Low Countries the merchants were ordered to pay their customs to royal officials in those parts and further they agreed to lend the king part of the proceeds from the sale of their own wool. Laurence de Ludlow also undertook to sell wool which had been confiscated to the crown from the Riccardi. It seems likely that in return the king agreed to delay the export of other wool so that the consortium might obtain the best possible price.

It has been said that the wool was carried in a fleet which left Yarmouth on 8 December and that this was led by Laurence de Ludlow, who was shortly afterwards wrecked and drowned off the coast of Zeeland. In fact Ludlow was already dead when the Yarmouth fleet sailed. All that can be said with certainty about this fleet is that it consisted primarily of ten heavily guarded ships carrying £25 000 in cash paid at the king's treasury to Robert de Segre, a royal clerk, for delivery to the continental allies. The only wool shipped from Yarmouth at this date was 127 sacks owned by seven local merchants. The wool fleet was separately organised and had sailed from London some two or three weeks earlier, although it is possible, or even probable, that for reasons of security it joined the treasure fleet at Yarmouth. Preparations for exporting the wool of the consortium had begun towards the end of September when the sheriffs of Kent and Essex and the bailiffs of all ports around the Thames estuary were ordered to assemble ships to take wool to Holland and Zeeland. The fleet gathered at London and wool began to be customed on 24 October, the work being completed by 14 November at latest. The total shipment comprised 83 sacks of better wool, 1797 sacks of other wool, 2522 fells and two lasts of hides, including 54 sacks and 223 sacks forfeited by the Riccardi.[41]

In charge of the expedition was Laurence de Ludlow and Master Roger de Lincoln, a royal clerk, who were to sail with the fleet and were to receive customs and loans after the sale of the wool. On 28 October letters of protection were issued to Laurence de Ludlow for the period of his absence and on 18 November further letters were issued to Ludlow, Lincoln and Robert de Segre instructing them to pay 6000 marks to the Archbishop of Cologne and 4000 marks to the Count of Bar. About two thirds of the total could be expected to be raised from customs payments and the sale of the Riccardi wool, leaving only a comparatively small sum to be lent by the merchants. The fleet must have left London soon after the date of the last letters for on Friday, 26 November, 'between night and day' at least one of the ships was wrecked off Aldeburgh in Suffolk and both Ludlow and Lincoln were drowned. Laurence's body was recovered and buried at Ludlow on 20 December. News of the shipwreck reached the Exchequer on Monday, 29 November, and gave rise to an immediate bustle of activity. Writs were made out to Ludlow's agents and those of all other English merchants in Holland, Zeeland, Brabant and Germany, instructing them to pay their customs to Robert de Segre, Master William de Kilkenny and Sir John Botetourte. Since the expedition could not do without the services of an experienced merchant Gilbert de Chesterton of Grantham and William de Belinges of London were appointed to sell the king's wool and that of Ludlow which was now appropriated to the king's use. Other writs were sent to all bailiffs on the east coast ordering them to assist royal officers commissioned to recover wool which had been washed ashore from the wreck and carried off by local people. There may have been more than one ship lost for something like 350 sacks of wool went missing and very little was recovered.[42]

The sum finally made available in the Low Countries from the proceeds of wool sales amounted to less than £5000[43] – a comparatively small amount beside the £25 000 which Segre had taken across in cash. However the abandonment of the prise meant that, for the time being at any rate, the wealth of the wool trade was to be tapped not by extraordinary operations in wool but by means of a greatly increased regular income from customs. In the four years 1290–4 the total custom on wool and hides had amounted to £46 256 19s and although precise figures do not exist it is safe to say that the annual average of wool exports was in excess of 30 000 sacks. Whether the government expected that revenue would increase proportionately after the imposition of the *maltote* is an open question. In the event exports were almost halved, the total for the three years from November 1294 to 23 November 1297 probably lying between 53 000 and 56 000 sacks.[44] It is clear that even without the *maltote* exports must have fallen, for the closure of French and Flemish markets and the dangers of the sea in wartime must have taken their toll. These extraneous factors make it impossible to determine how much of the shortfall in exports was due to the *maltote*, but it is certain that once the tax began to be passed on to the growers in the form of lower prices they became reluctant to sell their wool.

The total customs yield during the period of the *maltote* was around £110 000, for although exports may have been halved the rate of tax was increased sixfold. The fact that revenue trebled does not, however, entitle one to state without further consideration that the *maltote* was financially successful, for the burden of it may have impaired the ability of the king's subjects to support other forms of taxation.[45] Moreover the *maltote* was politically inexpedient in that it contributed largely to the general unwillingness to grant other taxes, although it would of course be absurd to suggest that without the *maltote* there would have been no opposition to taxation.

TABLE 8 *Wool exports, 1294–7 (quantities in sacks, to the nearest sack)*

Period	New-castle	Hull	Boston	Yar-mouth	Ipswich	London	Sand-wich	Totals[a]
1294–5[b]	112	3043	6052	667	60	6718	65	16 717
1295–6[c]	173	2323	3969	2511	34	5729	98	14 837
1296–7[c]	560	1936	5834	3760	19	8970	297	21 376

[a] Excluding Southampton.
[b] From various dates in late autumn to 29 September 1295.
[c] 29 September to 29 September.

From the outset of the war the summaries of exports provided by the enrolled customs accounts cover the period of the Exchequer year, running from Michaelmas to Michaelmas (29 September). As may be seen in table 8 they give the impression that exports were small during the first year of the war, fell during the second and rose again during the third year to give the highest total for this period.

Of greater interest, however, than the total of exports in a Michaelmas to Michaelmas period is the total for the twelve months following the shearing season. Unfortunately the only major port for which the pattern of exports can be redrawn is Boston, which provided the results shown in table 9.

It now appears that following the 1294 clip the export from Boston was very much down on a normal year. This stemmed partly from the fact that merchants were unable to make up leeway lost during the summer and autumn and partly from the diversion of much of the

TABLE 9 *Boston exports, 1294–8 (quantities in sacks, to the nearest sack)*

12 June 1294^a–14 May 1295	2959
14 May 1295^b–14 May 1296	5489
14 May 1296–1 July 1297^c	4898
1 July 1297–7 May 1298	4252

^a First shipment 20 November.
^b First shipment 5 June.
^c Last shipment 20 June.

Italian export from Boston to Hull. In 1295, despite a ban on Italian trade, exports increased considerably, though remaining below those of a normal year. In 1296 they declined somewhat, despite the partial resumption of Italian trade and despite the government's frantic efforts to force merchants to export, in order to increase the yield of the customs. In 1297 the total export again declined, despite the abolition of the *maltote* in November. Boston handled approximately thirty per cent of England's total wool export during this period and if this pattern was repeated in other ports one would be forced to assert that the Michaelmas to Michaelmas figures gravely distort the trend. However in the absence of details for London, which handled some forty per cent of the country's total export one cannot necessarily make this conclusion.

The year which has the greatest intrinsic interest is the third, that following the clip of 1296. Exports got off to a very bad start, for throughout the summer Flemish pirates were active in the southern parts of the North Sea.[46] Between 14 May and 29 September only 1570 sacks of wool left Boston, compared with 3112 in the same period in the previous year. At the end of September the government banned all exports until means of averting the danger could be discovered. The chosen remedy was a convoy system, details of which were announced in a proclamation published on 18 October. Exports were permitted only from London, Boston, Hull and Yarmouth and ships from the first three ports were ordered to hug the coast as far as Yarmouth and then cross directly to Zeeland. All ships were to cross in convoys of at least six and all carrying more than two lasts of cargo were to be protected by five armed marines. The expense was to be borne by the merchants, who were to pay conduct money at the rate of 35s for each last cargo. This charge added considerably to transport costs, for it was equal to double or treble the basic freight charge. A last of wool consisted of ten sarplers, a sarpler packed for the merchant being now larger, now smaller than the customers' sack. In 1297 the king's wool was freighted from Boston to Antwerp at rates of 10s 10d to 11s 10d per last and to Dordrecht for 18s. From Southampton to Bruges the rate was 20s.[47]

With the institution of convoys the export of wool began again and on 26 October 1363 sacks left Boston in twelve ships. However, it seems highly likely that by the winter of 1296–7 both growers and merchants were becoming thoroughly disillusioned with the state of the wool trade. One method adopted to avoid payment of the *maltote* was to spin wool into yarn and to partly tan the hides, in which condition they could be exported free of duty. In April 1297 the government declared this practice to be deliberate fraud and ruled that in future yarn and tanned hides should pay full customs.[48] This effectively stopped the loophole and from then until July 1297 only $2\frac{1}{2}$ sacks of yarn were exported through Boston.

It seems unlikely that any section of the merchant community experienced positive benefit from war-time conditions, for a slackening of competition in buying wool was more than off-set by the dangers of the sea and increased expenses. The most obvious casualties were the French and Flemish merchants, whose goods were confiscated at the outbreak of war.[49] Edward I made a treaty with Flanders in January 1297 and by May Flemings were once again exporting wool. However, other exporters were almost as seriously hurt.

It has already been shown that by 1294 the Italian share of the wool trade was virtually monopolised by eight Florentine firms and two Lucchese. These firms were not exempted from the projected prise of 1294 and to assist the Exchequer each firm was ordered to supply full details of all wool which it had already contracted to buy from English monasteries or which it expected to buy that year. With the cancellation of the prise the king allowed the Florentines to take delivery, but refused permission to export until they had agreed to make him a loan. The Lucca firms were a different proposition. For many years the Riccardi has been responsible for the collection of part of the royal revenues and the king claimed a large credit balance with them. Confidence in the firm had recently been undermined by crises in its European branches, particularly in France. The English government now bankrupted the firm in an effort to recover what it could and all the firm's assets, including wool, were confiscated to the Crown. The Bettri fell at the same time, since they were in debt to the Riccardi and on becoming debtors of the Crown were also bankrupted. In December 1294 the Exchequer of Ireland was informed that the debts of the Bettri to the Riccardi were assigned to the king, while in September 1295 the English sheriffs were ordered to levy on behalf of the Crown debts owing to the Bettri totalling £3312 8s 5d.[50]

Initially the Florentines were probably reluctant to make a loan to the crown for when the export of wool began in November 1294 all Italian wool was specifically excluded. Sometime that month an accommodation was reached and the Frescobaldi Bianchi agreed to lend the king £4000 while the remaining seven firms jointly lent £6000. The Spini contributed £745, Cerchi Neri £2457, Cerchi Bianchi £2132, Bardi £1576, Pulci-Rimbertini £1184 and Frescobaldi Neri £876 in return for which loan licences were issued permitting the firms to export a total of 2690 sacks of wool, presumably all the stocks they then held. Payment of customs was made in advance at the Exchequer. About half of the wool was exported through Hull, the remainder going through London and Boston, with a little through Newcastle.[51]

Licences were issued to the Italians on condition that, like all other exporters, they should take their wool only to Holland, Zeeland or Brabant. This they did, but they then obtained permission from Philip the Fair to import wool into French dominions.[52] This cannot have endeared them to Edward I and probably helps in part to explain the continued restrictions on Italian exports throughout 1295 and 1296. The ban was also part of the pressure exerted to obtain further loans. In the autumn of 1295 letters patent were drafted instructing royal agents to seize the wool of five of the companies, viz. Bardi, Cerchi Neri, Cerchi Bianchi, Frescobaldi Neri, and Frescobaldi Bianchi.[53] These letters were either not issued or else were subsequently cancelled, for there is no evidence that the wool was taken. However, it is not clear what happened to it, for the first four firms exported no wool in the season 1295–6. The relationship between the projected seizure and the refusal of these firms to make loans is suggested by the fact that the other three, whose wool was apparently to be exempted from the seizure, each lent 500 marks in October 1295, and were then allowed to export. It is not possible to discover the exact amount of their export in this season but the Mozzi received remission of customs on 58 sacks sent through Hull and Newcastle, the Spini were remitted custom of one sack at London and the Pulci-Rimbertini, while receiving no remission, paid cash for at least 125 sacks sent through Boston. The Frescobaldi Bianchi, after belatedly making a loan, were given permission to export and were remitted custom on 125 sacks dispatched through Hull and Boston towards the end of the season.[54]

In the season following the clip of 1296 it is likely that the Italian export increased, as the companies became more willing to meet the king's demand for loans. Details survive for the total export through Boston and Newcastle, while some of the export through other ports can be recovered through customs allowances. The Mozzi exported 160 sacks through Boston and at least 23 sacks through London, the Frescobaldi Bianchi took 228 sacks through Boston, 47 sacks through Newcastle and at least 134 sacks through Hull. The Cerchi Neri, who were given permission to export in December 1296, sent nothing through Boston but exported 29 sacks through Newcastle (and a further 24 sacks in October 1297) and at least 22 sacks through London. The remaining companies made no use of Boston or Newcastle, while there is no evidence of any export through Hull or London.

There is nothing to suggest that there was any significant Italian export of wool apart from that taken by the Florentine companies. The firm of Bellardi of Lucca advanced money to the crown and in part payment was licensed to export 450 sacks of wool free of custom. However, the bulk of the licence was assigned to German merchants and the firm exported no more than 36 sacks on its own account. In January 1295 Neapolonius Cardinale, canon of Lincoln, shipped 29 sacks from Hull, while at Boston in the 1296-7 season we find James of Pistoia with 36 sacks, Pagan de Pistoia with 22 sacks, Reginald Aldebrandyn with 19 sacks and Ricco Spilat with 20 sacks. The only exception to the statement made at the beginning of this paragraph is provided by the activities of the Florentine firm of Donati, probably based in Brussels, which exported wool in association with a group of Brabant merchants. The consortium received remission of customs in part payment of subsidies promised by the king to the Duke of Brabant. Lapus Boncare (or Bontate), the representative of the firm in England, was involved in the export of at least 290 sacks of wool from Boston and 71 sacks from Newcastle in 1295-6. The latter was the produce of Newminster Abbey, which at the outset of the war had been contracted to the Riccardi and the Frescobaldi Bianchi. In the following year Lapus seems also to have acted at Newcastle on behalf of the English branch of the Frescobaldi Bianchi.

It has been suggested that as a result of war-time conditions English merchants were able to capture a greater share of the export trade in wool.[55] In the absence of the all-important customs particulars for

London this possibility cannot be ruled out, although the surviving particulars of the provincial ports indicate that in these places the opposite was true. In Hull in the first year of the war 7 Englishmen exported 19 sacks of wool, compared with an export of 546 sacks in 1291–2. On the other hand 24 German merchants exported 890 sacks and 9 Brabanters 129 sacks, compared with totals of 603 sacks and 71 sacks in the earlier year. One Bordeaux merchant took 17 sacks and 34 sacks were taken by Zeeland sailors and ships' masters. Subsequently the fortunes of the English merchants improved somewhat, although their exports remained inferior to those of the Germans, if not to those of the Brabanters. At the beginning and the end of the 1295–6 season, accounts for the middle six months being missing, Englishmen handled 108 sacks compared with 539 sacks exported by Germans and 50 sacks by Brabanters. The respective figures for the first four months of the 1296–7 season were 80 sacks, 444 sacks and 38 sacks. Zeelanders probably handled less wool in these years than in 1294–5, while in each of the later years merchants of unknown nationality handled some 50 sacks. Details of known Italian exports through Hull have already been quoted.

Newcastle, where there had been a strong pocket of native wool exporters, was hit very badly by the war. The total export from the summer of 1294 to January 1298 amounted to some 915 sacks, which was little more than the average annual export of the pre-war years. The most important single exporter in this period was the king himself, who dispatched 286 sacks in 1297. Next came the Florentine companies with a total of 189 sacks. Twenty-five English merchants took a total of 160 sacks, while a further 43 sacks was the property of Isabella de Vescy, lady-in-waiting to the king's daughter in Brabant. In 1292 the leading four merchants of Newcastle had exported a total of 194 sacks. The remaining war-time exports were made up of 96 sacks taken by Brabanters, 50 by Germans, 12 by Flemings, 11 by sailors and ships' masters and about 20 by men of uncertain nationality.

Surviving customs particulars for the port of Boston cover the whole period of the war with the exception of May 1295 to May 1296. These make it quite clear that Englishmen were very much a minor force in the port throughout this time. Unfortunately only in the period 10 July to Michaelmas 1297 can nationalities be established with sufficient certainty to show the position numerically. In this period the leading non-Italian exporters were the merchants of Brabant, principally from Brussels, who handled 478 sacks; next came the Germans with 357 sacks and the Flemings with 257 sacks. Fifteen Englishmen, mostly from Lincoln and Grantham, exported only 144 sacks, and their ranks cannot be swelled much by recruits from merchants of uncertain nationality, who handled 259 sacks. The names of the last group suggest that most of them were aliens. The biggest English exporter was Roger de Belneyr of Grantham, with 42 sacks. It must be remembered, however, that the account does not cover a full season. Hugo fitz Adam of Lincoln, who exported 13 sacks, had exported 38 sacks the previous season, while John fitz Adam, with 42 sacks, may also have been an Englishman.

Throughout the war a steady stream of wool was sent abroad in the name of the king. After the export of 277 sacks of Riccardi wool from London in November 1294 the next consignment consisted of 142 sacks taken from Yarmouth in August 1295 by Reginald de Thunderly and William Cosyn, merchants of London. At least some of the wool was probably salvaged from the Ludlow wreck.[56] By this time more Riccardi wool was coming in and a total of 427 sacks from this source,

TABLE 10　*Royal wool exported 1294–7 (excluding prise wool)*[a]

	1294–5	1295–6	1296–7
Riccardi	277	427	78
Yarmouth	142	–	–
Holderness	–	27	30
French	–	83	–
Scots	–	58	–
Canterbury	–	96	–
York	–	–	41[b]
Lewes	–	–	20

[a] In sacks to the nearest sack.
[b] York wool of 1297 exported after Michaelmas – 34 sacks.

including 49 sacks from Ireland, was exported in 1295–6. The following year the supply was much reduced, amounting to 49 sacks in England and 29½ sacks from Ireland. In 1295–6 in addition to Riccardi wool the king shipped 265 sacks from other sources. From Hull went 58 sacks seized from Scottish merchants; from London 83 sacks and 12 000 fells confiscated by the sheriffs as a result of an enquiry ordered in August 1295 into concealed goods and debts of Frenchmen. Another source from which the king obtained wool was church estates in the hands of crown receivers, the archbishopric of Canterbury supplying 96 sacks in 1295, the archbishopric of York 41 sacks in 1296 and 34 sacks in 1297, and the alien priory of Lewes 20 sacks in 1296. Finally there were the royal estates in Holderness, which yielded 27 sacks in 1295 and 30 sacks in 1296.[57]

The continuity of royal exports meant that it was necessary to keep merchants stationed more or less permanently in the Low Countries[58] to dispose of the wool and this fact was no doubt considered when in the spring of 1297 thoughts turned to another prise. The government's main concern, however, was to force wool into the export market and it may have felt impelled to the prise by the reluctance of the growers to sell at current prices. If the customs revenue dried up then this was the only way in which the king could use the wool trade to finance the war. The origins of the prise are somewhat obscure, since all surviving departmental archives are silent about the early stages of the operation. From *post facto* statements it is clear that sometime in Lent 1297 the government decided to seize wool in all counties in England, except Devon and Cornwall, in the parts of Wales subject directly to the crown and in Ireland. Letters close under the great seal were dispatched to the sheriffs instructing them to make proclamation that all persons owning wool were to prepare it for sale and to carry it to specified towns in each county before the close of Easter (Sunday, 21 April).[59] All wool found outside the towns at that date was to be declared forfeit and was to be seized by officials appointed for this purpose. The proclamation gave no suggestion that wool carried to the towns would be taken as a prise, for clearly this would have invited disobedience. Whether a prise had been determined upon by the time that the letters were sent is uncertain, but the decision was taken before the expiry of the time limit. This is proved conclusively by events in Cambridgeshire and Huntingdonshire where, on Saturday 20 April, commissioners summoned the sheriff and all his bailiffs to the vill of Royston to seize into the king's hands all the wool brought thither, as one of the appointed towns. They found precisely nothing, but that is beside the point.[60]

The proclamation allowed no exception to the order that wool should be brought to the towns, but an ordinance authorising the prise apparently provided that wool belonging to native wool merchants should not be seized.[61] This lends support to the idea that the king was concerned primarily to force wool out of the hands of the growers and into the export market. Later, however,

> it was agreed and provided by Hugh le Despenser, John de Drokensford, keeper of the king's wardrobe, and by others of the king's council sitting in the exchequer, because the sum of wool provided could not be obtained by the ordinance, that the wool of well to do [*sufficientum*] and especially of wealthy wool merchants should be arrested for the king's use.

Later still the king disavowed this second ordinance:

the king has heard nothing previously of any such ordinance, and knows nothing of it [i.e. the second] or of any other ordinance except that by which it was ordained that wool and hides that had not been carried within the time after the proclamation limited for this purpose should be forfeited to him.[62]

Given the impossibility of dating either the letters sent to the sheriffs concerning the proclamation or the first ordinance, is it possible to date the second ordinance, that made by Hugh le Despenser and the others? If they spoke truly when they said that they extended the prise only when it became apparent that a target figure could not be reached then their decision must be dated either after 21 April or, if they had already received intelligence that the target was impossible of achievement, shortly before that date. On 24 April the Exchequer wrote to the sheriffs commenting on the massive disobedience given to the proclamation and ordering a stop to the movement of wool; each sheriff was to prevent any wool from leaving his bailiwick, even that which had been carried to the towns according to the terms of the proclamation; any merchant who disobeyed was to be imprisoned; the ban was to continue until the Exchequer had decided what move to make next.[63] It is tempting to see the extension of the prise to English merchants as having emerged from the ensuing deliberations at the Exchequer. Against this we must set the fact that as early as 20 April wool belonging to merchants of the Cinque Ports had been arrested at Sandwich. This was later restored to them on the grounds that the arrest was illegal, yet it is nowhere stated explicitly that it had been made by virtue of the second ordinance. The merchants successfully advanced the claim that the seizure, which took place within the port of Sandwich, was contrary to the liberties of the Cinque Ports. The second ordinance was cited in a vain effort by the Exchequer to warrant the arrest of wool belonging to these same merchants in London, but since the date of that arrest is not mentioned it is possible that it took place after 24 April.[64] The date of the second ordinance thus remains open.

Within a week of the seizures, orders began to be issued for the restoration of wool, at first purely as acts of royal grace. On 1 May orders were given for the release of wool belonging to the executors of Edmund of Cornwall, for wool belonging to Isabella de Vescy, who was in Brabant with the king's daughter, for wool of Ralph de Gorges, held prisoner in France, for the Abbots of Middleton and Shirburn, for the Bishop and Prior of Carlisle, for the abbey of Holmcultram and for the parson of Wendesle in Yorkshire. On 14 May the wool of the Carthusian priory of Wyttenham was ordered to be released 'for certain secret reasons' and on 15 May restoration orders were issued for the wool of Richard de Bosco, in Gascony on the king's service, and for the wool of Frampton priory and Thomas de Shelfing, customs collector at Sandwich. Later the king in acts of clemency pardoned and restored their wool to some of those who had disobeyed the proclamation; on 25 May a general pardon was granted to the men of the principality of North Wales and later three pardons were issued in favour of named individuals. All these restorations were qualified by the proviso that the wool must be exported by a specified date, for the king still needed the customs duty.[65]

By this time complaints were reaching the king of allegedly illegal acts on the part of the commissioners. The recorded complaints were confined to the ports of Sandwich, London and Southampton. The earliest probably emanated from the men of the Cinque Ports who alleged that in obedience to the proclamation they had assembled their wool at Sandwich ready for export to Flanders but that on Saturday 20 April, 'contrary to the form of the said order', it was seized by Harvey de Staunton, purveyor for Kent. On 17 May the king wrote to Staunton ordering him to release the wool and on 27 May, when it was still under arrest, he wrote to the Exchequer, repeating the order and instructing that Staunton be sent before him to purge his contempt. The Exchequer was still reluctant to part with the wool and it took a third letter dated 5 June, to secure its release. The following day the king ordered the release of other wool belonging to the men of Sandwich, which had been seized in the port of London.[66] Meanwhile on 28 May the Exchequer officials had written to the king explaining how they had issued a second ordinance extending the prise to English merchants.[67] As already shown the king disclaimed their action. Shortly after this orders were given to release wool belonging to a group of London merchants and one or two others, possibly on similar grounds.[68]

Meanwhile at Southampton another struggle was going on over wool taken in the prise. A number of merchants, short of ready cash, had deposited wool with the customers as a pledge of future payment of duty, this had been seized by Simon de Greenhill, purveyor for Hampshire. On 21 May the king wrote to Greenhill saying that 'it was not and is not the king's intention that wool thus delivered there or elsewhere within the realm for custom whereof the term of payment has not yet arrived shall be taken into his hands before the terms'. Greenhill was ordered to restore five sacks of this wool to Henry de Lym of Salisbury, 'unless there be reasonable cause why they ought not to be delivered to him'. Between 24 and 28 May the king ordered the Exchequer to restore the wool taken from five other merchants at Southampton. Although the Exchequer seems to have issued the necessary instructions none of the wool was recovered. The Southampton customers pleaded *salus regis*, the escape clause provided in the last sentence of the king's letter to Greenhill. They explained their failure to restore 24 sacks of wool to John de Shirley by pleading that on the very day they received the order from the Exchequer they had put the wool into a ship and could not unload it without great loss to the king.[69]

The number of surviving complaints of irregularities and orders for restoration are surprisingly few, considering that wool was also seized in the ports at Hull, Boston and Yarmouth. Possibly this may be explained by the fact that by the time the government began to address itself to complaints much of the wool was already aboard ship or had left the country. Subsequently some wool was restored in the Low Countries to its erstwhile owners, Agnes de Ludlow, for example, recovering 51 sacks and Laurence, son of John de Ludlow, 10 sacks.[70] On 10 May writs were sent to the sheriffs ordering them to deliver the wool to the ports of Newcastle, Hull, Boston, Yarmouth, Ipswich, Sandwich, Southampton and Bristol. On 13 May expeditors were commissioned to supervise the loading of the wool and on the following day writs were sent to the bailiffs of each port instructing them to cause the community of the vill to elect a merchant to take the wool overseas and sell it. John de St Ivone, the expeditor for the east coast, was at Ipswich on 18 May, Yarmouth on 20 May, Boston on 25 May and Hull on 28 May. He loaded all the wool which he found at each port, but once he had moved on the sense of urgency sometimes disappeared. At Yarmouth the merchants elected by the community did not take charge of the wool until 29 May and then sat out the Whitsun feast at the king's expense, only sailing on 3 June. At Boston, on the other hand, the bulk of the wool had been dispatched a week before the arrival of the expeditor. On 15 June writs were sent to all ports instructing that all wool still remaining should be exported as quickly as possible, but the final consignment from the Easter seizure was not dispatched until 9 July.[71]

The amount of wool taken in prise, some 2333 sacks,[72] was probably a disappointment to the government and this contributed, no doubt, to the decision to attempt a further prise after the summer shearing. The background to the second prise is even more shadowy than that of the first. During July the king was conceded an eighth of lay moveables by a body whose right to make such a grant was afterwards hotly contested. Since the collection of this tax would take some time it was decided that the king's immediate need for money must be satisfied by a prise of wool, to be sold abroad in the manner of the earlier one.

This decision was published in an ordinance of the council on 30 July.[78] A target of 8000 sacks was set and this figure was apportioned among groups of counties, the total amounting to 8300 sacks. Certain counties were excepted from the prise, those of the north and west probably because of their comparative remoteness, Kent, Sussex, Middlesex and

TABLE 11   *The prises of 1297 – wool taken (to nearest sack)*[a]

	Easter		July Target	Exported
Cumberland	81	Excluding 9 sacks condemned as unfit	–	–
Westmorland	34		–	–
Northumberland	158		–	–
Newcastle	14	Pledge wool	–	–
Lancs.	7		–	–
Yorks.				
NR	148			
WR	119		1500	–
ER	92			
Hull port	63			
Notts.	39		1000	20
Derbyshire	67			
Salop	} 17	Nearly all Salop	–	–
Staffs.			–	–
Lincs.	94		1500	485
Boston port	53		–	–
Leics.	30		400	8
Warks.	7			
Cambs.	} 8			9
Hunts.			200	15
Norfolk	} 138	Nearly all Norfolk	400	76
Suffolk				
Yarmouth port	62	Pledge wool	–	–
Gloucestershire	42		800	13
Worcs.	7			7
Hereford	33		–	–
Dorset	} 35	Excluding *c.* 25 sacks restored after delivery to Southampton	300	32
Somerset				
Wilts.				
Hants	} 383	Approx.	300	48
Southampton port				
Beds.	18		350	27
Bucks.	7			
Oxon.	20		600	13
Berks.	1			
Northants.	} 11		600	47
Rutland				
Essex	6		300	?
Herts.	7			
Middlesex	22		–	–
London	422	Excluding 46 sacks restored in England	–	–
Surrey	42		50	?
Sussex	16		–	–
Kent	*c.* 24		–	–
Totals	2333		8300	798

[a] Sources. King's Remembrancer Memoranda Rolls and Customs Accounts.

London for less obvious reasons. Groups of merchants, from three to
five in number, were commissioned to purvey the wool and, with the
assistance of the sheriffs, to get it to the ports. The ordinance laid down
no principles of selection beyond stating that the king did not wish the
wool of poor men to be taken. It was to be bought by the customary
weight of the country and to be valued according to current prices.

The prise was ordered at the peak of the season and for a time
brought trade to a standstill. At Boston 793 sacks were exported during
July and 373 sacks in the first three days of August. Then the port was
closed until 11 September, when 1072 sacks left in 14 ships, including
333 sacks of prise wool. Despite the cessation of private trade the
purveyors for Lincolnshire managed to export only 484 sacks and 19
stones out of their quota of 1500 sacks. On this occasion little, if any,
wool was seized at the port. Over most of the country the prise was
even less successful than in Lincolnshire; Yorkshire, for instance, exported none of its quota of 1500 sacks. By the autumn failure was
apparent and on 15 November it was decided to abandon the enterprise. Wool not yet carried to the ports was to be restored to its owners,
although subsequently orders were given to some customs collectors to
export wool still in their possession. The total export was only some 799
sacks. The reason given for the cancellation of the prise was that after
payment of expenses the king was losing money on it. It is impossible to
verify this statement or, in the absence of detailed accounts, to see
exactly how much profit accrued from the two prises taken together.
Wool exported from Southampton after Easter, despite the fact that it
proved difficult to sell, yielded a comfortable surplus over the price
which the king was committed to paying for it. However the success or
failure of the prises should not, perhaps, be judged by strictly balancing
income against expenditure. The sum realised by the sale of prise wool
was small in relation to the total cost of the war, but it came in at a
time when, and in a place where, the king was in urgent need of money.
Moreover he could choose his own time to pay for the wool. Finally
it is probably true to say that the threat of the prises forced wool into
the export market and so helped to swell customs revenue.[74]

This leads to a consideration of the questions of where the prise wool
came from and how much of it was eventually paid for? The main
source of the Easter prise was intended to be wool brought to the towns
in accordance with the terms of the proclamation, but disobedience
was widespread and the amount obtained in this way was undoubtedly
small. As already shown in Cambridgeshire and Huntingdonshire
resistance was complete and no wool was brought in. Juries were then
empanelled in each hundred to enquire about concealed wool, but so

successfully did the locals cover up for one another than only a few sacks belonging to strangers were discovered; the total for the two counties was only 9 sacks 8 stones, of which 8 sacks 8 stones were exported. Similar inquests in Hampshire and Wiltshire revealed a total of 17 sacks 35 cloves, ranging from 34 cloves in the Isle of Wight to 8 sacks 9 cloves in Salisbury. In these last counties, apart from confiscated wool, the prise was made up of 39 sacks 15 cloves taken from the Bishop of Winchester, 9 sacks 38 cloves from the Bishop of Salisbury, 41 sacks 18 cloves from the Abbess of Shaftesbury, 2 sacks 48 cloves from the Riccardi and a further 246 sacks taken from 24 individuals, most of them merchants; this last included at least 70 sacks pledged to the customers.[75]

Only in Warwickshire is there direct evidence, in the form of orders for bail, that appreciable numbers were imprisoned for concealing wool. These must have been very small fry, since the county contributed a total of only 7 sacks and it can only be concluded that the larger growers and the merchants ignored the proclamation with impunity. Towards the end of May the king was besieged with applications from distraught wives whose husbands had been imprisoned. At first writs were issued for the release on bail of named individuals, but on 28 May the king instructed the Exchequer to release all those in prison and writs to this effect were sent out on 31 May. This action did not constitute a pardon, for those released were required to give security to answer for their offence at a future date, and their wool remained forfeit.[76]

The July ordinance contained no provision for the confiscation of wool in cases of concealment and the prise was presumably conducted according to the customary rules of purveyance. It should not be assumed, however, that all those who supplied wool did so unwillingly. Since Robert Basing was one of the purveyors for Lincolnshire it can hardly be doubted that the 4 sacks of 'broken wool' bought from him for the very high price of 56 marks were taken with his consent. One consideration which may have made people willing to sell was the chance to get rid of otherwise unsaleable wool, this being balanced against the delay in payment. However, given the right connections a merchant might even avoid the inconvenience of having to wait for his money. Ralph de Fuldon of Lynn was one of the two merchants elected by the community of Yarmouth to export the Easter prise wool. No less than 52 sacks 8 stone of this wool had previously belonged to Ralph, although apparently pledged to the customers. He was credited with £167 13s 9½d, of which he recovered £17 18s 10d in customs allowances and assigned the remaining sum against his own debts to

Westacre Priory. Ten years later the priory was still waiting to receive payment from the Crown. The 75 sacks 22 stones exported from Norfolk and Suffolk during the second prise were apparently all bought in Yarmouth from fifteen individuals, of whom three supplied more than 10 sacks each. On the other hand the Lincolnshire purveyors seem to have travelled widely, for the patent rolls show that 429 sacks out of the 485 sacks taken came from 80 individuals, living mostly in inland market towns, although among them were the Master of the Templars, the Abbots of Thornton and Humberston and the Dean of Lincoln. In Hampshire and Wiltshire wool was forcibly taken in the manors of the Bishop of Winchester, both from the bishop and from some luckless merchants who had just bought from him, but it was not removed and was restored to them when the prise was abandoned.[77]

The purveyors appointed in July were instructed to give either tallies or letters patent, sealed with their own seals, in exchange for the wool. The same practice seems to have been followed at Easter, although no receipts were given to those whose wool was forfeit. Sometimes the purveyors refused or neglected to give a receipt, as happened to the Templars in Yorkshire and in Westmorland. This caused the seller great inconvenience, for he then had to obtain a writ from Chancery to hold an inquest to prove the debt.[78]

On the whole is seems highly unlikely that the king paid out much hard cash to redeem the promises given in exchange for the wool. Payment, when made at all, was made indirectly or in kind; thus St Swithun's Priory was paid in timber from the New Forest. Some persons were satisfied by cancelling their own debts to the Crown; the Archdeacon of Richmond was acquitted of £81 9s 9d of the £100 which he had borrowed from the Riccardi and which was now owed to the king. Others, less fortunate, were assigned crown debts and left to collect them as best as they might; Evesham Abbey, after waiting for 10 years, was assigned £20 against a former sheriff of Staffordshire. Less fortunate still were those who were not paid until they offended against the Crown and whose fines were then cancelled against the debt the king owed them; Walter Barre, a wool merchant of Hereford, was allowed a fine of £80 for coinage offences. In such ways some of the king's debts were paid, but a hard core remained – those who were not debtors of the Crown, did not offend against the law and were not in a position to receive payment in kind.[79]

Towards the end of the reign the cause of those who still awaited payment was taken up by Parliament and in 1304 a petition was presented to the Crown requesting that the King make satisfaction.[80] There is no evidence to suggest that the king acted upon this plea.

Three years later, during the parliament held at Carlisle, the matter was raised again, and on 11 April 1307 the king ordered the Exchequer to pay the outstanding debts. On 20 May the Exchequer announced that it would repay all those who could prove their debt, whether by tallies, scripts, inquisitions or any other means.[81] This move seems to have emboldened the Commons, or some of them, to press for a further concession, for they petitioned for a pardon for all those who had disobeyed the proclamation to carry wool in 1297 and asked that these too should now be paid. This wool had, of course, been forfeited for disobedience to a royal ordinance, but on 20 June the king's pardon and promise of payment was published.[82] This was one of the old king's last acts, for in less than a month he was dead. There is, however, little reason to suppose that there was any acceleration in the rate of repayment. Many years later the debts were still being paid off.

The reason given for the abandonment of the wool prise in November 1297 was that the enterprise had proved unprofitable to the Crown. This was probably a face-saving excuse, for hostility to the prise had been an important plank in the baronial opposition to the Crown. The wool prise was condemned, together with other prises and the *maltote* in the statement of grievances known as the *monstrauncés*, which were probably drawn up in July 1297. On 22 August the Earls of Hereford and Norfolk protested in the Exchequer against the second wool prise and against the levy of an eighth on moveables. That same day the king took ship at Dover, having made only minor concessions to the opposition. In particular he was determined not to give way on the matter of the wool prise, which was regarded as crucial to the financing of his coming campaign in the Low Countries. News of the outburst in the Exchequer reached him before he sailed and he immediately announced that the prise was to continue. Proclamation was to be made, however, that it had always been intended to pay for the wool. Edward added that he thought the king should be as free to buy wool as any other man.[83]

The opposition did not die down in the king's absence and on 10 October the regency bowed to the storm and issued the *Confirmatio Cartarum*, which was reissued by the king on 5 November. The barons, however, were not content with a simple confirmation of *Magna Carta* and the Forest Charter and demanded safeguards to provide against a repetition of recent abuses. *Confirmatio*, while reserving the royal right of purveyance, established that national prises, like those taken in recent years, should in future be exacted, like aids, only for the 'common profit' and by 'common assent'. It also dealt with the *maltote*. Bertie Wilkinson long ago observed that the legality of the *maltote* was not at issue during the crisis of 1297, but he believed that this sprang from the fact that the barons were preoccupied with the task of securing its permanent abolition. Edwards intimated that the barons recognised the legality of the *maltote*, but it remained to Harriss to spell out positively its legitimacy. He claimed that it satisfied the criteria of a constitutional aid, viz. consent – given by a merchant assembly, exceptional need – the pressure of war, and impermanency – it was conceded 'for two or three years if the war lasts as long'.

Confirmatio abolished the existing *maltote*, but for the future merely promised that the king would not exact more than half a mark without the *commun assent*. For Wilkinson this signified a compromise between the king and the barons, with the latter obtaining the immediate abolition of the *maltote* but not pressing the claim that it should never again be exacted. He believed that the barons understood the phrase *commun assent* to give them the right to refuse consent, while the king held that it gave him the right to levy a *maltote* with the formal assent of the merchants alone. Believing that the Commons were not involved in the grant of 1275 nor in the *commun assent* of 1297 Wilkinson claimed that 'Edward I never acknowledged the principle of national consent to the customs'. If one accepts Harriss' contention that the *maltote* was not a custom but an aid it would be possible to regard the preceding statement as true but irrelevant to the issues of 1297. Harriss, however, did not stop here, since he was concerned to destroy the dichotomy between merchant consent and national consent. He claimed that although the barons sought the cessation of the *maltote* in 1297 at no time did they ask for its permanent abolition, since this would have been an unconstitutional attempt to limit the king's right to seek an aid in a national emergency. Further, the safeguard provided in *Confirmatio* did no more, and sought to do no more, than spell out the existing state of affairs. Consent must be provided, although it might legitimately come from the merchants alone. However, the merchants spoke not merely for their own estate; their consent was given, or should be given, on behalf of the entire nation. According to this thesis it was only later, when the merchants could no longer be trusted to judge selflessly the national interest, that the Commons in Parliament were obliged to take away from them the task of judgment.

From mid-September, or even earlier, until the *maltote* was officially removed on 23 November 1297 private exports of wool were virtually at a standstill. Thereafter, despite the onset of winter there was a rush to export. Merchants were encouraged, no doubt, by a shortage of wool in the Low Countries and by the truce which had been made between England and France on 9 October. By 7 May 1298 4673 sacks had been exported from London, 1801 from Boston and 1562 from Hull. At the start of the new season there was no slackening of the pace and between 7 May and Michaelmas 1298 London dispatched 7199 sacks and Hull 3074. There is a gap of thirteen months in Boston's enrolled accounts at this point but the total export in the twelve months to Michaelmas 1298 was at least 26 216 sacks.

In the Exchequer year 1298–9 exports of wool totalled only 21 242 sacks, but this merely reflects the timing of exports and there was no real slump in the trade. Because of the continuing demand in the summer of 1298 most of that season's wool had been dispatched before Michaelmas; the clip of the following season, however, was delayed until after Michaelmas 1299 by monetary confusion in England. In 1298 the country had been flooded with foreign coins known as pollards and crockards. Some of them were brought in by returning soldiers but others were imported, no doubt, to finance wool exports. The coins circulated freely in England, much to the annoyance of the king, since this deprived him of seignorage profits. In 1299 was enacted the so-called Statute of Stepney. This ordered that all newly-imported pollards and crockards must be taken to the official exchanges and surrendered for sterlings. All imported sterlings must also be taken there to be tested for purity. Those which passed the test would be restored to their owner, but any which did not would be forfeit. Pollards and crockards already in the country remained legal tender for all transactions except the purchase of wool, hides, tin and lead, the principal export commodities. For this trade only sterlings or silver plate bearing the royal assay mark might be used. The penalty for breaking the law was confiscation of both the wool and the forbidden coin. This resulted in a general seizure of pollards and crockards in coastal towns and some seizure of wool. Erstwhile owners of wool found in possession of the forbidden money naturally protested that the deal had taken place before the proclamation of the statute. The resulting confusion in the wool trade was made worse by government orders of 21 and 23 August which banned both the sale and export of wool. The purpose of this was to facilitate enquiries about illegal transactions, which were alleged to have taken place on a wide scale. The ban on export was probably short lived, for at Hull shipments were halted only from 22 to 30 August. Sheriffs were ordered to deliver all forfeited wool to customs officials, but there is no evidence that this was done and the order was probably countermanded.[84]

In 1299–1300 wool exports totalled 31 621, but this figure is inflated by the delay in exporting the clip of 1299. It is likely that following each of the three shearing seasons beginning in 1297 exports did not differ radically from the average of the whole period, which was somewhat over 26 000 sacks. This figure is much the same as the average for the years 1279–90 when, as already mentioned, good wool may have been in short supply because of scab. If one accepts that the demand of the Flemish cloth industry was the main determinant of English exports then it seems likely that the industry was experiencing a period of depression or stagnation. It is not impossible that this was a continuation of a state of affairs brought about by a wool famine in the war years. Beyond this it is difficult to gauge the longer term effects of the war. Although major changes were soon to take place in the composition of the wool trade these seem to have been related more closely to other developments, which will be discussed in the next chapter.

4

The English triumphant

The fourteenth century commenced spectacularly with the greatest boom in the history of the wool trade. It is not clear just why the stagnation which followed the war gave way abruptly to a period of prosperity but it is impossible to doubt that the change was associated with developments within the Flemish cloth industry. The boom was retarded, although not reversed, by conflict between Flanders and France and surged ahead once that dispute was ended. The total export for the Exchequer year 1300–1 was 34 608 sacks and although that for 1301–2 was only 16 809 sacks most of this was the product of the 1301 clip. Not until the summer of 1302 did the Flemish market fail, with the result that very little of the current clip was exported before Michaelmas. In 1302–3 and 1303–4 exports were 31 381 sacks and 32 538 sacks, while in 1304–5 they reached 46 382 sacks. In fact this last figure is inflated by a delay in shipping much of the 1304 clip until after Michaelmas. The real explosion did not come until the summer of 1305, following the conclusion of peace between France and Flanders. Therefore the figures of 41 412 sacks and 41 574 for 1305–6 and 1306–7 are more conclusive proof that a boom was under way.

The Franco-Flemish dispute had its origins in the recent war with England. In 1298, once he had renewed the truce with England, Philip IV turned against Flanders to punish its count for his betrayal of France the previous year. Count Guy was imprisoned, the county declared forfeit and James of Châtillon installed as governor. On 18 May 1302 the men of West Flanders rose against the French in the so-called Matins of Bruges and on 11 July the craftsmen utterly defeated the chivalry of France at the battle of Courtrai. In September the French were forced to concede a truce, but this did not last and not until June 1305 was the Peace of Athis-sur-Orge concluded. The disturbances in Flanders in the summer of 1302 undoubtedly account for most of the fall in wool exports that year. The situation was probably aggravated by the behaviour of the citizens of Ghent. They chose this moment to revive monetary claims against the City of London dating back to the dispute of the 1270s. Although it is difficult to believe that this was anything but an excuse they imprisoned London merchants

and arrested goods to the value of £1000. A further source of trouble
was the robbery by Flemish sailors of Italian merchants enjoying the
protection of Edward I. All these matters were probably discussed in
England in the spring of 1303 by envoys representing John of Namur,
brother of the imprisoned count, and the towns of Ghent, Bruges,
Ypres, Lille and Douai. The main purpose of their visit, however, was
to request an alliance against France and to seek the aid of the fleet
of the Cinque Ports. This was refused.[1]

Towards the end of 1303 a further threat to the wool trade arose
from the prospect of English intervention in the Franco-Flemish dispute. Under the terms of the Treaty of Paris, sealed in May 1303, the
kings of England and France had agreed not to succour one another's
enemies. French envoys now persuaded Edward to expel Flemish merchants from England by midsummer 1304 and to withdraw his own
subjects from the county by the same date. The king's council dis-
agreed with the decision, declined to proclaim the ban on Flemings
and presented a reasoned argument against this course of action. In
April the king wrote from Scotland to the council, which was at York,
ordering them to publish the proclamation immediately. He said that
he had given full consideration to their arguments but that he did not
wish to break his word to France. At the same time he ordered the
Cinque Ports to mobilise twenty ships to assist the French. This was to
form part of a fleet going to the aid of Zeeland which, as an ally of
France, had been invaded by the Flemings. Despite the urgency expressed in the king's letter to the council the ban on Flemish merchants
was not proclaimed in the London husting court until 1 June 1304.
On 8 June Edward wrote to the Flemings saying that he had been
obliged by his treaty obligations to impose the ban but that he would
willingly labour to bring peace between them and the King of France.[2]

Rumours of the proclamation and the prospect of a cessation of
trade with Flanders probably led to a rush to export wool. The Hull
customs account reveals exceptionally large shipments in the spring of
1304 and then a lull in the summer months, leaving the bulk of that
year's clip to be shipped after Michaelmas. In fact the proclamation
did little or no damage to English trade with Flanders. Some Flemish
merchants managed to evade the ban by making their own peace with
the King of France and obtaining his letters of protection, which were
recognised in England. It is possible, moreover, that English local
officials, like the royal council, were reluctant to harass Flemish merchants in a cause which was not their own. The English still had
greater cause to dislike the French more than the Flemings. French
attacks on English ships had continued beyond the proclamation of

peace in May 1303 and claims for compensation were still being discussed at Montreuil.[3] It is not known when the ban on Flemings was formally removed, but by this date they played a very minor role in the wool trade. Therefore, as long as England refrained from damaging the Flemings and did not impose a ban on the export of wool any set-back to the trade would be kept to a minimum.

The tide of exports began to ebb slowly about the time that Edward II ascended the throne. It is difficult, however, to determine whether this was in consequence of growing friction between England and Flanders or because the Flemish cloth industry had momentarily reached a level of production which could not be sustained and from which the demand for wool could only fall. The estrangement was to result in 1313 in the setting up of the first compulsory staple of wool, an event of no small magnitude in the history of the trade. Before considering this development it is necessary to examine precedents and possible models for this staple. In 1320, during the course of a dispute about the legality of the staple, a group of English merchants advanced the claim that a continental staple had been in existence in the 'times of Henry III and Edward I',[4] a statement which has provided historians with considerable scope for their imagination. It is likely that the reference to Henry III is a memory of the arrangement made during the dispute of the 1270s to sell wool firstly at Abbeville and later at St Omer. The 'staple' of Edward I, if it does not refer to that same incident, can only allude to the provisions made for the sale of wool during the Anglo-French war of 1294–7, a setup which Tout described, not unhappily, as a 'preferential staple'.[5]

Although Edward I dispatched a wool fleet to Dordrecht at the end of 1294 this port was not constituted a staple. Writs sent to the customs officials after the fleet had sailed make it clear that merchants might now export to any place in Holland, Zeeland or Brabant. Once an alliance had been made with the Duke of Brabant the centre of royal operations was removed to Antwerp. The king had financial agents stationed there and in some instances English merchants paid their customs and made loans there. Although Antwerp was not a compulsory staple it remained the most convenient place for the sale of wool until peace was made with Flanders at the beginning of 1297. The Brabantine authorities were anxious to retain the business of the English merchants and in July 1296 Duke John II issued a charter conceding valuable commercial privileges in Antwerp.[6]

At the turn of the century there was a deterioration in Anglo-Brabantine relations, resulting mainly from the seizure by the duke of wool and other English goods. It is not now clear whether this was anything more sinister than the exercise of the right of purveyance, followed by reluctance to pay for the property taken. However, between 1300 and 1303 English merchants successfully demanded that reprisals be taken against Brabantine merchants in England. By 1305 the dispute had been settled and the duke renewed his charter to English merchants. Following this the English merchant community trading in Brabant assumed a semi-corporate character and elected a leader, described as mayor of the merchants. They may even have used the term staple to denote the centre of their operations. Within a few years there was a further period of coolness and at the end of 1310 the duke wrote to the English authorities complaining that the merchants had stopped going to Brabant, but declaring his readiness to renew his protection. It was then proclaimed in England that merchants might go to Antwerp to hold their staple as they had been wont to do.[7]

It can hardly be doubted that prior to 1310 English merchants trading with the Low Countries had adopted a more or less corporate organisation and took steps to direct their trade towards a staple, which they moved around as it suited their purpose. However, the limitations of the organisation must be kept firmly in mind. Although wool must have figured prominently in the trade it was not a society purely of wool merchants. Nor was there any legal compulsion on any merchant to follow the staple. The first compulsory staple of wool was authorised by a royal ordinance issued on 20 May 1313.[8] It laid down that all merchants, alien as well as denizen, wishing to export wool to the territories of Brabant, Flanders and Artois, must dispatch it to a staple which would be appointed by the mayor and commonalty of the staple. The location of the staple was not mentioned in the ordinance and, following Tout, it has been accepted that the earliest reference to the staple being held at St Omer is dated 30 May 1314. In fact, as will be shown later, it had already been decided to hold the staple in that town.

There has been considerable speculation about the motives which resulted in the setting up of the staple. R. L. Baker rejected earlier ideas that the Crown devised it either as a diplomatic lever or as a means of improving the efficiency of customs collection. He claimed that it was sought by the merchants themselves, although he was unable to show what they hoped to gain from it. W. S. Reid, in a reply, contended that the staple was imposed on the merchants in the interests of the Crown, and that it was an essential preliminary to a reform of the customs, which could then be pledged as security for loans raised from the merchants. However, the burden of his argument is that the staple was in large measure a direct consequence of Flemish involvement in the Anglo-Scottish struggle.[9] Although this is accepted it will be suggested that in considering Anglo-Flemish relations Reid managed to reverse cause and effect. It will also be shown that the English merchants stood to gain as much from the staple as the Crown did. The arrangement, in fact, was to their mutual satisfaction.

Reid points out that Scottish independence could not have been achieved without a continuous import of food and weapons, the main source of which was the marts of Flanders. He claims that Flemish failure to observe the blockade imposed by England led to a deterioration in Anglo-Flemish relations and that the St Omer staple was set up to convince the Flemings of the folly of their ways. It seems entirely unreasonable, however, to suppose that the Flemings valued trade with Scotland more than with England. Scotland was a small country; England was a relatively large one which supplied Flanders with most of her wool and took a large part of her cloth. Given normal relations with England it seems likely that the Count of Flanders would have given serious consideration to the English demands that he prevent the Scots from obtaining supplies in his country. The deterioration in Anglo-Flemish relations was independent of the Scottish rebellion, but in consequence the Flemings became more and more willing to trade with the Scots. In searching for the origin of the estrangement one possibly does not need to look much beyond Flemish resentment at England's refusal to lend assistance against the French in 1303.

The close rolls of Edward II are full of correspondence between the governments of England and Flanders about damage alleged to have been inflicted upon English sailors and merchants, both at sea and in Flanders itself. For the first eighteen months or so the complaints relate to incidents dating from the previous reign. Moreover, in their claims for compensation the English government adhered rigidly to accepted practice and was reluctant to distress Flemish merchants in England until its subjects had failed to obtain justice in Flanders. By the end of 1308 growing friction between the two countries is indicated in the correspondence, which now relates more and more to fresh incidents. In May 1309 Edward II, in writing to the authorities of Bruges, stated 'so many complaints come almost daily to his ears of the damages and wrongs inflicted by men of those parts upon his subjects that he is very much aggrieved and moved thereby, especially as he has no knowledge of his subjects inflicting any grievances upon them'. Some of the recent wrongs were actually alleged to have been perpetrated by the civic authorities of Flanders, including the seizure of wool and the unlawful detention of money taken to official exchanges.

The situation was exacerbated by the fact that German 'pirates', assisting the Scots and preying on English shipping, operated out of the Zwin estuary. In March 1309 Edward wrote both to Bruges and to the count requesting them not to harbour these 'easterlings'. It is significant that these first complaints about interference in the Anglo-Scottish business relate to Germans and not to Flemings.[10]

In the summer of 1309 the king persuaded the count to set up a special commission to hear the grievances of the English merchants. On 5 August it was proclaimed throughout England that all who had suffered wrong should go to Flanders to put their case by Purification next (2 February 1310). The English authorities seem to have determined that in the meantime they would do nothing to exacerbate the situation and refused to authorise distraints of Flemish property in England so long as there remained a prospect of a general redress in Flanders. However, the commission was either not established, or, alternatively, it proved powerless to compel civic authorities to provide a remedy for the complainants. In relation to at least one of the most serious cases the count 'excused himself' from doing justice and said that he was agreeable to the distraint of Flemish goods in England until justice might be done in Flanders. The English government still showed a preference for a general redress by the count himself and wrote to him to this effect in October 1310.[11]

In November 1310 the king wrote to the count asking him to suppress Flemish pirates and exiles from Holland and Zeeland who were operating from his territory against English shipping.[12] It needed only one more serious incident to complete the breach between England and Flanders. This was provided by the English themselves. On the night of 8 December 1310 a small fleet entered the bay of Graunzon in Brittany and plundered seven Flemish ships, laden with wine and salt, lying at anchor there. It was this episode, the 'battle' of Graunzon, not the question of Scottish trade, which became the insuperable obstacle to peace between England and Flanders.[13]

From this time it was not merely property which was endangered, for the persons of the merchants were now at risk if they ventured abroad without safe conducts. In February 1311 a number of merchants of Ypres were arrested in London in reprisal for the imprisonment of English merchants in Flanders. Writing to the count about this incident the king claimed that they were 'not kept in a vile prison', as had been alleged, 'but in a simple and fitting custody, going whither they liked in the city of London'. The Flemings were blamed for being the first to depart from civilised practice,

> whereat the king wonders because it has hitherto been observed between
> the king's and his [the count's] ancestors that no arrest of bodies or goods

was made for debts or trespasses until the lord of the persons, for whom amends of the trespass or payment of the debt were sought, had been properly requested and had failed to do justice.[14]

The escalation of the dispute was not to the count's liking and in April 1311 he sent Terry le Villeyn, a Flemish merchant well known in England, to give his version of the Graunzon affair and to ask the king to arrange a conference, at which representatives of either side would have full powers to make amends for their respective misdeeds. It was agreed that the meeting should take place at London on 13 June. In the event the king did not come to London until Parliament assembled in August. The council then began negotiations with the Flemish envoys, which was continued at York. Meanwhile open war had broken out between the sailors of the two countries, with the notorious John Crabbe and other Flemish pirates taking a heavy toll of English ships. Wool captured at sea was taken to Aberdeen, where it was sold to Scottish merchants and then re-exported to Flanders as Scots wool. On their side the English seized Flemish ships which traded with Scotland, justifying their action on the grounds that the Scots were rebels. The king himself declined to release such ships and on 1 October 1311 wrote to the count complaining about Flemish aggression.[15]

The discussions between the Flemish envoys and the council were concluded by the middle of March 1312 and letters were dispatched from York proclaiming the arrangements which had been made for the settlement of the dispute. The warden of the Cinque Ports and three royal justices were appointed to try, by the law merchant and the custom of the realm, all offences committed by the English at Graunzon and elsewhere. The hearing was to begin at London on 28 May at the latest, and letters of safe conduct were issued for Flemish merchants to come to England. The count named commissioners to hear the English grievances and complainants were to repair to Bruges by midsummer. The English hearing was prevented from taking place by 'divers hindrances that arose in this realm', which presumably means the pursuit and murder of Piers Gaveston. This was explained to the count in a letter delivered in November 1312 by William de Dene, knight, and Richard de Stury, the latter probably already mayor of the English merchants. In February 1313, following their return, the king again wrote to the count suggesting 15 August as the new date for the hearing of the tribunal. However on 25 March Flemish envoys appeared before the king and apparently demanded immediate justice for the wrong done at Graunzon. The commission of enquiry was immediately renewed, but according to the English version the count's envoys and subjects appeared and refused to sue any one for the damages aforesaid, but prayed that the damages, which they had assessed at a great sum, should be immediately paid to them; which request the justices refused to accede to as contrary to law and the tenor of the treaty; whereupon the count's envoys left London contemptuously.[16]

On 1 May the king wrote to the count, possibly in a last attempt to effect a settlement before the proclamation of the ordinance of the staple, which is dated 20 May. He requested that justice be done to his subjects and held himself ready to do justice to those of the count. Complaint was also made about fresh depredations by John Crabbe and about thirteen Flemish ships which had recently taken supplies to Scotland. The letter made no reference to the staple. However, a letter sent from Courtrai on 27 May, possibly in reply to that of 1 May, proves that the count already knew about the plans for a staple. He began by denying the stories that he had proclaimed the banishment of all English merchants and that Englishmen were already languishing in his prisons. He then went on to excuse his inaction in the matter of Scottish trade. He alleged that it was impossible to stop, since merchants came to Flanders from many countries, most of whom were unknown to his officers. He concluded with the veiled threat that if the English merchants continued with their plans to hold a wool staple at St Omer he would no longer be able to maintain his traditional favour towards the king. This suggests either that rumours of the staple had been circulating in London when the count's envoys had been there in March or even that William Stury may have threatened the Flemings with a staple before Christmas.[17]

The preceding narrative of the deterioration in Anglo-Flemish relations during the reign of Edward II should have made it clear why the English established a staple at St Omer in the summer of 1313. Short of imposing a total ban on the export of wool, which was probably unthinkable, they had little or no alternative. Any Englishman who ventured his person or his property to Flanders put them into danger. Because of this English merchants risked losing control of the wool trade to aliens, from whom they had so recently won it. Indeed the loss had probably already begun. After the imposition of an additional tax of 3s 4d per sack in 1303 the alien share of total exports seems to have fallen steadily. By 1309–10 aliens handled only 34 per cent of the trade and in the following year 35 per cent. In October 1311, however, the new custom was abolished; aliens and denizens again exported on equal terms as regards the burden of tax, but Englishmen were now severely handicapped by the situation in Flanders. The only way to redress the balance was to create a staple outside Flanders and to compel aliens as well as denizens to export there. An exception was made in favour of wool not intended to be sold within the territories of Flanders, Brabant and Artois. The object of the exercise was not to bring Flanders to her knees, for it was realised that the Flemings must still take most of the wool. However, at St Omer the exchange would take place on neutral territory, which was the attraction of the staple from the point of view of English merchants. The staple also had an appeal for the king. The count of Flanders and his subjects would suffer some financial loss and be put to inconvenience by the St Omer staple. They might thereby become more amenable to the king's demand that they stop trading with the Scottish rebels. Although not the original cause of the quarrel between England and Flanders this was now a matter of concern.

The removal of the wool trade to St Omer failed to effect a quick settlement to the Anglo-Flemish dispute, which was to drag on for many years. In the summer of 1314, however, a brief renewal of the war between Flanders and France inclined the count to seek an accommodation with England. On 25 July he wrote to Edward II requesting safe conducts for his subjects to come to England. He promised the safety of English merchants coming to Flanders and even suggested that they should remove the staple to Bruges. The urgency for a settlement was removed in September when the Flemings made their peace with France. However, the initiative had revived the prospects of serious negotiations. On 12 March 1315 a safe conduct until Christmas was given to all Flemish merchants coming to England to trade, although later that same month naval forces on the east coast were instructed to take all measures necessary to prevent ships from leaving Sluys with supplies for the Scots. In May burgesses of Ghent, Ypres and Bruges came to England on a peace mission. They promised to satisfy claims of Gascon subjects of Edward II and proposed that the Flemish injuries to Englishmen and the Graunzon affair should be referred to a diplomatic process. The talks went well and agreement was reached about the method of procedure. Unfortunately the terms of the agreement were not implemented, since once more war broke out between Flanders and France and the French king called upon Edward II to honour his treaty obligations.[18]

On 18 June, Louis of France wrote to Edward calling upon him to outlaw the Flemings as rebels against the French crown. The demand was repeated in a letter of 14 July, which reported that the peers of France had deprived the count of his fief and denounced his subjects as rebels. After some delay writs were issued on 1 September proclaiming that all Flemings must leave England by 23 October. France also requested that England should contribute ships to an expedition which was being mounted against Flanders. Some of the English council advised against sending aid, but they were overruled by the king. He argued that if France defeated the Flemings without English assistance she would refuse to help England in similar circumstances at some future date. He decided, therefore, to send six royal ships to assist the French since 'this will be an honour to the king and not much cost'. To the King of France Edward replied that most of the English naval forces were already committed against the Scots, but that he would send what ships he could spare and would do all he could to injure the Flemings. The formal ban on the presence of Flemings in England was not removed until the end of 1316 when Louis of France informed the king that he had made peace with Flanders. On 7 December writs were made out to proclaim the safety of Flemings coming to trade. The situation remained tense, for the renewed presence of the Flemings led to a clamour from English merchants that their goods be distrained to provide compensation for English losses. The recent hostilities had greatly increased the number of incidents for which claims had been submitted.[19]

The renewal of conflict between Flanders and France in 1315 obliged the English to remove the staple from St Omer. The Flemings could no longer resort to the town, while any Englishmen coming there from the areas in rebellion would also be harassed by the French. Some Englishmen began to export directly to Flanders, but the staple itself was officially established at Antwerp. At the end of the year the King of France requested that it be restored to his territory at some point between Calais and the Seine. On 16 December 1315 writs were sent to a number of English towns instructing them to nominate two or three merchants to discuss this proposition with the council when Parliament next met at Lincoln. Nevertheless, the staple remained at Antwerp until 1317 when, probably later than June, it returned to St Omer. This return was not caused solely by the conclusion of peace between France and Flanders; there had been friction in Antwerp between the English and the natives. Some Englishmen who had been robbed by Brabanters failed to secure justice in the duchy and caused property of Brabantine merchants to be distrained in England. This move was frustrated by the duke who persuaded the king to release the goods.[20]

In the summer of 1317 hostilities broke out between Flemish sailors and the men of the Cinque Ports, which later became known as the Rye affair. The king instructed his subjects to cease molesting the Flemings and letters of safe conduct were renewed for merchants to trade in England. The count also issued letters for Englishmen in Flanders. It is clear that both rulers were now genuinely anxious that peace should be made and each was willing to make concessions to this end. The count restored some wool which had been seized from English merchants and the king released a Bruges ship taken on a voyage from Scotland to Flanders. Later, at the request of the count, the king released a Zierikzee ship similarly captured. The crew of the latter were declared by an English jury to be 'pirates, robbers and homicides' but their release was granted 'in order to cherish peace and tranquility'. As early as January 1317 a number of English sailors were tried at Southampton on charges of piracy arising from the Graunzon affair. On the other hand English merchants claiming damages seem to have found it very difficult to obtain orders for the distraint of Flemish goods. Since it cannot have been the king's wish to deny justice to his own subjects one must assume that the government considered the situation to be too confused to be settled by the normal machinery of justice. The only way out of the impasse was by a diplomatic process.[21]

On 20 May 1318, in reply to an earlier request, the names of four English negotiators were communicated to the count and it was suggested that his representatives should be in London by 8 July. The messenger returned with the news that the Flemings would appear by 22 July, but because of events in the north the king could not be in London and postponed the conference until 30 September. When the king was still unable to come to London the Flemish envoys came to him at York and on 8 November an indenture was made recording the agreement which had been reached. This document did not establish peace between the two countries, being merely an agreement about the machinery which should be set up to remove obstacles to peace. On the Flemish side the major obstacles were the affairs of Graunzon and Rye. One of the points of the treaty was that these wrongs should be redressed by 22 July 1319, when the Flemish envoys would reappear to hear the king's judgment on them. On 8 February 1319 the king wrote to Walter de Norwich, the treasurer, and three others ordering them to drop all other business and to attend to their commission to enquire into the Graunzon affair in the counties of Norfolk and Suffolk. On 8 June a similar order was issued to the warden of the Cinque Ports and a number of justices with regard to an enquiry in Kent, Sussex, Hampshire and other counties. The English pirates had apparently scattered their loot far and wide.[22]

The enquiries into the Graunzon affair were conducted to no purpose, for in July 1319 the Flemish envoys did not appear to hear the judgment. This was probably not unexpected since at Whitsun the

Count of Flanders and the city of Bruges had written defiantly to
Edward II stating their refusal to stop the trade with Scotland. They
justified their stand with the boast that '*terra nostra Flandriae universis,
cuiscumque Regionis, est communis, et cuique Liber in eadem patet
ingressus: nec possumus Mercatoribus, suas exercentibus Mercaturas,
ingressum, prout hactenus consueverunt, denegare, quin ista cederent
in desolationen nostrae Terrae Ruinem*'. The city of Ypres was more
conciliatory, merely denying that its merchants had intercourse with
the Scots or with any other rebels against the king. In fact the breakdown in negotiations was probably caused less by the question of Scottish trade than by the refusal of the English merchants to remove their
staple to Bruges.[23]

The request for the transfer of the staple to Bruges was probably
made by the Flemish envoys who came to York in the autumn of 1318.
The matter was discussed in the parliament which was currently meeting there, but a counter proposal was made that staple towns should
be established in England. No decision was reached and John de Charlton, mayor of the staple, who had come to Parliament as a representative of London, was sent on an embassy to Flanders. At the same
time writs were issued for an assembly of merchants to meet with
Charlton in London on 20 January 1319. It is likely that this meeting
did not take place, possibly because Charlton did not return in time.
On 9 March 1319 fresh writs were issued for merchants to meet at
London on 24 April. The recommendations made by this assembly
have survived, although they are set out in rather summary form. It
was proposed that two staples should be established in England, one to
the south of the Trent and one to the north. Aliens would be permitted
to buy wool only in the staples and, apparently, would also be confined
to these places in the sale of their own wares. It was not specified what
part the staples would play in the denizen wool trade. Some of the
advantages which, it was alleged, would accrue from the new system
seem, logically, to imply that denizens would not be permitted to
engage in the export trade. This is not stated in the document, but
how else could the assembly guarantee that its plan would do away
with the personal violence, seizure of goods and unjust reprisals from
which Englishmen now suffered in foreign parts? Probably these
claims were merely extravagant, for there is no other evidence of an
intention to ban denizen exports at this date. It was also alleged that
the plan would halt the decay of English towns, dissuade the king from
borrowing money from aliens, prevent foreign powers from assisting
the king's enemies and inhibit the circulation of foreign and counterfeit
coin. This last result was to be effected by confining imports to gold,

silver plate and bullion. Bullion, in this context, apparently meant demonetised coin.[24]

The recommendations of the merchant assembly were not implemented and at the end of 1319 it was decided to enforce the St Omer staple more strictly. Between 6 December and 24 January 1320 a number of commissions were issued ordering John de Charlton to investigate allegations of large-scale evasion. Initially there was indecision about the most effective method of procedure. It was first decided to invite voluntarily confessions and to grant pardons in return for payment of fines. This was later replaced by enquiry and amercement, the penalties going to the Crown. In January Charlton was ordered to summon a council of the staple and to conduct his enquiry by oath. In the following month he was authorised to examine all customs particulars submitted since the issue of the staple charter. This implies that he possessed a record of wool brought to the staple which could be checked against that of wool legally exported from England.[25]

Opposition to the enquiry suggests that before this time the staple had been laxly enforced. The resistance was led by alien merchants, who had least to fear from exporting direct to Flanders. On 25 February 1320 a group of aliens went to the Exchequer alleging that they were not bound by the staple ordinance to which they had not given their consent, and that they were being vexed illegally by Charlton. They called for the immediate revocation of the staplers' charter and Charlton's commission. The sheriffs of London were ordered to bring the latter before the council at Westminster three days hence. On this occasion the commission was suspended and all parties were ordered to appear again on 7 April. After a further adjournment of one week the case was heard by the king and a large part of the council. The alien case was put by Italians, while Charlton was supported by a large number of English merchants. The former repeated their claim that they had never consented to the ordinance and quoted Magna Carta to the effect that they were free to trade wherever they wished. The English defence was that there had been an overseas staple in the reigns of Henry III and Edward I, but one which carried no penalties for disobedience. It was that lack which had caused both alien and denizen merchants to seek the present charter. The charter was then read before the council, but since they felt the need for further advice they ordered that it be placed in the king's wardrobe until further notice. Nevertheless they declared that the commission issued to Charlton should remain in force in so far as the levying of penalties for past offences was concerned. The charter was later restored to the staplers.[26]

The commissions of enquiry were renewed in June 1320 and the terms of reference were extended to discover instances of connivance by customs officials at the evasion of staple regulations. A number of prominent Londoners were imprisoned in the Tower when their offences were revealed, though all were released on bail. The enquiries seem to have thrown the wool trade into a state of confusion. It was alleged that 'many alien merchants, and especially German merchants, are guilty of the aforesaid offences, and that they propose leaving the realm with their wool and other goods, probably not intending to return'. To prevent this the sheriffs of a number of counties were ordered, on 18 June, to arrest the wool of aliens until they found security to answer any charges proved against them. Customs officials were instructed to take similar security from both alien and denizen exporters and to ensure that wool was exported only in the name of its true owner. On 25 July the severity of the precautions began to be relaxed. Denizens were permitted to export without giving security provided that they took an oath that the wool was their own. On 28 July sheriffs were ordered not to arrest any more alien wool and to release that already held. It was later alleged that some sheriffs extorted money to secure the release of wool.[27]

The need to reinforce the authority of the staple arose from the fact that a section of the English merchant community had recently taken to exporting to Bruges. After the issue of the commissions some of the rebels decided to return to St Omer, but others, led by Henry de Northwode, made a confederacy to prevent this. In 1321, however, the staplers began to exceed their powers by persuading the customs officials of some ports to take security from denizen merchants that they would export only to the staple. The government angrily put a stop to this when the matter was brought to its notice.[28]

Those Englishmen who wished to stay in Bruges in the spring of 1320 were probably encouraged by a slight thaw in Anglo-Flemish relations. After the breakdown of diplomatic negotiations in 1319 there had been a sharp increase in the number of orders for the distraint of Flemish property. It is unlikely that the English merchants gained much satisfaction from this, for the simple reason that few Flemings can have been so foolhardy as to come to England in this period. In January 1320, after receiving letters from Flanders, the government ordered that no more property should be arrested until 4 May and this protection was renewed several times until 1 August 1320. It declined, however, to release Flemings who had been imprisoned for communicating with the Scots. On 6 August the king wrote to the count accepting his request for the resumption of negotiations and proposed that Flemish envoys should come to Westminster on 12 October. In August authority was given for the arrest of Flemish goods in England, except for those at Boston fair and the Yarmouth herring fair, which were declared protected zones. Despite this apparent provocation the Flemish envoys arrived for the conference, with their powers sealed by the count and dated 1 October.[29]

The conference agreed that the process of Graunzon should be brought to a conclusion at Westminster on 4 May 1421, that the process of Rye should continue with all possible speed and that 'in the matters on both sides that are not clear the plaintiffs shall sue their plaints between now and [4 May], to wit the English in Flanders and the Flemings in England'. On 13 December 1320, the day following the enrolment of the above agreement, commissions were issued ordering new enquiries to be made into the Graunzon affair. It was now almost exactly ten years since the attack. The same day orders were sent to the sheriffs to make proclamation that all who had initiated suits against Flemings should come to Westminster on 4 May next. Those who wished to make new complaints should come to the Chancery without delay to obtain letters requesting the Count of Flanders to give them justice. In consequence of the agreement all arrests of Flemish property were suspended until 4 May 1321.[30]

The conference arranged for May 1321 duly took place between the council and envoys of Flanders. The king himself apparently played no part in it, but when the results were reported to him 'he accepted them and ordered them to be confirmed, although they were heavy terms'. In fact the treaty had not been confirmed by the time that Parliament assembled in July. The principal outcome of this gathering was the overthrow of the Despensers and the resumption of power by Thomas of Lancaster. While Parliament was sitting the Flemish embassy, or at least part of it, denounced the treaty and returned home. It is possible that they feared that the new government would not ratify it and preferred to make the break themselves. Edward II later alleged that the Flemings had behaved in this manner 'because of a disturbance moved against him in the realm'.[31]

Immediately after the departure of the Flemish envoys a large number of writs were issued ordering the distraint of Flemish property in favour of English merchants. The new government also took steps to secure the custody of Scots and Flemish prisoners, moving them from Suffolk to the Tower of London. In April 1322, following the defeat of the Earl of Lancaster at Boroughbridge, Edward II wrote to the Count of Flanders offering to conclude a treaty on the terms agreed the previous summer. There was, however, little prospect of a settlement at this time, since the Flemings were again actively assisting the Scots. Even while his letter was on its way the king mobilised the fleet of the Cinque Ports and ships of the east coast to fight the Flemings who were 'infesting the coast, despoiling the king's subjects, sparing no man and putting innocent persons to death'. In May the king wrote again to Flanders protesting at the imprisonment of English merchants. At the same time writs were issued for an assembly of wool merchants to deliberate with the council at York on 14 June. Unfortunately there is no record of the outcome of the meeting.[32]

In September 1322 Robert III of Flanders died and was succeeded by his grandson, Louis de Crecy. The new count immediately made overtures to Edward II and the king replied in favourable terms at the beginning of December. He made it clear, however, that a truce could not be granted unless the Flemings withdrew their assistance from the Scots. In February 1323 envoys came to England and the king agreed to a conditional truce. Since the envoys declared that they were unable to bind their countrymen to stop trading with the Scots the truce was not to be proclaimed in England until the warden of the Cinque Ports received intelligence that it had been proclaimed in Flanders together with a prohibition on trade with Scotland. The truce was proclaimed in England on 5 April 1323 and orders were given to release the Flemings imprisoned in London. Shortly afterwards all but one of these were permitted to return to their homes. The exception was to be detained until it was learned that the Englishmen imprisoned in Flanders had been released. On 18 April safe conducts were issued for Flemish merchants to trade in England. They were not to be punished for past offences against the staple but it was agreed that for the time being they should respect its privileges.[33]

The Anglo-Flemish truce was continually renewed but was not converted into a definite peace until Edward III, after a period of renewed hostility, made an alliance with Flanders during the Hundred Years War.[34] During the early years of the truce Edward II frequently admonished his subjects not to molest the Flemings. Minor breaches were committed by either side, but there was no serious trouble. The king was most careful to order the immediate investigation of any wrongs alleged to have been done by his subjects. The Flemish authorities were probably equally scrupulous, since there is no record of any reprisals being ordered against Flemish property in England. More importantly neither side used the weapon of distraint to hasten the settlement of earlier claims. Flemish envoys came to England several times during the early years of the truce and the processes probably continued at a leisurely pace. There is, however, no evidence that they were ever brought to a conclusion. Fortunately, neither side was ready to renew the war for the sake of ancient grievances.

In May 1325 the king ordered that the staple be established at Bruges. He promised that this should not be drawn into a precedent to the prejudice of the staplers' charter, which guaranteed that they might hold the staple wherever they pleased. Since July 1323 all aliens had been permitted to export wool to Flanders and it seems highly likely that Englishmen were allowed to do the same, since the penalties for offences against the staple had been suspended. The staple as an organisation remained in being during this period and there were at least two changes of mayor. John de Charlton was replaced by William de Merewelle by August 1324, and the latter by Richard de Betoigne by May 1325. All were Londoners.[35]

The Bruges staple was short lived, for in the spring of 1326 it was decided to create a number of staples in England itself. An ordinance to this effect was issued at Kenilworth on 1 May and was proclaimed at London twelve days later. The 'principal mover' of the new arrangement was alleged to be the younger Despenser, who was rewarded by the grant of a staple to his town of Cardiff. All the other staple towns, London, Newcastle, York, Lincoln, Norwich, Winchester, Exeter, Bristol, Shrewsbury, Carmarthen and three towns in Ireland, had the king as their immediate lord. The ordinance stated that all wool intended for export must pass through a staple town and must remain there for at least forty days. The writs directed to some towns had specified a period of fifteen days, but these were scribal errors which were corrected after a protest from London. The ordinance, unlike the legislation of 1353, did not prescribe the form the staple was to assume in each town.[36]

Despite a shortage of background evidence it seems not unreasonable to deduce, as was done by both Tout and Power, that the new policy reflects a division of interests among the towns and merchants of England. For the time being those interests which favoured home staples, as against an overseas staple, were in the ascendant. The interests may easily be identified, but the personalities are little more than shadows. Among the merchants who were actively engaged in the export trade there were those who would have welcomed a complete freedom from staple regulations but there can have been few who regarded home staples as preferable to an overseas staple. Although denizens were free to buy wool anywhere in the country the requirement that before export it must remain forty days in a staple was very much against the interests of the export merchants. London merchants were an exception to the general rule. The city was the only one of the four leading wool ports which had been constituted a staple. Since Londoners exported the bulk of their wool through their own port they would not have to go out of their way to pass through a staple. If the new policy had been suffered to continue London must inevitably have engrossed an even larger share of the export trade than it actually did. The official policy of the city was therefore in favour of home staples.

The ordinance limited aliens to buying wool in the staple towns. The purpose of this was to deny them direct access to the large producers and to channel the trade through the hands of native middlemen. They received a certain degree of compensation from the fact that the new staple policy might discourage denizen exporters and give them a greater share of the market. Moreover on leaving the staples they were allowed to take wool wherever they pleased. This was a distinct improvement on being compelled to take wool to an overseas staple, which might be out of their way. Later history was to prove that a compulsory overseas staple was highly detrimental to the alien trade.

Those who stood to gain most from the new policy were the middlemen, those who supplied export merchants but did not themselves venture into the overseas market. They were freed from the competition of alien buyers, while even denizen exporters might be driven to make greater use of middlemen, now that wool must remain forty days in a staple. English cloth manufacturers also stood to gain indirectly from the operation of home staples, which must inevitably add to the costs of the export trade. These costs would probably be passed on to the foreign cloth manufacturer, thus improving the competitiveness of the English producer, who was not required to buy his wool in the staples. The native cloth industry was also given protection by a series of measures, which were parallel to, rather than part of, the home staples policy. While the staple policy had been emerging the mayor of London had written to the king complaining that Flemings, Brabanters and other aliens were buying up teasels, bures, madder, woad, fuller's earth and other raw materials in a deliberate attempt to subvert the English cloth industry. He himself had arrested twenty tuns of these items. The king commended his action and imposed a general ban on the export of such raw materials. This protection was later reinforced by an order forbidding common people to wear alien cloth imported after Christmas 1326. Franchises were also promised to all the crafts in the industry.[37]

The only interest not considered so far is that of the wool growers. Beyond any doubt they would be best served by a policy which promoted competition among buyers of wool. Any staple, whether at home or abroad, was bound to limit competition. Under the present regulations alien merchants were forbidden to approach the growers on their home territory, a situation likely to encourage combinations among native merchants. This was recognised in the staple ordinance which banned confederations, either to force down prices paid to the growers or to prevent 'merchant-strangers' from buying wool. On 1 July 1327 a commission was issued to investigate allegations made in the East Riding that wool merchants of York, Beverley and other towns had confederated 'by writings and oaths' not to pay more than a certain price agreed between themselves.[38]

On 12 June 1326 two of the richest merchants from each of the staple towns met in London together with four Londoners and two Norwich merchants who had already been appointed by the government to examine the whole question of the staple. This assembly was ordered to elect a mayor of the staple. It passed over Richard de Betoigne, the last recorded mayor, and elected John de Charlton, a former mayor and one of the four London representatives. Charlton was apparently an associate of the Despensers and did not survive their downfall. Queen Isabella returned to England at the end of September 1326 and in mid-October London rose in her support. Charlton was driven from the city and his house was robbed. When order was restored and an ordinance was passed that all those who had fled might return in peace Charlton was the one person excepted by name, for he was classed among 'the common enemies of the land'. Nevertheless this same city ordinance decreed that all must respect the staple regulations until parliament should meet.[39]

With the disgrace of Charlton, Richard de Betoigne 're-emerged' as mayor of the staple. In June 1326 the customs officials had been ordered not to cocket any wool unless it was accompanied by a certificate, warranted by Charlton or a deputy, that it had been in a staple for forty days. In March 1327 orders were given at the behest of Betoigne, now recognised as mayor, that letters certified by Charlton or his deputies were no longer required. The staple ordinance, however, was not to be prejudiced in any way. It was later alleged that Betoigne had been elected overseas, but it is not clear whether this meant that he had been elected overseas by dissident exporters before the return of Queen Isabella, or whether his earlier election had taken place overseas and that he reassumed the mayoralty when Charlton fled from London.[40]

It is possible that, amid its other problems, the new government had little time to reconsier the staple policy and on 1 May 1327 it reissued the staple ordinance in precisely the same terms in which it had been published a year before. The previous day customs officials had again been instructed that they must not cocket any wool until they ascertained that it had been forty days in a staple. This meant that the staplers had to appoint an official in each town to certify wool. One John Gabriel had been a deputy of the mayor in Winchester in the previous year. In June 1327 denizen and alien merchants complained that they were unable to export wool taken to the York staple because no-one had yet been appointed 'mayor of the staple'. Thereupon the mayor of the city was ordered to issue the necessary certificates, authenticating them with the staple seal.[41]

The reaffirmation of the staple ordinance provided short-lived security for the present system. On 26 June 1327 a licence, valid until Michaelmas, was granted to all denizen and alien merchants that they might 'import and export their wares, and trade at the fair now begun at Boston, notwithstanding the ordinance for holding the staple at certain places'. This decision was made by the king and the whole council in view of the 'numerous complaints from magnates of the realm and others' that because of the ordinance alien merchants, who were wont to come to the fair to sell their goods and to buy wool, were proposing to boycott it. This would harm the price of wool and increase prices of imports. This partial relaxation in favour of Boston was soon followed by a complete suspension of the staple ordinance until Christmas 1327. However, this generosity to the exporters was accompanied by the demand that they lend the king 13s 4d on every sack of wool and 300 fells and 20s on every last of hides. The precedent for this demand was a loan taken by Edward II in 1317 and a subsidy in 1322.[42]

Writs instructing the customs officials to collect the loan from all merchants were dispatched on 2 July 1327. They alleged that native and alien merchants had begged the king to relieve them of the inconvenience of taking wool to the staple towns and in return had offered the loan in aid of the Scots war. The London officials protested at this claim, denying that any of the city merchants had been consulted by the king and council. London merchants refused to pay the loan and on 19 August a further writ was sent to the customers at the port, reproving them and demanding immediate compliance. A third writ, dated 23 September, excused the Londoners arrears of the loan provided that they paid what was due in future. Evidently they had continued to export wool while refusing the loan. It is clear that there had been no consultation with the merchant community on the scale implied in the writ. Indeed it is possible that consultation had extended no further than William de la Pole and the company of the Bardi. The former had advanced £4000 and the company a number of loans on security of the customs and a prest of wool.[43]

Although the ordinance was supposed to be revived at Christmas the future of the staple was clearly in the balance. On 2 December 1327 writs were dispatched to fifty-seven towns ordering them to send one or two of their most substantial merchants to York on 20 January 1328, to discuss matters relating to the wool trade. An account of some of the proceedings may be reconstructed from letters which were exchanged by the cities of London and York. The official representatives of London were John de Grantham and John Priour, but Richard de Betoigne was also present and was expected to protect the interests of the city. Towards the end of January the representatives of twenty-eight towns assembled in the chapter house at York. They were told to consider the future conduct of the staple and to deliver their verdict to the king via master Henry de Clif.[44]

On 29 January the city fathers of York wrote to the city of London complaining about the behaviour of Betoigne who, they alleged, claimed to be mayor of the staple and had recommended that the staple be removed overseas. The next day Grantham and Priour sent to the city for new instructions, but they made no reference to Betoigne. They reported that the whole 'commonalty' of merchants of England wished to remove the staple overseas, but immediately qualified this by saying that they, together with the merchants of York, Lincoln, Winchester and Bristol, had opposed the transfer. The first three towns, under the present arrangement, received wool which otherwise would have gone directly to Hull, Boston and Southampton. Bristol, on the west coast, normally had no share of the export trade. The majority of the assembled merchants, led by Richard de Edelmeton and William atte Pole (*sic*) of Hull, claimed that an overseas staple would benefit the 'commonalty of the realm' to the extent of 20s per sack. Just whom they meant by the commonalty of the realm is not clear, but there can be no doubt that the chief beneficiaries would have been the merchants themselves. The majority party recommended that two attorneys be appointed to put their case in Parliament, which was due to assemble at York on 7 February. The Londoners, however, urged that the assembly should not be divided in its counsel and succeeded in delaying a decision until they should have had time to consult the city.

On 4 February London sent separate letters to its representatives, to Betoigne and to the city of York. All stated that the city was in favour of home staples and that rather than have an overseas staple it would have none at all. On receipt of these letters Betoigne, Grantham and Priour wrote back to the city, absolving the former of any misconduct,

and attacking John de Charlton, now a burgess of York, for inciting
that city against Betoigne. The tenor of their letters was that when
Betoigne appeared in the chapter house, which according to him he
did only once, the majority party put it to him that he was their
mayor. When he denied this they became angry and said that he
should go to the place where he had been elected, which was overseas,
and surrender their charters and muniments, 'which had cost them
dear'. By these they meant not only the privileges obtained overseas,
but also the charter of Edward II. Betoigne replied that all their
charters were overseas with their 'other things' except for the charter
of Edward II, which was in the possession of John de Charlton.
Betoigne himself had only a copy of this charter which he had had
made at Dover, when the king was there in September 1325. From
these statements one may possibly deduce that the English staplers had
been divided among themselves as early as 1325, if not before. Moreover it is clear that even after the setting up of home staples an overseas establishment had been kept up.

As Betoigne was disclaiming the title of mayor John de Charlton had
had appeared in the assembly, robed in the livery of a burgess of York
and accompanied by the mayor and many of the commonalty of that
city. At this point Betoigne left the meeting since, as he piously claimed,
he could not remain in the presence of such a rebel without the consent
of the city of London. The city accepted this explanation and cleared
Betoigne of the charges made against him. Grantham and Priour, in
their letter, said that they had carried out the instructions of the city,
but that the will of the king and council was independent of the people.
What they meant by this is not clear, since on 1 March 1328 writs
were issued announcing that the policy of home staples was to be continued. However, when Parliament met at Northampton the following
month, all staples, both home and overseas, were abolished. Richard
de Betoigne was one of the two London members in this assembly.

The wool exporters did not long remain satisfied merely with the
abolition of home staples. Some of them set up a staple at Bruges and
tried to compel the rest of their number to observe this and to pay
staple dues. At the beginning of 1332 the government ordered the
authorities of London to conduct an investigation into the matter. In
fact the city merchants do not seem to have been involved in the staple
and clearly they were too powerful to be compelled to follow it against
their will. Only one Londoner is named in a mandate of May 1332,
addressed to forty-two merchants, ordering them to release the wool of
Nicholas Picheford of Bridgnorth, which they had arrested for exporting to Brabant in defiance of their wishes. Although it included a few

southern and East Anglian merchants the confederation was composed largely of the merchant community of Yorkshire and of midlanders who exported through the port of London. The names of merchants of Lincoln and the neighbouring towns, who exported through the port of Boston are notable for their absence, as are those of the numerically important community of Newcastle. The merchants ignored the order to release Picheford's wool and in September and November sheriffs were instructed to distrain their goods in England to obtain compliance.[45]

It is difficult to dissociate the illegal overseas staple from the decision, taken in the parliament of September 1332, to re-establish home staples, with effect from Easter 1333. They were to be held in the former staple towns and the regulations for the conduct of trade were substantially as before. Alien merchants were again forbidden to buy 'upland', but were apparently permitted to buy at fairs and markets, provided that they subsequently offered the wool for sale in the staples. One major difference from the earlier ordinance was that the king's duty was to be levied in the staples, even in the case of those inland towns which were not seaports. As before, the staple policy was accompanied by a measure intended to favour the native cloth industry. From the following Christmas no person with a revenue of less than one hundred marks from land or rent was to wear imported cloth for the space of two years. The revived home staples lasted for only one season, for in March 1334 it was proclaimed that, at the request of Parliament, they were to be abolished with effect from 4 June next. It is not impossible that staples were discussed at a conference of the council and a small group of merchants at York in July 1335, but in practice the staple was not revived until it became part of the king's diplomatic weaponry during the Hundred Years War.[46]

The home staple policy was accompanied by the second taxation of denizen exports, other than the ancient custom, since the *maltote* of Edward I. The impositions of 1317 and 1327 were, in theory, not taxes but loans, and in the former case at least some money was repaid. In the present instance the government alleged that the merchants had promised the king a subsidy on exported wool in return for the grant of home staples. Since most of the exporters were opposed to this policy such a promise can only have been given by the middlemen and was, understandably, disavowed by the former group. In fact the subsidy, 6s 8d for denizens and 10s for aliens, was first proclaimed by the authority of the magnates and prelates assembled in Parliament at York in January 1333. It was justified by the claim that the merchants had rumoured that the king was intending to take a subsidy, thereby effecting a reduction in the price of wool to the loss of the subjects and to their own enrichment. The magnates were persuaded, perhaps, that the merchants could be made to bear the incidence of the tax by the fact that it was to be largely retrospective. It was to be taken from all wool exported during the twelve months from 2 February 1332.[47]

A retrospective duty on exports proved impossible to collect even though commissioners, supplied with lists by the customs officials, were appointed to raise the sums from the goods and chattels of merchants throughout the country. In June 1333 the levy was abandoned and any money already collected was ordered to be restored. It was claimed that this was done to prevent a fall in the price of wool. In fact the king had already obtained the consent of the merchants for the levy of an identical tax on all wool exported in the twelve months following 14 May 1333. Writs of execution were not received at Winchester until 19 June and at London until 29 June and the collectors later pleaded that they were not responsible for the duty on wool exported before those dates. Although a tax levied at the time of export was easier to collect than a retrospective duty it had the disadvantage that by delaying their business merchants might avoid it altogether. Particularly towards the end of the twelve months many began to do just this. This was treated as fraudulent practice and even when the grant was officially at an end customers were ordered to continue to levy the subsidy on all old wool. The respite from additional taxation was short lived, for within three years Edward III was at war with France and burdened the wool trade with a large part of his military expenses.[48]

Having described the political and diplomatic background to the wool trade between Edward I's peace with France and the outbreak of the Hundred Years War it is time to consider the performance of exports in this period. The first question which must be asked is how reliable are the statistics from which the picture must be drawn? The English customs records have sometimes been discounted by critics on the grounds that widespread smuggling or fraudulent practices by officials minimise their value as a historical source.[49] In particular R. L. Baker has advanced the claim that the apparent fall in the level of exports during the late 1310s and the 1320s resulted largely from a breakdown in the administration.[50] He believes that this was caused by the failure of the government to check the activities of the collectors by an adequate system of controllerships. Baker revealed the fact that during the years 1315–17 the collectors of Ipswich apparently embezzled two thirds of the proceeds of the duty and went undetected until they were betrayed by an informer some years later. This is indeed an amazing case of fraud, but Ipswich handled a minute proportion of the country's total trade and Baker himself admits that there is no evidence of embezzlement on this scale at any other port. Several commissions of enquiry into malpractice produced largely negative results.

TABLE 12 *Wool exports 1297–1336*[a]

| | Averages 1297–1304 | | Averages 1304–11 | | | | | | Averages 1311–13 | | Averages 1313–23 | |
| | Denizen and alien | | Denizen | | Alien | | Denizen and alien | | Denizen and alien | | Denizen and alien | |
	Sacks	%	Sacks	%	Sacks	%	Sacks	%	Sacks	%	Sacks	%
London	10 412	37.5	8836	38.8	5367	31.8	14 203	35.8	15 464	41.0	12 584	46.6
Boston	5879[b]	21.2	4277	18.8	5805	34.5	10 082	25.5	10 798	28.6	5758	21.3
Hull	4307	15.5	2776	12.2	3927	23.3	6703	16.9	5274	14.0	3187	11.8
Southampton	2688	9.7	2233	9.9	967	5.7	3200	8.1	2679	7.1	2980	11.0
Lynn	1243	4.5	764	3.4	97	0.6	861	2.2	752	2.0	250	0.9
Yarmouth	1001	3.6	719	3.2	84	0.5	803	2.0	456	1.2	544	2.0
Sandwich	783	2.8	504	2.2	65	0.4	569	1.4	144	0.4	183	0.7
Ipswich	631	2.3	768	3.4	294	1.7	1062	2.7	475	1.3	396	1.5
Newcastle	541	1.9	1213	5.3	184	1.1	1397	3.5	814	2.2	366	1.3
Chichester	230	0.8	267	1.2	–	–	267	0.7	514	1.4	327	1.2
Others	56	0.2	395	1.7	42	0.3	437	1.1	387	1.1	452	1.7
All England	27 771		22 757		16 832		39 584		37 754		27 027	

| | Averages 1323–29 | | | | | | Averages 1329–36 | | | | | |
| | Denizen | | Alien | | Denizen and alien | | Denizen | | Alien | | Denizen and alien | |
	Sacks	%	Sacks	%	Sacks	%	Sacks	%	Sacks	%	Sacks	%
London	7044	47.2	4093	46.3	11 137	46.9	8945	38.9	3101	39.0	12 046	38.9
Boston	2049	13.7	2961	33.5	5010	21.0	3046	13.2	3302	41.6	6348	20.5
Hull	1978	13.3	962	10.9	2940	12.4	4661	20.3	651	8.2	5312	17.2
Southampton	1184	7.9	654	7.4	1838	7.7	2463	10.7	675	8.5	3138	10.1
Lynn	302	2.0	67	0.8	369	1.6	704	3.1	116	1.5	820	2.6
Yarmouth	431	2.9	21	0.2	452	1.9	607	2.6	22	0.3	629	2.0
Sandwich	126	0.8	8	0.1	134	0.6	139	0.6	14	0.2	153	0.5
Ipswich	203	1.4	11	0.1	214	0.9	169	0.7	1	–	170	0.5
Newcastle	1036	6.9	56	0.6	1092	4.6	1414	6.1	27	0.3	1441	4.7
Chichester	313	2.1	2	–	315	1.3	273	1.2	14	0.2	287	0.9
Others	248	1.7	–	–	248	1.0	577	2.5	24	0.3	601	1.9
All England	14 914		8835		23 749		22 998		7947		30 945	

[a] Sources. Carus-Wilson and Coleman, *England's Export Trade*. Baker, *English Customs Service*.
[b] Makes no allowance for gap of thirteen months in enrolled accounts.

In May 1331 the government made an ordinance for the reform of the customs system. Baker accepts that this increased the efficiency of revenue collection and accounts for the apparent increase in the level of exports during the 1330s. In fact export performance improved as early as the autumn of 1328 and was particularly marked in the denizen field, the area where one might most expect to find collusion between fraudulent officials and merchants. Denizen exports had totalled somewhat over 17 000 sacks in 1326–7 and about 14 000 sacks in 1327–8, but in the next three years they were over 22 000, nearly 24 000 and over 26 000 respectively. The most likely explanation for this was an increase in industrial activity in Flanders as a result of greater stability there. The export trade had failed to respond to the Anglo-Flemish peace of 1323, since a revolt by the city of Bruges initiated several years of civil war. The end of this civil commotion would inevitably be reflected more in denizen wool exports than in those of alien, since the latter included the wool of the merchants of Brabant and Italy exporting to their own countries, which were unaffected by conditions in Flanders. The present writer contends, therefore, that the fluctuations in the level of exports recorded in the enrolled customs accounts do not merely reflect the efficiency of revenue collection but provide a reasonably accurate picture of commercial activity. Similarly he is confident that the large amount of energy expended in analysing the particular customs accounts had not been misplaced.

During much of the period now being considered it is possible to distinguish between the respective totals of denizen and alien exports. This is the result of a higher rate of duty imposed on alien exports from February 1303. The occasion was the grant by Edward I to aliens of the so-called *carta mercatoria*,[51] which was intended to counter recent attempts by English urban communities, in particular the city of London, to limit the scope of alien trade within the country. In return for a statement and royal guarantee of their rights, alien merchants agreed to pay the king certain additional customs which included a duty of 3s 4d on each sack of wool. This came to be known as the new custom and was collected separately from the 6s 8d, now termed the ancient custom, which continued to be paid by both aliens and denizens. In the commission sent to the collectors of the new custom at London in April 1303 it was stated that any native merchant who would voluntarily pay the extra duty might share the privileges which the king had just granted to aliens. In fact the charter contained few rights which Englishmen did not already enjoy by prescription, while many of their number were bound to be angered by the threat of increased competition in internal trade. This view was doubtless expressed at an assembly of merchants, representing London and forty-two other towns summoned by royal writ to York on 25 June 1303. They unanimously refused to pay the additional wool custom or any of the other duties. The new custom on wool was retained when the other alien duties were suspended between August 1309 and August 1310, but it was swept away when the lords ordainers revoked the *carta mercatoria* in 1311. In 1322 the charter was restored, together with its concomitant duties.[52]

It is not easy to determine what effect the new custom had upon the distribution of wool exports between denizen and alien merchants. The amount was small in proportion to the overseas value of wool and might easily have been absorbed by an efficient organisation. On the other hand it must have acted as a disincentive to any aliens who could not show a marginal efficiency above that of native merchants. The actual figures for denizen and alien exports do not provide much of a clue to the problem, for in the early years of the new duty the latter fell by an amount far in excess of the slight increase in the former. The situation is complicated by the fact that the boom in exports may have been initiated by alien merchants while the subsequent decline in their totals may largely reflect a return to the normal pattern of trade. The highest alien export is recorded for the Exchequer year 1304–5 when it exceeded 24 000 sacks compared with under 22 000 for denizens but, as already mentioned, the figures for this year are freak in that they contain a disproportionate amount of the clip of 1304. The exact level of alien export in the year 1303–4 is not known, but the average for 1303–5 cannot have been less than 19 000 sacks. To what extent this figure had already been influenced by the new custom is difficult to say. In 1305–6 the alien total was still slightly more than 19 000 sacks and in the following year only slightly below that figure. It may be said, therefore, that at the height of the boom alien exports had a plateau of about 19 000 sacks. The denizen average was about 20 000 sacks in 1303–5 and exceeded 22 000 sacks in each of the next two years. Thereafter, denizen exports fell to rather less than 22 000 sacks in 1307–8, but exceeded 23 000 sacks in the years 1308–10 and exceeded 24 000 sacks in 1310–11. Alien exports, on the other hand, were no more than 15 000 sacks a year in 1307–9, below 12 000 sacks in 1309–10 and rather more than 13 000 in 1310–11. In later years it is no longer possible to distinguish between the two communities.

During the years 1304–11 exports of wool from England averaged about 39 500 sacks a year compared with an average of less than 28 000 sacks during the previous seven years. Although the boom had passed its peak exports remained at a high level, the average for the years 1311–13 being nearly 38 000 sacks. The 32 000 sacks exported in each of the two years following the establishment of the St Omer staple is a significant reduction but pales besides the drop to less than 21 000 sacks in 1315–16. The factor immediately responsible for this latter fall was the outbreak of war between France and Flanders, but exports remained far below 30 000 sacks in each of the next three years. The great famine which affected much of Europe in the years 1315–17 must probably carry some share of the blame. Demand for wool remained uncertain into the 1320s and overall the annual export from 1313 to 1323 was about 27 000 sacks, rather less than that of the period 1297–1304. It has already been pointed out that the settlement of the dispute between England and Flanders was followed by several years of civil strife in the latter country, which adversely affected the demand for wool. The average export for the years 1323–9 was less than 24 000 sacks. This suggests that commotion in Flanders, whether caused by war with France or by domestic quarrels, had more damaging effects on the English wool trade than did the Anglo-Flemish dispute. Even when at war England and Flanders were dependent on one another. It is possible that historians have tended to exaggerate somewhat the degree of permanent damage which was caused to Flemish industry by the wars of the early fourteenth century, for in the period 1329–36 English merchants exported an average of 23 000 sacks a year, overwhelmingly to the Low Countries. Clearly the export trade was far from moribund on the eve of the Hundred Years War.

As may be seen from table 12 the share of the nation's total export enjoyed by each of the authorised ports did not remain constant during the period under review. During the war London had become the leading port and in the 1310s and 1320s it increased its share of the total trade to almost one half. The latter resulted from the fact that during the depression London's exports were more buoyant than those of the provincial ports. During the recovery of the 1330s the capital's share reverted to the level of earlier years. London's resilience was probably due to changes in the composition of the trade which passed through its port, a point which will be discussed later. Boston remained England's second wool port throughout the period but lost ground relatively, its share of total trade declining from 26 per cent in 1307–11 to 21 per cent in 1329–36. Comparison with Hull is instructive. Both ports lost a large volume of alien trade but Hull was able to recoup much of the loss by increasing its denizen trade both absolutely and proportionately, while Boston's denizen trade declined on both counts. Hull's success reflects the rise of a dynamic group of Yorkshire merchants; Boston's loss does not necessarily establish the decadence of the local merchant community but it strongly suggests that it was unable to retain trade which had been acquired during the boom. Among the four leading ports Southampton presents the interesting spectacle of increasing its share of total trade in the first part of the depression but losing ground in the later stages. It is tentatively suggested that this phenomenon reflects the trade links between Southampton and France, which cushioned the town against troubles in Flanders but which were a liability during the tension between England and France in the later years of Edward II. The town's rough handling of Italians in the 1320s may be another factor which is reflected in the trade figures of the period.

Among the lesser ports Newcastle stands out because of its extremes of fortune. During the period of boom Newcastle's exports had done particularly well and even as late as 1313 were up to the pre-war level. Thereafter, however, they plummeted. Although any analysis of Newcastle trade cannot afford to overlook conditions along the Scottish border there can be little doubt that the major cause of the fall in wool exports was the establishment of the St Omer staple. Northern wool was of poor quality and, as in the later middle ages, could not bear the expense and competition which resulted from a compulsory staple. This diagnosis is supported by the fact that when the overseas staple was abolished Newcastle's exports revived more quickly than those of the country as a whole. Lynn is another port whose wool trade seems to have been crippled by the staple, although it must be pointed out that its exports had been declining throughout the period of general boom. Unlike Newcastle, Lynn did not recover its trade when the overseas staple was abolished. In the case of the other minor ports the direct effects of the staple cannot readily be distinguished from those resulting generally from the recession.

As already mentioned the enrolled customs accounts of the early fourteenth century are supplemented by a relatively rich survival of particular accounts. Most of these have been thoroughly analysed by the present writer but unfortunately there is insufficient space for the findings to be presented in full. All that can be offered are summary descriptions of the characteristics of the trade of individual ports. The best served port is Hull, for which ancient custom particulars, together with a few new custom particulars, have survived for the entire period from May 1298 to March 1315, with the exception of twelve months commencing in May 1301.[53] There are also a few accounts for later years. These documents are not only the best-written and best-preserved of all surviving medieval customs accounts they are also, until about 1305, especially informative as to the places of origin of both merchants and vessels engaged in the export of wool. Thereafter less information is provided so that newcomers to the trade can seldom be identified with a town. Before dealing with the merchants who traded through Hull the particulars have been used to recalculate the port's exports on the basis of twelve monthly periods beginning of June 1 rather than Michaelmas (table 13). This means that all the wool from a particular shearing is included in one period of account instead of being spread over two accounts according to the practice adopted by the Exchequer. The former presentation is of much greater value to the historian and it is suggested that the Hull figures may well reflect the export pattern of the country as a whole. The exercise demonstrates that oscillations were sometimes less extreme than is indicated by Exchequer figures and that the best year was that following the clip of 1305.

The main value of the Hull particulars consists of the detailed evidence which they provide about the rise of local capitalist merchants as a major force in the wool trade. Few in number at the end of the thirteenth century they increased rapidly during the period of boom. Only the fact that the total volume of exports increased enormously explains why denizen traffic did not exceed that of alien merchants until near the end of the first decade of the fourteenth century. Behind

TABLE 13   *Exports from Hull, 1297–1315*

	June to June	Michaelmas to Michaelmas
1297–8	–	4636
1298–9	3900	2800
1299–1300	3782	3953
1300–1	4063	5833
1301–2	(4471)ᵃ	2138
1302–3	4124	4725
1303–4	6170	6062
1304–5	6087	8812
1305–6	7693	7288
1306–7	6590	7055
1307–8	6277	6018
1308–9	6017	5828
1309–10	6086	5604
1310–11	6150	6312
1311–12	5193	5580
1312–13	5743	4968
1313–14	4957	3530
1314–15	3959	3198

ᵃ By deduction – no particulars extant.

the bare figures there may lie a struggle for the control of local wool between Yorkshiremen and merchants of the Hanse, a contest which was ultimately won by the former group. Nevertheless the Hull accounts indicate that there was still scope in the wool trade for the small exporter and the occasional exporter. During the period under consideration approximately 2100 individuals exported a total of 86 791 sacks of wool (excluding that of 1301–2). Some 750 of these can be identified as denizens and 870 as aliens, while among those of uncertain status the balance probably inclined slightly towards denizens. An average struck from these figures would be misleading, since the great majority appeared once only, most of them handling very small amounts of wool. The bulk of the trade was in the hands of a much smaller number of regular exporters. For example, the three leading German exporters between them handled 9849 sacks, while eight other Germans, each with over 1000 sacks, reached a total of 9357. Although native enterprise was not on such an heroic scale, four Englishmen exported more than 1000 sacks each, their combined trade being 4821 sacks. Between them these fifteen men owned well over a quarter of all the wool exported from Hull from 1298 to 1315.

The bulk of the denizen trade which passed through Hull was handled by Yorkshire merchants. The most important centre was Beverley, whose citizens invested more frequently and on a larger scale than those of any other town. Between 1298 and 1305 about 70 Beverley men and women can be identified, from the customs accounts alone, as wool exporters, while the true total is certainly larger. Three of the four merchants who exported more than 1000 sacks came from Beverley; John de Cotingham, 1184, Richard Tirwhit, 1109, and Walter de Kelsterne, 1244. From the standpoint of numbers engaged in the trade, York was second to Beverley; some 56 citizens are named in the accounts from 1298 to 1305 and again the actual total of exporters was undoubtedly larger. However they tended to export less frequently and on a smaller scale than those of Beverley. In 1303 (June to June) 29 York merchants dispatched 312 sacks compared with 682 sacks sent by 46 Beverley men. Two years later, at the peak of the boom, the respective figures were 20 men with 205 sacks and 34 men with 752 sacks. Barton on Humber and Pontefract vied with York for second place among the local centres of the wool trade. In each of these towns the total number of participants was considerably smaller than at York but the leading figures exported more regularly and on a larger scale. John Metal of Pontefract, with a total of 1282 sacks had the largest export of any English merchant, while John de Gaskerik of Barton, 743 sacks, was in fifth place. Hull itself could not boast an important group of wool merchants. Although not a few exporters were described as being of Hull the amounts of wool involved were invariably very small and many of the men were probably sailors, since they are found chiefly in English ships. It is likely that Hull, a new town, was still overshadowed by Beverley which lay only a few miles away. Richard de la Pole exported hides in 1305 but did not export wool (27 sacks) until 1311.

In addition to those places already mentioned well over a dozen Yorkshire towns and villages, mostly in the east and north ridings, are recorded as the domicile of exporters. Places outside Yorkshire occur comparatively infrequently and it is clear that merchants from the midlands and the south of England made little use of Hull. For reasons which will later become clear reference must be made to the exports of Londoners. Except in two or three instances these were not of great importance and apparently dwindled in the later years. William Cosin dispatched 85 sacks in 1299 and 1300 and 262 sacks in 1302 and 1303, while William de Combemartin sent 283 sacks between 1303 and 1305 and 48 sacks from 1306 to 1309. The exports of Elias Drury cannot always be distinguished from those of a Bawtry man of the same name, while a couple of the people bearing the surname de London paid alien rates of duty.

Besides the accounts for 1298 to 1315 there are particulars for Hull covering 1319–21 and 1324–5, the former being two good years in the middle of the depression and the latter being a very poor year. These accounts confirm the dominant position occupied by Yorkshire merchants. In the absence of separate alien taxation the amount of wool carried by aliens in 1319–21 cannot be determined precisely, but proportionately it was far smaller than the pre-1315 level. Further discussion of the role of aliens in Hull's trade will be reserved until later.

Evidence for the study of denizen exports from Boston is less satisfactory than that for Hull. Ancient custom accounts survive for the periods November 1308 to Michaelmas 1309 and Michaelmas 1310 to April 1312, while there are fragmentary accounts for several short periods in later years of Edward II's reign and for February to July 1333.[54] Only some of these documents are matched by corresponding new customs accounts so that by no means all denizen exporters can be conclusively identified. Furthermore towns of origin are only sporadically recorded. This means that, taking the accounts of Edward II's reign, out of about 250 positive identifications of natives we find that 103 can be provided with a town, while a further 41 took their surname from a town. The latter does not provide foolproof identification, since John de Leicester and Walter de York, for example, were citizens of Lincoln. There appears to be no means of determining whether this sample is representative of all denizen exporters. The customs clerks may have been ignorant of, or less concerned about, the domiciles of the more distant merchants, while the mere fact that these may have been less regular exporters than local men means that there is inherently less chance of their towns being put on record. If we disregard this possible bias we find that native exporters were drawn overwhelmingly from towns and villages in the eastern plain and the fenlands. The most westerly citations are 2 for Warwick, probably one for Ludlow and possibly 2 for Coventry, all taking the less satisfactory form of the town being used as a surname rather than as a definite statement of domicile. There are only 4 certain identifications of London merchants, including the ubiquitous William de Combemartin who exported 122 sacks in 1308–9 and 82 sacks in the summer of 1311.

The most important centre of denizen trade was Lincoln, with 48 positive identifications and 5 merchants who were surnamed 'of Lincoln'. Next came Spalding with 10 and 7 respectively, Grantham with 9 and 5, and Boston with 9 and 2. No other place contributed more than 5 merchants, including the less certain form. During the 29 months which make up the first two periods mentioned above a minimum of 41 Lincoln merchants exported 2062 sacks, while the exports of 2 others cannot always be separated from aliens of the same name. Seven of the group dispatched more than 100 sacks each, making 1044 sacks in all, the leading exporter being Walter de York with 248 sacks. Over the same period a minimum of 10 Boston men sent 947 sacks, 2 of them having more than 200 sacks each and 2 more than 100 sacks; the front runner was John de Tumby with 264 sacks. For Spalding the figures are 15 men with 1109 sacks, of which Richard de Spalding took 442 sacks, while 2 others had more than 100 sacks each. Eleven Grantham merchants exported 601 sacks, of which William Carpenter took 191 sacks and one other more than 100 sacks. These figures do not include the exports of the Chesterton family, which probably still hailed from Grantham. Gilbert had 58 sacks, Gilbert fitz Gilbert 23 sacks and John 398 sacks.

The comparatively few surviving customs particulars for London were utilised by G. A. Williams in his thorough survey of the social and economic history of the capital.[55] He drew attention to a considerable increase in the proportion of London exports owned by London merchants themselves. The proportions he quotes are 12 per cent for 1297–8, 14 per cent for 7 months in 1303, 13 per cent for 5 months in 1306, 41 per cent for 1312–13, 38 per cent for 6 months in 1322–3, 31 per cent in 1324–5 and 43 per cent for 9 months in 1332. Although the identification of Londoners must be left to a specialist in London history the present writer suggests that the first figure quoted must be revised to 18 per cent. Williams' figure is based on a London ownership of 1218 sacks out of a total of 10 030 sacks exported in 1297–8. In fact the accounts are damaged and incomplete so that ownership can be recovered for only about 6850 sacks exported between December 1297 and the following June. One difficulty in the way of accepting that these figures accurately reflect a large increase in the volume of wool exported by Londoners is that they imply that during the fourteenth-century boom city merchants were exporting as little, or even less, wool as they had done in the 1270s. The dilemma might be resolved if it could be established just how much use Londoners made of provincial ports in the early years of the fourteenth century. It is possible that at this time a not insubstantial part of Londoners' exports were being

channelled through provincial ports. Diversion of this traffic to their
own city during the depression might account for some of the increase
in their share of London's trade but would not imply a corresponding
increase in their overall trade. In support of this contention it may be
pointed out that the greatest city merchant in the early fourteenth
century seems to have been William de Combemartin, whose recorded
exports of 841 sacks from London before 1313 are almost equalled by
recorded exports of 798 sacks from Hull, Boston and Southampton.
Unfortunately this line of enquiry cannot be pursued far because of
the dearth of accounts, other than those of Hull.

Even if the explanation suggested above is correct it is unlikely to
account for all of the increase in the city men's share of London exports.
There must have remained some real increase in trade. The next
question is, therefore, at whose expense was this gain made? Table 12
suggests that the main losers were alien merchants. It is quite likely that
some Londoners stopped being middlemen supplying aliens and became
exporters in their own right. However, the Londoners may also have
gained a certain amount of trade from provincial merchants. If over
the entire period 1304–11 Londoners owned 20 per cent of the city's
exports their average would have been 2840 sacks, leaving 5996 sacks
for the provincials. If they improved their share to 40 per cent in
1329–36 their average becomes 4818 sacks, leaving only 4127 sacks for
the provincials. The lower one sets the Londoners' share in the first
period the greater becomes the loss of the provincials in the second.

It is not easy to distinguish Londoners from provincial merchants
since the customs clerks seldom bothered to record the domiciles of
exporters, while town surnames are particularly unreliable indicators
of immediate origin because of large-scale immigration into the city.
However, there are specific references, as early as 1297–8, to merchants from Shrewsbury, Coventry, Banbury, Worcester, Abingdon,
Hertford and Winchester. In the later accounts Hereford, Bridgnorth,
Warwick and other midlands towns occur frequently and there can be
no doubt that London was the main outlet for the wool of central
England, the Cotswolds and the Welsh March. Even some of the wool
of the east midlands, whose natural outlet was the Wash, may have
been directed to London. Walter Priest, the leading merchant of
Melton Mowbray, exported from London as well as from Boston.
Another point to be remarked is that at the start of the fourteenth century, in contrast to the 1270s, wool merchants were widely distributed
throughout central England. Despite a citation of Dunstable in 1297–8
there is little evidence that this place was still an important business
centre and it is possible that the trade of the region was now handled

from London. Shrewsbury, however, remained a thriving centre and its exporters in 1297–8 included the family of the late Laurence de Ludlow; his widow, Agnes, exported 67 sacks and his brother, John, 199 sacks. Richard Stury of Shrewsbury, later first mayor of the compulsory staple at St Omer, exported 61 sacks in the same year.

Southampton is provided with full ancient custom particulars, and with some new custom particulars, from December 1307 to June 1311 and from April 1313 to April 1315.[56] The documents provide another good illustration of the large number of individuals who made at least an occasional venture into the wool trade. Disregarding Italian exports we find that 483 people exported wool or fells during the two periods under consideration. Of these 275 can be positively identified as denizens and 77 as aliens, while there can be no doubt that a majority of the remainder were denizens. The pattern of ownership is similar to that of the late thirteenth century, which was analysed in the previous chapter. Taking an average of 30 sacks a year as a significant export we find that 15 denizens and one alien exported over 100 sacks in the first period and the same number dispatched over 60 sacks in the second period. Six denizen names and the alien name are common to both groups. Collectively they dispatched 2995 sacks (33 per cent) out of a total of 9049 sacks in period one and 2293 sacks (44 per cent) out of 5224 sacks in period two. The foremost exporter was John Goudhyne of Marlborough, 401 sacks and 245 sacks, who was the only man to receive a personal summons to the first of the merchant assemblies which punctuated the Hundred Years War. Roger de Inkepenne, of Winchester, 317 sacks and 219 sacks, also figured prominently in the wool dealings of Edward III in that war. A third figure who stands out is William Dounton, 287 sacks and 209 sacks, while mention must be made of William de Combemartin of London who exported 262 sacks in the first period. John de Burford, who exported 74 sacks in the second period, was probably the Londoner who was buying wool from the Bishop of Winchester at this time. The alien who exported 235 sacks in period one and 76 sacks in period two was named Roger de Bristol and it is quite conceivable that he was permanently domiciled in England. Thomas de Bristol was also an alien, as was Guy de Arundel. The surnames of the other aliens indicate that most of them were Picards or Normans. Since the customs clerks seldom or never record the domicile of exporters it is impossible to determine exactly the hinterland of Southampton's wool trade, but it may have been quite extensive. Four merchants surnamed de Warwick were regular exporters, and the fact that they frequently exported

together, and in the company of one Henry de Coventry, suggests that
they may have been midlanders who cooperated in dispatching their
wool to the port. The most distant town which appears as a surname is
Swansea. The bulk of the trade, however, was probably handled by
comparatively local men, among whom we find survivors or descen-
dants, of the families of the 1270s and 1280s, such as the Kerdyfs of
Southampton and Bristol and the Dalryons of Winchester.

Yarmouth has one of the better collections of surviving records from
the reign of Edward II, with an alien account for 1307–8 and ancient
custom particulars, together with some alien accounts, for a total of 11
years 4 months over the period 1308–27.[57] These enable one to obtain
a fairly comprehensive impression of the port's wool trade. Table 13
shows that Yarmouth's alien trade was small and fast disappearing. In
the early years of the period covered by the particulars it was handled
mainly by Picard merchants on a regular basis and may possibly have
been a remnant of a pre-war enterprise. This trade died away altogether
and most of the wool exported in later years belonged to German merchants, although there also seem to have been one or two Italian shipments. These later exports were far more sporadic than can be detected
from the bare totals of the enrolled accounts.

As a wool port Yarmouth was normally inaccessible to all but local
merchants, but during the war, when it had offered one of the shortest
direct crossings to the Low Countries, its exports had boomed. This
cannot have engendered much permanent traffic from the rest of the
country and the high level of post-war exports, compared with those
of the thirteenth century, is attributable to the emergence of a local
community of wool merchants. It is, of course, possible that these in
some measure owed their start to the war-time situation. Although
there were a number of merchants at Yarmouth itself the most important centre of the local wool trade was Norwich. It was for this reason
that the city was created a staple. When home staples were established
for a second time the bailiffs of Yarmouth were warned not to hinder
merchants from taking ships up the river to Norwich.[58] Although some
exporters took their surnames from Norfolk villages there is no doubt
that many of these were inhabitants of boroughs. The writ returned by
the sheriff for the assembly of 1322, which is unusually detailed, states
that there were only three wool merchants dwelling outside the liberties
of towns.[59] Two of these, Ralph de Reynham and David de la Doune,
may be traced in the customs accounts. The former exported 120 sacks
in 1308–12 and 73 sacks in later periods; the latter took 71 sacks and
42 sacks through Yarmouth, but he seems to have directed more of
his trade through Lynn.

During the years 1308–12, the longest period for which there are consecutive accounts, only three merchants achieved an average export of 30 sacks a year or more, their combined efforts reaching 572 sacks, 21 per cent of the port's traffic.[60] The total number of denizens who exported wool in the same period was 95. However although the enterprise of Norfolk merchants may have been modest they tended to be regular exporters. This helps to explain why only just over 200 names can be culled from the Yarmouth particulars, which is not a large total having regard for the number of accounts and the length of time over which they extend.

The surviving customs particulars from Lynn date mainly from the period of depression in the wool trade, during which time the port's exports suffered more than those of most towns.[61] The longest period with consecutive accounts runs from Michaelmas 1312 to January 1316. These accounts indicate that there was no recovery in the alien exports of Lynn, which had been falling steadily since the introduction of the new custom. However this was not necessarily a case of cause and effect and the town probably suffered more from a boycott by the German Hanse, imposed because of injuries allegedly done to its members. Before the war the Germans had brought a large volume of trade to Lynn, which must have made a substantial contribution to the then relatively high level of wool exports. In August 1303 the aldermen of the Hanse in England wrote to the magistrates of Rostock requesting them to secure strict enforcement of a prohibition against Baltic shipping coming to the town.[62] An alien customs account for February 1303 to June 1304 names 3 or 4 German merchants but most of the 199 sacks exported in this period belonged to Frenchmen, Flemings and Brabanters. It is possible that some of Lynn's thirteenth-century alien trade was overspill from Boston which was lost in later years.

As far as denizen exporters are concerned far more names are common to the accounts of Lynn and Yarmouth than to those of Lynn and Boston. This is probably due only partly to the fact that there are considerably fewer accounts for Boston than for either of the other places. More importantly many of the merchants who exported through Yarmouth conducted some of their business through Lynn. This means that any attempt to assess the business of Norfolk merchants must embrace both ports. The total number of those exporting through Lynn, and the distribution of their wool, is similar to that of Yarmouth, though the patrons of the former port were possibly the less regular in their business. It must be emphasised that the last observation is merely an impression which has not been proved statistically. Lynn, like Yarmouth, had its own community of wool exporters, the most prominent being Roger de Fliccham, who exported 94 sacks between Michaelmas 1308 and August 1309.

The main evidence for Newcastle relates to 1308, when the boom had passed its peak although business was still healthy, and 1325–6, when the town's trade began to recover following the abolition of the compulsory staple.[63] Although the earlier account covers only the period 25 April to Michaelmas it includes 1208 sacks out of 1245 denizen sacks and 191 alien sacks exported in the twelve months of 1307-8. In 1322 the sheriff of Northumberland stated that there were no wool merchants in the county outside the liberty of Newcastle. The leading exporters in the accounts can certainly be shown to be city merchants. In 1308 a total of 126 men, only a handful of them captains of ships, shared in the trade. Excluding one obvious Italian only 5 exported as many as 30 sacks, their combined efforts yielding 312 sacks, 26 per cent of the total. The leading exporter was Richard de Emeldon, 133 sacks, who was Newcastle's leading citizen. During the depression the larger merchants may have fared less badly than the small men; at any rate they handled a larger proportion of the trade in 1325–6. Disregarding a small number of illegible entries we find that 11 men exported more than 30 sacks each, amounting to 542 sacks (57 per cent) out of a total of 944 sacks taken by 56 denizens. Richard de Emeldon took 50 sacks, a figure which was exceeded by five others, including Robert de Haliwell with the largest amount, 71 sacks. Out of a total alien export of 65 sacks the Bardi took 25 sacks, 6 merchants took half of the remainder and the rest was taken in small parcels by captains and sailors.

The enrolled customs accounts, summarised in table 12, establish the fact of the absolute and relative decline of alien wool exports so clearly that it needs no further comment. What this source does not do, however, is to show how the alien trade was shared between different national groups. The most important point which emerges from an investigation of the division of alien trade is that leadership passed from Italian merchants to Germans in the early fourteenth century, but probably returned to the former within a few years. The first change can be proved conclusively from the particular accounts, but the latter happened in a period from which few particulars have survived.

German merchants became the leading group of alien exporters in the first decade of the fourteenth century, at a time when many of the old-established Florentine companies were experiencing acute economic crises. The possibility of a cause and effect relationship between these two events cannot be ruled out, although the explanation must be couched very tentatively. The demise of the companies in the Flemish market, at the time of an expansion of demand, may have provided the Germans with a greatly-enlarged stake in this trade. However, even before the Florentine bankruptcies the grasp which these companies had exercised on the wool trade had been shaken by the emergence of new Italian companies and individual exporters, both Florentine and non-Florentine. At first the exports of the newcomers were not sufficient to compensate for the shortfall in those of the old companies but the ranks of the former grew as the century progressed. The wool trade seems now to have been wide open to Italians and besides Florentines one may note the participation of merchants of Lucca, Piacenza, Pistoia, Sienna, Asti and Genoa. As German exports declined these may have become collectively the most important group of aliens, although whether Italian exports were in absolute terms as high as they had been in the late thirteenth century is an open question. The question is difficult to answer because of uncertainty about the way in which Italian exports of the thirteenth century were divided between the cloth industry of Flanders and that of Italy. A growing demand for English wool in the peninsula may have compensated Italian merchants for the loss of market opportunities in Flanders. If this was so the total volume of their exports may have been little less than that of the earlier period. There can be no doubt that in the early fourteenth century the bulk of Italian exports was destined for the peninsula and for this reason wool exported direct to Italy was excused the staple. Difficulty arose, however, about wool which was sent to Flanders merely to be loaded into galleys. Unless they obtained a licence for this route Italian merchants could be, and were, prosecuted for breach of staple regulations.

Although the war of 1294–7 undoubtedly caused inconvenience and financial loss to the Italian merchants in England it cannot be shown to have been directly responsible for any bankruptcies, with the exceptions of the Riccardi and the Bettri. Among the Florentine companies the Falconieri disappeared before the war began, while the Frescobaldi Neri had gone by 1299, apparently reabsorbed by the Frescobaldi Bianchi. The first company to disappear in the post-war period was the Cerchi Neri, which was still in existence in August 1301, but which was omitted from a directive of April 1303 ordering representatives of all the leading companies to appear before the Exchequer at York. It was probably wound up in an orderly manner for there is little or no record of its passing. The Mozzi became bankrupt in 1304 and before the end of that year its English representatives were being prosecuted for debt. The company remained active in the wool trade almost until its demise, exporting 124 sacks from London between March and Michaelmas

1303. Towards the end of 1305 all the members of the Pulci-Rimbertini fled secretly from England, taking with them money deposited by native merchants and magnates.[64]

By the beginning of 1306 there remained only four of the pre-1294 Florentine wool-exporting companies, the Spini, the Cerchi Bianchi, the Frescobaldi and Bardi. The Spini and the Cerchi were still independent companies in 1310 when they were charged with disobedience of a recent proclamation banning the use of foreign coin. A jury of denizens and aliens found that the Cerchi had spent or exported 4000 gold florins and the Spini 10 000 florins. Shortly afterwards members of the Spini were arrested and charged with being in arrears of payment of customs but were able to produce receipts. The company was nominally still in being in 1314 when it was granted half of the temporalities of vacant bishoprics and abbeys to extinguish the king's debt which was currently £3448. Whether it was still involved in the wool trade is open to doubt, and Matthew Clarrisimi, formerly its chief wool exporter, seems to have been a member of the Peruzzi since at least 1311. Francis Grandon, chief wool agent of the Cerchi, and Maneutus Francisci, of the same company, became members of the Bardi, although it is not clear whether this happened before or after the demise of the Cerchi. It is probably significant that neither the Cerchi nor the Spini were among a number of companies pursued by the Crown in 1318 for debts to the now defunct Frescobaldi and one may reasonably assume that neither was still in existence at this date.[65]

The Frescobaldi, which seems to have been the most flourishing of the companies, became Crown banker about 1303, occupying a position similar to that which the Riccardi had before 1294. It continued in this role in the reign of Edward II until it was overthrown and ruined by the ordainers in 1311.[66] Although engaged in a wide range of financial and commercial activities it had still invested in the wool trade. In one of its periodic statements of account with the Crown the company was awarded 4000 marks in compensation for damage which its wool trade had suffered in consequence of expenditure of time and money on royal business.[67] After a brief interval in which a Genoese financier acted as Crown banker the mantle was assumed by the Bardi, the last of the old Florentine companies. It continued in this role until it could no longer meet the king's demands for money during the Hundred Years War. Over-involvement with the English Crown was one of the chief reasons for the company's bankruptcy in 1346. The wool trade was probably always the mainstay of Bardi commercial, as opposed to financial, activity. In November 1320 it reckoned that it had exported 4800 sacks of wool since the imposition of the staple in May 1313, of which only 650 sacks had ben in breach of staple regulations. The only sort of check which can be used to test the figure of 4800 sacks is the total of 1052 sacks which the company exported between July 1317 and Michaelmas 1318, perhaps the greater part of two seasons' exports. In that period the Bardi were excused the loan of 10s per sack imposed on all other alien exports.[68]

Even before the dissolution of the Cerchi Neri about 1303 at least four new Florentine companies made their appearance in England. Two of these, the Veluti and the Galenani, had only a fleeting existence and there is no evidence of any investment they may have made in the wool trade. The other two, the Peruzzi and the Portinari, immediately became and remained major forces in the trade. The Peruzzi exported 386 sacks from London between March and Michaelmas 1303, while the Portinari exported 161 sacks in the same period and 124 sacks between April and Michaelmas 1304. In 1320 the Peruzzi were fined 2000 marks for staple offences, but a quarter of the sum was excused at the request of the King of France.[69] Another Florentine company, the Scali, was a major wool exporter from the second decade of the fourteenth century until it was made bankrupt in the years 1323–6. Although a Francis de la Scala sent 51 sacks of wool overland from London to Southampton in August 1307 it is unlikely that there was continuity in England between this company and the thirteenth-century Scali.

Among non-Florentine Italian wool exporters company affiliations are generally more difficult to determine and it is possible that these merchants were organised to a lesser degree, although it must be admitted that not all the Florentines were associated with the well-known companies. The biggest contrast with the Florentines is provided by the Genoese who, on the evidence of surviving customs particulars, appear to have been the second most important group of wool exporters. Few Genoese merchants resided permanently in England. They arrived in a galley or dromond, bought up a large amount of wool while the vessel remained in port and then departed with their purchases. There were, however, a few very significant exceptions to this general rule. One such was Anthony Pessagno, whose role as financier to Edward II after the collapse of the Frescobaldi has been recognised but not fully appreciated. By November 1314 he had advanced, and had been repaid, no less than £102 914. He remained in England, supplying royal armies with victuals and munitions, and tried to recruit 5 Genoese warships for service against the Scots.[70] In 1313–14 Pessagno exported 103 sacks of wool from Southampton. Another who remained in England for a long time, Anthony Ususmaris, acted as shipping agent for Italians of all cities.

During the thirteenth century the main ports used by Italian exporters had been Boston and Hull, but in the fourteenth century it is possible that even together they handled only a minority of the total export. Of the Bardi export of 1317–18 551 sacks went through Southampton, 79 sacks through Hull and 41 sacks through Boston. The total Italian export through Hull in the years 1298 to 1301 was 2291 sacks, while the total from 1302 to 1315 was 5824 sacks. Exports through Boston were 29 sacks between February 1303 and July 1304 and 2686 sacks between November 1308 and April 1312. The reason for the abandonment of the east coast ports was a major change in the method by which wool was sent to Italy. Originally most wool had been sent overland by the Alpine passes, although some may have always been sent through Gascony and the French Mediterranean ports. From the 1270s, however, the Genoese regularly sent ships to Flanders and wool began to be consigned to Italy in these ships. Although Genoese galleys loaded wool in London in 1281 and in Sandwich in 1287 there can be no doubt that in the thirteenth century most of the wool destined for Italy continued either to be sent overland or had to be delivered to Flanders for transhipment. This pattern changed immediately after the war of 1294–7, or even during the war itself, while the pressure to ship directly from England to Italy became even greater after the staple ordinance made it illegal to send wool to Flanders.

Italian vessels had little stomach for the east coast and in 17 years Genoese galleys visited Hull on only two occasions; Andalus de Nigro loaded 175 sacks of wool in August 1307 and 246 sacks in August 1309. With this exception Mediterranean ships seem to have confined their visits to London, Sandwich and Southampton. Although most of the shipping was Genoese a Majorcan galley loaded wool in London in September 1304 and use of the direct route was not confined to Genoese merchants. The latter, however, seem to have owned the whole of the 1417 sacks which left London in 4 galleys on 20 August 1306. Much of the Italian wool which was exported from London was sent to Sandwich where it was transferred to galleys. This is stated explicitly only in the alien account for 1311 but there can be no doubt that the same thing happened in 1297–8. In that year an unnamed galley loaded 249 sacks, but most of the Italian wool was dispatched in very small boats or barges which returned time and time again for fresh loads. It is inconceivable that these can have gone further than Sandwich.

The first organised voyage of Venetian galleys to northern Europe did not take place until 1314 and there is no record of their presence in England before an ill-fated visit to Southampton in 1319. Trouble between the townsfolk and sailors was the first of a number of incidents which seems to have led not only to the Venetians' avoidance of England thereafter but a boycott of the town by all Italian vessels.[71] The only Venetians who traded in England at this time under safe conducts were described as merchants and servants of the Bardi.

Reference has already been made to what can only be described as a highly successful challenge to the Italian stake in the wool trade by Hanseatic merchants in the early fourteenth century. The contrast between the rivals is seen at its starkest in the port of Hull. Between 1298 and 1315 Italians dispatched 8115 sacks of wool from Hull, 9 per cent of its total export. Germans sent at least 33 643 sacks, 39 per cent of the total, and the figure might be revised slightly upwards by the inclusion of wool owned by some whose nationality has not been determined. At national level, of course, the disparity between the two groups was not as great as is suggested by these figures. For the Italians the port of Hull was of declining importance, while the Germans undoubtedly made it the stronghold of their enterprise.

From 1298 to 1301 (June to June) German exports from Hull averaged 1043 sacks a year, 27 per cent of the total. In 1302–3 the figure was 2079 sacks, in the following year 3126 and in the next year 3442. This last figure, 57 per cent of all wool exported, was the high-water mark for the Hanseatics. In 1305–6 the port total was 7693 sacks but their share was only 3160 sacks (41 per cent). The increase in the Hanseatic presence at Hull coincided with their boycott of Lynn and a significant fall in the wool exports of that port. Furthermore the growing German pressure in Hull seems to have squeezed out the merchants of Brabant and Flanders who until about 1305 were sending several hundred sacks a year from the port. Picard merchants, who were not competitors of the Hanseatics, seem to have been unaffected. Without developing too elaborate a theory, therefore, it seems very likely that the German descent on Hull was a matter of design.

Some mention has already been made of the very large amounts of wool exported by the leading German merchants who operated from Hull for years on end. Even exporters of the second rank, however, owned quantities which were large by English standards. Unfortunately little appears to be known about German business methods and the English sources offer few clues. Although the foremost exporters appear to have been members of extended families or clans, wool was generally exported in the name of one owner. There is nothing to suggest that each member of the family actually came to England and it is possible that many investments were made by one or two active members. There was generally a considerable imbalance between the wool credited to the leading member of a 'family' and that exported by all the others. Conrad Clipping, for example, exported 4064 sacks, while the total of seven other Clippings was 1572 sacks. Martin de Rasceburgh exported 3223 sacks, but six others had only 117 sacks. Hardelef Spicenayl had 2561 sacks and Godfrey 1364 sacks, but seven others had only 538 sacks. Since John Clipping, who exported only very small amounts, was often described as the servant of Conrad, it is quite possible that some of the others were also apprentices or factors, named after their masters, who did a small private trade of their own. One leading German merchant, Lothewyc Dorring (1055 sacks) had an English factor (*garcio*), who occasionally exported on his own account. It is possibly significant that Lothewyc was the sole exporter bearing the name Dorring.

German exports from London and Boston are less readily identifiable than those at Hull. The customs clerks seldom entered the nationality of exporters and because of a not inconsiderable Brabantine and Flemish trade from the larger ports a Germanic-sounding name is inconclusive evidence. Nevertheless German exports from Boston and London, although separately not as large as those from Hull, were substantial. At Boston in 1303–4 and 1308–12 the Germans easily outstripped the Italians. It is, perhaps, only to be expected that those who had the greatest stake in Hull were less prominent in the other ports. Taking the leading three Hull families we find that Conrad Clipping sent only 13 sacks from Boston and three other Clippings 61 sacks, Hardelef Spicenayl sent 116 sacks and one other 21 sacks while the Rasceburghs did no trade at this port. The leading German family at Boston was that of Revel; Walter sent 617 sacks and six others 911 sacks. The total export of 6 or 7 Revels from Hull was 728 sacks over a much longer period.

As late as 1313–14 German merchants dispatched at least 2291 sacks of wool from Hull, 46 per cent of the total export, while from June 1314 to March 1315 they sent 1500 sacks, 38 per cent of the total. In 1324–5 all aliens exported 905 sacks from the port compared with 1544 sacks owned by denizens. Of the alien wool 205 sacks was owned by an Italian while most of the rest belonged to Germans, although probably by no means all. This poor performance by Germans was not merely a reflection of the fact that it was a bad year for all Hull exporters. They had fared little better in the good years of 1319–21 and it is quite clear that their domination of the port was at an end. The Spicenayls exported 45 sacks in 1319–21 and 27 sacks in 1324–5, the

Clippings nil and 27 sacks, the Rasceburghs nil and 3 sacks. Even the current leader among the Germans, John Sudermann, exported only 141 sacks and 79 sacks in the respective periods. It is unlikely that these figures merely mean that the Germans had transferred much of the business to other ports, since alien exports fell heavily in all ports. Clearly the Hanseatics lost a very large part of the stake in the wool trade which they had acquired in the early years of the century. It is suggested that this may have been a direct consequence of the compulsory staple. However great the evasion of the staple may have been in its early years it seems to have been successful in its obvious intention of winning the north European market for English merchants. The Hanseatics were strong in Flanders but were probably reluctant to follow an English-dominated staple where they would be treated as second-class members. The German merchants do not seem to have been able to recover their stake in the wool trade when the protection of a compulsory staple was removed. Although there is a dearth of particulars for the 1320s and 1330s it is clear that much of the reduced volume of alien exports was taken by Italians to their protected market in the peninsula. The English became the dominant force in the northern European market but whether they would have achieved this without the protection of a staple during the dispute with Flanders and without the reimposition of a differential custom in 1322 is an open question.

5

Edward III – woolmonger extraordinary

Once England and France were committed to the struggle which became the Hundred Years War it was probably inevitable that the wool
trade should fall prey to the king's diplomatic and financial needs.
Edward III needed to command large sums of money, not merely to
pay his own forces but also to buy allies on the continent. No matter
how amenable Parliament might prove he could not depend upon
direct taxation to yield the requisite sums with the speed necessary for
his plans. Manipulation of the wool trade, however, seemed to be the
solution to the problem of raising money quickly.[1] In the summer of
1337 the government and the community of English merchants agreed
upon a plan by which almost the entire stock of the nation's wool was
to be made available to finance the king's war. Thirty thousand sacks,
or more correctly the proceeds of the sale of 30 000 sacks, estimated
at £200 000, were to be lent to the king in a foreign staple. Disposal of
the wool was to be left to the merchants, for without their cooperation
the scheme was hardly practicable. Details of the agreement were formally embodied in an indenture drawn up on 26 July, the day after
an assembly of wool merchants came together at Westminster. On the
same day commissions were issued for the purveyance of wool by virtue
of the king's prerogative. Following Unwin most historians have accepted that this agreement was the culmination of a scheme set on foot the
previous summer, which from the first had aimed at monopolising the
wool trade for the king's profit. Although it is beyond dispute that some
months of negotiation lie behind the July agreement, it must be questioned whether measures taken in the summer and autumn of 1336
were indeed preliminary steps in a grand design which took more than
a year to come to fruition.

On 8 May 1336 writs were sent to London and twenty-one other
towns instructing them to send merchant representatives to Oxford on
27 May. It is not known what was discussed, or even whether the
assembly met, but on 28 May orders were sent to all sheriffs to squash
a rumour that the king proposed to increase the wool custom by 20s
per sack. This was said to be a falsehood spread by merchants to depress
the price of wool. On 1 June fresh writs were issued for merchants to

assemble at Northampton on 28 June, but again nothing is known about any deliberations. On 12 August instructions were sent to customs collectors to prevent the export of wool until further notice. The ban on the export of wool has been interpreted as an integral part of the monopoly plan, its purpose being to keep wool in the country while arrangements were made for a purveyance. At the same time this action would create a shortage in the Low Countries which would help the price when wool began to be exported once more, the profit now going to the king. However, it can be argued that a ban on export was already overdue even if there were no thoughts of a royal monopoly. The government was anxious to increase the rate of duty, but could not do this without obtaining the consent of at least the merchant community. This had not yet been given but rumours of an impending increase doubtless acted as a spur to exporters to accelerate their business. In these circumstances a temporary ban on exports would incline the merchants to be more sympathetic to the king's request for an increase in duty and at the same time would hold back the flow of wool until the higher rate was in force. Beside this fiscal consideration it is possible that by August the government had decided that a ban on export might provide useful pressure on Flanders to join the English alliance.

A third assembly of merchants which met at Nottingham on 23 September finally accepted the need for an increase in the rates of duty and granted a subsidy of 20s on each sack of wool and 40s on each last of hides in addition to the ancient custom. Subsequently alien merchants agreed to pay the subsidy together with an equal sum as a loan. As well as the increase in duty there emerged from the Nottingham meetings a schedule of wool prices, later known as the Nottingham prices. While the subsidy was later said to have been the gift of the merchants the price schedule was the work of a Great Council in which the merchants participated with the magnates. Although it is almost universally accepted that the schedule was drawn up for the purveyance of wool for the king's use, it is equally explicable as a price floor to protect the growers from the additional export subsidy. For the time being both the Nottingham prices and the subsidy remained in abeyance, since the export ban was not lifted. Its continuance, however, was not necessarily a deliberate manoeuvre to create a scarcity of wool in the Low Countries and so to enhance the price. The Flemish response to the ban – a counter prohibition of all trade – may have been unexpected and certainly minimised the value of England's unilaterally raising the embargo. Moreover negotiations were in progress for the setting up of a foreign staple for wool. In December 1336 the king promised to send envoys to the Duke of Brabant to discuss his request for a staple, although he stipulated that one could not be established until the duke provided for the safety of English merchants and guaranteed that wool would not be allowed to reach Flanders. In February 1337 an ambassador was sent to Brussels, Louvain and Malines carrying the king's conditions for a staple in Brabant. In April, however, the Bishop of Lincoln was authorised to discuss the terms of a staple with any potential ally.

In the absence of conclusive evidence the question of when the decision to create a royal monopoly in the wool trade was taken remains open.[2] It cannot be doubted, however, that the project was thoroughly debated at the two merchant assemblies which met in June 1337. In this period many of the country's leading wool merchants must have pledged their support. As already mentioned the terms of the agreement between the king and the merchants were formally embodied in an indenture made on 26 July in the course of a third assembly. In the last resort the whole of the 30 000 sacks which it was intended to raise might be taken as a royal purveyance. The target figure was apportioned between all the English counties, with the exceptions of Lancashire, Devon and Cornwall, and from two to seven merchants were commissioned to purvey wool in each county or group of counties. It was agreed that for the best wools the purveyors should pay the prices determined at Nottingham the previous September. For lesser wools they were to bargain with the owners. They were not required to hand over any ready cash at the time of purchase, but half the sum due was to be paid within six months of the wool being delivered to them and the remaining half within the year. One feature which distinguished this from a normal purveyance was that those surrendering wool did not receive royal letters obligatory; instead they were given the personal bonds of the merchants. In effect the king was using the credit of the country's leading merchants to obtain wool for himself. The purveyors would be reimbursed out of funds made available to repay all those who joined in the venture.

The right to participate was not confined to the 99 merchants who were appointed purveyors. It was open to all those willing to accept the conditions which had been determined in the assemblies. The chief of these was that all proceeds of sales on the continent should be lent to the king. It is pertinent to enquire why any merchant should willingly engage himself in this company. The truth is that the alternative was even less palatable. If he declined to participate any wool in his possession was liable to be taken by the purveyors. If he successfully concealed it he could not export it since the king pledged himself to maintain the ban until all of the 30 000 sacks had been disposed of. There were, however, certain positive advantages to be gained from joining the venture. All the participants were to have their property protected from further royal prises and they were not to be impleaded for debt for wool bought before the drawing up of the indenture as well as for that bought afterwards. This was important for those who had bought wool on credit, payment for which might now be due. Creditors would have to wait until the merchants had themselves been paid. Finally by participating in the scheme a merchant stood to make some profit, even though it might be a long time before it was realised. Strangely the question of profits was not touched upon in the agreement of 26 July, but later it was recorded that all profit should be divided equally between the king and the merchants. This meant that repayment by the king of any money lent to him would be reduced by a sum equal to half the profit, profit being the sale price less the purchase price and all other expenses.

The leaders of the merchants who had made this agreement with the king were William de la Pole of Hull and Reginald Conduit of London. They were charged with the disposal of the wool and made responsible for the king's share of the profits. They were also the agents for the ultimate repayment of the merchants. In the name of the community they were to hold one leaf of the cocket seal in all ports and once normal trade was resumed they were to collect all payments of custom, which was to be the fund out of which the merchants would be repaid.

Despite the provisions for a purveyance there was no arrest of wool in the summer of 1337 nor any other hindrance to its sale. All were free to buy new wool to contribute to the grand design although ordinary merchants, unlike the purveyors, could not insist on taking wool on credit. Since purveyors also had the right to buy wool for ready cash the way was opened to extortion. In at least one case a Lincolnshire purveyor was charged with giving sellers the option of taking cash at well below the Nottingham price or of having wool forcibly taken in a credit transaction.[3]

It was intended to dispatch the 30 000 sacks of wool in three shipments to Dordrecht in Zeeland and to pay the king three instalments of 100 000 marks at Christmas, Easter (12 April 1338) and Ascension (21 May). Although it had been agreed that customs duty should be paid in the foreign staple it was eventually decided that the subsidy of 20s should be collected at the English ports and that the first instalment of cash abroad should be reduced by an equivalent sum. The ancient custom of half a mark was not levied at this stage. The wool collected by the merchants left the ports of Newcastle, Hull, Boston and Sandwich in the last days of September and in early October 1337. The ships carrying it assembled into two convoys in the Orwell estuary and at Sandwich before setting out for Dordrecht in early November. They arrived there on 28 November, having deposited a small amount of wool at Middelburg. In the convoy were representatives of the merchant community, who were to sell the wool, and the king's envoys, led by the Bishop of Lincoln, who were to pay out the proceeds of the sales as subsidies to the king's allies.

In the Netherlands events took a radically different course from that which had been planned at the beginning of the venture. On 19 December a conference was held at Gertruidenberg between the king's envoys and the merchants who had travelled with the wool, none of which had yet been sold. When asked how much money they could now advance the merchants refused at first to name a definite sum, alleging that the wool had deteriorated and that because they were debarred from selling to Flemings prices would be poor. Finally they declared that if they were allowed to sell to whomever they wished they would pay 100 000 marks by the beginning of Lent (25 February) or at latest by Easter. The king's envoys replied that this was insufficient for their needs and that between 2 February and 22 March they had to raise £276 000, a sum greater than the merchants had agreed to lend on the entire 30 000 sacks of wool. The envoys then cited a subsidiary agreement made some time between July and the departure of the wool fleet. This established that the first 10 000 sacks were to be entirely at the disposal of the envoys who might use them as they wished, provided that they paid the merchants sufficient cash to cover their previous expenses so that they might fit out a second fleet. When the merchants declined to advance more than that to which they were bound by the original agreement the envoys decided that they must take over the wool. With some difficulty the merchants were persuaded to hand it over, subject to their receiving £20 000 in cash; enough to provide £2 for each sarpler surrendered. The king's agents apparently succeeded in getting hold of all the wool which had been officially exported except for 335 sarplers, for the detention of which certain merchants were later prosecuted.

The handling over of the wool began in February 1338 and continued at least until May. Despite the bad odour which has surrounded the so-called 'Dordrecht seizure' this was not a confiscation and a careful record was kept of the king's obligations. The merchants were even allowed to set their own price upon the wool, the valuation of it being made by thirty of their number who had travelled with the expedition. The amount of wool taken, together with a record of the king's obligation, was put into indentures, 317 in number, made between the king and each of the merchants in whose name the wool had been exported. The king's remaining obligation to each merchant was the value of the wool less the cash paid at Dordrecht, at the rate of £2 per sarpler, and less the ancient custom of half a mark per sack, since this impost had not yet been paid.

The total value of the wool taken over for the king at Dordrecht and Middelburg was approximately £114 000. The amount of wool involved has been a matter of dispute among historians. Terry and Unwin gave a figure of 11 497 sacks, but Fryde criticised them for failing to observe that these sacks were of the weight of Middelburg and Dordrecht. Only a very small, though undetermined, proportion were of Middelburg weight, the sack consisting of 60 cloves of 6 lb each. The great majority were delivered to Dordrecht, where the sack allegedly contained 54 cloves of 6 lb each, plus 4 lb, a total of 328 lb. Fryde takes at face value the assertion of William de la Pole and Reginald Conduit that the indentures on which their account was based recorded wool by Dordrecht and Middelburg weights.[4] There is, however, no room to doubt that this was a lie and that the indentures recorded English weights. The evidence is provided by an inspection of the wool delivered at Dordrecht by the purveyors. The number of sacks of wool credited to them are identical in the Dordrecht indentures and in the enrolled accounts of the purveyors relating to purchases of wool in England. Fryde was aware of this but he chose to assume that the purveyors' accounts recorded wool by Dordrecht weight.[5] This is not only implausible; it is directly contradicted by the internal evidence of the accounts. Time and time again it is stated that these are English sacks, for example 30 stones of 12 lb in Yorkshire, 28 stones of 13 lb in Leicestershire, 26 stones of 14 lb in Staffordshire and many other counties. When details of sales are provided the correct totals are arrived at using these standards. Furthermore when a purveyor had wool which was assembled too late for delivery to Dordrecht he handed it over to collectors of the next levy in February 1338. There can be no question of the latter having any truck with Dordrecht weights, yet again the number of sacks is the same in each set of accounts.[6] Since all the purveyors' wool was recorded in the indentures in English weights one must assume that the same is true of wool belonging to other merchants. The only wool which can be said to be quite definitely of a non-English weight is the king's own, but chances are that here the figures are entirely fictitious, concocted by someone who had little knowledge of the true relationship between English and Dordrecht weights.

The total amount of wool accounted for by Pole and Conduit was 11 414¼ sacks 4 lb taken over from the merchants, 21½ sacks from the king's Holderness estates and 61¼ sacks 11 cloves presented to him by the Archbishop of Canterbury, making 11 497¼ sacks 2 cloves 1 lb in all.[7] In order to maintain the pretence that Dordrecht weights were being used the king's wool would have to show an increase in the number of sacks, but by how many? The Canterbury wool had weighed 49 sacks 8 cloves or 17 892 lb at the London customs and should therefore have weighed 54 sacks 30 cloves at Dordrecht. It weighed 61¼ sacks 11 cloves or 20 056 lb, a real increase in weight of 12 per cent. The enthusiasm of the fabricator seems to have run away with him.

Why, it will be asked, should Pole and Conduit deliberately state that the weights recorded in the indentures were those of Dordrecht and Middelburg if they knew them to be English weights? Probably because it was their only immediate defence to the charge brought against them that they had been involved in a massive criminal conspiracy to defraud the Crown. Someone at the Exchequer had observed that in many of the indentures merchants were credited with surrendering at Dordrecht a larger number of sacks than that which they had declared to the customs.[8] This led to a general enquiry and the revelation that a vast amount of uncustomed wool had sailed in the fleets which sailed to Dordrecht. By claiming that the indentures referred to Dordrecht sacks, smaller than those of the English customs, Pole and Conduit may have hoped to confuse the issue, since this would appear to account for the increase in the number of sacks between England and Dordrecht. Naturally this deception did not stand up to a full-scale investigation.[9] At first the Exchequer advanced the claim that 5000 sacks of wool had been smuggled but later accepted an estimate that the correct total was about 2500. This seems a very likely figure. The enrolled subsidy accounts record a total of 9312 sacks 6 stones of wool, including the king's and 15 154 fells as having left Hull, Newcastle, Boston and London either just before or just after Michaelmas 1337. Pole and Conduit accounted for 11 497 sacks, including the king's, while something like 350 sacks were not handed over. It is difficult to apportion blame for the breakdown of the 1337 venture, although it is clear that neither party to the original agreement was completely blameless. The king must be acquitted, however, of the charge of having confiscated the wool at Dordrecht. There are no grounds for supposing that it was not intended ultimately to pay the merchants in full. The blame attaching to the king is that he failed to honour successive arrangements made for repaying the debt.

Reverberations of the dispute in the Low Countries between the king's agents and representatives of the merchants brought the collection of wool to a virtual halt in the winter of 1337–8. This did not deflect Edward from his goal of obtaining 30 000 sacks, but it may have persuaded him of the advisability of seeking parliamentary approval of his actions. The parliament which met on the morrow of Purification (3 February) 1338 made a grant of half of all the wool in the country, conveniently estimated at 20 000 sacks, the amount thought to be outstanding from the original loan. It must be emphasised that this was neither a free gift nor a new loan. It was merely a confirmation of the king's right to continue levying the remainder of the 30 000 sacks which he had already determined to borrow from his subjects. Any wool remaining in the hands of the purveyors appointed the previous summer was to count as part of the 20 000 sacks and, more significantly, further purveyance was to be restricted to wool already shorn – none was to be taken from the clip of the coming season. Furthermore, while wool could be taken from the clergy as well as from the laity no more than half of each man's stock was to be taken and all were to be free to dispose of the remainder as they wished. If the chronicler Murimuth may be believed it was intended that no wool should be taken from men owning less than one sack. As before, Nottingham prices were to be paid for the better wool in each county and the price of lesser grades settled by agreement. The main difference between the arrangements of 1337 and those of 1338 was that in the later year the purveyors were not required to give personal bonds in exchange for wool; vendors were to be provided with royal letters obligatory as was usual in the case of purveyance. The term of repayment was two years.

On the same day that the commissions were made out writs were dispatched for an assembly of merchants to meet on 16 March. It may have been hoped to settle the differences between the Crown and the merchants and to re-enlist the support of the latter in disposing of wool. If this was the case the hope had been abandoned before the assembly met, for on 11 March the government formally concluded an agreement with the Bardi and Peruzzi, although later, on 11 May 1338, this was modified and a new indenture made.[10] It was finally agreed that 4000 sacks of royal wool should be exported before the king left England and placed at the disposal of the companies, in return for which they would lend him £15 000 before his departure and a further £22 000 as soon as he arrived overseas. At the same time another 6000 sacks were to be exported, disposal of which was retained to the king. The next 10 000 sacks were to be assigned to the companies in settlement of old debts, although the king reserved the

right to send another 4000 sacks with these. If he elected to have the
additional wool sold by the companies they were to pay him four marks
per sack in cash within a month of delivery and to account later for
all remaining issues. The two companies were authorised to export
2000 sacks of their own wool to be sold for their own profit. They also
had an assignment of the second year of the current tenth and fifteenth
granted by the clergy and the laity. In the first indenture it had been
provided that, with the exception of 3700 sacks recently licensed to be
exported by Brabanters and Germans, the general embargo on export
would continue until all the wool which was subject to the agreement
with the Italians had been sold. In the modified agreement this protection was guaranteed only until 1 August. The change was necessary
because of an agreement just made between the king and the English
merchants about the method of paying for the wool taken at Dordrecht.
This will be discussed later.

Despite the fact that a ban was placed on the sale of wool by private
individuals the results of the February levy were disappointing in the
extreme. The collectors managed to raise only 1867 sacks, although
additionally they acquired up to 940 sacks remaining from the purveyance of the previous year, which had been assembled too late for
shipment to Dordrecht.[11] From the beginning there was considerable
resistance both by clergy and laity and no doubt this increased once
the government had set a date at which the general export of wool
might be resumed. Shortage of canvas for packing wool added to the
problems of the collectors and meant that delivery was disappointingly
slow. No wool was exported before June and when the king left
England on 16 July the total dispatched, including that taken with him,
was less than 2000 sacks, far short of the 4000 sacks mentioned in the
agreement with the Italians. However about this time the two companies received a total of 3610 sacks of the Dordrecht wool.

On 24 July, two days after his arrival at Antwerp, Edward wrote
to the council in England complaining of his embarrassment at not
finding all the wool which he expected to be in the city. His estimate
that only 2500 sacks were there appears to include the wool belonging
to the Bardi and the Peruzzi just exported in the king's fleet according
to their agreement. He urged the council to raise the 17 500 sacks
which remained from the 20 000 sacks as quickly as possible. The
king's command was transmitted to the Great Council which assembled
at Northampton at the end of July 1338 and this body confirmed the
arrangements now made to put it into effect.

In one respect the Great Council seems merely to have provided
further confirmation of the king's right to collect what remained of

the original 30 000 sacks, although it was agreed that new wool might now be taken as well as the old. It also accepted a new method of collection, which spread the burden among all who paid taxes instead of restricting it to owners of sheep and wool merchants. All persons contributing to the lay tenth and fifteenth and the clerical tenth were required to provide wool for the king's use. It is a moot point whether initially the grant was regarded as a tax in kind or a loan to be repaid, either directly or by remission of taxes, but whatever the intention there was no repayment so the levy undoubtedly became a tax in kind.

Commissions for collection were made out on 1 August 1338.[12] In each county there was a group of assessors to inform every taxpayer of the amount of his contribution and to ensure that he delivered it, at his own charge, to collection centres where receivers assumed responsibility for delivering it to the ports. The assessors were armed with current lists of those paying the tenth and fifteenth. Each of these was charged in proportion to his assessment to the money tax, ten stones of wool being required for every 20s paid to the fifteenth and pro rata for the tenth. All who paid a tenth, which in the case of the laity meant inhabitants of boroughs and ancient demesne, had their money assessments reduced by one third before their quota of wool was calculated.

Although it was realised that many taxpayers had no wool of their own all were required to pay in kind. Persons without wool were expected to buy it, at Nottingham prices, from those who had more than they were liable for. The government may have hoped that the prospect of a market with ready cash would discourage hoarding, but the reverse seems to have happened. An abundance of prospective buyers created a sellers' market and many refused to part with wool at Nottingham prices, holding out for a higher figure. Three weeks after the first commissions were issued it was necessary to instruct the officials to assist taxpayers to buy wool. If any person with a large stock remained obstinate in his refusal to sell it was to be taken forcibly at Nottingham prices, the cash being provided by those who could not otherwise obtain wool. Only in Essex is it certain that officials actually bought wool with cash provided by taxpayers and on 16 October the instruction was countermanded and receivers were ordered to retain any cash given in lieu of wool Over the whole country only about 6 per cent of the estimated yield of the levy was rendered in cash, mostly in counties short of wool.[13]

The intention of the Great Council had been to provide the king with the 17 500 sacks remaining out of the 20 000 granted or confirmed by the Commons in February 1338. The government calculated, however, that on the basis of the current tenth and fifteenth the yield should be 18 972 sacks, of which nearly 5000 sacks represented the clerical contribution. The collection of wool from the clergy soon met strenuous opposition on the grounds that consent had not been given. On 20 August 1338 collection was suspended until the two convocations should meet. Canterbury met on 1 October and while refusing to give wool offered to give an extra tenth instead. York met on 12 November and refused to give either wool or alternative aid. The bishops and greater abbots who had received summonses to the Great Council at Northampton, were treated as being personally liable, whether or not they had been present when the grant was made. Their contribution totalled 814 sacks, although as a result of exemptions only 443 sacks were collected. Furthermore this wool was treated not as a tax but as a loan.[14]

As a result of the refusal of the clergy to contribute and because of miscalculations in converting the money tax into wool the government was obliged to reduce its estimate of the probable yield from 18 972 to 14 509 sacks. The actual amount handed over by the receivers within twelve months of the commencement of the levy in August 1338 was 12 354 sacks.[15] The first wool began to reach English ports in late September, shortly after the dispatch of the last of the wool from the February levy, and shipments were made intermittently for the next twelve months. The king complained incessantly to the council about the delays in shipping wool, as well as about its quality and the fact that the quantity fell far short of the original estimate of 19 000 sacks. In fact there is nothing to suggest that the delays were other than inevitable given the onset of winter and war-time pressure on shipping. When Southampton was sacked by the French in October 1338 the wool collected there was either burned or in the confusion looted by Englishmen.

Between the summer of 1338 and the autumn of 1339 some 7689 to 7827 sacks of wool were exported in the name of the king, of which several hundred sacks were lost at sea by enemy action.[16] This total is considerably lower than the combined results of the grants of February and July 1338. The difference is accounted for largely by the wool handed over in England to the king's creditors who exported it in their own names. The chief recipients were William de la Pole, William de Duvenvoorde, lord of Oosterhout in the Low Countries, and the Bardi and Peruzzi, each of them receiving over 2000 sacks. The king's agent Paul de Monte Florum also took possession of over 1000 sacks in England in addition to royal wool delivered to him overseas. The authority for the delivery of wool in England took the form of writs of privy seal emanating from the king who was abroad throughout this period. The assignments were based on the council's original estimate of the yield of the July grant and suitors appeared to claim wool which the authorities in England did not have at their disposal. None of the creditors was able to obtain the full amount assigned to them, while some, such as the Hanseatic merchants, got nothing at all.

Despite deliveries of wool from England and despite loans raised both from his own subjects and from aliens Edward was in a state of perpetual semi-bankruptcy throughout his stay in the Low Countries. Therefore when Parliament met in October 1339 he sent messengers, including William de la Pole, to ask for further financial assistance. In response to this request the magnates offered to give for two years the tenth lamb, fleece and sheath from their demesnes, sparing, however, the lands of their villeins. At the same time they sought the abolition of the *maltote* on exported wool which, since March 1338, had consisted of a subsidy of 33s 4d, making with the ancient custom a total duty of 40s. The Commons backed this demand but declined to grant aid until they had first consulted their constituents. Accordingly writs were issued for Parliament to meet again on 20 January 1340. In the new Parliament the Commons, after a month's deliberation, offered 30 000 sacks of wool, subject to redress of grievances. On the same day the magnates renewed their offer of a tenth of their produce. After repeated pressure from the king's ministers the Commons offered 2500 sacks of wool – either as an advance of 30 000 sacks if their demands were met or as a free gift if they were not. These demands were so far-reaching that the ministers could not accept them without the king's personal consent, so Parliament was adjourned until his return. Edward returned to England on 21 February, 1340, for the first time since July 1338, and met Parliament on 29 March.

When Parliament assembled the Commons offered the ninth lamb, fleece and sheath from the produce of 1340 and 1341. This was the same proportion as the tenth offered by the magnates in the earlier parliament, since the Commons allowed for the church tithe, which was taken at source. Townsmen were to pay a normal tenth, merchants and other non-agriculturalists living outside towns were to pay in cash at the rate of one fifteenth, but husbandmen were actually to pay the ninth in produce. In return for the grant the Commons won from the king important concessions touching the taxation of exported wool. This matter had become more urgent than ever since a recent deal between the Crown and the merchants had resulted in the duty being raised to a staggering £4 per sack for denizens and £5 3s 4d for aliens.

The Commons were unable to obtain a reduction to the pre-war rate but they were able to bring the duty down from these heights and to obtain an assurance that in future the level of taxation would be determined by Parliament and not by a mere assembly of merchants. Statute two, made on 16 April, recited that the Lords and Commons had granted the king a duty of 40s on every sack of wool, 300 fells and last of hides, to continue until Whitsun 1341. As a result of this the subsidy for aliens, as well as denizens, became 33s 4d, while both paid the ancient custom and the former continued also to pay the new custom. The grant was followed by a promise that after Whitsun 1341 the king would never again demand of Englishmen more than the ancient custom of 6s 8d per sack. Statute four merely guaranteed that the king would not increase the duty beyond this level without the consent of Parliament.[17] Even this, however, was a considerable advance on earlier assumptions.

The ninth of 1340 afforded the government valuable breathing space in its financial difficulties. The tax would be yielded up only in instalments as the farming year progressed, but it might be anticipated. This might be done by trying to persuade people to buy the produce and pay in advance or by borrowing on security of future sales. It seems never to have been the intention of the government to collect the produce itself, for lambs and grain in sheath were a different proposition from sacks of wool. Italian bankers and English merchants were found willing to lend money in return for assignments of the proceeds of the tax but at first actual buyers of the produce were reluctant to stand forward. This is hardly surprising since it would be some months before the final yield would be known. Moreover in the summer the possession of wool became less attractive in the light of a new forced loan set on foot by the government. Commissions for the administration of the ninth, issued on 20 April, were followed in July by instructions that it might be sold in gross at the valuation of churches according to the taxation of 1291, but not below that figure. The government seems previously to have resisted this course of action on the ground that the taxation was no longer, if it ever had been, a *verus valor*. In fact in many cases the taxation figure was undoubtedly still higher than the produce of the ninth since it included glebe land, tithe of hay and other issues which were not subject to the present tax. The new instructions did not result in many sales, so that as the ninth was assessed and collected it had to be committed to the custody of four men in each vill. Only after this stipulation for minimum prices was abolished in January 1340 did disposal of the ninth go ahead fairly smoothly. It is likely that in many cases taxpayers 'bought' their own goods, so that what had begun as a levy in kind ended as a simple tax in cash.

Within a short time of his return to the continent in June 1340 Edward was virtually bankrupt. Funds from alien financiers dried up and in his extremity the king was forced to call upon his subjects to anticipate the newly-granted ninth with a loan in wool. When Parliament met in July some of the lords and knights present offered to lend their own wool, but this was superseded by a loan of 20 000 sacks from the nation at large. It was to be collected concurrently with the present ninth but was made first charge on the ninth of 1341. Thus anyone surrendering wool in excess of his assessment was guaranteed repayment out of the following year's tax in his own area. To facilitate collection of the grant the Commons agreed that until Michaelmas all buying and selling of wool should be suspended. Thereafter, all might buy and sell and export at the current rate of duty. The conditions under which wool from the new loan was to be disposed of seem to have been determined by, or at least in, Parliament.[18] These were that the king should buy the wool from his subjects at Nottingham prices and should sell it to merchants at one mark less. The buyers were to pay the money, together with the duty of 40s per sack, to the king's representatives overseas.

Some of the most prominent English merchants were either members of Parliament or were at Westminster while it was in session. Immediately Parliament rose they came before the council and made indentures for the purchase of part of the wool. Whatever Parliament's intention may have been some of them were able to obtain the concession that part of the price should be set against earlier loans. A group of Yorkshire merchants who bargained for 1500 sacks for a total of £6750 were allowed to deduct £1000, provided that they paid a first instalment of 3000 marks at Bruges by 1 September 1340. Altogether 15 merchants grouped into 5 syndicates agreed to take a total of 4300 sacks on similar conditions. Following another assembly convened on 21 August a further 18 merchants in 6 groups made indentures for 3200 sacks. William de la Pole had already agreed to take 1200 sacks and subsequently half a dozen merchants in 2 groups bargained for over 158 sacks. This accounts for about 9000 sacks, less than half the amount which the government hoped to have at its disposal. Thereafter wool began to be assigned to the king's alien creditors and allies, a course dictated perhaps less by choice than by the reluctance of English merchants to offer cash.

The loan of 1340 turned out to be the most unsuccessful of all the attempts to raise wool for the king's use and neither English merchants nor royal creditors laid their hands on very much. The largest amount, 340 sacks, went to the Duke of Brabant, but the exercise as a whole put a mere 854 sacks at the king's disposal.[19] Of this no less than 564 sacks were taken at London, mainly from Hanseatics and the Peruzzi. A considerably greater amount had actually been seized, but most was restored to its owners for various reasons. Outside London the levy was almost a total failure, although no single reason can be adduced for this. In some counties the government at a relatively early date ordered collectors to stop taking wool, since it could not, or would not, cancel assignments already made on the ninth of 1341, which was supposed to provide a fund to repay those from whom wool was now taken. However, there were other counties where no such order was given which yielded not a single sack. The main reason for the lack of success was probably the sheer resistance of the population. Efforts to collect wool continued throughout the winter of 1340–1, fair words alternating with threats in the government's proclamations. In February it was announced that while the king fully intended to pay for any wool taken now, all that was found after Easter would be declared forfeit. Not until 1 April 1341 were orders issued for the levy to be suspended.

The government totally disregarded the condition written into the parliamentary loan of 1340 that after Michaelmas all might buy and sell and export wool. Without a licence, which normally was granted only to official purchasers and assignees of the loan, it was impossible to deal openly in wool. In January 1341 even licensees were ordered to export by the first Sunday in Lent (25 February) or else surrender their wool. In March, however, it was decided to allow the export of certain types of wool which the king's creditors refused to take. Such wools could be exported under licence at the full rate of duty. The suspension of the loan in April was accompanied by an announcement that better wools might be exported upon payment of a double duty of £4 per sack. At this rate there were few willing to export apart from creditors who were allowed to set half the duty against existing debts. The government attempted, not very successfully, to overcome the resistance by threatening to confiscate all wool not exported by Ascension (17 May). It was claimed that merchants were holding back their wool until Whitsun (27 May), when the subsidy granted by Parliament was due to expire. Parliament itself assembled on 23 April 1341 and cannot have avoided a discussion of the doubling of the rate of duty. Although the rolls of Parliament do not record any complaint by the Commons the issue is covered by implication in a new grant of wool. All dealing by merchants in wool of the coming season was forbidden until Michaelmas 1341 and anyone discovered exporting it before that date would forfeit the wool and incur a three-fold penalty. Thereafter the trade was to be thrown open to all on payment of the ancient custom of 6s 8d. Parliament agreed that meanwhile old wool might be exported under licence for 40s. From 4 May onwards, while Parliament was still in session, the government actually took 50s from denizens and 53s 4d from aliens, initially for old wool but later for new.[20]

The wool grant of 1341 was made in the light of a vast accumulation of royal debt and the prospect of a renewal of the war, which had been suspended since the truce of Esplechin (September 1340). It was not a loan but a tax of 30 000 sacks of wool, to be paid by the laity and by the lords spiritual who had been summoned to Parliament. The rest of the clergy were exempted, except for such of their property as was normally assessed to lay taxes, that is lands acquired after 20 Edward I. Twenty thousand sacks were to be collected by 1 August 1341 and the remainder by 1 August 1342. The tax was not an addition to that granted the previous year since the ninth of 1341 was immediately cancelled in its entirety. Anyone who might already have paid it was to be reimbursed out of the present grant, as were all who had contributed to the wool loan of 1340.

Responsibility for distributing the burden of the new tax was committed to the Bishop of Chester, Robert de Sadington, Treasurer from 5 May 1340 to 26 June 1340 and previously chief baron of the Exchequer, and Thomas Wake of Lidell, chief of the justices charged with hearing complaints of the king's subjects about tax gathering and similar matters. They submitted to Chancery, almost certainly before 1 June, an indenture which fixed a quota for every county, except Chester and Durham, with separate assessments for London, Bristol, York and Newcastle. On 15 June writs were sent to the Bishop of London and Thomas Wake ordering them to attend a meeting of the council on the following Thursday to consider complaints made by 'certain magnates and others of the council' about the unfairness of the recent assessment.[21] Since there is little doubt that these complaints were made after the delivery of the above-mentioned indenture their nature may easily be guessed at. The magnates were probably puzzled by the fact that some counties were required to produce a much greater amount of wool than they had paid in the levy of July 1338, while the assessment of others rose hardly at all. Once the principle of the assessment had been explained to them they were probably satisfied, since the county quotas remained unchanged. The new assessment, merely described as having been made *iuxta sortem lanarum et ratam Quinte-*

decime triennalis, represented a deliberate attempt to avoid the inequity of the wool tax of July 1338. The earlier levy had enjoined the provision not of a given value from each county but of a given weight, ten stones being demanded for every 20s paid in a fifteenth. This established a certain degree of fairness within each county, where equal weights of wool might be assumed to be more or less equal in value. It was, however, highly inequitable as between county and county, since here there were wide differences in values. The 1338 assessment weighed much more heavily, therefore, on counties with good wool than on those with poor wool. The revised assessment was fairer since it took account of differences in the quality. Although the quota of each county was expressed in weight it had undoubtedly been determined on the basis of value, the Nottingham schedule providing the standard of reference. The result was that counties with good wool found their quotas increased very little, and in one case reduced, while those with mediocre wool had theirs increased. Thus the Herefordshire quota, valued at 12 marks per sack, was reduced from 156 sacks to 141, that of Shropshire, at $10\frac{1}{2}$ marks, was increased from 232 sacks to 237, while that of Norfolk, at 6 marks, rose from 1238 sacks to 2207.

While the use of Nottingham prices equalised the burden of the tax over the country as a whole it tells nothing about the relationship of 30 000 sacks of wool to the product of a fifteenth, which can be determined only by comparing the value of the wool to the value of a fifteenth. This exercise makes it clear that each county was required to produce in 1341 an amount of wool equal in value to $2\frac{3}{4}$ times the product of one fifteenth, boroughs and ancient demesne having their assessment cut by one third. The total amount of wool which would be raised in this way was actually 20 323 sacks 2 stones $9\frac{1}{4}$ lb. The burden on individual taxpayers was rather less than $2\frac{3}{4}$ times their contribution to a fifteenth since in reckoning the county quotas the contribution of the higher clergy had not been taken into account. After some initial confusion about the way in which this clerical wool should be collected it was established that it must not be included in the quotas of the villages where the clergy had their lands for this would have provided relief for a limited number of places.[22] Instead the contribution was rendered on a county basis, so that the relief would be enjoyed by the entire county. Thus in Berkshire the county quota of $538\frac{1}{2}$ sacks $\frac{1}{2}$ lb was relieved by 34 sacks 8 stone 1 lb provided by the Bishop of Salisbury and 6 abbots, and the assessment of each lay taxpayer was reduced to fractionally less than $2\frac{1}{2}$ times one fifteenth.

On 1 June 1341 commissions were issued appointing assessors and collectors of the wool tax in each of the areas named in the Bishop of

Chester's schedule, the only exception being London, which presumably had already arranged to give cash in lieu of its quota of 504 sacks. Subsequently the collection was postponed in Northumberland, probably on account of the Scots invasions. The exemption was not intended to apply to Newcastle, but no wool was collected in the city either in 1341 or 1342. At some point the entire quota of Cornwall was commuted to cash, because of the remoteness of the county and the poor quality of its wool. The tin-miners of Devon resisted the tax and at one stage the collectors complained that almost one third of the entire county was refusing payment. The government gave ground very reluctantly, instructing the collectors to ensure that only working tinners were exempted. Finally the Cinque Ports were excused the tax and the collectors of Kent and Sussex were given an allowance for the wool of these places, which had been included in the county quotas. As well as collectors there were in each county a group of receivers who were to have custody of the wool and to dispose of it as instructed by government warrants. They usually handed it over directly to attorneys of the king's creditors or of merchant contractors who then assumed responsibility for it. In some instances sheriffs had a hand in further delivery and subsequently claimed allowance for expenses.[23]

On 20 June commissions of oyer and terminer were issued in each county in compliance with a promise made in Parliament when the wool had been granted.[24] These were designed to hear complaints made by subjects about misbehaviour on the part of the officials responsible for the levy. Where the interest of the king was involved charges against officials were dealt with by the central government. Complaints against receivers seem mainly to have been confined to those involving neglect of duty. The Hertfordshire receivers refused to accept wool until ordered to do so on pain of exemplary punishment, while those of Lincolnshire were charged with refusing to deliver wool to the attorneys of the Duke of Guelders, even though they had some in their custody. The charges against collectors were more serious, since they involved attempted fraud. On 10 October an order was given for the arrest of the collectors in Sussex to answer charges that they accepted wool by the statutory weight and delivered it to the receivers by a lesser weight, keeping for themselves from two to four cloves in every sack. Similar charges were made against collectors in Somerset and Dorset. The Worcestershire collectors were charged not only with using two sets of weights but also with putting sand in fleeces and with taking cash from taxpayers and using this to buy inferior wool at 6 or 7 marks although the county price was $9\frac{1}{2}$ marks. The alleged offences came to light when the merchants who had contracted to buy the wool refused to accept the inferior fleeces offered to them. The false weights and the rejected wool were ordered to be brought to Westminster to be examined by the council. The same group of merchants brought similar charges against the Shropshire collectors.[25]

The wool was brought to appointed centres in each county at the expense of the taxpayers, often being delivered by the constable of the vill or by agents of landowners. In Bedfordshire the abbot of Ramsey paid nearly 5 sacks beyond his quota so that he might be spared from assisting in the collection.[26] In some instances at least the wool seems to have been weighed in the villages, although it may have been re-weighed when delivered to the centres. The collectors were evidently involved in the business of weighing since all disclaimed any liability for increment beyond very small amounts which sometimes arose in the process of converting cash quotas into wool. Their defence was that they received the wool *per strictum pondus*. Even the Sussex collectors, who had been charged with attempting to defraud the receivers, disclaimed any responsibility for increment alleging that they had accepted the greater part of the wool in whole sacks from the Archbishop of Canterbury, the Bishop of Chichester, Earl Warrenne and other magnates for themselves and their tenants, and the remainder *per strictum pondus*. The *strictum pondus* was the statutory weight of 14 pounds to the stone and 26 stones to the sack whose use in the levy had been enjoined in Parliament. The requirement was probably written into the grant because of the trouble caused by the question of increment in earlier levies. The receivers were not charged with any increment except in Norfolk and Middlesex. In Middlesex the increment, amounting to nearly 4 stones in every sack, was alleged to have arisen because all the wool, although weighed *per strictum pondus* was delivered directly to the receivers by the taxpayers unsacked and in small particles. There is, however, some reason to suppose that this statement was an accounting fiction. The matter may be tested by reference to a case involving the receivers of Suffolk. The latter were summoned to the Chancery on 22 December 1341 to answer a charge that they

> refuse to make indentures for the wool received by them and delivered to them by single persons of the county by the half sack, stone or pounds, but only for a sack weighed by the beam, intending to appropriate to their own use the emolument arising from such receipt and to defraud the king thereof.[27]

Once this matter had been cleared up the Suffolk collectors were not charged any increment. Some wool must have been received in small amounts in most or all counties and one cannot accept that the Middlesex receivers were singled out for a hefty increment on these grounds alone. An alternative explanation is that not a single Middlesex tax-payer actually paid his contribution in wool. What may have happened is that all, apart from defaulters, paid their quotas in cash which was then used by the officials to buy wool in gross. A sack of wool, weighing 364 lb, could be bought more cheaply than 364 pounds of unpacked wool since the former included the weight of the canvas wrapper which was worth less than wool. The increment represented the difference in price. A similar explanation may be put forward for Norfolk where the receivers were charged with increment, at the rate of one stone per sack, on only part of their wool. In this county some taxpayers undoubtedly paid in wool and others in cash.

As in the case of the levy of July 1338 it was inevitable that many taxpayers, perhaps even a majority, should have no wool of their own and would have to buy in order to meet their obligation. It was for this reason that Parliament suspended all dealing in new wool until Michaelmas 1341, except for purchases by taxpayers who could buy at Nottingham prices. As in 1338 owners of wool may have been reluctant to sell at these prices, while merchants were keen to obtain wool in expectation of the freedom of export which had been promised from Michaelmas onwards. In August it was alleged that in Oxfordshire merchants were buying up wool for their own use, thereby impeding the collection for the king.[28] In some counties serjeants-at-arms were commissioned to search for and to confiscate wool bought by merchants prior to Michaelmas.

The government was concerned that as far as possible each county should meet its obligation by supplying wool, since large quantities had been promised to creditors and merchants. Until arrears became desperate there was no question of official commutation, with the exception of a number of villages in Kent which were allowed to pay cash instead of contributions totalling 199½ sacks 4¾ stones. They later complained that they were compelled to pay 9 marks per sack whereas the official price of Kent wool was 6 marks. The difference was apparently intended to compensate the king for loss of export duty. In some counties there was undoubtedly an unofficial or semi-official arrangement between taxpayers and collectors by which the latter received contributions in cash and used this to buy wool to fill the county's quota. The Middlesex collectors bought at least twenty sacks in Hampshire and Wiltshire for this purpose.[29] In Norfolk a similar arrangement between collectors and taxpayers was supplemented by another between taxpayers and a merchant. The latter was placed on a fully official basis by a contract between the merchant, John de Wesenham of Lynn, and the king.[30] An indenture, made shortly after Michaelmas, recited that Wesenham agreed to buy 600 sacks of Norfolk wool at $8\frac{1}{2}$ marks per sack, paying 1000 marks within fifteen days and the balance at Christmas and one month after that. Because of the shortage of wool in the county he could buy it anywhere in England, making his own arrangements to recover his outlay from Norfolk taxpayers still in arrears. A similar contract was made in July 1342 with John atte Fen of Lynn to buy 136 sacks still in arrears; the exports of both men can be identified in the customs accounts. Kent, which also experienced a shortage of wool, does not seem to have hit upon this method of solving its problem and the officials became actually embarrassed with arrears. However, it may not merely have been counties with a shortage of wool where taxpayers contributed cash instead of wool. In Hereford-shire the collectors' accounts record that the wool was received *de mercatoris de quibus empte fuerunt per homines ad hoc electos ex parte communitas eiusdem comitatus.*[31] It must be observed that if all the taxpayers of Herefordshire voluntarily gave cash so that wool might be bought from merchants it can only be because their own wool com-manded a higher market price than the official valuation of 12 marks, already the highest in England.

It was intended that the wool should be collected by 1 August and that any still unpaid at Michaelmas, when trade was thrown open to all, should be charged for at a treble rate. The government was con-cerned that this time-table should be maintained and as early as 1 July wrote to all the collectors accusing them of being lukewarm and negli-gent in their duty. From mid-July serjeants-at-arms were appointed to act against obstinate taxpayers. A fair amount of wool was collected by Michaelmas and some had already been exported. A Bedfordshire account[32] shows that in the vill of Eton 163 people had paid a total of 5 sacks 4 stones 1 lb by 1 August, leaving 71 people owing 16 stones $12\frac{1}{2}$ lb. By Michaelmas the entire Berkshire quota of $538\frac{1}{2}$ sacks had been paid except for 20 sacks 19 stones $12\frac{1}{2}$ lb, of which more than one third represented the contributions of the Bishop of Salisbury and the abbots of Westminster and St Albans. The remaining arrears were confined to 16 vills. The use of the word 'paid' in this context must be qualified, since there is no certainty that all the wool had yet been taken to the reception centres. It is clear, however, that it must all have been viewed by the collectors or sub-collectors, accepted as fit for the king and marked or sealed in some way. Its owners were thereby offi-cially absolved from being in arrears. All the Berkshire wool had been assigned to the Bardi, whose attorneys took delivery at Abingdon and Reading. They acknowledged receipt of a total of 397 sacks 8 cloves on 5 occasions between 4 September and 4 October 1341, 107 sacks on 3 days from 30 October to 6 December, 11 sacks 44 cloves on 20 February and 3 April 1342 and 21 sacks 3 cloves 2¾ lb on some other occasion.[33]

At first the government was slow to act against those in arrears, if only because many collectors failed to submit lists of defaulters. They did this at their own peril for if they did not account satisfactorily for all the wool at which the county was assessed they would, eventually, be charged personally for the missing amount. Because of the repeated disregard of instructions to send lists of arrears all collectors and receivers were ordered to come in person to the Exchequer in the first and second weeks in Lent, bringing with them all particulars relating to the levy. Where there had been genuine reasons for delay in delivering wool the government did not attempt to exact the treble penalty, although it still demanded its due. In March the collectors in Lancashire, Cumberland and the North Riding of Yorkshire, which had been harried by the Scots, were ordered to stop trying to levy treble the arrears in wool and to collect the original assessment in cash. In April the king wrote to the Exchequer instructing them to show leniency towards poor men in the matter of the treble penalty, but to extract it from rich men.[34]

Accounting for the wool was a slow process since collectors and receivers frequently made excuses to delay their appearance. Even when they did arrive the account was often delayed by their inability to produce satisfactory quittances for wool which they claimed to have delivered to creditors. By early June, however, a picture began to emerge of the amount of wool which had still to be collected and new arrangements were made for disposing of it. Contracts were made with merchants for the purchase of 860 sacks of arrears in various countries. The customs and other accounts prove that the merchants obtained most of their wool, but there is no certainty that any large part of it came directly from taxpayers since the contracts had conceded that the merchants might receive arrears in cash and use the money to buy wool. The 860 sacks mentioned above is by no means the total of arrears and among the counties not included is Kent, possibly the county which had caused most disappointment to those who had been assigned wool here. The county's original quota of 1274 sacks, or even the 938 sacks which remained after official commutation and exoneration, could not be raised out of local production. Norfolk, which was required to raise over twice as much wool, solved a similar problem by arranging to have wool bought outside the county. The Kent officials did not do this. When they first accounted at the Exchequer they had a *debet* of 264 sacks, none of which, they claimed, had yet been collected, although they had in their possession distresses equivalent to 60 sacks of wool, which they asked permission to sell. The arrears were reassigned and eventually the collectors produced quittances for virtually the entire amount. Although the quittances speak of the delivery of wool it is quite clear that the most of it was handed over in cash.

A small part of the wool which was not collected, something over 70 sacks, represented official government remissions in favour of various taxpayers. These consisted mostly of acts of charity towards impoverished priories and hospitals, but there were a few writs in favour of whole communities; Carlisle was allowed 9 sacks towards the cost of fortifying the city against the Scots; Southampton and Portsmouth, still recovering from sack by the French, were allowed $15\frac{1}{2}$ sacks; half a dozen villages in Suffolk, whose crops were destroyed by a tempest in June, were allowed $5\frac{1}{2}$ sacks. A few individuals were allowed to set their own tax contribution against money owed to them by the Crown, William fitz Waryn, banneret, for example, being allowed 5 sacks in Northamptonshire in lieu of wages.

Despite a certain amount of delay the levy of 1341 was the most successful of all the wool levies ordered by the government of Edward III or, for that matter, of any English king. Allowing for London, Northumberland, Newcastle, Cornwall, the Cinque Ports, the Devonshire stanneries, the official commutation of 200 sacks in Kent and the 70 sacks exonerated the original assessment of 20 323 sacks is reduced to 18 942 sacks. The addition of increment brings the total back, in round figures, to about 19 000 sacks, of which something like 18 350 sacks were raised within a little over twelve months of the beginning of the levy.[35] At least 117 sacks of wool collected were sold by the collectors and the proceeds given to some of those who had contributed to the loan of 1340. The sales represent acceptance of Parliament's demand that the 1340 loan should be repaid out of the proceeds of the present tax. After these sales there remained over 18 000 sacks for creditors and contractors who may be classified, very broadly, as English merchants, alien creditors and allies, English soldiers and persons associated with the royal family and household.

In making arrangements for the disposal of wool from the levy of 1341 the government was more or less obliged to make the first assignments to those foreign allies and creditors who had been promised wool from the abortive loan of 1340. However, the council reserved the right to withdraw assignments if it subsequently sold the wool to English merchants. In this event, of course, alternative arrangements would have to be made to guarantee the sums owed to the creditors.

This degree of flexibility was possible because in most cases the wool had not been sold to the assignees and at no time became their property. It was given only as a pawn or pledge and the price named in the letters of assignment was merely a rough guide to the value of the security. Wool was handed over by the county receivers to attorneys of the creditors and conveyed by the latter to the staple at Bruges. Both the expense and the risk of the transport were borne by the king. At Bruges the wool was sold by English merchants answerable both to the king and to the attorneys. The proceeds of the sale, up to the amount indicated in the letters of assignment, were handed over to the attorneys and any balance applied to the king's use. Any shortfall would be made up from another source.

Where the wool was held only in pledge an assignee could have no real objection to its being withdrawn, provided that he received adequate alternative security. Thus the Duke of Brabant surrendered his claim to the wool of Warwickshire and Nottinghamshire on the understanding that he would be paid in Bruges by the merchants who bought the wool.[36] John de Hanona, Lord of Beaumont, surrendered his claim to wool of Wiltshire on a similar basis. The Bardi, being a commercial organisation, wanted wool not merely as a pledge but to sell and declined to surrender their claim to the wool of Gloucestershire.[37] In this case it was the English group who had to withdraw, the government alleging that it had forgotten about the prior assignment to the Bardi. The importance of the possession of wool as a security is demonstrated by the treatment of the Duke of Guelders in October 1341. Because there was no wool to be had in Kent where he had been assigned 330 sacks to the value of 3960 marks he had to be provided with other security. Part of this was provided by an assignment of Buckinghamshire wool, now withdrawn from an English group, while the rest was secured on Lincolnshire wool. The Lincolnshire group was to pay the duke £10 from each of $124\frac{1}{2}$ sacks after they had been taken to Bruges and sold, but if his attorneys were not satisfied with the security which the merchants offered as a token of payment they were to take over 93 sacks of wool, rated at 20 marks, out of those sold to the merchants.[38] To such a state had the credit of the King of England been reduced after the fiasco of 1340. Edward's word had to be backed up by wool, unless it was bolstered by the private bonds of his own subjects. There is no doubt that attorneys took physical possession of wool assigned to their principal and speeded it on its way. Suffolk wool assigned to the Duke of Brabant was taken to Ipswich where the customs collectors had been ordered to pay the cost of freight. Since the collectors had no money and the sailors wanted cash in advance the attorneys paid the charges on the understanding that these would be refunded by the king.

Having assigned wool to creditors it is unlikely that the council would have withdrawn the assignments unless it saw some positive advantage to the Crown in alternative arrangements. It is not clear whether the hoped for advantages of the 22 contracts made with English merchants between June and August 1341 were regarded as being mainly organisational or as financial.[39] At first glance there seems to be no doubt about their financial attraction, but closer examination of all the facts leads one to question this. Unwin was impressed by what he calls the remarkably high prices recorded in the indentures which, on his reckoning, would afford the king a 'monopoly profit' of over 50 per cent.[40] This 'monopoly profit' was supposed to arise from prolonging the general embargo on the export of wool until all of the 20 000 sacks had been exported. The only exception was 1500 sacks which might be exported under special licence. However the king had made such a promise before and there is no reason whatsoever for believing that merchants could be induced to offer prices greatly in excess of those bid twelve months earlier on such a flimsy foundation. In fact Unwin misunderstood the indentures. While recognising that the prices included export subsidy and insurance, since losses at sea would be allowed for, he overlooked the fact that the king was committed to refunding the costs of delivery. More importantly each indenture stated that if the king and council sold wool at a lesser price than that now recorded the merchant contractor would be called upon to pay only such price or else he could withdraw from the bargain. All things considered it is clear that the indenture prices, like those mentioned in assignments to creditors, were nothing more than sums which the merchants would be charged if they failed to give a satisfactory account of any wool committed to their custody. The real price would not be known for some time. In this context it is interesting to note that in November 1341 the government wrote to the staple officials in Bruges saying that it had heard that some of the merchants who had bought the king's wool were insufficient to answer for the price.[41] If the officials had any reason to believe this they were to arrest the wool until the merchants provided security for payment. In the light of the new understanding of the indentures it is clear that government drew the merchants into the levy not because they offered higher prices than anyone else but because their expertise was needed in disposing of the wool. For the merchants one of the main attractions of the business was the prospect of recovering debts owed to them by the king at the rate of £2 for every sack handled.

Although the indentures make it quite clear that the merchants were to recover their expenses, no claims for allowances have survived with the exception of one account which covers only costs in England. This is explained by the fact that before the merchants were called to account the terms of the bargain had been renegotiated, in consequence of a dispute which had arisen about the price of the wool. On 18 April 1342 Chancery wrote to the Exchequer saying that because of the dispute the merchants were to account not in sterling but in the Flemish imitation of sterling, generally described as *monete Flandre vocate Englishe*, a coin which had a wide circulation in the Low Countries at this date. It was in this coin that the merchants had paid for the wool, delivering the money either directly to the king's creditors or to William de Kelleseye, a royal clerk who acted as the king's receiver in the Low Countries from 21 August 1341 to 14 February 1343. The rate of exchange notified to Kelleseye on 11 September 1341 was 5d *Englishe* for 4d sterling, in other words for every 20s sterling at which the wool had been priced the merchants were to render 25s *Englishe*. In the Chancery writ of 18 April 1342 it was stated that accounts were to be settled on the basis of 3d *Englishe* for 2d sterling. This represents a 20 per cent depreciation of the *Englishe*, although it was agreed that even if it depreciated further the merchants should account at the present rate. However the dispute had not been about the rate of exchange but about the currency of the marks in which wool was priced in the indentures made between the king and the merchants. There can be no doubt that the government had intended that these should be marks sterling, but the vital word had apparently been omitted. In the assignments of wool to alien creditors, or in at least some of them, valuations had been made in marks Flemish or *Englishe*, the number of marks per sack being correspondingly higher. However, this fact seems to have led to a claim by the English merchants that the prices fixed in their indentures were marks *Englishe*. The way in which the Exchequer acted upon the Chancery order is explained in a note preceding the enrolment of the merchants' accounts. It agreed that the marks mentioned in the indentures should be regarded as *Englishe* but that in return the merchants must renounce all their claims for expenses. This meant that a merchant who had agreed to pay fifteen marks paid that price in *Englishe*, exported free of subsidy and paid the expenses out of his profit.[42]

Because of the apparent fluctuation in the value of the *Englishe* it is impossible to determine exactly how much each merchant actually paid for his wool. The accounts were rendered in terms of *Englishe* and only the balance, if any, rendered into sterling at the rate of three to two. At this rate the London syndicate which bought the wool of Surrey and Middlesex would have paid £5 6s 8d sterling per sack, including export subsidy. The Nottingham price for the wool of these counties was 6 marks sterling, the same as that of Kent. In this period William de Cusance, *custos* of the wardrobe, sold Kent wool at Bruges for £5 19s sterling having incurred expenses of 13s 9d per sack. On the analogy of Cusance's account it is likely that all the merchants gained a certain advantage from increments in weight. Being a royal servant he was obliged to account for the increment while they did not. The increment was not large and in some instances may later have drawn upon merchants unfounded charges of smuggling. All the wool handled by the English merchants arrived safely at its destination, except for 11 sacks lost at sea and 21 sacks damaged by sea water.

The original distribution of wool between alien assignees and English merchants is no guide to the final division since the government frequently changed its mind, while many assignments were frustrated because of delays in collecting wool. It made little real difference to the king whether wool went to his creditors or to merchants, since the great majority of it had to be sold under the direction of his own agents at Bruges. For the record it may be mentioned that the collectors and receivers of the 1341 levy handed over 5649 sacks to English merchants and something like 8300 sacks to the attorneys of alien allies and creditors. Some of these attorneys were themselves English merchants, who must have received some consideration for their services, but others were aliens.

About 1392 sacks of wool from the 1341 levy were delivered to military leaders or to royal clerks in charge of war finance. This figure does not include the 700 sacks delivered to attorneys of Henry of Lancaster for his 'ransom'. The so-called 'ransom' was the money paid to secure the release of the earl from personal pledges he had given relating to the king's debts in the Low Countries. During the summer a considerable amount of wool was assigned to provide wages for the indentured companies which were being raised for the forthcoming expedition to Brittany. In September instructions were issued to all collectors south of the Trent that they were not to hand over any more wool on this account, since the king had postponed his passage.[43] However, Brittany was not the only front where military activity was funded directly by the wool levy. Ralph Neville and Henry Percy, defending the north against the Scots, received at least 130 sacks out of an assignment of 200 sacks. Sir William Stury, who remained in Flanders with a company of archers, received and exported 40 sacks. The customs accounts prove that most of the wool 'delivered' to soldiers was actually exported in their names. It is obvious that they can have had very little personal involvement in the business and most probably had arrangements with English merchants. Neville and Percy sold their wool to a syndicate of Yorkshiremen.

The last small group of assignees has already been described as royal family and household. Chief among them was William de Cusance, keeper of the Wardrobe until 25 November 1341 and Treasurer from 3 October 1341 to 12 April 1344, who was assigned 2500 sacks in various countries. Initially he obtained 1477 sacks, of which 1389 sacks were exported by his own agents, and later obtained cash in lieu of 84 sacks of arrears. He managed to get another 362 sacks out of the levy of 1342, all of which was taken in cash. The king's mother, Queen Isabella, obtained all of the 250 sacks assigned to her for arrears of dowry, while his wife, Queen Philipa, received at least 334 sacks. Finally mention may be made of John de Cologne, the royal armourer, as an example of the depths to which the king was reduced in meeting his personal expenses. John was assigned relatively small amounts of wool from the arrears of a number of widely scattered counties, which must have been exceedingly troublesome to collect. At least 16 sacks can be traced in the accounts, while 24 sacks were exported in his name after Michaelmas 1342.

Despite the promise made to Parliament that after Michaelmas 1341 all would be free to export wool there was no question of lifting the embargo when that date came. In his contract with the English merchants the king had pledged that until all of the 20 000 sacks from the 1341 levy had been dispatched the general ban would be maintained. He reserved only the right to license the export of 1500 sacks outside the levy. In August 1341, after licences for 200 sacks of this had been granted to John de Beaumont in lieu of wages and 80 sacks to someone else, licence for the remaining 1220 sacks was granted to Hugh de Ulseby, Henry Goldbeter and Walter Prest, who were to pay in cash a subsidy of 43s 4d beyond the ancient custom for every sack exported. These three were virtually commercial civil servants and Ulseby was mayor of the newly reorganised staple. In the spring of 1340 when the Flemings joined his grand alliance Edward had promised that the staple would be held in Flanders and soon afterwards Bruges became the appointed place. However, until August 1341 there seems to have been no real effort to enforce the staple policy. The new regulations were designed to give teeth to it. Unwin has interpreted the staple, still held at Bruges, as being a monopoly company of 43 English merchants who were involved in contracts with the king. In fact the staple was at first virtually a department of state, designed purely to safeguard the interests of the Crown. It had the dual function of arranging the sale of the king's wool and the prevention of smuggling. Clearly the staple officials in Bruges could do little about wool smuggled out of east coast creeks and taken to Brabant or elsewhere. Their duty was to prevent licensed exporters from exceeding the amount of wool specified in their warrant. Export to places elsewhere than Bruges was made prohibitively expensive by the imposition of a surcharge of 60s per sack beyond all other duties. The new staple ordinance laid down that henceforth customers were to make their cocket letters in the form of an indenture, retaining one half themselves and sending the other with the wool. Ships' masters were commanded to go directly to Bruges and there to unload their cargo only in the presence of a staple official who would check it against the indenture. To prevent fraud the two halves would eventually be compared in the Exchequer.

Until the end of November 1341 exports were restricted to wool from the levy and the 1500 sacks. Then, however, it was decided to allow the export of lambs' wool, 'peltwolle' and 'cobbewolle' for a subsidy of 26s 8d and of *lana mera*, or pure wool, for 40s per sack. A qualified permission for merchants to export continued until the following spring. On 5 May 1342 instructions were sent to the sheriffs to arrest all wool, particularly that from the coming shearing, until taxpayers had bought whatever they required for the second instalment of the 30 000 sacks.[44] There was no need for a new assessment, since each was required to give half as much wool as in the previous year.

The wool of 1341 had gone a long way towards meeting the king's obligations to his continental allies, but the Margrave of Juliers and the Duke of Guelders received 469 sacks and 777 sacks respectively out of this year's levy. Apart from the king's butler the other alien recipients were all Italian creditors, Paul de Monte Florum, a couple of merchants of Lucca, the Leopardi of Asti, the Acciaiuoli, the Portenari, the Peruzzi and, above all, the Bardi. William de Cusance received 360 sacks, English merchants 1117 sacks and some 1600 sacks went to earls and lesser military leaders in payment of wages for the expedition to Brittany. For reasons which will be discussed shortly it is impossible to ascertain just how much of the tax was taken in wool and how much in cash accounted for as wool. Although the burden was only half that of the previous year in some respects the general economic situation of the country seems to have been worse and this was a complicating factor.

Before the end of May contracts had been made with six syndicates of English merchants to buy a total of 1356 sacks of new wool, as well as some of the arrears of last year's levy.[45] In each case the price was made up of the Nottingham price for the county plus 40s, which allowed export free of subsidy, although the ancient subsidy remained to be paid at the ports. This was a firm price; there was no question of the king refunding expenses or lowering the price if sales were poor in the Low Countries. Both in the case of arrears and of new wool it was specified that the merchants might receive cash from the taxpayers and use this to buy wherever they wished. It was probably on account of this that a further clause was written into the indenture stipulating that the merchants should pay only for the assessed amount of wool and should not be charged for any increment in weight arising either in England or overseas. The fact that the merchants buying the wool of Shropshire, Derbyshire, Yorkshire and Westmorland 'received' every last pound of the wool of these counties indicates quite clearly that they made full use of the power of commutation.

Some of the assignments to leaders of the Brittany expedition expressly stated that cash might be taken in lieu of wool and it is likely that this was implicit in all the grants. Unfortunately the value which the government had put on the wool was the Nottingham price plus 40s per sack for export subsidy. This made it virtually impossible for the assignees and the county officials to agree on a simple cash transaction. The wool of Norfolk, on which three earls had assignments, was valued at £4 per sack and taxpayers would be unwilling to pay in cash more than this rate. In order to pay the wages of their retinue, which in the case of the Earl of Oxford numbered a banneret, 9 knights, 29 esquires and 30 mounted archers, the assignees had to get £6 for every sack. The only way out of the impasse, short of taking wool and selling it or exporting it themselves, was for the assignees to sell their claim to a merchant. The latter could receive the bare county price from the tax collectors, using the money to buy wool which would be exported free of subsidy in the name of the original assignee. In the normal order of things the merchants would demand a discount which, since it could come only from the assignee, would reduce the sum available for wages. Fortunately there was one factor which, whether intended or not, operated very strongly in favour of the assignees. Wool from the levy of 1342 could be exported without its owners having to deposit plate to secure the import of bullion. This must have been a strong inducement to merchants to deal in levy wool, regardless of any discount which they might obtain. The origins and significance of the bullion deposit will be explained shortly.

Despite assurances that the general ban on exports would be maintained until all 10 000 sacks from the 1342 levy had been dispatched, at the height of the season the government altered the very basis of its policy towards the wool trade. A merchant assembly was convened on 8 July 1342 and within a week it was decided to throw open the trade to all.[46] The two factors which counselled this may easily be guessed at. In the first place the king was due to receive this year a maximum of 10 000 sacks, leaving a large surplus which had to be exported. Secondly it is difficult to doubt that experience of the depressed prices of wool in the Low Countries had convinced the government of the futility of trying to make a profit out of a state monopoly of wool exports. It was better to leave the trade to merchants and to take a share of the profit in the form of high rates of duty. Only after an interval of five years was a further wool levy attempted, at a desperate moment when it looked as though the assault on Calais might fail because of a shortage of cash. Before examining the consequences of the policy change of 1342 it is necessary to review the events of the preceding five years from the standpoint of the merchants.

Once he became committed to war with France, Edward III's financial hopes centred in large measure on the community of English merchants. At first it may have been looked upon merely as the body whose consent was necessary for the imposition of a *maltote* on the export of wool. Soon, however, it came to play a much more important part in his plans. It is impossible now to determine from which direction came the suggestion of greater merchant involvement; whether from the government or from ambitious and enterprising individuals in the merchant community. Active cooperation between the king and the whole community lasted for a very brief period and for this, as already seen, each side must bear some blame. The king, however, found that he could not dispense with the services of the English merchants in one form or another, for alien financiers could not indefinitely support the heavy demands he was making of them. On their part the merchants either corporately or, more frequently, as individuals or small groups, found it difficult to resist the king's requests for assistance. The key to the king's control over them was his right to stop overseas trade at will. This right was in some respects more fundamental than the right to tax trade, which has received far greater attention at the hands of historians. At the beginning of the war it was generally admitted that the king could not increase customs duties without the consent of the merchant community. With the prospect of permanently enhanced rates of duty this consent came to be regarded as insufficient and the consent of the Commons assembled in Parliament came to be the necessary qualification. On the other hand there was no denial of the king's right to stop overseas trade, or to resume it, whenever he deemed it to be in his own or the country's interest. This meant that the merchants, either collectively or individually, had to accommodate the king so that he would either raise an embargo on trade or license exceptions to it. The right to stop trade was, of course, a doubled-edged weapon and one which the king could not wield for too long or too frequently. Stoppages were disliked by the merchants but they also harmed the Crown by depriving it of customs revenue.

The earliest of Edward's incursions into the wool trade, that which ended sadly at Dordrecht, not only involved a larger number of merchants than any of the later ones but may have engaged their cooperation with a certain degree of willingness, for they had not yet been made cynical by the king's repeated disregard of his obligations. Nevertheless table 14 suggests what appear to be regional differences in the response to the government's appeal for the involvement of the merchant community. Although the table is largely self-explanatory it is necessary to give a brief description of the sources upon which it is based, while a few other comments may be in order.

The only source listing all the wool received by the king's agent at Dordrecht and Middelburg is the enrolled account of William de la Pole and Reginald Conduit, which contains a summary of 317 indentures drawn up as it was delivered.[47] The parties to the indentures were those in whose names the wool had been exported, although they were not necessarily its owners. Additionally we have an enrolment of accounts rendered at the Exchequer by the purveyors of 1337. These usually distinguish between what is described as the purveyors' own wool and that which they had bought, the names of vendors sometimes being recorded and sometimes not. Furthermore, the accounts do not exhaust the wool handled by the purveyors. Some of them returned a nil account or rendered no account at all but nevertheless delivered wool at Dordrecht. In such cases wool cannot be divided into own or bought although most of it, perhaps all of it, clearly belongs to the former category. For convenience the labels 'own', 'bought' and 'indeterminate' have been used in table 14 to differentiate wool handled by the purveyors. In the same table the term 'free merchants' merely denotes those named in the indentures who were not purveyors. One further group of sources remains to be described – royal letters obligatory. The indentures made at Dordrecht did not constitute a promise of repayment; they were merely receipts against the delivery of wool, the matter of the outstanding balances not being touched upon. The first of many promises of repayment were made in May 1338 in the form of letters patent allowing remission of customs against future exports of wool. At this stage many of those named in the Dordrecht indentures, both purveyors and 'free merchants', took the opportunity to bring the real owners of the wool into the picture. Instead of personally accepting a letter for the oustanding value of wool which they had delivered at Dordrecht they caused separate letters to be made out to each person who had contributed to their consignment. This did not happen in every case for some merchants received a letter representing all their delivery, later having it cancelled in favour of individual letters. There were many opportunities for readjustment, for the letters issued at this stage proved to be worthless and had to be cancelled in favour of new ones. Many of the new issues were equally valueless.

The characteristic features of the south-western counties which fill the first five places in table 14 may be described as a lack of private participation and the neglect of purveyance until a very late stage in the operation. Consequently most of the 560 sacks out of an original target of 1900 sacks came out of the purveyors' own stocks. East of the previous region four London purveyors had a target of 4000 sacks to be raised in the city and in the counties of Middlesex, Surrey, Kent and Sussex. Although they returned a nil account they delivered a total of 384 sacks at Dordrecht, which must have come from their own stocks. Behind the 59 private London merchants who delivered 1367 sacks stood an indeterminate number of merchants and citizens, many of whom later received their own letters obligatory from the crown. In the eight counties to the north of London, divided into three commissions, the wool raised was distributed more evenly between private merchants, purveyors' own stocks and purveyance than in any other region. Norfolk and Suffolk formed a joint commission with a modest quota of 400 sacks, of which 249 sacks were sent to Dordrecht from Norfolk alone. Although three purveyors were active in the county not one of them seems to have supplied any of his own wool. Behind the 11 merchants of Norwich and Lynn who supplied 117 sacks stood others who afterwards received their own letters obligatory. A marked feature of nine west midland counties was the almost complete neglect of purveyance and the active cooperation of private merchants. Most purveyors failed to return accounts or else stated that they had bought no wool. Nevertheless eleven of them delivered a total of 910 sacks at Dordrecht, presumably most of this coming from their own stocks. Most of the 1263 sacks supplied by 45 merchants came from Shropshire and Warwickshire. In four east midland counties there appears to have been no great enthusiasm on the part of private merchants, only ten of them supplying 162 sacks. This seems to have called for great effort by the purveyors, sixteen of them contributing 914 sacks of their own wool and buying another 404 sacks. In the north, Cumberland and Westmorland provided nothing, despite a quota of 600 sacks, but elsewhere there seems to have been active cooperation among the

TABLE 14　*Regional participation in Dordrecht export*[a]

County	Target (sacks)	Contributions of free merchants		Purveyance				County total at[b] Dordrecht	Remained for February levy
		Merchants	Wool	Purveyors	Wool bought	Own stocks	Indeterminate		
Gloucs.	400	1	10	1	–	–	18	29	62
Somerset	1000	–	–	1	–	–	39	39	20
Dorset			–	1	18	–	–	18	61
Wilts.	500			1	–	196	–	196	2
Hants	4000	2	74	5	–	–	204	278	112
London	400	59	1367	4	–	–	384	1751	–
Herts./Essex	800	2	21	3	11	29	106	167	7
Beds.	1000	–	–	1	20	13	–	32	–
Bucks.				1	62	15	–	67	–
Cambs./Hunts.		4	118	1	62	12	–	191	21
Oxon.	400	1	12	2	47	149	–	207	85
Berks.		3	43	1	34	30	–	107	–
Norfolk/Suffolk	400	11	117	3	132	–	–	249	96
Worcs.	600	1	23	3	–	111	–	134	–
Warks.		8	330	4	–	–	394	724	–
Staffs.		1	11	1	–	–	30	41	7
Chester/Flint	200	2	45	1	–	–	24	68	–
Hereford		2	18	3	–	162	–	180	–
Salop	300	31	735	2	–	–	89	824	–
Northants.	1500	3	36	7	170	173	–	379	–
Leics.	1200	4	78	5	83	488	–	648	–
Notts./Derby	1200	3	48	4	151	252	–	451	–
Northumb.	600	24	161	5	13	58	–	232	–
Durham	500	10	265	3	–	232	–	497	–
Yorks.	6000	45	1062	5	37	757	–	1856	–
Lincs.	4500	22	750	5	644	605	–	1998	–
Totals		239	5324	73	1484	3270	1288	11 363	473

[a] Sources. Enrolled accounts of Pole and Conduit and county purveyors. E358/10.

[b] Because amounts are rounded to the nearest sack totals may differ from the sum of individual entries.

merchants. Lincolnshire seems, at first sight, to differ from the other northern counties in that nearly one third of its 1998 sacks came from purveyance. However, most of the people from whom wool was bought were undoubtedly wool merchants themselves, who may well have had private arrangements with the purveyors for the sharing of profits. Most of them received allowances in their own right at the first issue of Dordrecht bonds in 1338. It might be dangerous, therefore, to make a rigid distinction between them and the 22 'private' merchants who were mentioned in the original Dordrecht indentures. Moreover the Lincolnshire evidence shows that even wool definitely stated to be the purveyors' own sometimes belonged to other people. Overall the northern region delivered at Dordrecht a total of 4584 sacks out of a target of 11 600. This degree of success undoubtedly reflects the enthusiasm of the northern merchants for the enterprise.

Since the break-down of the contract has already been described the next point to be considered is the effect which this had upon the fortunes of the merchant community. In their original agreement Edward had undertaken to prevent the export of wool until all of the 30 000 sacks subject to the contract had been sold. While his agents were disposing of the wool taken at Dordrecht he had little incentive to raise the ban and for Englishmen the prohibition remained in force until the summer of 1338. The only exceptions were 28 sacks sent to Gascony during the winter, 200 sacks exported by Geoffrey le Scrope in April 1338 and a number of fells exported in the spring. Retention of the ban was also desirable in view of the fact that the king was trying to collect the 20 000 sacks which he still regarded as his due and which had been confirmed to him by the February parliament. However, the dispute with the merchants could not be allowed to continue indefinitely since it was depriving the king of much-needed customs revenue. In December 1337 and in the following March all the merchants named in the purveyance commissions of the previous summer were summoned to Westminster. The later assembly presumably considered the question of repayment for the wool taken at Dordrecht and by the beginning of May a formula had been worked out. This had the unfortunate side-effect of giving recognition to an increase in the rate of subsidy to 33s 4d, which with the ancient custom made a total duty of 40s. The king was given the choice either of providing letters obligatory promising payment in cash at the Exchequer, half at Easter 1339 and half the following Easter or, alternatively, of allowing the export of wool free of customs duty. The latter was the method of payment adopted in the overwhelming majority of cases and letters patent began to be made out in May. It was agreed that

English merchants might export wool from 1 August 1338 and that between then and Michaelmas they might use their bonds to secure remission of half the duty. From Michaelmas they were to be relieved of all duty until the king's debt to each man was extinguished.

The choice of 1 August for the lifting of the ban on export was presumably determined by the hope that by then all of the king's 20 000 sacks would have been collected and dispatched. As already seen this hope was frustrated and at the end of July a Great Council authorised the levy of 17 500 sacks according to the rate of one fifteenth. On 1 August commissions were issued for its collection, which contained the provision that no-one might buy, sell or export wool until the king was served. Endorsement of this action was probably demanded of the merchant assembly which met on 3 August. Unlike the previous two assemblies this one was not composed solely of the 1337 purveyors, for the writs had commanded the election of four merchants to represent the community in each county. Despite the collection of wool for the king the government did not attempt to maintain a strict ban on exports. Instead it used the formal prohibition to frustrate the promise to settle the Dordrecht debt by means of customs allowances. Merchants were licensed to export on condition that they paid duty in cash and between late July and Michaelmas 1338 about 2675 sacks of wool and fells were dispatched, mainly from Hull and Newcastle. In the same period almost 1000 sacks were exported free of subsidy in the name of English magnates who had gone abroad with the king. The allowance was intended to meet part of their claims for wages. Some of the wool probably came from their own estates, but some was bought in England and some may have been exported under this cover by merchants.

The ban on the export of hides and fells was lifted in October 1338 but that on wool remained in force theoretically until 20 March 1339. On that date the order was given that anyone might export provided that he took his wool to the staple which had been established at Antwerp the previous August. In fact the ban had not been strictly enforced and a great deal of wool had been exported under licence. As a general rule licences were granted only to merchants who were willing to advance money in foreign parts. Those who did this not only obtained a licence but in many cases were able to strike a bargain which actually spared them payment of part of the subsidy. The licences show that an individual might easily secure remission of one third or more of the full rate of duty. Between Michaelmas 1338 and Michaelmas 1339 denizen merchants exported roughly 18 000 sacks of wool and fells, a considerable proportion of this going before 20 March. Most of the rest of the denizen wool exported this year belonged to the Crown, but again some hundreds of sacks were dispatched duty free by magnates. After March English merchants were able, for a short time at least, to utilise their Dordrecht bonds to obtain some relief from duty. In January 1339 the customs of all ports except London had been assigned to William de la Pole in repayment of sums he had personally advanced to the king. He agreed, however, that Dordrecht bondholders should be allowed 20s on each sack they exported until Michaelmas 1339 and the full 40s thereafter.

In the summer of 1339 the freedom of export which English merchants had enjoyed since the spring began to be curtailed. On 6 August the customs collectors of London were ordered not to let any wool go to Flanders since French ships were gathering in the estuary of the Zwin. On 2 September a total ban was imposed on exports until the sea was cleared of pirates since, it was alleged, a number of ships sailing without escort had been lost to the enemy. Such warnings were repeated at intervals throughout the winter. It would be easier to accept such statements at their face value were it not for the exemptions granted to the English and alien merchants who were supporting the king with loans. Between Michaelmas 1339 and 6 March 1340, for example, aliens exported from London 1911 sacks compared with only 285 sacks sent by denizens. On 16 February, however, even licensed export was brought to a halt with the order that all wool then on board ship was to be unloaded and no more was to be exported until the king's return to England, which would be very soon. Shortly after his return Edward made known the conditions under which exports might be resumed. On 6 March writs were sent to all ports announcing that old wool might be exported until Whitsun. Merchants were advised to be expeditious in their business since from that feast no further export would be allowed until all wool granted to the king had been dispatched. No grant had, as yet, formally been made. As a condition of export, merchants were required to take their wool to Bruges where they were to make the king a gift of 40s per sack within one month of delivery. While all merchants were to pay this gift those who held Dordrecht bonds might use them to obtain relief from the payment of the 40s due at English ports. As a method of raising ready cash the gift was a total failure since all merchants who exported during the short period during which it was charged were able to get it set against sums owed to them. It did, however, help to reduce the king's indebtedness by a fractional amount. It must also have served to increase the resolve of Parliament to bring the customs under its own control.

This it managed to do although, as already seen, it was obliged to confirm that the duty should stand at 40s for a limited period.

There are two slightly different versions of the origin of the additional duty of 40s, although each represents it as a 'gift' of the merchants. The writs of 6 March state that it was offered by the merchants in a petition requesting the resumption of exports. Further writs of 20 March say that it was given in the last 'parliament' before the king's return. This presumably means the assembly of merchants which met simultaneously with Parliament on 20 January 1340. This assembly, to which 44 merchants were called by personal writs, was the first to have been summoned formally since August 1338. Although Unwin states that an assembly met in December 1338 after having been thrice postponed, this was in reality a series of meetings of the king's council to which different groups of merchants were called in turn. From January 1340, however, the merchants assembled with growing frequency. The next meeting, in March, was called at the explicit request of the Commons. Presumably it thought that if the merchants were to deliberate together it would be better for them to do so when Parliament itself was also in session. Personal writs of summons were sent to 154 merchants for the March assembly and the same group was called again in the following May. For an assembly in August writs were sent to the sheriffs to secure the election of 272 merchants from the counties and boroughs, the largest number ever summoned. A fifth meeting in September 1340 is treated by Unwin as a merchant assembly, although it was probably a somewhat different type of gathering.

The reduction in the rate of customs duty which had been achieved by the Easter parliament became effective on 8 May 1340, but the concomitant freedom of trade was short lived. It was effectively brought to an end by the July wool grant, for although there was no formal ban on export, Parliament had decreed that there should be no buying and selling of wool. After this all wool owned by Englishmen was liable to be taken by the king's collectors. Aliens were allowed to own and to export only wool bought before 14 July, the date of the parliamentary grant. From the beginning of August their exports were suspended while enquiries were made to ensure that they had not bought wool since that date. Rightly or wrongly the government believed that there was massive collusion between Englishmen and aliens in this matter. The total export by denizens and aliens between 8 May and Michaelmas was something less than 5000 sacks, most of it probably dispatched before the end of July.

The precise total of wool exported between Michaelmas 1339 and

Michaelmas 1340 is impossible to determine since the terminal dates of some accounts do not accord precisely with the Exchequer year. Moreover the division between aliens and denizens is complicated by the fact that for part of the time Flemings were treated like denizens in regard to taxation. The combined legal exports of denizens and aliens probably did not exceed 20 000 sacks, but during this period the government became increasingly concerned about smuggling. In November 1339 it was alleged that over 1000 sacks had been smuggled through Boston, while in the same month the London customers were ordered to make a new cocket seal, since wool was being exported under forged seals.[48] The main feature of the legal trade throughout 1339 and 1340 was the continuing dominance of northern merchants. The basis of their success was their ability and willingness to advance large amounts of cash, mostly paid into the wardrobe overseas. These loans were not made individually but out of pooled resources. A syndicate of six Newcastle men lent £4000, which was to be repaid out of the customs of Newcastle and Hartlepool. In June 1340, when they had recovered £2100 from this source, they advanced a further 2000 marks on the security of the ninth of the north riding.[49] Several syndicates of Yorkshire merchants advanced even larger sums and in September 1339 they gained the concession that York should become a customs port.[50]

The parliamentary wool loan of 1340 had the effect of concentrating the trade even more narrowly into the hands of the limited number of merchants who were able and willing to meet the king's demands for cash. Parliament had been promised that from Michaelmas 1340 export would be allowed to all who paid the 40s duty. However, as already described, the government maintained the ban on export throughout the winter as it vainly attempted to collect the loan. Despite the collection a not insubstantial amount of wool was exported under licence, although most of this cannot now be distinguished from that dispatched after March 1341, when the export of poor wools was permitted. The decision to allow good wool to be exported from the beginning of April produced few takers and as far as ordinary merchants were concerned the whole of 1340–1 was a wasted year. However, even for merchants who were willing to cooperate with the Crown the year was far from satisfactory. Of the dozen syndicates of English merchants who had contracted to buy some 9000 sacks from the loan of 1340 only four received any wool, and that a meagre total of 88 sacks. While waiting to obtain the official wool some of them had been authorised to buy wool themselves and export it, but this was not without its own hazards. Such wool was frequently arrested by the official collectors of counties through which it passed en route to a port and was only released on production of yet another royal warrant.

The fiasco of the 1340 loan may explain why only one third of the 39 contracting merchants are to be found among the 42 merchants who agreed to participate in the first 22 contracts made for the levy of 1341. The contracts of 1340 had been distributed fairly evenly among merchants from different regions of England, but those of 1341 were heavily weighted towards Yorkshiremen. One York merchant, Henry Goldbeter, figured in no fewer than five contracts. Some of the merchants were subsequently charged with having exported free of duty a greater amount of wool than they had received from the royal collectors. A rough memorandum outlining charges against seven syndicates has an overall excess of $113\frac{1}{2}$ sacks 12 stones (wrongly added up to $123\frac{1}{2}$ sacks 12 stones.[51] In fact in only one instance was there a really serious discrepancy; William Shirburne and Robert Bayhous of York received 281 sacks 9 stones and exported $348\frac{1}{2}$ sacks 7 stones. In other cases comparatively slight excesses may easily have been caused by increments arising from the fact that the customs collectors weighed more accurately than the local officials.

Freedom to export non-royal wool between November 1341 and May 1342 was restricted to those holding a licence, which could be obtained only by paying the subsidy in advance at the Exchequer. This provision was not necessarily designed to speed the flow of cash into the Exchequer, which was probably willing to accept its own bonds in payment, Dordrecht bonds always excepted. It is as likely that it was an attempt to avoid difficulties imposed on exporters by a shortage of ready cash, which was aggravated by enforcement of the very legislation designed to end it. For some years there may have been a net outflow of silver from England; in the opening phases of the war a trickle became a flood. The amount of silver physically exported in connection with diplomatic and military manoeuvres from 1336 onwards cannot be measured but it was less significant than the losses caused by the virtual stoppage of wool exports. It is quite likely that earnings from these no longer sufficed to pay for the country's imports. In this context it must be understood that the Dordrecht wool and all the wool subsequently exported by the king or delivered by him to creditors, allies or merchants made very little contribution to the balance of payments since most of the proceeds were expended abroad. In addition wool of non-royal origin was also exported by magnates to meet their expenses while abroad.

By 1339 Parliament was fearful that a shortage of silver money might bring internal trade to a halt and requested legislation that all exporting wool be required to import silver bullion to the value of at least 40s per sack. In 1340 it was enacted that within three months of export all Englishmen and 'other residents' should deliver to the king's exchanges plate to the value of two marks per sack.[52] They were required to deposit plate of equal value with the customs collectors prior to export, which would be restored to them on the production of a certificate that bullion had been delivered to the exchanges. The government seems to have valued the legislation more as a means of securing obedience to staple regulations than as providing for the import of bullion. In June 1341 and again in September it ordered all customers to enforce the law strictly, and in November wrote to them in the strongest possible tems complaining about the neglect of this duty, which had resulted in smuggling and the delivery of wool to places other than Bruges.

When the government decided to allow the export of poor wools in November 1341 the bullion regulations became even more restrictive. Before export an ordinary merchant would have to find in cash or plate 6s 8d for ancient custom, 26s 8d or 40s for subsidy and 26s 8d for bullion security, an utterly impossible requirement. Rather than remove the export deposit the government probably decided to allow Exchequer bonds, other than Dordrecht bonds, to be taken in payment of subsidy, but required that they be paid directly into the Exchequer where they could be authenticated and cancelled. This widened the trade hardly at all, for the simple reason that most of the wool merchants who held such bonds were already heavily committed to exporting the king's wool which paid no subsidy. Everybody paid ancient custom since this had been assigned to the Hanseatics and no exceptions were allowed.

The only way in which trade might be widened further, short of removing the export deposit, was by deferring payment of subsidy; this was done by writs sent to the ports in February and March 1342. Merchants were to be allowed to export now and to pay the subsidy within one month of Easter (8 April).[53] When Easter came the government may have decided to allow those owing for 6 sacks or less to pay in bonds at the ports, but those who wished to give bonds for a larger amount were required to come in person to the Exchequer.[54] The obligation to give security in the form of plate does not seem to have been removed and would appear to have been more important than ever since the subsidy had not yet been paid. In consequence of the new regulation over 2000 sacks were exported between February and the beginning of the new season, when exports were once more stopped.

By the terms of the settlement made in the merchant assembly which met on 8 July 1342 the export trade was to be thrown open to all until midsummer 1343 on payment of a subsidy of 40s beyond the ancient and new customs.[55] There was also to be complete freedom of trade within the country, with the Nottingham scale of prices providing a floor to protect the producer. Finally anyone detected smuggling was to be expelled from the community of merchants. The agreement had virtually no effect on the level of exports, for the simple reason that merchants did not have the liquidity to pay duties of 46s 8d and bullion security of 26s 8d per sack.[56] Not until the government relaxed the demand for security in late December did exports improve. In all ports outside London merchants not exempted from payment of subsidy exported only 589 sacks of wool and 17 000 fells between 15 July 1342 and January 1343, but 2314 sacks and 39 000 fells from January to July 1343.[57] Londoners exported 1058 sacks of wool and 32 542 fells between 15 July 1342 and 20 July 1343. In the winter of 1342–3 silver coin was desperately short in England and it was alleged that the debased foreign imitations of sterling were imported to alleviate the shortage.[58] This naturally encouraged the exportation of any remaining good sterling. The continuing shortage of coin was probably a factor in the major reorganisation of the wool trade which occurred in the summer of 1343, although the dissatisfaction which must undoubtedly have been generated in the merchant community during recent years also demanded a settlement. However, before examining this development it seems worthwhile to complete the picture of the early war years by examining the fortunes of alien wool exporters in that period.

At the beginning of the war the principal Italian contingents in England were made up of merchants of Florence and Lucca. For some time relations between England and Genoa had been strained, apparently because of the plunder of a Genoese vessel by Hugh Despenser while in command of ships of Edward II. In 1336 Edward III agreed to allow the Genoese 8000 marks out of the customs on their merchandise and granted a safe conduct for their ships to come to England. The reconciliation did not take place and once fighting began Genoa provided naval assistance to the French.

The king expected all the Italians enjoying his protection in England to make a contribution to his war finances and in June 1337 ordered the arrest of all except the Bardi and Peruzzi. Subsequently we find a number of them agreeing to make loans, which ranged from 40 marks to 200 marks for individuals and small groups, with correspondingly larger sums for important companies. The Acciaiuoli promised 1000 marks, the Albertini 500 marks and the Buonaccorsi 300 marks. Two years later all the Italians in London were again summoned before the council and requested to give assistance. After being given time to consider they refused to lend the £1000 which was demanded of them and declined to apportion the amount between themselves. Thereupon the officials of London were instructed to assess each individual and company according to their means and to levy the amounts on their goods. With this some of the merchants gave way, but representatives of the Acciaiuoli and the Albertini and three private merchants carried off wool and other goods to Bristol, in a vain attempt to get them out of the country. Eighteen months later it was complained that little or nothing of this money had yet been paid.[59]

Although there was a general ban on the export of wool throughout 1337, by that summer the government had decided that wool might be sent to Italy since this would not interfere with the monopoly the king was preparing for himself in northern Europe. Licences were granted, of course, only to those who were willing to assist the king with loans. In July 1337 the Acciaiuoli, the Portinari and two other Florentines were granted permission to ship 420 sacks in two Genoese galleys which were expected at Southampton. The Bardi had been issued with export licences as early as the previous January, but had not yet dispatched any wool. The expected galleys failed to arrive and the stocks of Italian wool became an obvious prey for the English purveyors commissioned in July 1337. Letters were issued for the protection of wool and for the restoration of that already taken, including some owned by a couple of merchants of Asti. During the winter the Italians managed to bring Spanish ships to Southampton and by 10 January 1338 a total of 1395 sacks had been dispatched from that port.[60]

The king was unwilling that the Bardi and Peruzzi should export all their stocks of wool to Italy and in the spring of 1338 demanded that the company lend him 2000 sacks for his expedition to Brabant. The greater part of this amount was actually handed over, 882 sacks being sent from Hull, 530 sacks from Boston and 451 sacks from London. The main obstacle to export to Italy, apart from the king's will, was a scarcity of shipping. The Genoese had allied with France and the Venetians had suspended the northern galleys because of the war in the narrow seas. There remained only Spanish and Gascon ships, in which wool was shipped to Bordeaux and from there taken overland to the Mediterranean. Even in Gascony wool was not safe from the king and a quantity was seized from the Peruzzi by royal officials. Despite these difficulties the Bardi managed to ship a further 515 sacks from Southampton in the spring and summer of 1338, while the Peruzzi sent no less than 1010 sacks. About November 1338 the Peruzzi also sent 70 sacks from Bristol. This was not wool diverted from Southampton because of the French raid; permission to export it had been given in August. In the spring of 1339 the two companies arranged for Spanish ships to come to Bristol to collect wool, but the vessels did not arrive until August. They were further delayed when the attorney of William de la Pole, to whom the customs had been assigned, refused to affix his half of the cocket seal, thereby preventing the wool from leaving free of duty. The Bristol customers were then ordered to clear the cargo merely with their own half of the seal, a most irregular procedure. Finally, in October, the Bardi managed to get away 700 sacks and the Peruzzi 1354 sacks.[61]

Because of the shortage of southern European shipping the Bardi and Peruzzi sent wool to the Low Countries whenever such exports were not forbidden. Before their collapse they exported at least 7388 sacks free in whole or in part of duty. They continued to trade privately in wool, including among their suppliers the Archbishop of York. However, part of their export was made up of wool handed over in repayment of royal debts. They were first promised wool in January 1338, when the government began to suspect that far more than 10 000 sacks had been dispatched to Dordrecht. The Bishop of Lincoln was then ordered to deliver 1500 sacks to each company. After the breakdown of the contract with the English merchants the Bardi received $3105\frac{3}{4}$ sacks of the Dordrecht wool, the price of which was set against the king's debt. The Peruzzi took $604\frac{1}{2}$ sacks, but paid for it in cash. As well as Dordrecht wool, both companies received on the continent a small part of the wool which was exported for the king during 1338. The Bardi had 282 sacks and the Peruzzi 449 sacks, all of which were set against the king's debts.[62]

In England the Bardi and Peruzzi were jointly assigned 5000 sacks out of the royal levy of July 1338, but later agreed to relinquish 2000 sacks in consideration of a twelve month monopoly of export by sea to Italy and an assignment of the customs at London. By virtue of this agreement they restored 1077 sacks out of 3359 sacks which were delivered to them. The Bardi was assigned a further 1000 sacks and received this wool at Boston, but subsequently restored all but 47 sacks to the king's agents on the continent. Neither company received any wool from the abortive levy of 1340: on the contrary they were required to lend their own wool to meet the claims of disappointed creditors. Out of the proceeds of the 1341 wool tax the companies jointly received 1198 sacks from Gloucestershire and Berkshire. The following year the Bardi received slightly more than 3000 sacks, while the Peruzzi 'received' 230 sacks out of 1342 levy, but all of this went to their own creditors, 60 sacks to the Acciaiuoli and 170 sacks to Bernard de Syster, papal nuncio.[63] The great wool seizures of Edward III provided no salvation for the Bardi and Peruzzi since the proceeds had to be shared between too many of the king's creditors.

As the Bardi and Peruzzi found it increasingly difficult to meet the king's need for money during the late 1330s he turned more and more to other companies for loans. Some of these already had business interests in England, while others, such as the Venetians, remained on the periphery even after lending money. The Portinari had been one of the main recipients of Dordrecht wool, but purely as a commercial transaction, and the company did not begin to lend money on a large scale until after the king's arrival in Brabant. Some of their advances, which reached a total of about £20 000, were repaid by allowances of customs and by assignments of wool. In 1339 and 1340 they were excused duty on 691 sacks bought privately, 39 sacks being sent to Italy and the rest to the Low Countries. In 1341 they were given royal wool in Bruges but did not get any in England until the levy of 1342, when they received 335 sacks of Essex wool. The Portinari's associate company, the Buonaccorsi, had also bought wool at Dordrecht and later lent £1950 on the continent. This was repaid by the duty-free export of 650 sacks of wool which left London between October 1339 and January 1340, despite the opposition of the Bardi and Peruzzi who had an assignment of the customs of that port. The Buonaccorsi failed in 1342, the first of the major companies to go under in the wave of bankruptcies which shook Florence in that decade.[64]

Another Florentine company which endeavoured to maintain its stake in English trade until it too went bankrupt was the Acciaiuoli. In July 1341 the company agreed to contribute to the ransom of Henry of Lancaster who was a hostage for the debts incurred by the king during his continental campaign. To provide the necessary funds they were licensed to avoid the general ban on export by sending 180 sacks, later increased to 300 sacks, from Southampton to Flanders. They were required to pay duty at the port and by March 1342 had exported 281 sacks. On 6 February 1342 they agreed to advance another £1000 on the continent, to be repaid by the export of 500 sacks duty free. The wool might be sent to any parts friendly to the king and 184 sacks were consigned from Bristol to Italy in a Majorcan ship. By July 1343 they had dispatched a further 339 sacks of duty-free wool from London. The fact that the total exceeds 500 sacks is perhaps to be explained by their receipt of 60 sacks of royal wool originally assigned to the Peruzzi.[65]

As well as the major companies some smaller groups of Florentines were tempted to advance money in the hope of gaining an opening into the now closely-regulated wool trade. These plans did not always work out. In the summer of 1341, for example, a consortium led by James Siralbys agreed to pay certain monies on the king's behalf and to recover the debt by the duty-free export of $787\frac{1}{2}$ sacks of wool to Catalonia or Majorca in 2 Catalan ships. In October this wool was prevented from leaving Bristol and Southampton as planned, since the merchants had not yet accounted with the king. The following spring they were authorised to send 120 sacks from London and the customs accounts duly record the export of $98\frac{1}{2}$ sacks in repayment of money advanced at Bordeaux.[66]

After the Florentines the most active Italian community in England in the early 1340s was that of Lucca. Several groups made loans and were partially repaid by duty-free export, small grants of wool and finally, in 1342, by an assignment of half of the export subsidy. Although the ancient custom had frequently been assigned, the subsidy had previously been reserved for the king's own use. To complete the picture of the main groups of Italians involved in the wool trade at this time mention must be made of the Leopardi of Asti. By the summer of 1340 the king was heavily indebted to the company, who demanded to be repaid in wool. It was agreed that they should receive 2006 sacks from the loan authorised by Parliament and another 500 sacks which the Bardi and Peruzzi were to lend to the king from their own stocks. Although the Leopardi received all or most of the latter amount they obtained only about 136 sacks from other sources at the king's disposal. Nevertheless they managed to export 600 sacks from Southampton before 24 February 1341, another 57 sacks from that port in the following September and at least 548 sacks from London before Michaelmas 1341. The 143 sacks which they exported duty-free from London after Michaelmas 1342 was probably the wool which they received from the levies of Sussex and Somerset.[67]

Although the king was willing to let wool go to Italy by the summer of 1337 he refused to countenance any breach of his monopoly of sales in northern Europe until the following spring. The relaxation which then took place was probably a political concession to his ally, the Duke of Brabant. At the beginning of the war the duke had requested that a wool staple be appointed in Antwerp. This was not conceded, probably because Edward yet hoped to woo Flanders to his cause. Antwerp was not proclaimed to be the staple until August 1338. By the spring of 1337 the cloth workers of Brabant were probably beginning to feel the effects of a shortage of wool and a plan was devised to meet their needs without allowing wool to fall into the hands of the Flemings. In May instructions were given to issue letters of protection to Brabantine merchants to buy wool in England. Each cloth-manufacturing town was to be allowed sufficient wool to employ its looms for a year and a day. The merchants were to bring certificates from the échevins stating the number of artisans in each town and were to swear that they would not export in excess of their quotas.[68]

The plan outlined above was itself a direct threat to Edward's monopoly. Since he was concerned that the Flemings should not obtain wool his own sales would be aimed at the Brabant market. Whether or not the Brabant merchants actually received letters of protection they were not allowed to export wool. They did, however, accumulate a considerable stock, some of which was seized by the officials commissioned to raise the loan of February 1338. When the Duke of Brabant committed himself to the king's cause instructions were given for the release of the wool and Brabant cloth was allowed to enter the country. In March the Brabantine merchants were authorised to ship 2200 sacks, permission subsequently being given for an additional 360 sacks. This seems all to have been wool belonging to them before the date of the commissions for the February levy. After several changes of plan the wool was still aboard ships of Holland and Zeeland at Ipswich at the beginning of May. When the sailors threatened to take the cargo to their own country the admiral was ordered to ensure that they delivered it to Brabant.[69]

While the king was in Antwerp in 1338 he was prepared to favour the merchants of Brabant in the matter of trade with England. He confirmed a charter of privileges granted to Louvain in 1331 and issued licences to all the principal towns allowing them to sell their cloth and to buy wool in England. However, the Duke of Brabant proved a lukewarm ally and in consequence the duchy could not press too strongly for special treatment, particularly as Flanders inclined slowly towards the English cause. On the other hand the king probably had no wish to alienate the duke by withdrawing his concessions and the Brabanters had scant cause to complain about their treatment in England. In 1339 some, although apparently not all, were given the privilege of paying denizen rates of subsidy on exported wool. In November 1340 all of them requested that they be relieved of the new custom on wool and cloth, payable under the terms of the 1303 charter. Although a final decision was deferred until the spring it was agreed that in the meantime payment should be postponed. In the event the decision was favourable to the merchants and they did not pay the custom on 467 sacks exported from London. Any allowances made in other ports are less easy to detect. A final example of the king's indulgence was the treatment of Brabant merchants during the early days of the loan of 1340. A number of them refused to swear that wool in their possession had been bought before 20 July, the date when private trade was to stop. Nevertheless, because the king wished to favour them it was agreed that they might export it. Apart from these collective privileges individual merchants of Brabant, like most of the groups from whom the king borrowed money, received licences for the export of wool free of duty.[70]

The request of the merchants of Brabant to be excused the new custom was, in effect, a claim for parity of treatment with the Flemings who had been granted the privilege of trading as denizens between 29 March 1340 and 27 May 1341. Under this warrant Flemish merchants exported 583 sacks of wool from London. The concession was one of a number given to Flanders in return for the treaty of alliance into which it entered at the beginning of 1340. Another was the transfer of the staple from Antwerp to Bruges. Although there seems to have been little attempt to enforce the staple until the autumn of 1341 Bruges was probably the main destination of wool exported from England from 1340 onwards. This was by no means the first wool to reach Flanders and the real shortage had long since ended. During the course of 1338 the Flemish towns, led by James van Artevelde and the burghers of Ghent, had renounced the authority of their count and declared themselves neutral in the struggle between England and France. From that time the embargo on the export of wool to Flanders had been relaxed.

The last group of aliens of whom mention must be made are the merchants of the German Hanse. From the outbreak of the war they were regularly issued with letters of protection to trade in England but, like everyone else, they were strictly forbidden to export wool. Not until the spring of 1338 were they licensed to export 1552 sarplers which had been theirs before the announcement of the February levy. In their case the contribution which the king expected towards his cause was financial. As a condition of export they were required to advance money to the king's agents on the continent. Between August 1338 and April 1339, despite the formal continuation of the ban on export, German merchants were licensed to dispatch 1700 sacks, the duty having been paid in advance overseas. They continued to send similar quantities in later embargoes. The greater part of this wool was acquired in private trade; comparatively little came from the royal wool levies, although they were promised more than they received. It must be acknowledged, however, that their trade was frequently conducted under royal licence at times when private trade was forbidden and their stocks were protected from purveyance. When the German loans became so large that they could no longer be repaid out of the duty-free export of their own wool they received a general assignment of the ancient custom.

Most of the advances received from German merchants came from syndicates which probably existed only for the purpose of making a loan. The group received a collective export licence to recover its investment but it is unlikely that it traded as an entity within England. In consequence we find that a particular individual appears now in one syndicate and later in an entirely different group. In the various syndicates may be found many of the leading wool exporting families of the early fourteenth century; the Clippings, Revels and Spicenayls who dominated the later years of Edward I and the early years of his son, the Sudermanns and Mudepennyngs who later came to the fore and the second rank families who may be found in both periods. Although it is impossible to determine whether the absolute volume of German wool exports in war-time was larger or smaller than that of the early 1330s there can be little doubt that the Hanseatic share of non-royal trade was proportionately much larger than it had been in the earlier period. Such was the advantage that they derived from their ability to raise loans for the king.

6

Quest for a staple policy

Throughout the winter and spring of 1342–3 the wool trade was in a state of crisis, caused partly by political and partly by monetary factors. Total exports were at a lower ebb than at any time since the beginning of the war. It was inevitable that the matter should be debated in the parliament which was summoned for 26 April 1343 and it was probably for this reason that the government caused an assembly of merchants to come together one day earlier. The writs for the latter body were identical with those sent out in June 1342. The petitions of the merchants were copied onto the dorse of the parliament roll, although presumably they had been presented first in their own assembly.[1] They began by stating that it would be to the greatest profit of the king and his subjects if the staple was held in England, since this not only would enhance the price of wool but would also inhibit the entry of debased coin into the country. Their objection to the present staple in Bruges was twofold. In the first place they protested that the towns of Ghent, Bruges and Ypres, which exercised a corporate dictatorship in Flanders, sought to manipulate the staple for their own profit. This they did by trying to suppress the manufacture of cloth in the smaller Flemish towns and by preventing wool from leaving the staple in sea-going ships, thus hampering the Italians who were important customers. The English merchants did not refer directly to the Italian market since elsewhere in their petition they were complaining about the competition of the Bardi, Peruzzi and other companies. Their second objection to the Bruges staple was that the gold florins, for which they sold their wool, were overvalued in the Low Countries, causing them to lose one third or more of the value of their goods. Having stated their preference for an English staple the petitioners said that if it had to be held overseas, export should be open to all men; both alien and denizen. They expressed themselves willing to pay a subsidy of 40s per sack provided that half of this be allowed to the holders of Dordrecht bonds or to the heirs of those who had died. This demand was repeated no fewer than three times in the course of the petition.

Following discussions in the assembly an indenture was made between the king and twelve merchants representing the entire com-

munity concerning payment for the wool taken at Dordrecht. It was
agreed that bond holders should be paid by means of an allowance of
20s on every sack exported in the twelve months from Midsummer
1343 and 6s 8d per sack in the following two years. All who exported
wool were required to take it to the staple and to sell it under the direction of the mayor and merchants of the company of the staple. The
object of this was to maintain the price of wool and to protect the rate
of exchange. In order to prevent smuggling all wool was to be unloaded
in the presence of staple officials and the company was to receive
one third of forfeitures for its trouble. The export of wool was to be
restricted to 8 English ports, afterwards reduced in number to 6.
On 20 June the king confirmed the appointment of Thomas de
Melchebourn, elected by the merchants to be mayor of the staple at
Bruges.[2]

The indenture mentioned above is dated 29 April, but it is impossible to determine precisely how the agreement fits into the contem-
poraneous discussions in Parliament. The Commons at first demanded
that the export duty on wool be reduced to 6s 8d per sack on the
grounds that it was beyond reason that the merchants should grant a
subsidy of 40s when the Commons paid the tax. The government's
reply was that the merchants had only granted what was theirs to give
since the growers were protected by minimum prices. Eventually the
Commons were obliged to concede a subsidy of 40s beyond the ancient
custom, to last until Michaelmas 1345. They coupled the grant with a
revision of the minimum prices which was substantially higher than the
Nottingham scale. The new schedule was to last for as long as the
subsidy was levied and anyone buying for less was to forfeit the wool.[3]

The settlement between the king, Parliament and the community of
merchants was soon followed by a revolutionary development in the
administration of the customs. Until this time a large part of these
revenues were going directly to alien creditors in satisfaction of royal
debts. Now the assignments were revoked and on 8 July 1343 the king
made an indenture with a 'company' of 33 English merchants, valid
from Midsummer 1343 to Michaelmas 1346, the period of the parliamentary subsidy.[4] Throughout this time the company was to have
the entire management of the customs, receiving the ancient custom, the
40s subsidy and all other duties except that on imported wine. The company did not at this stage farm the customs, but was to pay the king
1000 marks in cash every month and was to account for the balance
every quarter. It was also to pay 10 000 marks a year beyond all the
issues. If trade was stopped for any reason the company was to receive
a rebate in its payments. The Dordrecht bond holders were to receive

the allowances which had been promised to them, but the company was granted the privilege of buying up the bonds of those who were too impoverished to export wool. It was also granted half of all forfeitures for successful prosecutions of those buying wool below the statutory prices.

In order to appreciate the significance of this development it is necessary to understand the true nature of the so-called company of 1343 and its relationship to the wider community of English merchants. Sayles, who has written most extensively on the subject, was adamant that it was a private company which enjoyed a complete monopoly of export until this was rescinded by Parliament in 1344.[5] Unwin, writing earlier, was somewhat vague about the legal status of the company, although he, too, clearly stated that it enjoyed a monopoly which was destroyed by Parliament.[6] Fryde, on his own admission, followed Sayles, although it is not clear that he accepted the idea of a monopoly, and he certainly stressed that the company was wider than its 33 nominal members.[7] Although it is impossible to disprove conclusively the private status of the company it seems more likely that the 33 were formally representative of the merchant community as a whole, otherwise the company of the staple. This statement is made primarily in the light of an explanation which will shortly be proposed for the adoption of the new method of customs administration.

Whether or not the thirty-three formed a private company or merely represented the staple they certainly did not enjoy a monopoly of export. Unwin and Sayles were led to this belief by a misunderstanding of the parliamentary petitions of June 1344. The relevant petitions neither state nor imply that there had been any monopoly in the preceding year. The first asks for the abolition of minimum prices, which had proved harmful to the country at large, leaving buyer and seller to negotiate a fair price. It also requested that no-one be prosecuted for having bought wool below the minimum prices. All this was granted without comment. The second petition complained of the arrogance of the Flemings, who had put a total ban on the export of wool from Flanders, thus frustrating purchases by Italians and Spaniards. It did not propose a remedy, but prayed for redress of the grievance. The reply was that this was a reasonable complaint and that all merchants, both alien and denizen, should be free to buy wool in England as they used to do and that the sheriffs should be informed of this. The answers to the petitioners were then incorporated in an ordinance which concluded with the statement '*la Mier soit overte a tote manere des Marchantz de passer ove lour Marchandises*'. The writs sent to the sheriffs, also entered on the parliament roll, state that aliens and denizens may buy wool at any price but make no reference to its export.[8]

Logically, acceptance by the government of the Commons' complaint about the selfishness of the Flemings should have ensured the removal of the staple from Bruges or at least that aliens be exempted from carrying wool there. It is impossible to determine whether either of these measures was implied in the answer which was given. In practice, however, the staple remained at Bruges and there is no record of any steps to relax regulations in favour of aliens. Representations were made to the Flemings about restrictions on access to the staple and in November 1344 it was announced that the mayor had been given assurances on this point and that therefore all exporters must take their wool to Bruges.[9]

Unwin and Sayles were encouraged in their idea that the company of 1343 had a monopoly of export by the fact that it was willing to pay the king 10 000 marks a year beyond the issues of the customs. How, other than by monopoly profits, was that sum to be raised? The company had been granted the right to buy up Dordrecht bonds and it was envisaged, no doubt, that these might be obtained at a discount. However, in the absence of a monopoly the bond holders were at liberty to export wool themselves and there is no doubt that many did so. Moreover there is no proof that the company had been guaranteed the sole right to acquire bonds. The bonds might be transferred only by royal licence, but at a slightly later date we find that outsiders, including aliens, were given permission to purchase them. Some contribution towards the 10 000 marks might come from the forfeitures of wool sold below statutory prices, but this was likely to be small. We are left, then, with the problem of explaining why any body of merchants should be willing to pay 10 000 marks a year for the privilege of managing the customs.

It is suggested, as a hypothesis worthy of consideration, that the company of 1343 represented the entire community of English merchants, which was willing to pay 10 000 marks in order to be free of the operation of the bullion law which threatened to bring their trade to a complete standstill. It has already been shown how in 1341 and 1342 ordinary merchants found it virtually impossible to export wool under the dual burden of duty and bullion deposit. The parliament of 1343, greatly concerned with the shortage of coin, re-enacted the regulation and required that all merchants give security to import two marks of silver for every sack of wool exported. If the law was strictly enforced every merchant would again be required to advance 73s 4d for each sack exported, an impossible requirement. By taking the administration of the customs into their own hands the merchant community might reap two advantages. Between themselves not only might they devise a form of bullion security which was less onerous than hard cash or plate but they might also be able to defer part of the payment of duty. They were required to pay the king the relatively small sum of 1000 marks per month, the balance being accounted for every quarter. This allowed them ample time to export their wool and to repatriate the proceeds. Ten thousand marks a year was a small price to pay for these considerations. In fact some time after the merchants took the customs into their own hands the bullion regulation seems to have fallen into abeyance. It was reintroduced in the parliament of January 1348, not, however, at the request of the Commons, but at the instigation of the council. A few weeks later, in the Lent parliament, the Commons asked for its repeal on the grounds that the Flemings would not allow bullion to be exported and that the regulation was adversely affecting the price of wool.[10]

The parliament of 1343 seems deliberately to have renewed the bullion ordinance as an alternative to a debasement of the coinage, a course of action it heartily condemned. An explanation of this hostility is provided by a Commons complaint that the king's ministers, unlike everyone else in the land, refused to receive taxes proffered in the debased halfpence and farthings made since 1335 at a rate of 252d to 254d to the pound Tower, instead of the old standard of 243d. Recent mint activity might seem to suggest that the bullion ordinance could provide an effective remedy to the money shortage. The average amount of silver coined in the London mint in the years 1324–35 was £407, rising to £1834 (in halfpence and farthings) in 1335–41. In 1341–2 the amount was £5363 and in 1342–3 £14 750, the only new factor being the bullion regulation. The king refused, however, to be bound by the parliamentary ordinance forbidding debasement and at the end of 1343 made arrangements for the coinage of pennies to recommence at a lower weight than those made between 1279 and 1335. By 1346 the weight of the penny had been progressively lowered to 270 to the pound Tower. After rising to £40 830 in 1343–4 the amount of silver coined in the London mint fell to £25 129, £7746 and £4612 in the following three years. Since we do not know just when the bullion regulation was abandoned it is impossible to determine how much of the decline was due to this fact and how much to the failure of the policy of debasement. The temporary increase in mint output had little effect on the money supply and counterfeit sterlings continued to pour into England and to circulate in lieu of native coinage.[11]

Besides considering the question of the silver coinage the parliament of 1343 was obliged to take account of the complaint of the merchants relative to the losses they incurred when they sold their wool for gold florins. Although they no doubt exaggerated when they set their loss at one third they had a legitimate cause of complaint, particularly in respect of the Florentine florin (*florenus auri de Florentia*). The other principal florin in use at this time was the French *florin de l'ecu* (*florenus auri de scuto*) or florin with the shield. Between the late 1330s and 1343 the exchange rate of the latter coin in terms of sterling fell from 4s 6d to 3s 4d. The rate of the Florentine coin was largely determined by the official dealings between the government and the Italian financiers and remained steady at 3s sterling throughout the period.[12] Although it retained its purity it seems to have been overvalued both in terms of the *ecu* and the market price of gold but little could be done to bring it down because of the financial and economic importance of the Italians. After the matter had been raised in Parliament the council commissioned the services of a number of goldsmiths to determine the basis of an English gold coinage, which hopefully would enjoy an international circulation. Production began in January 1344 but the coins were first overvalued and then undervalued so that not until 1346 were nobles made at a rate which properly reflected the market price of gold.

Following this discussion of the coinage it is necessary to revert to the company of 1343 which had assumed the entire management of the customs. The nominal head of the company was Thomas de Melchebourn, mayor of the staple, but Sayles has shown that the key figure in the enterprise was none other than William de la Pole.[13] Although not formally a member of the company Pole was later said to have been its originator. The reason for the secrecy probably lies in the fact that his disreputable past made him suspect amongst ordinary merchants. Pole was also responsible for the expulsion of no fewer than 21 of the 33 members of the company in July and August 1344. It was at this stage, presumably, that the company ceased to represent the entire merchant community and became concerned primarily with the profit of a few.[14] In March 1345 the rump, which until now had been held to account for all the issues, was granted the customs at farm and the arrangement was made retrospective to midsummer 1343. It was merely required to pay the king a rent of £50 000 a year. In the same indenture[15] the rump was granted the half of the forfeiture of smuggled wool which had previously been granted to the staple company. In the parliament of January 1348 the mayor and merchants of the staple protested at this deprivation.[16] Thomas de

Melchebourn, still mayor in 1348, had been a member of the rump but was not associated with the group currently farming the customs.

The rump of the Melchebourn company did not hold the farm very long, for in August 1345 it was surrendered in favour of another group led by John de Wesenham. The new agreement was made retrospective to Midsummer, Melchebourn accounting for the £100 000 owed up to this time and Wesenham for anything due thereafter. In fact the export of wool had been banned since midsummer, if not before, allegedly because of dangers at sea and the arrest of shipping.[17] This stoppage was given as one of the reasons why the Melchebourn company was unable to continue with its contract. The other reasons apparently included its inability to raise a large loan which the king demanded in addition to the farm. The group was far from bankrupt, however, for as part of the terms of surrender it undertook to raise a new loan of 10 000 marks, secured by an assignment on a tenth and fifteenth. The condition was later cancelled in return for a release of part of its claim against the king. In settlement of earlier loans the outgoing group was given an assignment on the ancient custom and granted a share in a monopoly of the export of wool until 13 October 1345.[18]

The other part of the monopoly was vested in the new farmers, Wesenham and company, who had obtained the farm by undertaking to raise a loan of 20 000 marks. Their contract lasted until Michaelmas 1346, but as early as May the group was outbid for the renewal by a fresh syndicate led by Walter Chiriton and Thomas Swanland, former members of the Melchebourn company. The terms of the 1346 contract appear to exclude the ancient custom from the farm, although the rent remained at £50 000. It is far from clear, however, how much benefit the previous farmers had received from this source, since there were a number of fees charged to it. The Chiriton–Swanland contract, made initially for a period of two years, was renewed in May 1348 for a further period of three years. Gilbert de Wedlinburgh, who had long been associated with the group, was now brought in formally as a co-principal. In March–April 1349 the syndicate became bankrupt and management of the customs was handed over to a group of 32 merchants headed by John Malwayn. This group was required to render a strict account for all the issues until Michaelmas 1351, but all income beyond the sum of £50 000 a year was to count in the settlement of Chiriton and company's debts to the king.[19]

A major factor in the bankruptcy of Chiriton and company was the exorbitant demands for loans made upon them by the king, which forced them to adopt self-damaging financial practices.[20] A further source of weakness was the hostility of Parliament and many merchants which was evident by the beginning of 1348. Much of the hostility arose from the levy of 20 000 sacks of wool which was currently taking place. In March 1347 a great council, summoned in the absence of the king by Lionel of Antwerp, had been told that unless the king was assured of the means of continuing the war during the summer all that had been spent so far would be utterly wasted. Thereupon the council granted the king 20 000 sacks of wool. Although represented as a loan there was little prospect of repayment, since it was to be collected according to the method of assessment devised in 1341. The only difference was that anyone wishing to do so might pay cash instead of wool.[21]

The wool from the levy was to be disposed of by a syndicate of English merchants with whom an indenture was made on 2 April 1347.[22] They were to buy it at 23s 4d below Nottingham prices, paying £40 000 by 8 July, £10 000 between 1 August and Michaelmas, £16 666 13s 4d between the last date and Christmas and the balance at Purification (2 February). All expenses were to be borne by the merchants, but the king was to find the ships and to make allowance for any wool lost at sea. The syndicate was guaranteed a monopoly of export until Easter 1348. The contract seems to have attempted a reconciliation between the present farmers of the customs and their predecessors, since it was drawn up between the king and John de Wesenham, Walter Chiriton and their fellows. It also stipulated that the same group should have the farm of the customs for three years from Michaelmas 1348. In the event the Chiriton and Wesenham groups seem to have acted entirely independently, each taking the wool of different counties.

Commissions for the assessment and collection of wool were issued as early as March but in order to accelerate the levy men were added throughout the summer. The wool was handed over by the receivers to attorneys of the merchants, who were responsible for it thereafter. In deciding whether to pay his assessment in wool or in cash a man would have had to take at least three factors into consideration; the price of wool was depressed by the ban on export, the price of grain in 1347 and in 1348 was far higher than at any time in the preceding fifteen years, and money may still have been in relatively short supply. In fact given the consistency with which most counties were assessed either entirely in wool or entirely in cash it is doubtful whether individuals had a freedom of choice. It was later alleged in Parliament that pressure was exerted for the delivery of wool and that anyone who insisted on giving cash was made to pay 2s 6d to 3s in the pound more than the value of wool. One of the few counties where there does seem to have been freedom of choice was Suffolk. The county as a whole paid 286 sacks 6 stones $10\frac{1}{2}$ lb in wool and £2690 11s $4\frac{1}{4}$d in lieu of 672 sacks 8 stones 12 lb of wool. In the hundred of Thyngowe, with 18 vills, 10 gave all wool, 4 gave all cash and 4 gave a mixture of cash and wool. Counties assessed entirely in cash were London, Middlesex, Kent, Devon and Cornwall. Surrey gave almost all in cash. Norfolk supplied two thirds of its quota in cash and Sussex and Bedfordshire almost one half, while five other counties supplied quite small proportions in cash. The remainder were assessed entirely in wool.[23]

Parliament met in January 1348 while collection and export of the 20 000 sacks was still going on. Never before had there been so many separate complaints about the conduct of the wool trade. It was alleged that the customs farmers were robbing the king by buying wool at 23s 4d less than its value and that they were cheating his subjects by using weights of 16 lb and 17 lb to the stone. The ban on export deprived the Commons of a market for their wool, but the farmers were granting export licences in return for a payment of 26s 8d a sack beyond the custom and subsidy. There were complaints about rich merchants oppressing the poor in the acquisition of Dordrecht bonds and about the farmers buying up all manner of royal debts at 1s and 2s in the pound and presenting these at the Exchequer in payment of their rent. There was a revival of the charges that the Flemings were restricting access to the staple and that the florin was overpriced. As always, of course, there was a prayer for the abolition of the *maltote* on wool. The answer given to this was that the subsidy still had some time to run. On the last two occasions on which the subsidy had been granted consent had been provided by non-parliamentary bodies. In February 1346 authority was provided by an assembly of bishops of Canterbury province, although the merchants had concurred, for its collection for two years from the following Michaelmas. When Parliament met in September of that same year the Commons unsuccessfully protested against the continuance of the levy. The Great Council of March 1347, which authorised the wool loan, provided that the *maltote* should continue for three years from Michaelmas 1348 to finance the repayment. This grant was finally confirmed by the Commons in March 1348.[24]

A similar answer was given in the January parliament for the abolition of a subsidy of 2s per sack imposed for one year by Lionel of Antwerp's great council. Ostensibly this money was to provide warships to protect the wool convoys. Parliament, however, had good reason to be cynical about the tax because of apparent misuse of a similar subsidy of 1s levied during the time when Wesenham and company had held the customs. In November 1346 Thomas le Brewere and other merchants sued Wesenham and John Pyel before the mayor and sheriffs of London, alleging that they had received the money but failed to provide protection, with the result that the plaintiffs suffered great losses at the hands of the enemy. The case was abandoned on the instructions of the Crown, which claimed that since the subsidy had been imposed by the government any matters pertaining to it could only be heard before the king and council. In any event Wesenham may have been blameless, since on 10 January 1346 writs had been sent to all customs collectors instructing them not to pay the money to him. The collectors were themselves to pay archers to sail with the wool. In January 1348 Brewere and other merchants presented a petition in Parliament alleging that many of their fellows had been killed and goods valued at over £20 000 had been lost because of the lack of escorts. The government promised an enquiry, but commissions were not issued until March shortly before the next meeting of Parliament.[25]

On 17 January 1348, following the complaint of the Commons, the customs farmers surrendered their monopoly of export and were rewarded with a licence to export 5000 sacks a year, for the next three years, to wherever they wished. This presumably means that they were exempted from the obligation to follow the staple. In fact the export trade does not seem to have been thrown open to all, for in March the Commons again complained that the ports were closed and that the value of their wool was reduced by half. The same parliament also requested the lifting of the bullion regulation which had recently been reimposed by the council. The government gave an evasive answer, merely saying that it would consult with the Flemings. But why had the council acted as it did? Was it a genuine attempt to meet renewed complaints about a shortage of coin, did it reflect the weakening of the Flemish alliance or was it a thoroughly devious attempt to negate the promise of free export? Confronted with a strict enforcement of the regulation many merchants would be effectively prevented from exporting.[26]

Until 1348 the staple was held at Bruges for purely political reasons. In his anxiety to preserve the alliance Edward was obliged to disregard the economic interests of his own subjects and to appease the Flemings in the event of clashes between the two communities. In 1347, for example, following disorders on Cadzand he promised to build and endow a Carthusian priory on the island and a hospital on the mainland. However, Louis de Nevers, the exiled Count of Flanders, was killed fighting for the French at Crecy and in 1347 his son and heir, Louis de Mâle, returned to Flanders and began at once to restore the comital authority. Ghent, the most independent of the towns, submitted to him in January 1349. The restoration of the count resulted in a corresponding diminution of English influence in Flanders and made the king less willing to maintain the staple in the face of obvious disadvantages. In February 1348 he wrote to Ghent, Bruges and Ypres voicing the complaints of his subjects about the restrictions on access to the staple. Although discussions continued into the summer it is clear that there was little or no export to Bruges from January 1348 onwards. The customs farmers were exempted from following the staple and it is probable that no-one else was allowed to export before Michaelmas. On 20 October it was announced that the staple was removed from Bruges to Middelburg.[27]

Merchants had apparently been informed that they might export wool from Michaelmas 1348, but they had not been told that this would be conditional upon their lending the king 26s 8d per sack beyond the custom and subsidy. This was announced after they had paid the duty, but before the first wool had cleared the ports. They then had little choice but to pay the loan, since the customs collectors were instructed to arrest the wool of all who refused. This action must have caused consternation and delay and it is more than likely that, with the exception of wool belonging to the farmers of the customs, no wool was sent abroad other than 489 and 821 sacks recorded as having left Boston and Lynn respectively between late November 1348 and early February 1349. The merchants were given vague promises that the loans would be repaid by allowances of duty on future exports. Nothing came of this, for on 15 March 1349 a complete ban was imposed on export, presumably in consequence of the bankruptcy of Chiriton and company. When the matter of non-payment was later raised in Parliament the king at first denied responsibility. In a later parliament he accepted that the claim for allowances was reasonable, but still held that the late farmers should pay them. The resumption of exports was not authorised until 10 June 1349, with the announcement that the staple was to be located once more at Bruges.[28]

The bankruptcy of Chiriton and company proved to be indirectly beneficial to the historian in that the new managers of the customs were required to account for all issues. This means that trade figures, lacking for 5 out of the preceding 6 years, are available once more. Details of wool exports from Michaelmas 1350 have been published, but there is a certain amount of evidence relating to the previous year and a half. This shows that the income from all customs, excluding that from wine and the new duties on exported cloth, totalled £49 392 in twelve months beginning 21 April 1349. Although slightly less than the rent of the farm it must be borne in mind that this was the period of the plague. Moreover in this twelve months the export of wool did not begin until 10 June 1349 and ended early in April 1350. Between 28 February and 6 April 1350 no fewer than 4209 sacks of wool were exported. On the latter date the government announced the imposition of an additional subsidy of 20s per sack, authorised only by 'prelates, earls, barons and others of the king's council at Westminster lately assembled'. A mere half dozen sacks were exported before the subsidy was withdrawn on 28 June 1350. However it was not only the extra subsidy which served to depress trade for by 20 April at latest all ships of 50 tuns and more had been arrested.[29]

The comparatively low income from customs between 21 April and Michaelmas 1350 is to be explained by a slow start to the new wool season. The government was trying to negotiate a new treaty with Flanders and not until the end of August did the parties agree upon a formula for a settlement of outstanding commercial disputes. Once more the location of the staple seems to have been used as a bargaining factor. In mid-August the London customs collectors were instructed that wool was to go only to Zeeland, but by October it was to go only to the staple in Flanders. Between Michaelmas 1350 and Michaelmas 1351 nearly 36 000 sacks of wool were exported, a figure which includes the first wool of the 1351 season as well as that from 1350 and earlier years. Exports were stopped on 8 April 1351 but seem to have been resumed about mid-July. However, by 21 September 1351, if not earlier, trade was once again at a standstill and did not recommence until early November. The stoppage was undoubtedly used to extract forced loans from the trading community. Receipts of loans ranging from £3 to 1000 marks were acknowledged in the patent roll between the middle of August and the end of November. Lenders were promised that they would be repaid by allowances or assignments on the wool duties.[30] Despite the bad start to the season exports seem to have picked up quite well, for it is likely that the majority of the 21 000 sacks dispatched in 1351–2 were taken before the beginning of July 1352 when restrictions were placed on trade and the export of wool may even have stopped completely, although this is less certain. By far the greater part of this wool had been consigned by denizens, but this was the last time for several years that they were permitted legally to export wool. In the twelve months after Michaelmas 1352 they exported no wool at all, although in the same period aliens dispatched nearly 17 000 sacks.[31] Thus denizen export ceased a year before it was formally forbidden by the ordinance of the staple.

There is no mystery as to why the ordinance abolished the overseas staple, held at Bruges as late as March 1352, in favour of home staples. The impossibility of continuing at Bruges must have been self evident. As early as 3 September 1352 the export of wool was banned until further notice 'because the king has learned that the mariners of Flanders, by order of their superiors, are preparing to set out to sea to inflict what damage they can on the king and his subjects until they recover the damages which they pretend they have received from the king's subjects'.[32] What has to be explained is why the ordinance saw fit to exclude Englishmen from the export trade. The explanation advanced by Unwin has found universal acceptance, indeed it has been the most widely publicised of all his ideas. He stated,

> The taxpayers, the wool growers and the smaller merchants were united in opposition to the continuance of the monopoly embodied in the staple at Bruges. Fifteen years' experience of a succession of syndicates of native monopolists led them to demand the exclusion of English capitalists from the export trade and the re-establishment of the home staples through which it was hoped both the grower and the small dealer would get the benefit of free access of foreign capital. The King in return for his abandonment of a bankrupt monopoly system received a grant of wool subsidy for three years, and willingly consented to an exclusion of native exporters which secured him a higher rate of export tax from aliens.[33]

There is, however, no evidence that the monopoly system survived into the 1350s and fifteen years is certainly too long a period over which to trace the antecedents of the staple ordinance. Unwin's analysis of the events immediately preceding the publication of the ordinance does nothing to justify his conclusion.[34] He failed to take account of all the available evidence and misinterpreted that which he did examine. He relied almost exclusively on mere lists of names and allowed free range to his intuition. The lists in question are the writs of summons to a great council of August 1352, a merchant assembly of July 1353 and a great council of September 1353. There are no records of any of these gatherings except the last, from which emerged the formal version of the staple ordinance.

For Unwin the initiative of the lesser merchants and the Commons was of paramount importance, the approval of the king being a secondary matter. The first paragraph of the ordinance roll gives a very different picture. It states that the king had decided to hold the staple in England *per assent des ascuns Prelatz et Grantz* and that the ordinance had been framed with *l'assent et avisement des ditz Prelatz et Grantz*.[35] Unwin briefly acknowledged this but he seemed to attach little importance to the words themselves, even though they are not simply part of the formal preamble to the ordinance. He subordinated these statements to the fact that the Commons summoned to the September great council demanded copies of the ordinance and then *apres grande deliberation eue entre eux, monstrerent au Conseil leur Avis en escrit; quele escrit lue et debatue per les Grantz, si furent les Ordinances de l'Estaple faites en la forme qe s'ensuit.* From this Unwin deduced that 'the Commons took an active part in framing the ordinances'. There is little justification for this statement. The observations made by the Commons are among their petitions, which are copied onto the ordinance roll. They number only two.[36] Firstly the Commons requested that eight more staple towns should be added to the eight already designated; the government accepted Canterbury 'for the honour of St Thomas' and dismissed the rest. Subsequently Chichester, not among the towns asked for by the Commons, was added to bring the total to ten.[37] The second request was that between now and Easter the king should consult with the Lords and Commons about the making of a new assise of wool prices. The government reserved its answer to this, but in the event nothing was done.

Unwin seems to have been unaware of the fact that although the Commons did not discuss the ordinance until the early days of October 1353 the home staples had been operational since the beginning of August. As early as 10 June writs had been sent to all sheriffs instructing them to proclaim that home staples would open at Lammas. This move was clearly designed to ensure that there would be a market for wool in the coming season. The fact that the new policy was proclaimed before the meeting of the merchant assembly on 1 July suggests that this body was summoned primarily to implement the policy. On 10 July writs of appointment were issued for a mayor and two constables in each of the eight English staples already announced. In view of Unwin's theory about the anti-monopolist nature of the ordinance it must be mentioned that officials of the Westminster staple were John Wroth, Hugh Ulseby and Thomas Perle, all colleagues of the so-called monopolists. The officials of the provincial staples also included many prominent wool exporters. On 14 July and 31 July letters of protection were issued for Flemings and Genoese merchants based in Flanders to come to the staples.[38]

For Unwin the resentment of growers and small merchants against the monopolists is the keynote to the politics of the wool trade in 1353. Suppose, however, that the key to the situation was not this but the state of relations between England and Flanders. This enables the ban on denizen exports to be seen in a quite different light. It is suggested that in 1353 relations between England and Flanders were not too dissimilar from those which had existed in 1313. On each occasion they had recently abandoned an alliance against France into which Flanders had been dragged by her dependence on English wool. On each occasion, moreover, the alliance had been followed by a period of tension during which English merchants ventured to Flanders at their peril. In 1313 the escape had been provided by the establishment of a staple at St Omer. In 1353 Calais might have served the same purpose, but the English had recently set up a staple there for cloth and other goods, only to abandon it almost immediately. Middelburg had been tried in 1348 and apparently found wanting. There remained only the home staples. The ban on denizen exports meant that any losses at sea or in the Low Countries would cost England nothing and the government would not be embarrassed by the demand of its own subjects for reprisals. Finally it is likely that one should attach greater significance than Unwin does to the fact that, provided aliens could handle all the wool previously carried by Englishmen, the king's revenue would benefit from the prohibition of denizen export. This accords with the evidence that the change of policy was made on the initiative of the government. Although Unwin constantly asserts that the Bruges staple had operated to the benefit of the so-called monopolists there is no evidence that this was the case. Edward III had maintained the staple at Bruges in his own diplomatic interests. By the 1350s it no longer suited his purpose to have it there.

When Parliament met in April 1354 the ordinance of the staple was drawn into a perpetual statute. This was done at the specific request of the Commons, for having experienced the new policy they found it to their liking. The measure of their satisfaction may be gauged from the fact that when Parliament next met in November 1355 the commons *uniement et d'un acort* renewed the wool subsidy for six years, the first time that this had ever been done without protest.[39] It had last been authorised by the great council in 1353, following the expiry of a parliamentary grant of February 1351.

The ordinance, and later statute, of the staple was designed primarily to implement the adoption of a policy of home staples in the wool trade. However, it created an elaborate machinery which was used to regulate all manner of mercantile activity and which even came to be used to register non-mercantile debts. This machinery continued in use long after the home wool staples had been abandoned. For the purposes of this study, however, the statute is of consequence only in so far as, and for as long as, the use of home staples was compulsory in the wool trade.[40] The original staple towns in England were

Newcastle, York, Lincoln, Norwich, Westminster, Winchester, Exeter and Bristol. Canterbury and Chichester were added in October and November 1353 and Hull in March 1354. Carmarthen[41] was a staple in Wales and there were four in Ireland. The trade in wool outside the staple towns was open to all, denizen as well as alien, although this clause was quickly amended to read that within three miles of a staple town wool might be sold only by the grower. All wool intended for export, although not that going to the home cloth industry, had next to be brought to a staple. It was at this stage that wool still owned by a native had to be sold to an alien, since all Englishmen, Welshmen, and Irishmen were forbidden to export. The wool was weighed and sealed in the presence of staple officials and charged with a duty of 8d per sack, reduced in November 1354 to 4d. This was intended to pay the salaries of the officials and to defray other staple expenses. Thereafter the wool was carried to an appointed port, except in the few instances of staples which were also ports, weighed once more, charged with the king's customs and finally exported. All exporters had to swear on oath that they would not make another staple abroad.

Alien merchants probably retained their legal monopoly of the export of wool until the summer of 1357. It seems generally to have been assumed that natives were allowed to export from Michaelmas 1356, following the convening of a large merchant assembly in the previous June.[42] If correct this means that the king had gone back on his solemn promise, enshrined in the statute of the staple, not to license any exceptions to the ban on native exports. In fact there is no proof that Englishmen began to export at Michaelmas, while there is one piece of evidence strongly suggestive of the contrary. On 8 September 1356 the king granted a licence to John and Walter Permay in reward for great labours at sea.[43] They had captured a cargo of Scottish wool and brought it to Boston as a prize of war. The licence did not authorise them to export it but absolved both them and the alien merchants to whom they were to sell it from carrying it to the staple at Lincoln.

Authority for the resumption of native exports was provided by the parliament which met on 10 April 1357. It is unfortunate that no rolls have survived for this assembly, since discussion of the wool trade seems to have been protracted and may have been acrimonious. A proclamation by the sheriffs of London announcing decisions of Parliament had twice to be amended.[44] Parliament authorised natives to export wool from 5 May 1357 to the following Michaelmas, provided that they paid the higher alien rate of duty. The statutory record of this decision was immediately followed by a further clause which stated that the Chancellor and Treasurer might, by the advice of the council, extend the period of export if they saw fit.[45] There is, therefore, no justification for Unwin's statement that 'when the six months expired the native merchants continued to export wool in defiance of Parliament under licence from the King'.[46] The king's guilt on this occasion lay in his dismantling the safeguards which Parliament had provided to protect the growers and, apparently, the native cloth manufacturers. The first were to be protected by a new schedule of minimum prices, made and proclaimed while Parliament was still in session.[47] This was not simply a reissue of either of the earlier schedules but a completely new assessment. The very best wools were priced a half mark below Nottingham values, second qualities at a half mark above and the poorest wools about the same. Overall prices were lower than those claimed in the schedule of 1343. Parliament broke up on 16 May and on 5 June the government proclaimed that the price ordinance was repealed. It is not even mentioned in the statute. This was the second time in less than four years that the king had disregarded the Commons' plea for minimum prices – an indication of how much, or rather how little, influence they had upon the staple policy of the 1350s.

The statute did incorporate an amendment of the statute of the staple, which seems to have been designed to protect cloth manufacturers. All wool bought in the country had to be lodged in a staple for at least fifteen days and apparently had to be offered for sale there. Only wool which could not be sold might then be exported. It is unlikely that manufacturers derived much benefit from this law. On 1 September the government wrote to the officials of the Winchester staple instructing them to disregard the fifteen day rule and to allow wool to leave the staple immediately it had been weighed and the dues paid.

Once English merchants were legally permitted to export wool it was not long before the Bruges staple was re-established in all but name. In July 1359 the king and the Count of Flanders restored all the liberties formerly enjoyed by the community at Bruges. In the same month the king confirmed the election by the merchants of John Malewayn, not as mayor but as *gubernator*. All natives exporting wool were required to take it to Bruges and to unload it only in the presence of officials of the community. In March 1360 regulations concerning alien exports were tightened up on the grounds that they had assisted Englishmen to avoid the staple. The English merchants evidently felt some insecurity about the terms upon which they were suffered to export, for when Parliament met at the end of January 1361 they petitioned the king to confirm their right while Parliament was in session, lest they should be impeached for their activities. Whether their plea was debated by the Commons is not clear, for the patent roll states that 'the king, with the assent of his whole council in the present parliament, ratifies the passage'. Nevertheless the right of the English merchants to export on a permanent basis was established by the statute issued after Parliament dispersed.[48]

The *de facto* staple probably continued at Bruges until the autumn of 1362; in the following spring a staple was established at Calais. For Unwin, preoccupied as ever with his thesis of monopoly, the Calais staple represented an act of revenge by the king against the Commons, who in 1362 conceded a subsidy of 20s beyond the ancient custom for three years, on condition that thereafter only the 6s 8d should be levied.[49] He wrote that

> the wool tax had been finally secured in 1353 by a bargain. The Commons had received an equivalent in the abolition of the foreign staple and in the 'free trade' enactments of 1353–4. As they now proposed gradually to withdraw the wool tax, there was nothing left for him but to withdraw the equivalent and to re-establish his hold upon indirect taxation by a system of monopolies such as had been in existence before the Statute of Staples was passed. That this was a main motive for the institution of the Calais Staple in 1363 is scarcely open to question.[50]

This motive can, and should, be questioned. The decision to transfer the staple to Calais had been taken, and proclaimed, long before the parliament of 1362 assembled in October. Moreover the Calais staple was not, in the first instance, a monopoly.

In May 1361 the merchants of each of the home staples were instructed to elect representatives to attend a conference to discuss the question of wool staples.[51] Since the men of Calais were also told to send six persons there can be no doubt that the question of a staple at Calais was to be discussed. The Calais staple was first proclaimed in the summer of 1362, but its operation was postponed, probably because the town was not yet ready for a large influx of wool. Orders were given, however, to build premises to receive wool.[52] At Michaelmas 1362 exports were stopped and did not resume until the following February when the Calais staple became operational. Parliament was informed of the decision to establish the staple immediately it assembled in October 1362 and was invited to express its opinion on the matter. The Commons, however, declined to say either yea or nay. The knights of the shire

> disoient, Q'ils avoient parlez as pluseurs Marchantz de la matire, desqueux les uns disoient que le Repeir serroit bone a la dit Ville, et les autres le contraire. Et par tant prieront q'ils feussent deschargez de dire un ou autre, depuis que en nul autre, depuis que la conissance de cel matire gist en Marchantz pluis que en nul autre. Et issint demoert cel Article sur avis et tretee ove Marchantz et autres.[53]

The statute which emerged from this parliament reaffirmed the right of natives to export wool but made absolutely no reference to Calais. The sole authority which we have for the setting up of the Calais staple are the letters and 'charter' enrolled in the French Rolls, formally dated 1 March 1363.[54] These are said to have been made by the advice of prelates, lords and others of the council. This point is critical to a later discussion of events in the Good Parliament of 1376.

Parliament had been told that the Calais staple was designed to increase the price of wool which was alleged to have fallen because it was sold outside the king's jurisdiction. However, there can be little doubt that the principal motive was the hope of making the town financially independent of the Crown. During the war years Calais had been a severe drain on the king's resources. From 19 February 1356 to May 1358 it had received £34 462 from the treasury and from 10 May 1359 to 9 May 1360 £10 095, as well as £4721 from other external sources.[55] The Peace of Bretigny, 1360, offered a chance of reducing the garrison, without which burden means might be found of making the town self-supporting. A thriving wool trade might ensure this. The town was sufficiently near to Flanders to enable the Flemings to travel there themselves, thus ensuring that the transactions took place on English territory.

The new arrangements for Calais removed the government of the town from the hands of the governor and treasurer and transferred it to a 'new company' of 26 English merchants, 24 of whom had the status of aldermen.[56] There were two mayors, probably one responsible primarily for the town and one for the staple, as in England. This company did not have a monopoly of the wool trade. Indeed its main, possibly even sole, function was to govern the town, although this duty was widely defined and included complete authority over trade. If permanent residents in Calais were not to be discouraged by high taxation it was inevitable that trade should be made to bear the brunt of the town's expenses. The problem was to fix the correct level of duty. Even allowing for the initial expense of preparing for the reception of wool it is likely that the duty was set too high and was certainly regarded as such by the wool exporters, who seem to have staged a protest strike. From mid-February to Michaelmas 1363 wool exports by natives totalled 22 069 sacks, but in the following twelve months only 12 217 sacks. Alien exports in the same periods were 7175 and 7001 sacks. In the first year of the new regime (1 March 1363 – 29 February 1364) income from wool duties totalled £6116 7s 6½d, while another £133 17s 4d was received from forfeited wool.[57] Wool coming into Calais was charged 3s 4d per sack and fells 'at least' 3s 4d per hundred; the export duties were 6d per sarplar and 2d per hundred.

When Parliament met in October 1363 the damage caused by the high rate of duty and by other *Subtiltees et Ordinances* of the Calais company were brought to the attention of the government, which promised to enquire into the matter.[58] The letters of March 1363 had already provided that a commission would be sent to Calais after one year to review the situation. The date of this commission was not advanced, but because of the disquiet its terms of reference seem to have been widened. Fortunately the findings of the commission have survived.[59] Its report shows quite clearly that all was not well at Calais. Apart from the fact that some of the aldermen were using their positions to line their own pockets the company was divided into at least two factions by general policy differences. The complaints voiced by the five juries examined by the commission extend beyond the wool trade, but only those relative to the latter need be mentioned here. Apart from the excessive rate of duty the wool merchants had two major grievances. They complained that at Calais they were denied their *fraunchises*, by which they apparently meant the body of privileges which they had enjoyed at Bruges. A group of aldermen led by John de Wesenham, one of the mayors, was willing to allow these privileges, but was opposed by the rest led by John Wroth, the second mayor. The other complaint related to the price of wool. The company had ruled that the wool of each English county should be sold at a uniform price. This seems to have been unwelcome to many merchants and in assertion of its authority the company forbade the sale of wool for a day, at a time when many foreign buyers were in the town. After protest the utmost concession which the company would make was that six merchants should join with six aldermen in an assise to determine prices. Less notice need be taken of a third complaint, that merchandise might not be unloaded without a *bille* from an alderman. Although it may have provided scope for corruption the company was obliged by law to do this to deter smuggling.

The commission of 1364 fined certain of the Calais aldermen for misdemeanours and returned to England. There the matter appears to have rested until Parliament met in January 1365. According to Unwin the Calais scheme was then abandoned at the request of Parliament.[60] This is an oversimplified, indeed erroneous, statement of the situation. In order to see what really happened it is necessary to examine the Commons' petitions and the king's answers one by one. Number xvi requests that the staple shall be held in England and that all merchants, alien and denizen, shall be free to import merchandise and to buy wool. This appears to mean that the Commons wished the wool export trade to be open to native merchants. The government's reply was that the statute of the staple of 1354 should be re-introduced, together with its *Declarations, Additions, et Modifications.* The latter would have ensured denizen export, were it not for the fact that the king had already stopped this traffic in his reply to petition number III. In this the Commons asked for the repeal of legislation of 1363 which limited every man to one trade, the wording stating that aliens and denizens should be free to buy and sell throughout the realm as well as to export. The king conceded this request, but excepted the export of wool and fells by natives. It is quite likely, however, that the ban was never intended to be more than a temporary measure, pending a new settlement of the Calais question. As regards Calais itself neither did the Commons request, nor the king concede, any major change of policy. Petition number XVII asked for the removal of the 3s 4d duty at Calais and *toutes autres impositions nient resonables*, and that writs be sent to the collectors informing them of the decision. The government replied laconically that all manner of unreasonable impositions and charges would be removed. If there was any contest about the wool trade in this parliament, victory lay with the king. The export subsidy was once more increased to 40s beyond the ancient custom, with little conceded in return.[61]

Denizen export of wool was banned on 31 January 1365 and resumed on 17 May. In the interval aliens had been permitted to take their wool wherever they wished, but from the later date both groups were compelled to export to Calais. Aliens wishing to sell wool north of the Alps were required to do so at Calais, but Italians were apparently permitted to ship direct to Italy. Despite the temporary cessation of exports to Calais there appears to have been no formal removal of the staple and a statute of 1369 clearly regards it as having been there continuously since 1 March 1363. There was, however, one significant difference between the periods before and after January 1365. In the earlier period wool exported to Calais was not required to pass through a home staple. The statute of 1365, re-establishing home staples, clearly intended that wool must pass through them even though destined for Calais. If strictly enforced this would have caused considerable expense and inconvenience to some exporters. This may explain why in 1368 Canterbury ceased to be the staple and Sandwich the wool port for Kent and both were located at Queenborough.[62]

During the interval in which no wool was sent to Calais the regime of 1363 was dissolved and a new system of government established, which restored the authority of the governor and treasurer. Administration of the town was vested in a mayor and 12 aldermen, 6 of whom had to be merchants.[63] One of the latter also served as mayor of the staple. This was neither the company of 1363 nor the fifteenth-century fellowship of the staple. It was basically an ordinary English staple, although having additional duties at such times as the town was the entrepot for the wool trades. Revenues from wool imports and exports, now fixed at a more modest level, went into the coffers of the treasurer.

Because of the complete dearth of customs particulars for the 1350s, as indeed for the greater part of the reign of Edward III, it is impossible to analyse the composition of the export trade. Before 1363 it is impossible even to separate denizen from alien exports, for only in that year were natives freed from the higher rate of duty. Although aliens at no time enjoyed a real monopoly of export the formal ban on the native trade must have been of considerable assistance to them. One must beware of reading too much into the evidence of exports by Flemings, since they were frequently used by English merchants as cover men. Hanseatic merchants appear still to have been active, but there is little doubt that most of the genuine alien trade belonged to Italian merchants, drawn from a considerable number of cities. The most important group was probably the Genoese who, after assisting the French during the early years of the war, had made their peace with England in 1347. Both the ships and the merchants of Genoa reaped considerable dividends from the wool trade in this period. Despite the bankruptcies of the 1340s there also remained a considerable Florentine presence. The Alberti now represented the financial interests of the papacy and a *popolano* company, the Strozzi, were here by at least the early 1360s, if not before. Collectively more important, however, were the large numbers of individual merchants. It has been estimated that at least 60 Florentines were active in England between 1350 and 1376.[64] Ruddock has rightly insisted that the letters of safe conduct issued for the Venetian galley fleet from 1357 onwards do not prove that it came to England.[65] They were intended to ensure that the fleet was not molested by English ships while passing up the channel to Bruges. Nevertheless the request for a safe conduct by the Venetian consul at Bruges in 1347 certainly gives the impression that some Venetian merchants were thinking of coming here. Nicholas Negrobon, a Venetian dealing in wool in Bristol, in 1355 was still, or again, in London in 1366.[66] Merchants of Lucca also had a considerable stake in the wool trade.

The legal prohibition on denizen exports did not restrict the activities of the greater English merchants. In fact it probably enabled them to obtain a larger share of the native trade. They were much better placed than the small men to act in collusion with aliens or to bribe customs officials to allow them to export under false names. In a case involving 840 sacks exported under cover of Flemings 360 sacks were owned by William de la Pole and another 360 sacks by John Goldbeter, one of the biggest and most unscrupulous of the merchants of York in the 1340s. By 1361 Goldbeter had succeeded John Malewayn as governor of the English merchants at Bruges.[67] The ban may also have encouraged the smuggling of wool from places outside the ports. Considerations such as these, as well as the desire to improve the price of wool, undoubtedly counselled the freeing of denizen trade in 1357. Two Commons petitions of the early 1370s recall this period; both were seeking an end to prosecutions of denizens for exporting under cover of aliens.[68] That of 1372 recites that the ban on denizen trade, supported at first by the penalty of life and limb, acted to the great profit of aliens, but adversely affected the price of wool. The severity of the penalty was then reduced to one of the forfeiture of land and goods, but still *la greindre partie* of the English merchants declined to buy wool and the price remained low. For this reason the ban on denizen exports was removed.

The Commons was historically correct in stating that the price of wool had been low during the 1350s but wrong in its attribution of this to the lack of a market. From the early 1350s to the establishment of the Calais staple the export trade enjoyed a boom such as it had not seen since the early years of the fourteenth century. From the summer of 1353 to Michaelmas 1362 total exports were about 327 000 sacks. Since less than 10 full shearing seasons were involved the average is considerably more than 33 000 sacks a year. The only years in which exports fell markedly below the average were the war years 1355–6, 1358–9 and the plague year 1360–1. In the latter year exports, at little more than 26 000 sacks, were the lowest of the entire period. However the trade was merely delayed, not lost, for in the following year exports rose to nearly 43 000 sacks. In London the Exchequer and the law courts were closed at the end of May 1361 because of the pestilence and the city's overseas trade must have been at a standstill that summer.[69] This explains why its exports of wool totalled only 12 676 sacks in the twelve months before Michaelmas 1361 and 22 265 in the twelve months thereafter.

The buoyancy of England's premier export trade in the 1350s is an indication of how quickly the European economy recovered from the first ravages of the Black Death. England undoubtedly benefited from the improved situation in Flanders. In that country the 1350s seem to have been more free from civil strife and war than any other decade in the entire fourteenth century. Its cloth industry, although not the workers themselves, received an unintended stimulus from the currency depreciation of Louis de Mâle.[70] In the 1350s also Florence made a remarkable recovery from the financial disasters of 1343–6 and the plague. A contemporary noted that the city's cloth industry was flourishing, although total output was never again as high as in the great days of the early fourteenth century.[71]

In England, as elsewhere in Europe, there was a considerable degree of inflation in the period following the Black Death. Wool prices, almost alone, stagnated.[72] It has already been shown how two attempts to establish minimum prices for wool were abandoned, presumably because they could not be enforced. In the light of the general inflation and of the export boom how is the level of wool prices to be accounted for? It is difficult to think of any explanation other than the fact that export merchants were determined to pass the high taxation of wool onto the grower. Before 1337 alien exports carried a duty of 10s per sack and denizen exports 6s 8d; now all paid a duty of 50s. There can be little doubt that sheep farmers paid the greater part of the additional taxation.

The overseas staple for wool remained at Calais until June 1369, when it was abolished by act of Parliament in consequence of the renewal of the war.[73] Although the period had been one of peace and, with the exception of 1368,[74] relatively free from plague there appears to have been a definite reduction in the level of exports in comparison with the earlier period. Following the stoppage of trade between Michaelmas 1362 and February 1363 exports totalled nearly 169 000 sacks up to Michaelmas 1368, of which slightly more than one quarter were handed by aliens. The denizen 'strike' of 1363–4 was not followed by a quickening of exports as had been interruptions in earlier years. Since the period includes 5 entire growing seasons and parts of two others the average export cannot be set higher than about 28 000 sacks a year. It is tentatively suggested that at least part of the drop was occasioned by the withdrawal of Hanseatic merchants from the wool trade, probably because they were unwilling to follow the staple to Calais, where they could expect nothing but second-class treatment. To compensate for this withdrawal they increased their investment in English woollen cloth. From 1358 to 1363 Hanseatic cloth exports averaged 396 a year; in 1363–4 the total was 2044 and in the following year 2292.[75] Thereafter the investment in cloth fell somewhat, although precise figures are not obtainable, probably because of dispute about access to the Baltic markets. In the 1360s the incidence of civil strife in Flanders began to increase again, although not until 1379 did the situation become really desperate.

Table 16 (p. 264) gives details of the wool passing through the Calais staple between 1 March 1365 and 19 March 1368. The figures cannot be compared with the amount of wool leaving England since the periods of account are different. The import duty settled down at 4d per sack and per 100 fells compared with 3s 4d levied in the days of the 'new company'. This is the same rate as that charged on wool in the home staple. The export duty of 8d per sack was rather more than twice as much, since the sack was probably smaller. Calais used the system of weights and measures of Artois. The poke in which Italian wool was packed was probably about half of an English sack, giving a total of about 4420 sacks over the three year period.

When the staple was removed from Calais in June 1369 the statute of 1354 was re-enacted and with it the ban on denizen exports. At the same time the subsidy, which in May 1368 had been reduced to 36s 8d, was increased to 53s 4d beyond the ancient and new custom for aliens and 43s 4d for denizens. Naturally the latter duty must remain in abeyance until the ban was lifted. In consequence of the ban on denizen trade alien exports increased from just under 5000 sacks in 1367–8 to well over 14 000 sacks in the following year, although there was probably an element of collusion in the summer of 1369. What is more surprising is that despite the continuance of the ban throughout 1369–1370 the alien export totalled only 17 526. It seems likely, therefore, that English merchants generally refrained from collusionary sales in the summer of 1370 because of pressure being exerted on the government to lift the ban on denizen exports. If they waited a while they would be spared the burden of an additional 13s 4d for alien subsidy and new custom.

On 10 August 1370 proclamation was made that as from 26 August denizens might again export, and on the following day writs were sent to the ports.[76] Calais was once more made the staple for denizens and aliens. Although denizen trade was freed on 26 August the customs accounts record no export before Michaelmas. This may merely reflect clerical carelessness or disregard in the dating of the enrolments. The Londoners, however, seem to have been in no rush to export. On 9 September there was a meeting of the merchants of the staple to consider the safe passage of their wool, estimated at 2500 sarplers, to Calais. They also complained bitterly about having to send their wool to Westminster for staple registration, which was reckoned to add 4s to the cost of every sack. Since June 1369 Westminster and Winchester had been the only two staples which were not also ports, other inland

towns having been removed. As a result of the complaints of the
Londoners it was decided to rescind the provision that exports from
London and Southampton must pass through their respective staples.
With this action home wool staples were, to all intents and purposes
abolished, although the name remained attached to those ports from
which exports were allowed.[77]

When Parliament met in February 1371 the opposition to government which characterised the last years of Edward III was much in
evidence and the state of the wool trade was already becoming one of
the main grievances. The Commons demanded that there should be no
charges or impositions on wool other than those authorised by Parliament. Although this demand was conceded writs of proclamation and
of notification to customs collectors were delayed until 13 June, following a further petition presented in the great council which met in
Winchester on 9 June. According to Thomas Walsingham this council
was held because of rumours of rebelliousness among the merchants
of London, Norwich and other places. In fact it had been announced
at the end of the earlier parliament. The great council, which included
merchants, conceded a duty of 2s on the tun of wine and 6d in the
pound on the value of all other merchandise except wool and hides.
The government evidently felt uneasy about this grant for it does not
seem to have been announced until shortly before it was to become
effective on 28 October. The writs then sent out did not merely order
collection of the duties; they requested the authorities of each port to
secure the consent of the merchants there.[78]

In the middle of December 1371 the government began to issue
licences for the export of wool to Middelburg or Dordrecht instead of
to Calais. The first were issued to aliens, who were required to pay in
addition to custom and subsidy a total of 1s 7d which would have
been paid at Calais. A few days later denizens were permitted to export
to these places but were required not merely to pay the Calais duties
but the full alien rate of export duty. Although the imposition of alien
rate is a clear case of extortion the actual bypassing of Calais may have
been necessary at this time, because of tension between England and
Flanders. When the war had been renewed these two countries had
begun talks about the right of Flanders, as a neutral, to trade with
France. Unless there was a convention about this they would soon be
fighting a naval war between themselves. By 24 July 1370 it had been
agreed that the Flemings might trade peaceably with France but that
all weapons and foodstuffs should be declared contraband. Moreover
Flemish ships should not carry any goods belonging to Frenchmen or
to their Spanish allies. It is possible, although of this there is no proof,

that the resumption of wool exports by denizens was delayed until after the agreement. Edward III confirmed the treaty on 4 August 1370, but it was not ratified by the Flemings until 27 April 1371 and because of the delay the terms were not publicly proclaimed in England until 8 May 1371. After ratification talks began about the release of Flemish ships already seized by the English, but these made little progress. In August 1371 order was given for the arrest of all Flemish subjects in England, although their confinement was to be honourable, while English merchants were also arrested in Flanders. Calais may have been rendered useless as a wool staple since the Flemings could not come there. Under the year 1371 Thomas Walsingham reports that the English captured a fleet of 25 Flemish salt ships. Despite the hostilities, talks between the two sides continued at Marck near Calais and on 20 March 1372 it was decided to reaffirm the treaty of July 1370. This was to be proclaimed simultaneously in Flanders, England and Calais at Easter (28 March), and prisoners were to be released on both sides. A more substantive treaty was made in the following July.[79]

From April 1372 licences for the avoidance of Calais specified that wool might be taken to Middelburg, Dordrecht or Flanders. On 4 May proclamation was made that the council had ordained that from Whitsun both aliens and denizens might take wool only to Calais. Nevertheless licences of exemption continued to be issued down to 23 September. On 14 September writs were sent to the ports stating that, in pursuance of the council ordinance, wool might be taken to Calais until Michaelmas. It is likely that until now unlicensed export of the new season's wool had been hampered or entirely prevented by a general arrest of shipping, for on the same day orders were given to release ships of Germany, Flanders and Zeeland. The stoppage was presumably associated with preparations for the coming campaign in France. Plans for the latter were changed into an expedition to raise the siege of la Rochelle, but this was abandoned after being delayed by bad weather.[80]

Hardly had the export of wool been resumed when, on 23 September, writs were sent to the collectors of customs stating that all export must cease until further notice. Wool cocketed before Michaelmas might leave after that date, provided that a licence was obtained. The reason for this was that the parliamentary grant of subsidy was about to expire and had not yet been renewed. Parliament had been summoned for the beginning of September but had been prorogued until November, because the king was planning to lead the expedition to France in person. Nothing demonstrates more clearly than this stoppage the control which Parliament had now established over customs duties. On 16 October customers were instructed to permit the export of wool provided that merchants gave security to pay whatever customs 'and other duties' might be granted by the coming parliament. Two days later licences for the avoidance of Calais began to be issued on the same condition.[81]

When Parliament assembled it renewed the wool duty for two years at the existing rate.[82] It also renewed for one year the grant of tunnage and poundage which had been made by the Winchester great council. This was immediately farmed to the London merchants Richard Lyons and John de Medingham and soon afterwards all the petty customs were added to their lease. The transaction was to figure prominently in the later impeachment of Lyons.[83] Two petitions were presented in this parliament by 'cities and boroughs', one of which has already been discussed. The other expresses dissatisfaction with the conditions under which denizens were currently exporting wool. It complained that export was made, to Middelburg and elsewhere, under authority of royal letters patent, *quele passage est contre l'Ordinance en la darrein Parlement*.[84] This can only be a reference to the fact that the ban on denizen exports, imposed by the statute of 1369, had never been repealed by Parliament. The petitioners requested a reassurance that notwithstanding the 'ordinance' they would not be prosecuted for exporting according to the patent. They further complained that the staple was held in various places and was changed suddenly to their great loss. They therefore requested that a single staple should be named and adhered to. The king answered only the first part of the petition, saying that he would allow no-one to suffer on account of his patent.

Throughout 1372–3 licences continued to be issued for avoidance of Calais. Denizens who availed themselves of them were no longer charged alien rates of duty, merely paying the 1s 7d which should be paid at Calais. However, behind the scenes they had to pay heavy fines to acquire the licences. The attack on this system was renewed when Parliament met in November 1373. A Commons petition makes the first recorded claim that the staple had been established at Calais by authority of Parliament.[85] It demanded that it should now be restored and that no more licences of exemption should be issued. The king answered that he would be guided in this matter by '*son grant Conseil*'. Licences continued to be issued right down to the assembly of the Good Parliament in April 1376.

The Good Parliament secured the temporary discomfiture of the court party which was held responsible for the country's current misfortunes. The wider constitutional and political significance of the proceedings is irrelevant to the present study.[86] We shall be concerned only with the impeachment by the Commons of Richard Lyons and Lord Latimer, the king's chamberlain, and even in this only the charges relating directly to the wool trade can be dealt with. Although both men were found guilty there is good reason for disquiet about the verdict, which was to a large extent politically motivated. It is necessary, therefore, to reconsider the charges.

The Good Parliament assembled on 28 April and on 30 April the Commons, sitting alone in the chapter house of Westminster Abbey, began a protracted debate about the state of the country. The second speaker, not a merchant but a knight, complained about the removal of the staple from Calais. He alleged that the government of the town by the merchants of England had saved the king £8000 a year. Then, however, the staple was removed and the merchants thrown out, for the personal profit of Latimer, Lyons and others. This knight claimed that the staple had been established at Calais *par commune conseil en parlement*. Later the claim became even more specific. After some political manoeuvring Latimer, Lyons and a number of lesser functionaries were arrested and formally prosecuted by Sir Peter de la Mare, spokesman or Speaker of the Commons, who began by saying that *une estatute fiust fait en parlement par commune assent*. Latimer pointed out that the removal of the staple from Calais was done before he became a minister. However, his observation that it had been legally removed by the king and his council seems to have angered de la Mare who replied:

> *Que ceo fuiste encontre la ley Dengleterre et encontre lestatute ent fait en parlement, et ceo qest fait en parlement par estatute ne serra poynt defait saunz parlement et ceo vous moustra par lestatute escript. Et le dit sire Peirs avoit une liver des estatutes prest sur luy et overa le liver et luyst lestatute avaunt toutz les seignours et communes issint qil ne purroit estre dedist. Et fuist graunt altercacioun parentre eux.*

The editor of the *Anonimalle Chronicle*, from which these descriptions are taken, was rightly worried about all this talk of statutes, particularly about that from which Sir Peter claimed to be quoting.[87] He searched in vain for a statute creating the Calais staple, while he pointed out that it had indeed been removed by statute. However, is it certain that the *lestatute escript* from which Sir Peter quotes is in fact the alleged statute which created the staple? Galbraith assumes that this is the case. Another reading of the text suggests that the *lestatute escript* is actually some statement, for which the authority of a statute is claimed, that a statute made by Parliament can only be unmade by Parliament. This still leaves us with the problem of the alleged statute creating the staple, of which there is no record. It does, however, remove the greater embarrassment which is caused if we accept that Sir Peter was actually quoting from such a statute.

On balance it seems that the claim that the Calais staple had been established by parliamentary statute must be dismissed as political propaganda. What about the charge that it was unlawfully removed by the counsel of evil men for their own profit? Latimer can hardly have been involved in the original removal, but what about Lyons? The removal was effected by a lawful statute, the preamble of which says that it was made at the prayer of the prelates, lords and commons. The parliament roll appears to confirm this statement.[88] In 1369 the removal of the staple from Calais may have seemed a very necessary measure. It had never been held in the town in war-time and there was good reason to doubt the practicability of combining a staple and a base for military operations. The soldiery might interfere with the business of the merchants and foreign buyers might be deterred from coming to the town. On the other hand although the merchants may at first have welcomed the removal to England they cannot have been a party to their own exclusion from the export trade. Who was responsible for this latter step it is impossible to say. The ban may have been regarded as a temporary measure or, in certain circles, it may still have been held to be a necessary feature of a home staple policy. Further experience of the new regime convinced the English merchants of the necessity of returning to Calais and of strictly enforcing the staple policy. Above all others the factor which influenced their thinking was the expansion of exports by aliens now that they were freed from the Calais staple. During the period of the staple aliens had handled a quarter of the trade, exporting an average of 7200 sacks a year. From 1368–72 denizen and alien exports cannot be distinguished, but from 1372–5 the latter enjoyed nearly 40 per cent of the trade, handling an average of 10 000 sacks a year. Denizen exports in the respective periods shrank from an average of nearly 21 000 sacks to about 15 800. It is suggested, therefore, that the English dissatisfaction may not date back to the original decision to remove the staple from Calais. Their complaints may well have been born of hindsight during the period in which licences were issued to take wool elsewhere than to Calais.

The licences provided the substance for further charges against Latimer and Lyons that they had counselled the levying of extra-parliamentary duties on wool and that they had personally profited by this action. There was no dispute about the fact that 11s was paid by exporters for every sack of wool which they were licensed to send elsewhere than to Calais. What was at issue was the authority by which these fines were levied and what had happened to the money. Latimer was implicated because the proceeds were paid into the chamber, which was his department. He claimed, however, that the practice had begun before he took office and that although it continued thereafter he made no personal profit. He said that 10s went to the king and 1s to the clerks responsible for issuing the licences. Lyons could not deny that he was involved in the origins of the scheme, although he claimed that he had acted throughout on the personal authority of the king. He was also unable to deny that he had received some part of the 1s fee but claimed that the 10s was strictly accounted for in the chamber. It was alleged that the first licences were issued for the export of wool to Genoa and Venice, places which would not interfere with the English trade, but that they were then requested by other merchants who offered money of their own free will.

The third charge made against both Latimer and Lyons was one relating to a loan of 20 000 marks made by the latter to the king. Lyons was accused of receiving interest of 50 per cent and Latimer of taking the loan on the king's behalf in return for a consideration. The seriousness of the offence was compounded by the fact that Latimer refused the offer of an interest free loan of £10 000 made by William Walworth on behalf of the Calais staplers. Their only condition was that the staple should be strictly enforced and that they should receive repayment out of wool duties. Walworth was called to give evidence on this point and there is little reason to doubt his statement. A loan of £10 000 would have been a small price to pay to ensure that all exports went through Calais. The remaining charges against Lyons relate to his extortion of 4d in the pound from Italian bankers in return for licences to issue letters of exchange. Those against Latimer were concerned with his former military commands.

Events in the parliaments of the 1370s, culminating in the Good Parliament, signify a major step forward in the political considerations which determined the direction and regulation of overseas trade. Prior to the outbreak of the Hundred Years War control of trade remained with the executive and there is no evidence that Parliament ever sought to interfere in this department. Despite Unwin's assertion of the contrary it is unlikely that Parliament took the initiative in the setting of the home staples of 1353 and as late as 1362 the Commons as a whole seem to have been indifferent to the location of the staple. In the 1370s, however, the Commons claimed that they had been the originators of the Calais staple and that it ought not to be removed without their consent. Although historically incorrect the claim was allowed and right of Parliament to be consulted in the location of the staple was firmly established. In the following reign the Commons was able to enforce its wishes in this matter by the expedient of withholding authority for the collection of the export subsidy. The establishment by Parliament of its right to be the sole authority for the levy of the major source of customs revenue was a necessary precondition of any claim to regulate trade. Although there may be doubts as to exactly when the right ceased to be contested it was unequivocally admitted in September 1372, when the government halted wool exports as the current parliamentary subsidy came to an end. Once Parliament controlled the subsidy its control over other aspects of the wool trade was inevitable.

7

The evolution of the Calais staple

The return of the staple to Calais at the command of the Good Parliament in 1376 did nothing to halt the decline of the English wool trade. The fall in exports which had begun in the 1360s continued unabated throughout the last quarter of the fourteenth century. In the search for an explanation of this decline particular attention must be given to three matters of policy, namely the staple, the taxation of exports and monetary regulation. Before examining each of these, however, one must recognise the importance of events over which the English had little or no control. Civil strife in Flanders and Florence had damaging effects on the cloth manufacturing industries of each of these regions and led, in turn, to a reduction in the demand for English wool.

The civil war which racked Flanders from 1379 to 1385 has been described as a 'total disaster' and the opinion advanced that 'it is questionable whether the Flemish economy recovered from this conflict before the modern period'.[1] The material damage was probably greater than that caused at any time since the struggle with France in the early fourteenth century. The English were themselves partly responsible for this, with the suburbs of Ypres being destroyed in the siege of 1383. The experience of these years probably accelerated the movement of the Flemish cloth industry from the towns to rural areas. This encouraged the use of cheaper native, Scots and Spanish wool at the expense of the English product. The same tendency is observable in Brabant. This reduction in the demand for English wool in the southern Low Countries was only partly compensated for by new customers in Holland, whose cloth industry dates from the late fourteenth century. The revolt of the Ciompi in Florence in 1379 dealt a blow from which the cloth industry of that region never properly recovered. The city continued, however, to buy English wool, as did Milan and Venice and other textile towns in northern Italy. Unfortunately it is difficult to gauge the Italian demand for English wool in the late middle ages. Fiscal policy acted as a disincentive to Italian merchants to export wool from England and encouraged them to buy it at the Calais staple. This was shipped at Antwerp or Bruges or taken to Italy via the Alpine passes. This trade is less easy to detect than direct exports from England.

None of the groups who successively governed in England during the reign of Richard II was firmly committed to the principle of maintaining the staple at Calais. Some of them, indeed, were actively opposed to its presence there, while for others the location of the staple and the degree to which it was enforced were matters of expediency. With the return to Calais, however, the wool merchants quickly reorganised the semi-corporate nature of the trade. One indication of this is a mandate to the merchants of the fellowship of the staple to build at their own cost a fifty-oared balinger. Another is a request to Parliament for permission to tax themselves for the safe conduct of their goods between Gravelines and Calais. In this period the trade was still dominated by Londoners and in return for financial support the government agreed to allow them to regulate the flow of exports. In the summer of 1377 the merchants advanced £10 000, which was to be repaid out of the wool duties of the leading ports. The loan was underwritten by the London capitalists, although others, including the provincial merchants, were expected to contribute and for a time export was to be confined to those who did so. The Londoners tried, not very successfully, to dictate the timing of exports. In August it was ordered that the new season's wool should cross to Calais between 14 September and 13 October and that no more should be sent until Christmas. Shortly afterwards it was agreed that merchants who contributed to the loan might export at their leisure until Christmas and that thereafter no more should pass until Purification (2 February 1378). In mid-December the Londoners, impatient with merchants of Boston and Lincoln who had agreed to take a share in the loan, complained that they were deliberately delaying their shipments and threatened that unless they exported immediately others would be allowed to take their quotas. On 8 January 1378 it was proclaimed that wool might be exported freely between 20 January and the end of March but that thereafter none might leave until September. Although alleged dangers at sea were cited in justification of this restriction it was a clear statement of intent to control the export of wool in the following season. This attempt to regulate the flow of exports seems to have been abandoned in March 1378, when it was announced that all merchants might export at any time at their own risk.[2]

In the parliament which sat in the spring of 1379 a petition was presented from the town of Calais which alleged that all the wools of England, Wales, Ireland and Berwick should be sent to its staple and which complained that this law was not observed. In consequence of the complaint an ordinance was made that aliens must ship wool only in company with Englishmen and that they must find security of Englishmen to take it only to Calais. The evidence of the surviving customs particulars shows that this law was generally observed. Except in the case of Italian vessels shipments containing only alien wool are very exceptional. However, the ordinance did not restore the monopoly of the Calais staple in which a breach, already legally established, was widened as a result of representations made in this same parliament. As late as July 1377 the council had reaffirmed the monopoly of Calais and ruled that both aliens and denizens might take wool there and nowhere else. In the parliament which sat at Gloucester in the autumn of 1378 an ordinance was made which allowed Italian merchants to export wool to 'western parts', that is to the Mediterranean via the Straits of Gibraltar. The concession was drawn into a statutory right, recognised by successive kings whenever they confirmed the liberties of the staplers. Sometimes the Italians were required to give security that they would take the wool only to Italy and to bring back certificates that this had been done. There is no evidence, however, that this was the general rule.[3]

In the same parliament of 1379 which had legislated on the Calais petition a complaint was made by the town of Newcastle on Tyne that no wool had been exported from that port for two years because northern merchants took their wool to Berwick where the rates of duty were lower. No action was taken in Parliament, but a few months later the king issued a licence to the merchants of Newcastle allowing them to export 1000 sacks direct to Flanders or elsewhere, paying the English customs and the 1s 7d which would have been charged at Calais. At the same time every effort was to be made to prevent English wool being taken to Berwick. The right of Newcastle merchants to avoid the staple depended on royal licence until given statutory authority in the late fifteenth century. Because the staplers consistently opposed the granting of the licences, when their liberties were confirmed at the accession of Henry VI the government specifically stated that it was within the king's prerogative to license northern wools to go elsewhere than to Calais. The position of the Newcastle merchants in the reigns of Richard II and all three Lancastrians depended on the relations between the Crown and the staplers. Whenever the king wished to conciliate the staplers he refused, or revoked, the Newcastle licence, while at other times he granted it willingly. What consideration, if any, was given by Newcastle is not recorded. The licence always specified that export was to be restricted to the poor wools of the northern counties which, allegedly, could not bear the expense of going to Calais and still return a profit. Because of this the staplers based their objection on the claim that the licence was used as a cover to export the better sorts of wool which should go to Calais. In the fifteenth century the licence frequently specified that the wool should be taken for one year to Bruges and the next to Middelburg. This may have been intended to prevent the traffic with either town from being drawn into a precedent.[4]

The right of the merchants of Berwick to export elsewhere than to Calais was intermediate between that of the Italians and that of the Newcastle men. It began as a royal concession but was accepted as a right by Henry IV. Scope for the royal prerogative remained in the power to adjust the levels of duty and the regions from which wool might be drawn. In the 1390s, 26s 8d duty was charged on wool grown between the rivers Cocket and Tweed, 13s 4d on that grown in Teviotdale and other parts of Scotland in the allegiance of Richard II and 6s 8d on that from parts recognising the King of Scotland. In 1410, after the burning of Berwick the duty of the first sort of wool was reduced to 13s 4d. In 1426, when the Scots refused to sell their wool, Berwick merchants were given permission to buy in England.[5]

Once the government had breached the monopoly of the Calais staple by allowing Italians and the merchants of Newcastle to export elsewhere it seems to have been ready to permit further exceptions, provided that it derived some benefit from the concession. On 2 October 1379 it was proclaimed that all merchants might export wherever they pleased provided that they paid the custom in advance, together with the 1s 7d due at Calais. This offer, which found no takers, was clearly inspired by a desire to anticipate the customs revenue. It was not provoked by any threat to the Calais staple, since the Flemish insurrection began only in September 1379 with the rising of the weavers of Ghent. In the parliaments of January and November 1380, however, the chancellor alleged that the revolt was discouraging the Flemings from buying wool and that in consequence the customs revenue was declining. These complaints appear premature since there seems to have been little or no reduction in exports before Michaelmas 1380, although thereafter the shortfall was serious. Nevertheless the revival of plans to bypass the staple did not spring from a threat to Calais but, again, from the government's desperate shortage of cash. In the parliament which sat during the winter of 1381–2 the Lords and the Commons agreed that with the advice of the council the king might issue licences to export elsewhere than to Calais to all who would lend money. Immediately Parliament broke up on 25 February a great council was held at Windsor, to which two or three merchants from each of the main towns were summoned. When the merchants refused to lend any money, Parliament was reconvened in May 1382 and told that £60 000 must be raised to finance a campaign led by the king in person to recover his French throne. The leading merchants were again asked for loans and again refused. They justified their stand by reciting the melancholy example of Pole, Wesenham and other English financiers of Edward III and stating that they feared a similar fate for themselves. The government thereupon announced that if it could not raise money by one means it must do so by another and rushed through an ordinance, which was published on 11 May, only four days after Parliament assembled. This appealed to merchants to pay export duties in advance at the Exchequer by 19 July next. All who did so would receive a rebate of 6s 8d per sack and might export wherever they wished from 1 September 1382 to Michaelmas 1383. Very few took advantage of this offer.[6]

The parliament which sat from 6 October to 24 October 1382 was largely taken up by a discussion of rival military plans. One party desired finance for an expedition to Portugal by John of Gaunt, but the Commons favoured a campaign in Flanders. To facilitate an alliance with Ghent it was agreed that the staple might officially be removed from Calais. Although not specified, the new staple was intended to be held at Bruges where English merchants already had what Thomas Walsingham called a 'countour'. He commended the men of Ghent for their treatment of English merchants when they captured that town in 1382 but charged the French, who took it later that same year, with slaying English apprentices there. The French invasion of West Flanders in the autumn of 1382 and their victory at Roosebeke on 27 November not only prevented the removal of the staple to Bruges but also brought the wool trade to a standstill. Merchants refused to export lest their wool be captured at sea. On 10 December the government wrote to the customers of Boston and Hull saying that merchants might take wool wherever they pleased provided that they paid the English duty and that due at Calais. About the same time it received intelligence that the merchants were fearful of exporting because of the news from Flanders. The following day it sent again to Boston saying that all who had already loaded wool on which the duty had not yet been paid might unload it for safe keeping provided that they paid half the duty. They could reship it at their pleasure, paying the other half at such time. On 12 December similar authority was issued to the London customers, but there merchants were required to pay the full duty before they might unload. Letters were sent to Hull on 18 January 1383.[7]

With West Flanders under the control of the French it became imperative to find an alternative venue for the staple, not now for diplomatic reasons but simply because the Flemings were denied access to Calais. On 14 December 1382 credentials were issued for an embassy to the Duke of Holland and Zeeland to discuss the affairs of the merchants. Among the envoys was the London merchant William Brampton. In the spring of 1383 wool began to be sent to Middelburg in Zeeland. This was well-situated for trade with Ghent and Brabant but it was not yet designated a compulsory staple. As late as 12 October 1383 the English customers were informed that merchants might take wool to any parts within the king's friendship.[8]

When Parliament met on 26 October 1383 the Commons requested that attention be given to the question of the staple which, it said, had been unsettled for two or three years. It did not, however, make any firm proposal in its petition. The government's reply was that if peace was made or a general truce agreed for three years or more the staple should be in Calais, otherwise it was to be held in England in such place or places as would be ordained by the council. An English staple implied freedom to export to any place not at war with England, which was the existing state of affairs. The situation was complicated by the fact that the king was still levying 1s 7d on all exports in lieu of the duty charged at Calais. The Commons petitioned against this, presumably on the grounds that it was illogical to do so when Calais was unusable and no wool at all was being sent there. The Lords trying the petition stated that this was reasonable and allowed the claim. Ministers of the government, however, crossed out the endorsement and noted that the king did not wish to allow it. Subsequently they were forced to concede the claim and on 26 November the customers were informed that denizens were no longer to pay the Calais dues. Aliens were forced to continue the payment, probably on the grounds that they had always paid it when not exporting to Calais. The defeat of the government on the matter of the Calais dues probably influenced its attitude towards the staple question. Without this income it had nothing to gain from supporting the right of merchants to export wherever they wished. It therefore sanctioned the establishment of a compulsory staple at Middelburg and William Brampton was elected governor. The royal letters of confirmation, dated 24 January 1384, stated that all the former privileges and obligations of the staple were to be enforced at Middelburg.[9]

The Middelburg staple did not long remain unchallenged, for when Parliament met in October 1385 the chancellor, Michael de la Pole, urged that the staple should be held in England. He claimed not only was this preferable from the monetary stand-point but that it was also worth an additional 1000 marks a year in customs revenue. There is no indication of how this figure was arrived at, but the surrender of the Calais dues had cost at least that amount. Pole was supported by a Commons petition urging the same course of action. As a result an ordinance was made stating that the staple was to be in England, but leaving all details about timing and regulations to be decided by the council. There is no indication that the council took steps to implement the ordinance, but it may have been on the strength of it that some London merchants resumed exports to Calais in 1386. They could legitimately do this, since an English staple permitted them to export to wherever they pleased. They may have been influenced in their decision by the fact that the rebels of Ghent came to terms with their count at the end of 1385 and the prospect of peace in Flanders meant that the Flemings might once more be able to come to Calais. Some of the Londoners apparently regretted the decision and obtained permission to ship their wool from Calais to Middelburg, while a renewal of fighting between England and France in 1387 seems to have prevented further efforts to revive the use of Calais. From the end of 1386 at latest Middelburg seems to have been regarded as the official staple and government organised convoys were dispatched there from London in December and from the Orwell in January 1387.[10]

In the Merciless Parliament of February 1388 there was a call for the removal of the staple from Middelburg to Calais by the following Michaelmas. The answer was given that the staple would be removed but that the council would decide whether it was to be to Calais or to England. In the event nothing was done and instructions were given to the customers that all wool was to continue to go to Middelburg. The demand for a return to Calais was repeated in the parliament which met at Cambridge in the following autumn and this time the government gave way. On 24 October a proclamation was issued that henceforth all wool should be exported to Calais and the same day orders were sent to William Brampton to remove himself and all the instruments of the staple to Calais by 1 December. Subsequently he was instructed to remain at Middelburg until 2 February 1389. By this time negotiations were going on for a truce with France, which was concluded at Leulingham in June 1389. In 1396 it was renewed for a period of thirty years. It was necessary to include Flanders in the terms, for since the accession of the Duke of Burgundy in 1384 England had been at war with the county. However even before the first truce was formally signed safe conducts were being issued for Flemish ships to come to Calais.[11]

General satisfaction with the return of the staple to Calais was short lived, for when Parliament met at the beginning of 1390 it demanded that the staple be established in England by the following Michaelmas and that thereafter it should not be removed without the consent of Parliament. While accepting this request the king stated that, for sound reasons and on the advice of the Lords, the return should be delayed until St Andrew's day (30 November). It was proposed that when home staples were established, exports by denizens should once more be prohibited. The Commons, however, realised the impossibility of preventing denizens from exporting under the cover of alien factors and were apparently prepared to tolerate this, provided that alien rates of duty were paid. They requested the repeal of the Edwardian law which decreed forfeiture of all wool cocketed in a name other than that of the real owner. This the king declined to accept.[12]

The staple was still at Calais when Parliament met again on 12 November 1390. This parliament, which sat until 3 December, was concerned almost exclusively with matters of trade and its determination to secure the return of the staple was given statutory sanction. The staple was to return to England by 9 January 1391 at the latest and was to be held in those towns named in the statute of 1354. To enforce its decision, Parliament decreed that the authority to collect the subsidy on exported wool should cease if the staple had not been brought back by that date. It was also to cease if the staple was removed from England at any time in the next three years. In an effort to improve the prices of wool, restrictions were placed on the activities of English middlemen. Outside of the staple towns denizens might buy wool only directly from the owners of sheep or tithes and within the staples they might not buy it for the purpose of regrating. This allowed cloth manufacturers to buy their raw material either in the country or in the staples but confined broggers to a single transaction between the growers and the home staples. Instructions were sent to the customs officials banning all exports by denizens on 6 January and 16 January 1391.[13]

The legislation of 1390 proved to be a total failure and was reversed in the parliament which sat during November 1391. The need to improve the price of wool was cited as the second of three reasons for summoning this assembly. It was enacted that the present home staples should remain until midsummer 1392, but that then they should cease. Instead all ports authorised to export wool were to be designated home staples and Calais was to be once again a compulsory overseas staple. The ban on denizen exports was removed immediately as were the restrictions on the trade in wool within the country. This meant that both natives and aliens might buy wool from any person anywhere within the realm and that the former might again export in their own names at denizen rates of duty. Merchants were authorised, although not compelled, to export to Calais from March 1392, but on 30 May instructions were given that henceforth all wool was to go to Calais. The ban on denizen exports was replaced in this parliament by new bullion regulations which provide a clue to the thinking behind the former prohibition.[14]

The theoretical monopoly of the Calais staple remained intact for only a few weeks, for on 24 June 1392 writs were sent to at least Southampton and Hull stating that denizens might export from those ports to western parts, that is to the Mediterranean. On 26 June 1394 similar instructions were sent to all ports. Those who took advantage of the offer were apparently required only to pay an additional 8d per sack in lieu of Calais dues. This was lower than the former rate since the Calais staple fee had been reduced in consequence of all wool now being required to pay a registration fee in the staples at the English ports. Merchants at first tried to evade this latter fee but were ordered to pay it to the mayors of the staples. The general absence of this 'Calais money' from the English customs accounts suggests that few natives were exporting to Italy at this period. However, William Venour of London regularly exported Welsh wool to Italy throughout the 1390s. There was also an attempt to breach the monopoly of the Calais staple in other directions. The truce with France restored the prospect of the wools of the southern counties feeding the looms of Normandy as they had done before the beginning of the Hundred Years War. There is evidence of French merchants buying wool from Lettley Abbey and commissions were issued to enquire into allegations that wool was smuggled to France from Sussex and Hampshire. In the parliament of January 1394 the commons of Berkshire, Hampshire, Wiltshire, Dorset and Somerset petitioned that their wools were slight wools which could not bear the expense and competition of the Calais staple and requested that they be allowed to export them to Normandy. This request was refused.[15]

In June 1396 the general concession that denizens might export direct to the Mediterranean was apparently withdrawn, for instructions were issued that henceforth all wool must go to Calais, except that for which special licences were issued. This did not mean that the king was willing to enforce the monopoly of Calais, merely that he wished to be paid for permission to take wool elsewhere. In the parliament of January 1398 the Commons complained that the sale of licences was destroying the Calais staple. The reply to the petition was evasive, conceding that no more 'licences' would be issued, but excepting the *especiale congie* of the king. On 30 September 1399, the first day of the reign of Henry IV, instructions were sent to the customers of Southampton stating that all merchants, including denizens, might export to Italy and the western parts. This concession was revoked in the parliament which met a few days later. As already mentioned Henry IV, in confirming the liberties of the staplers, guaranteed the monopoly of Calais, saving only the position of Berwick and the right of Italians and Spaniards to export to the western parts.[16] Despite the promise by Henry IV to respect the monopoly of Calais the staplers continually complained that he issued licences for wool to be taken elsewhere. They presented a petition to this effect in the parliament of January 1401 and another in October 1402. On the latter occasion the king again promised to respect the monopoly. Nevertheless while discussing the location of the staple in 1404 the Commons called for the revocation of licences to export elsewhere than to Calais. In November 1406, after renewed complaints from the staplers, the customers of Newcastle were instructed to take security from all who exported from there that they would ship wool only to Calais. These instructions were repeated in May 1407. However, certain Newcastle merchants complained that by virtue of the earlier licence they had bought a large quantity of wool which was too poor to go to Calais and that this was now deteriorating. In June 1408 they were told that they might export this after Martinmas. In July 1410, however, the Newcastle merchants were given a fresh licence to export 2000 sacks of wool. It was probably this grant which provoked another protest by the staplers in the parliament of 1411.[17]

The complaints of the staplers about licences seem to relate mainly to the concession granted to the merchants of Newcastle. There is no evidence that the king authorised any other breach of their monopoly. He did sanction at least two attempts by English merchants to obtain a foothold in the Mediterranean trade, but this did not threaten the staplers in quite the same way. Evidence of the first attempt is provided only by a fragmentary Exchequer account, which shows that in 1403 a London ship, the *Anthony*, was sent to the Mediterranean with a cargo which included 19 sacks of wool. The fate of this ship is not known, but there is nothing to suggest that it provoked a diplomatic incident as did the next recorded expedition. In November 1411 a group of London merchants asked for a licence to send wool and other merchandise to the Mediterranean. Their request was granted and in April 1412 they freighted one Dutch and one Castillian ship with goods alleged to be worth £24 000. Royal letters of safe conduct were addressed to all authorities who might be met with on the way, but there is no suggestion that the ships had a specific destination. On reaching the Mediterranean the cargoes were seized by the Genoese and in March 1413 the London syndicate which had sponsored the voyage was granted letters of marque against Genoese merchants.[18]

The reign of Henry V was almost entirely free from complaints by the staplers about breaches of their monopoly, satisfaction being found, no doubt, in the fact that for the greater part of this period there was no export of wool from Newcastle. The complaint of the staplers in the penultimate parliament of the reign, May 1421, was directed not against licensed export but against the smuggling of un-customed wool to Holland and Zeeland. More revealing are the charges made by the Commons, both in this and in the previous parliament (December 1420), that the growing use of Scots and Spanish wool was damaging the sale of English wool in Flanders. It was alleged that in former times there had been an agreement that only English wool would be sold in Flanders and that in return England would not sell her cloth there. The Commons demanded that since England and Burgundy were now allies the duke should be made to enforce this agreement.[19]

The conquest of Normandy by Henry V reopened the question of the direct export to that province of the wools of the southern English counties. In October 1419 it was agreed in Parliament that wool might be sent there for the use of the king's subjects, but purely as a temporary measure. However when it became necessary to confirm the charters of the staple at the accession of Henry VI a proposal was made that the slight wools of Hampshire, Sussex, Kent and Yorkshire should be exempted from staple regulations. The staplers presented a reasoned argument against this suggestion, but the matter was not dismissed out of hand. It was agreed that these wools must go to the staple until the next parliament should meet and that the royal pre-rogative to license exceptions should be reserved. The prerogative was exercised, on the advice of the council, in 1427 when it was agreed that the Bishop of Winchester might export 800 sacks to Normandy. Already in 1423 the Earl of Westmorland had been licensed to send 500 sacks of northern wool to Holland or Zeeland. This appears to have been a grant to an individual of the licence formerly vested col-lectively in the merchants of Newcastle. Later in the reign of Henry VI the subject of licences to avoid the staple became a serious grievance, but before examining that matter consideration must be given to the question of fiscal policy.[20]

When the reign of Richard II began it was clearly understood that the subsidy on wool, as opposed to the hereditary custom of 6s 8d paid by denizens and 10s by aliens, could only be levied with the consent of Parliament. It was equally clearly recognised that unless Parliament was prepared to continue the subsidy it would be obliged to vote the king larger and more frequent amounts of direct taxation. On the whole the former course of action was preferred. The subsidy of 43s 4d on both denizens and aliens was not due to expire until Michaelmas 1379, but in November 1378 Parliament extended it until Easter 1380 and also agreed that from Easter 1379 it should be increased by 13s 4d. Before the addition came into force it was rescinded in favour of a poll tax modelled on that levied two years previously. History was to prove that a higher rate of wool subsidy was a lesser evil than the poll tax. After this the subsidy was twice renewed at the same rate, each time for short periods but well before it was due to expire.[21]

When Parliament met in November 1381 in the aftermath of the peasants' revolt complaints about the nation's poverty and demands for retrenchment were voiced more loudly than ever. The subsidy was to expire at Christmas and it was desirable to renew it before Parliament adjourned for the festivities. However, in order to demonstrate their independence the assembly deliberately allowed it to expire, renewing it only from 1 January to 2 February, thereby ensuring that they would have to be recalled. In the final session of the resumed parliament, on 25 February 1382, the subsidy was continued until Midsummer 1386. At the next renewal, in December 1385, the members again made a token demonstration of the fact that they controlled the purse. They reduced the denizen rate from 43s 4d to 42s 4d, left a gap between Midsummer and 1 August 1386 and granted the subsidy for one year from the latter date.[22]

The Wonderful Parliament, which met on 1 October 1386, secured the resignation of the Chancellor and the Treasurer and impeached the former. One of the main grievances against him was his failure to implement a commission set up in the previous parliament to investigate royal finances. The present parliament appears to have suspended the authority by which the subsidy was currently being collected, restoring it only in December after they had attained their political objectives. At the same time they slightly extended the duration of the subsidy to 20 November 1387, or to Christmas if Parliament had not met by the earlier date. However the grant was limited by the provision that it would become invalid and that the subsidy should not be collected if the king dismissed or annulled the powers of the continual commission which Parliament appointed to investigate and control royal finances for one year from 20 November 1386.[23]

Parliament did not, in fact, meet again until 3 February 1388. This was the Merciless Parliament in which the lords appellant, following the royalist defeat at Radcott Bridge in the previous December, secured the condemnation of many of the king's supporters. Authority for the collection of the subsidy had expired at Christmas and on 30 December all ports had been instructed to stop the export of wool until further notice. Orders for the resumption of exports were issued on 20 March 1388, the day on which Parliament renewed the subsidy until Whitsun. On 2 June, two days before it broke up, Parliament renewed the subsidy until Midsummer 1389, now restoring the 1s which had been symbolically cut from the denizen rate. The lords appellant were awarded £20 000 for their expenses to be paid out of the wool subsidy.[24]

The subsidy granted in June 1388 continued to be collected beyond Midsummer 1389. Therefore unless it was levied without authorisation it must have been renewed at the same rate in the parliament which met at Cambridge in the autumn of 1388, an assembly for which no official record survives. The next parliament assembled on 17 January 1390 and on 2 March it made a grant operative from the previous day until the following Christmas. The rate of subsidy was reduced by 10s for both denizens and aliens. This reduction may have been intended to ensure that the government carried out its promise to bring the staple back to England, for in December 1390 the old rates were restored with effect from 30 November and the subsidy was renewed for three years.[25]

The history of the wool subsidy in the last years of Richard II is an apt comment on the degree to which the king had gathered the reins of power back into his own hands. Although the previous grant expired on 30 November 1396 the government seems neither to have stopped the export of wool nor to have relinquished its claim to the subsidy. The parliament which met on 22 January 1397 renewed the tax retrospectively for a period of five years and there is no record of any complaint about the irregularity of the proceeding. In this parliament the Commons planned to protest against the extravagance of the royal household, but they were compelled to withdraw their bill and to tender apologies. Worse was to come, however. In the Shrewsbury Parliament of 1398 Richard forced the Commons to grant him the subsidy for life, at the same time increasing the alien rate by 6s 8d. He did this by the device of withholding the royal pardon from fifty un-named persons, who were alleged to have been involved in the activities of the lords appellant. The Commons could do no more than to protest feebly that the life grant was not to be a precedent for future reigns.[26]

When the first parliament of Henry IV met in October 1399 there were complaints about the award of the subsidy to Richard II for life and the present grant was made for the duration of three years only. This being the case there was unease when the king began to reward his supporters with life-time annuities charged against the subsidy, since this implied that it would be renewed indefinitely. In the next parliament the king was compelled to cancel such annuities, but in 1404 it was agreed that an exception should be made in favour of the Duke of York.[27]

The grant made by Parliament to Henry IV specified a denizen duty of 50s and an alien rate of 60s, and this award was continued for a further three years when it expired at Michaelmas 1402. In 1404, however, the Exchequer began to demand an additional 6s 8d per sack from both aliens and denizens. It claimed that the parliamentary grant was a subsidy only and the extra sum represented the ancient custom. When Parliament met in October 1404 it protested against this interpretation and stated that the sums mentioned in its awards had been intended to embrace the ancient custom. It claimed that confusion had arisen because of carelessness on the part of Chancery clerks. In view of the time-lag between the grants and the present controversy this explanation must be considered suspect. It is by no means impossible that the Commons had been engaged in a subtle attempt to bring the king's hereditary custom within the control of Parliament and that the plan misfired as a result of the vigilance of officials of the Crown. The dispute was settled by a compromise. The government maintained its claim that the 60s and 50s were merely subsidy, but the king relinquished his right to ancient custom on all wool exported between his coronation (12 October 1399) and Martinmas (11 November) 1404. In return he was to receive the subsidy of 60s and 50s plus the ancient custom on all exports from Martinmas to Michaelmas 1405. The new grant of subsidy for two years from Michaelmas 1405 made it quite clear that the rates of 53s and 43s 4d did not include the ancient custom. Thus the king's hereditary right to this duty, as well as to the 3s 4d paid by aliens under the terms of the charter of 1303, remained firmly outside the control of Parliament. The first parliament of Henry V granted him the subsidy for four years from Michaelmas 1413. However, in November 1415, probably in a mood of euphoria following news of the victory at Agincourt, the king was awarded the subsidy for life. This generosity was not repeated at the accession of his son in 1422. Henry VI was granted the subsidy for only two years in the first instance, while the denizen rate was reduced from 43s 4d to 33s 4d.[28]

During the reign of Henry IV native merchants gained an important concession as regards payment of duty. Until now they had been required to pay the full duty when the cocket letters were issued by the customs officials. Only occasionally, and by royal licence, were they allowed to postpone payment. In August 1403 the king's council decided that henceforth denizens should be required to find only 16s 4d at the time of export. This sum was earmarked for the expenses of the customs and for the defence of Calais. Half of the balance was to be paid within three months of export and the remainder within the following three months. Until the accession of Henry VI this concession remained dependent upon royal favour. Then, however, it was incorporated by Parliament within the grant of subsidy. Merchants were not required to pay anything at the time of export, but were to pay half of the duty within six months and the remainder within the following six months. It was also determined that no duty should be demanded for any wool lost at sea.[29]

Consideration of the relationship between the wool trade and English monetary policy requires us to retrace our steps to the reign of Edward III. It will be recalled that the bullion regulation of the 1340s had been designed to promote the flow of silver into England for the purposes of internal trade. The problems resulting from the silver shortage were more effectively solved by the Black Death, for with the great loss of population and a lower level of commercial activity coin became relatively abundant. However, if government proclamations may be credited the situation was soon threatened once more by the illegal export of coin. This movement may have been encouraged by the debasements of Louis de Mâle in Flanders or by some other factor which made it more profitable to export coin rather than commodities to the marts of the Low Countries. The government's response in 1351 was to carry out its own debasement of both the silver and gold coinage. One cannot rule out the possibility, however, that the prospect of the seignorage profits to be derived from a general recoinage was an important factor in deciding this course of action. The debasement was enormously more successful than that of the 1340s in attracting silver and gold to the mint. Unfortunately the mint records of this period no longer draw a distinction between bullion of foreign origin and native issues brought for recoinage. During the first three months of the debasement the value of gold coined was more than five times that of silver, but during the course of the next two years the position was reversed and nearly twice as much silver was minted as gold.[30] In the following two years the situation was again dramatically reversed and gold out-valued silver by more than two to one. Although it must be pointed out that the latter reversal co-incided with the legal monopoly of wool exports by alien merchants I do not wish to draw any conclusions from that fact. It will not be possible to formulate any meaningful theory about the important fluctuations in English mint output during the 1350s and early 1360s until all aspects of overseas trade have been thoroughly examined.

The opening of a mint in Calais in 1363 undoubtedly affected the output of the London mint and the former establishment must always be reckoned with in any attempt to calculate England's total supply of treasure. From about July 1351 to Michaelmas 1362 the output of the London mint averaged about £100 200 by value per annum of gold and £36 300 of silver. From Michaelmas 1362 to Michaelmas 1368 the respective values averaged £21 119 and £1611, no silver at all being struck in the years 1365–7. At Calais from February 1363 to August 1368 the annual output of gold averaged about £51 000, while £3165 of silver was produced from February 1363 to April 1365 and nothing thereafter. In the early 1370s minting at Calais was presumably hit by the fact that a great deal of wool was licensed to be sold away from the staple and from August 1368 to November 1374 the average production of gold was slightly less than £23 000 a year. Nevertheless London gold production in the period 1368–74 increased only to an average of £26 072 and silver production remained negligible. The re-establishment of the Calais monopoly of wool exports in 1376 does not seem to have given much of a fillip to minting in the town since gold production in the period November 1374 to May 1381 totalled only £29 843. The revolt of Flanders and the disruption of the Calais staple then put an end to all mint activity until 1387.

One of the main commercial considerations for the establishment of the staple at Calais had been the desire to make foreign buyers pay for wool in English coin. For years the exporters had complained that in Flanders they had been paid in foreign minted gold which, according to English standards, was overvalued. Merchants would lose by bring-ing this coin to England. With the staple at Calais, together with a mint producing English coin, it was possible to insist that buyers ex-change bullion or foreign coins for nobles before purchasing wool. The gold would then be valued according to the English standard. In fact this practice was not rigidly enforced. A few surviving schedules of the Calais mint indicate that although a considerable amount of gold was brought to the mint by Flemings and by Italians coming from Flanders some was brought there by Englishmen and by Italians exporting wool from England to Calais.[31] This meant that the latter must have accep-

ted payment in bullion or in foreign coin. It is likely that most of the
nobles struck at Calais found their way to England. This mint must
have been particularly useful to provincial merchants who had no
business in London, since it spared them an unnecessary journey to
the Tower mint.

TABLE 15 *Gold minted at Calais 1363–1404*[a]

Period	Value (£ sterling)
20 Feb. 1363 – 10 Apr. 1364	52 929
10 Apr. 1364 – 13 Apr. 1365	10 248
13 Apr. 1365 – 13 Apr. 1366	95 805
13 Apr. 1366 – 20 Mar. 1368	113 960
20 Mar. 1368 – 27 Aug. 1368	7750
27 Aug. 1368 – 26 Nov. 1370	51 923
26 Nov. 1370 – 16 Oct. 1371	15 464
16 Oct. 1371 – 4 Nov. 1373	70 084
4 Nov. 1373 – 14 July 1374	1654
14 July 1374 – 4 Nov. 1374	1469
4 Nov. 1374 – 15 May 1381	29 843
15 May 1381 – 7 Jan. 1384	90
7 Jan. 1384 – 17 Jan. 1387	Nil
17 Jan. 1387 – 28 Feb. 1388	32 537
28 Feb. 1388 – 17 Jan. 1390	Account missing
17 Jan. 1390 – 17 Jan. 1393	6618
17 Jan. 1393 – 17 Jan. 1394	22 184
17 Jan. 1394 – 17 Oct. 1395	19 680
18 Oct. 1395 – 18 Oct. 1397	10 564
18 Oct. 1397 – 25 Aug. 1399	363
25 Aug. 1399 – 29 Sept. 1401	12 745
29 Sept. 1401 – 30 Mar. 1403	2597

[a] Source. Calais Treasurers' Accounts, Enrolled and Particular (E101, E364,
E372).

The decline in minting at Calais during the 1370s was not compensated for by any increase in production in England. In the years
1374–84 the Tower mint coined a mere £54 320 in gold and £16 156
in silver. In the face of this inexorable slowing down of total mint
activity after 1362 it is impossible to avoid the conclusion that the
balance of trade was turning against England. Merely as a working
hypothesis, which needs to be tested more rigorously than is possible
in the present study, it is suggested that during the 1350s England may
have recovered part of the treasure which had been squandered during
the opening years of the Hundred Years War. The main factor operating in her favour was a positive balance of trade. The fall in population must have resulted in some reduction in the level of general

imports, while home-produced cloth was substituted for all but the
most luxurious of imported fabrics. On the other hand England's
principal export, raw wool, was in greater demand than at any time
since the boom of the early fourteenth century. The commercial success
was not negated by misfortune in war. This period was one of the
few in which the country may have gained some positive benefit from
its indulgence in the military arts, in the shape of booty and ransoms
extracted from the Scots and the French. This strong position was
weakened during the peaceful 1360s when wool exports began to
decline. After 1368 it was eroded even more rapidly as the continuing
fall in exports was combined with the unsuccessful prosecution of war.

By 1379 the deterioration in the balance of trade was sufficiently
serious to be brought to the attention of Parliament. The Commons
complained that no gold or silver was being brought into the country,
while both metals were being exported. However, the legislation which
was passed in an effort to reverse this trend was limited to the period
which should elapse until the meeting of the next parliament. It was
not then renewed. It was enacted that merchants importing certain
luxury commodities must, within six months, bring to the mint one
shilling's worth of gold for every pound of their value. Similarly wool
merchants were required to render 1s in the pound within twelve
months of export. The proportion was only half of that which had
been suggested by the Commons and the yield of gold was very disappointing. Nothing seems to have been extracted from importers and
only £2515 worth of gold from certain wool merchants, from whom
the customs officials of London and Boston had taken security.[32]

In the parliament which sat from November 1381 to February 1382
there were renewed complaints about the export of specie and a commission of mint officials and goldsmiths was summoned to advise on
this and allied monetary matters. The experts were agreed that in
order to preserve the nation's stock of precious metals the value of
imports must not exceed that of exports, in other words trade must be
in balance. They also recommended that controls against the export
of money should be tightened, including in their definition of money
not merely coin but letters of exchange. The latter advice was accepted
and incorporated in a permanent statute. However, in their pursuit
of the letter of exchange the legislators had been led astray by their
detestation of the use made of it to transfer money to Rome. The law
proved to be too severe in its application and in the next parliament,
October 1382, it was amended to allow the use of the letter of exchange in commercial transactions. A joint petition from the Commons
and Italian bankers claimed that the letter of exchange was essential

to the conduct of the wool trade.[33] There was no further legislation on monetary policy until the parliament of 1390 which secured the return of the staple from Calais to England. Then it was enacted that all alien merchants must buy English goods to at least half the value of any merchandise imported. Further, whenever letters of exchange were sent abroad English goods must be bought to their full value. It is suggested that these measures provide a clue to the thinking which resulted in aliens being vested with a monopoly of the export of wool. With the establishment of a compulsory staple at Calais the alien share of the wool trade had declined even more than the overall fall in exports. Although there was no legal impediment to their trading at Calais they could not compete in this market with Englishmen since they were burdened with a higher rate of export duty. Aliens continued, however, to handle a large part of the import trade. They were embarrassed by the lack of a suitable investment for the proceeds resulting from the sale of their goods, since the overseas market for English cloth was not yet sufficient to employ much of their capital. Legally prohibited from exporting bullion, aliens could only repatriate their money by means of the letter of exchange about which Parliament was still uneasy. The new regulations were a compromise, which allowed aliens to transmit half of the proceeds of the sale of imports as a letter of exchange and half in the form of English products. In order to provide aliens with a suitable export commodity Parliament was willing to vest them with a monopoly of wool exports. It is quite certain that Parliament expected Englishmen to evade the ban, but it presumably believed that the legal monopoly would enable aliens to increase their share of the trade sufficiently to engage much of the capital generated by the sale of imports.[34]

For English merchants the cure proposed for the country's monetary problem was worse than the disease and, as already seen, the alien monopoly of wool export was swiftly rescinded. The restoration of the denizen trade was accompanied, however, by a new bullion regulation. In December 1391 it was ruled that all merchants, denizen as well as alien, must import one ounce of gold in foreign coin for every sack of wool or 240 fells exported. After Midsummer 1392 the gold was to be taken to the mint at Calais. After Parliament dispersed, the council, apparently on its own authority, decided that merchants might pay an additional duty in lieu of importing gold, the rate being 13s 4d per sarpler or 480 fells. In fact this sum had to be paid to the customs by all wool exporters as security for importing gold. If, within six months, they produced delivery receipts from the mint the money would be refunded, otherwise it was forfeit. In March 1392 the penalty was reduced to 6s 8d per sarpler or 480 fells and when the Calais mint became the delivery point it may have been abandoned altogether.[35]

The Calais mint had resumed production in 1387, before the return of the staple from Middelburg. In the period 17 January 1387 to 28 February 1388 gold had been coined to the value of £32 527 and £9 15s 4d had been spent on repairs to the mint. This gold was presumably the proceeds of wool taken to Calais by Londoners in 1386. It is most regrettable that in the next period, 28 February 1388 to 17 January 1390, there is a gap in the Calais treasurer's accounts, but there is no reason to doubt that with the official return of the staple to Calais the mint was in full production. From 17 January 1390 to 17 January 1393 it produced only £6618 in gold, but this low figure is explained by the return of the staple to England and the order that merchants must bring gold to the London mint. When the law was amended mint output in Calais recovered and between 17 January 1393 and 18 October 1397 £52 428 was coined. This figure would probably have been higher had it not been for a further change in the bullion regulations in January 1397.[36]

Despite the reservation made at the end of the last paragraph it is clear that during this period the proportion between gold struck in Calais and the amount of wool sold there was much less favourable than it had been during the reign of Edward III. Since the difference is not entirely accounted for by the fall in the price of wool two other factors must be taken into consideration. Some wool was undoubtedly exchanged at Calais for Flemish imitations of the English noble. Philip the Bold had been requested to produce these coins by the échevins of Ghent in March 1388 and he authorised the work in the following October.[37] Although intended to pass for the genuine article the coins had a lower gold content than the English noble and yielded Flemish merchants a slight profit compared with the price paid for gold at the Calais mint. However even this explanation is inadequate to explain the comparatively low level of mint activity at Calais. The entire gold production of the Burgundian Low Countries added to that of Calais did not nearly approach the value of wool delivered to the staple. The difference was presumably met by the extension of credit. While not denying the use of credit in earlier times it is suggested that this period may have been decisive in the establishment of the credit mechanism which dominated the late medieval wool trade. Under this arrangement buyers coming to the staple put down only a proportion of the total price. The staplers collected the balance at a later date in the Low Countries and with it purchased letters of exchange, by means of which they transmitted their money to England.

The influx of Flemish nobles, the increasing use of credit and the failure of the staplers to bring gold to the Calais mint probably combined to provoke the parliamentary ordinance of January 1397 that henceforth all merchants, denizen and alien, must bring to the London mint one ounce of gold in foreign coin for every sack of wool exported. Security was to be provided at the customs in the form of 13s 4d per sarpler or 480 fells. Twelve months later in the Shrewsbury Parliament there was a joint petition from English and alien merchants protesting at being made to bring gold to London when there was a mint at Calais. Much was made of the inconvenience caused to provincial merchants, who exported only 10–20 sacks of wool, by having to make an unnecessary journey to London. It was also pointed out that the Duke of Burgundy had banned the export of bullion from his dominions. The only reply afforded to the protest was that the king would raise the matter with the duke. No remedy was provided until the first parliament of Henry IV when it was ruled that henceforth merchants might take bullion to the Calais mint. The king also pardoned the merchants for past offences against the bullion regulations and ordered that all outstanding securities be cancelled.[38]

In January 1401 Parliament complained about the renewed export of coin and demanded that the measures designed to prevent this should be more strictly enforced. It also charged the staplers with accepting Flemish nobles and importing them into England. It was alleged that in every payment of £5 a man was sure to receive three or four spurious nobles, which were worth 2d less than the genuine coins. To remedy the situation it was enacted that all foreign coins, including the false nobles, should cease to be legal tender and must either be exported or brought to the mint by the following Christmas. The problem of the Flemish nobles soon solved itself, or at least became less acute, with the closure in June 1402 of the last Burgundian mint at Bruges. In fact the closure provided the English with cold comfort, since it seems to have been brought about by an acute shortage of bullion which was soon to close the Calais mint and bring that at London to a near standstill. From October 1397 to August 1399 only £353 of gold was minted at Calais. With the decision of Henry IV that merchants need no longer bring their gold to London minting increased to £12 745 in the next period, to Michaelmas 1401. From the latter date to 30 March 1403 production totalled £2597. Thereafter certainty disappears. The treasurer's account for 1403–4 is incomplete, that for 1404–5 suggests that there was no production, while by 1405–6 the mint had definitely closed down and the pix, with its triple lock, was sold for the sum of 5s.[39]

J. H. A. Munro, surveying the period 1384 to 1402, draws a picture of conscious mint competition between England and Burgundy which he describes as the 'war of the gold nobles'.[40] Whether or not he is correct in his general analysis he is mistaken in his conclusion that England lost the war. On the figures which he presents the London mint coined 21 098.3 *marcs de Troyes* of gold in this period compared with a combined production of 22 347.6 *marcs de Troyes* in the mints of the Burgundian Low Countries. Given the fact that the latter mints were the first to close this is hardly a major defeat. Further, on Munro's own statement most of the 8554.1 *marcs de Troyes* coined in the Low Countries in the first two years of the period were recoinages of earlier issues. More seriously, however, Munro failed to discover the figures for production at Calais and believed that this mint was closed from 1384 to 1422. When the Calais figures are added to those of London total English production of gold considerably exceeded that of Burgundy. The surviving Calais accounts record the coinage of £107 288 in gold, 10 221 *marcs de Troyes*, while accounts are missing for two important years, when production may easily have reached £50 000, 4763 *marcs de Troyes*. England therefore won the 'war of the gold nobles', but only at the cost of losing the 'battle' for silver. The more attractive price for silver in Flanders gave her a minting superiority over England of twenty-two to one. This redressed the combined values of gold and silver minted in favour of Flanders. The lead was significant, although not enormous.

At the end of 1411 England reduced the weight of both gold and silver coins, although the standard of fineness was retained. This led to an enormous influx of gold into the London mint, a total of £288 692 in the first two years and £313 503 during the next four years. Much of this was undoubtedly old issues brought for recoinage, but there may also have been an accession of bullion. To cope with the initial flood it was planned to reopen the Calais mint. On 30 October 1411 John de Newerk was appointed changer (*campsor*) and assayer at Calais, a post he had held during the previous period of minting. This was a salaried office under the Crown and was not filled when the mint was closed. On 23 April 1412 Richard Wandeford was appointed controller and assayer at the Calais mint. Despite these appointments it is unlikely that minting was resumed in the town. There is a gap in the Calais accounts between May 1412 and March 1413, but those before and after that date have no record of any seignorage profits.[41]

Although the English silver coins had been reduced in weight by a greater proportion than gold coins, thereby altering the bullion prices in favour of the former metal, the response of silver to the debasement was disappointing. In the six years to Michaelmas 1417 only £36 442 was coined. This was an improvement on recent years, during which the flow of silver had completely dried up, but it was trifling compared with the results of the recoinages of the thirteenth and fourteenth centuries. The English mint price for silver still could not compete with that of Flanders, which had debased its coinage and reopened a mint at Ghent in 1409.[42]

The position of the bullion regulations during the first two decades of the fifteenth century is somewhat obscure. It seems generally to have been assumed that the law requiring the import of gold in return for exported wool was in abeyance after the accession of Henry IV. In view of the small amount of gold coined before 1412 this belief may well be justified. However the question is complicated by proceedings in Parliament in 1420.[43] Briefly the Commons proposed the reopening of the Calais mint, the success of which was to be assured by hosting regulations. All alien merchants coming to the town were to host with officially registered brokers, with whom they were to deposit all bullion and coin which they had brought with them. This was to be submitted to the inspection of the officers of the mint. All English coins of full weight would be returned, but underweight coins and all those of foreign origin were to be exchanged for lawful money. The host or broker would then conclude a bargain between the aliens and the staplers. Out of the purchase price the stapler would be allowed to retain a sum to cover local expenses and any English customs which he had been instructed to pay at Calais. The balance would be put into a bag, sealed by the mint officials and reopened only in the presence of the mayor of London. The suggested procedure was cumbersome and apparently would have allowed no room for the extension of credit from the stapler to his customer. However, if strictly enforced it would have ensured that the greater part of the value of the wool was brought back to England in gold or silver coin. The Commons proposed that if their bill was carried merchants should be released from the 'anciently ordained' obligation of importing two marks of bullion for every sack of wool exported. This suggests either that the Edwardian bullion regulation was regarded as still having the force of law or, alternatively, that there had been some talk of re-enacting it. The government rejected the proposal and ordered that the old 'statutes and ordinances' should be enforced. It did, however, give approval to a second petition that aliens exporting direct to the Mediterranean should be required to import one ounce of gold for every sack taken.

In May 1421 the staplers renewed their plea for a mint at Calais, on the grounds that the treasurer would accept payment only in nobles, a demand which required them to break the law forbidding the export of these coins from England. On this occasion the request was refused, possibly because some thought was being given to the removal of the staple from Calais. Parliament made an ordinance which authorised the king and council to establish the staple, for a period of three years, in whatever place seemed most fitting. It is difficult to determine which place was being considered. In view of complaints made in the present parliament about declining sales of wool in Flanders it is possible that there was demand for a Flemish staple. On the other hand it may have been thought that home staples would encourage the sale of wool in Normandy, now a province ruled by Henry V. However the staple was suffered to remain at Calais and when the request for a mint was repeated in December 1421 it was now accepted. It probably received force from a petition of the garrison demanding payment of the arrears of their wages.[44]

After an initial period of success, in which production was on a scale comparable with that of the 1360s, the output of the Calais mint was severely curtailed. This experience may have contributed to the legislation of 1429, which has rightly been regarded as a turning point in the history of the late medieval wool trade. However, before examining this legislation and its consequences it is necessary to review the trend of exports since 1376 and to investigate the evidence relating to the composition of the trade.

In the previous chapter it was shown how the suspension of the Calais staple in the early 1370s resulted in a large increase in alien exports; in the period 1372–5 aliens averaged 10 000 sacks a year compared with a denizen figure of 15 800 sacks. The return to Calais immediately put an end to a part of the alien trade. Ignoring the transition year, 1375–6, we find that the alien average for 1376–9 was little more than 2700 sacks. On the other hand denizens increased their trade only to an average of 17 500 sacks, leaving a shortfall of 5500 sacks a year. It would be unwise to attribute all of this loss merely to the reimposition of the Calais staple, for some undoubtedly resulted from the misfortune which befell Florence at this time. In 1375 hostilities broke out between Florence and the Pope, the War of the Eight Saints, as a result of which the city was placed under an interdict. Wherever civil authorities heeded the Pope's message the trade of Florentines suffered. The ban was proclaimed in England and merchants arrested at the beginning of 1377.[45] The misery generated in this period was a contributory factor to the revolt of the Ciompi in 1379.

In 1379–80, at the beginning of the civil war in Flanders, total exports of wool from England still exceeded 20 000 sacks. Thereafter there was a sharp fall. In 1380–3 denizen exports averaged rather less than 13 500 sacks a year, although alien trade increased slightly to an average of 3300 sacks. In 1383–6 denizen exports averaged 13 400 sacks against an alien trade of 3800 sacks, while in 1386–9 respective figures are 15 200 and 3900 sacks. Since the higher denizen figure in the later period reflects a total ban on exports from June to December 1376 it is probably advisable to strike an average for 1383–9, which gives a figure of 14 300 sacks, not much better than in the worst years of the Flemish troubles. Alien exports, despite some revival, still fell short of 4000 sacks a year. At this level of trade alien merchants may have had difficulty in finding an investment for the money realised from the sale of their imports. It has already been suggested that this problem may have influenced the decision to vest aliens with a legal monopoly of wool export in 1391.

After the fiasco of the home staples denizen trade settled down at a steady level, averaging about 15 000 sacks a year during the 1390s. Alien trade, however, fell a prey to fiscal policy. Until 1398 aliens and denizens paid the same rate of subsidy, but that year the alien rate was increased by 6s 8d. Virtually the whole of the alien trade was now handled by Italians who were prepared to pay some premium for the convenience of sending wool direct to the peninsula. However, as the margin between alien and denizen duties widened it became advantageous for them to buy from Englishmen at the Calais staple. Alien exports, which averaged 4034 sacks in 1391–6, averaged 2296 sacks in 1396–8 and fell to 1632 sacks in 1398–9.

Despite the decline of alien exports denizens failed to improve their trade in the fifteenth century, indeed their own record was considerably worse than that of the 1390s. Renewal of the war with France and a privateering war with Flanders account in part for the poor performance of the early years of Henry IV's reign. However, the truces of 1408 brought little real improvement. Not until about 1412 does it seem possible to talk about a limited recovery. Denizen exports averaged about 12 400 sacks a year in 1399–1412 and 13 300 sacks in 1412–22. The latter figure includes a spell of comparatively good trade in the years 1417–19, after which exports again declined. From 1422, however, it is possible to detect a real improvement. Despite a temporary setback in the years 1424–6 denizen exports averaged about 14 500 sacks in the period 1422–8.

Although Henry IV made limited fiscal concessions to Italian merchants their stake in the wool trade continued to decline in the fifteenth century. Alien exports averaged 1321 sacks a year in 1399–1412, 946 sacks in 1412–22 and 933 sacks in 1422–8. In November 1404 the king granted a licence to John Torell and his partners of Bologna to export 1000 sacks a year, paying only denizen rates of custom and subsidy. Half was to go to Calais and half to Italy. To what extent this grant was honoured is difficult to detect. Of more general concern was the question of the alien rate of subsidy. In the parliament of 1404 Italian merchants presented a petition complaining about the additional 6s 8d with which they had been burdened in 1398. They alleged that this had led to an increase in Italian purchases at the Calais staple. This was not only unfair to those merchants who continued to export directly from England but was also harmful to the king's revenue. The petition was overshadowed by the dispute between the Crown and the Commons as to whether the grants made by the previous parliaments had or had not included custom as well as subsidy. The Commons stated that it had been their intention to grant a denizen and alien subsidy of 43s 4d and 50s. However, in their clarification of the situation they fixed the rates at 43s 4d and 53s 4d.[46]

In April 1405 the king granted the Albertini a rebate of 3s 4d on their wool exports. Three years later the Italians protested against the 53s 4d rate of subsidy and the merchants of Lucca and Venice were given a rebate of 3s 4d on wool exported between Martinmas 1404 and Michaelmas 1408. All the Florentines probably already enjoyed this concession since they were given a rebate for 1408–9. All three groups continued to be granted the reduction of 3s 4d on an annual basis. The alien rate of subsidy was reduced to 50s in the first parliamentary grant to Henry V, but increased to 60s in the life-time grant of 1415. In 1417, however, the king reduced the rate to 50s for a period of four years.[47]

The analysis of late-fourteenth-century exports must commence with the London particular for the twelve months following Michaelmas 1365.[48] The total trade of the port was over 16 000 sacks, of which almost 12 000 sacks belonged to denizens, the second highest figure ever recorded. The most important fact to record is the marked degree of monopoly. The denizen trade was handled by only 92 individuals, more than half of whom exported over 50 sacks. To leave the matter there, however, would be to disguise the extent of the monopoly. Although it is not possible to determine exactly how much of the denizen wool was owned by London merchants it was certainly a very large majority. Later accounts confirm that midlands wool exporters, who in the early fourteenth century had conducted a thriving trade through London, had largely disappeared. Only four exporters can certainly be identified as provincials in 1365–6; Henry Mulsho of Northamptonshire, 198 sacks, Nicholas Michel of Coventry, 382 sacks, John Olneye, senior and junior, of Coventry, 468 sacks. The younger Olneye, allegedly the first Englishman to be born in Calais after its capture from the French, later settled in London, became a member of the grocers' company and continued into the fifteenth century as one of the most prominent of the wool merchants.

The London exporters were dominated by a small group of merchant capitalists drawn from the mysteries of the grocers and the fishmongers. The biggest individual export was the almost incredible 1432 sacks dispatched by Nicholas Brembre, grocer, later executed by the lords appellant. The amount is particularly revealing since this date was apparently early in Brembre's career.[49] Apart from Brembre there were at least six other grocers, including William Baret, 540 sacks, Fulk Horwode, 375 sacks, John Philpot, 353 sacks, Richard Preston, 312 sacks, and John Hatfield, 273 sacks. Henry Penshurst, 230 sacks, may also have been a grocer, since in 1358 he was in Prussia acting as factor for Horwode and John Salman.[50] Horwode was mayor of the Westminster staple from 1365 to 1368 and Brembre from 1385 to 1388.

If it were not for Brembre's enormous export the performance of nine merchants identified as fishmongers would have been quite on a par with that of the grocers. In this group the most prominent were John Curteys, 677 sacks, John Lovekin, 544 sacks, Edmund Oliver, 470 sacks, John Southam, 237 sacks and John Torngold, 106 sacks. Torngold was mayor of the Calais staple, while Lovekin's servant and heir, William Walworth, although not exporting in his own name this year, was mayor of the Westminster staple from 1369 to 1385. The other great mysteries do not appear to have been as well represented in the wool trade as the grocers and the fishmongers but among the leading exporters we find John Barton vintner, 325 sacks, John Bernes mercer, 169 sacks and James Andrew draper, 91 sacks. In the ranks of those whose craft affiliation has not been identified the most prominent were Adam Franceys, 538 sacks, Laurence Wight, 254 sacks (possibly a fishmonger), William Vine, 300 sacks, and Thomas atte Lee, 221 sacks. Several others only just failed to reach the figure of 200 sacks.

The economic activities of the merchant capitalists were not restricted to the wool trade but extended into many branches of wholesale commerce. There were, however, a half dozen or so exporters who are generally described in London documents as woolman, woolmonger or fellmonger. Although it seems reasonable to suppose that the greater part of their substance came from the wool trade their individual exports fell noticeably short of those of the great capitalists. The most important of them were John Permay, 187 sacks, and Matthew Broun, 162 sacks.

The London capitalists were the main proponents of the Calais staple, a fact which is reflected in their refusal to export elsewhere during the 1370s. In the period 1371–6 over 90 per cent of the 31 000 sacks of denizen wool exported from London went to Calais, a proportion far higher than that of any other port. On the other hand rather less than one third of 293 000 fells were sent to Calais. A suspicion that the fellmongers may have used this occasion to dispute the leadership of the capitalists is strengthened by a study of the licences issued for export to places other than Calais.[51] Licences to export from London were issued to a number of city woolmen and fellmongers, to a few provincial merchants and to a larger number of undetermined status and origin, but not a single city capitalist from the 1365–6 account acquired a licence throughout this period. Paradoxically the fact that the capitalists denounced the system makes the London lists of licensees more useful than those for provincial ports. In the capital, licences were granted to individual merchants, but in the provinces after the first couple of years block licences were issued to the entire denizen community trading from a particular port.

The next surviving London particular which is worth analysing is that for 1384–5.[52] The staple had recently been transferred to Middelburg and the denizen export from London, 5211 sacks, was the second lowest of any twelve month period in 1380s. The total number of exporters, 92, was the same as that in 1365–6. The degree of monopoly, although less than that of 1365–6, is still impressive. The leading seven exporters, each with more than 200 sacks, handled 42 per cent of the trade. The largest amounts belonged to the mercers Robert Haringey, 528 sacks, and John Shadworth, 326 sacks. The former had acquired licences to avoid the Calais staple in 1372 but thereafter seems to have abjured the practice. William Staundon, grocer, had 252 sacks, William Wotton, frequently described as woolmonger, 210 sacks, and Laurence Wight, 342 sacks. Nicholas Brembre, 294 sacks, and the Olneyes, 213 sacks, were noted in the previous account. It is not impossible that Brembre was also exporting from other ports, since in 1379–80 he had dispatched at least 66 sacks from Hull. One London merchant notable for his absence is William Brampton, fishmonger and mayor of the Middelburg staple.

During the 1390s the circle of London wool exporters seems to have become even more restricted. Accounts covering the period 17 February 1397 to Michaelmas 1398 show that only 58 men were needed to handle a denizen trade of rather more than 6863 sacks, details of four ships being illegible.[53] The leading eleven exporters, each with more than 200 sacks, owned 67 per cent of the total. In cases where craft affiliation is known the grocers easily led the field. By this time, however, craft membership, although remaining a necessary qualification for entry into the freedom of the city, is an uncertain guide to a man's economic interests. Richard Reynolds, one of the lesser fry, who exported 27 sacks in this period, had been admitted to the freedom as a tailor in 1394. In 1400 he confessed that he was totally unconnected with this trade and transferred to the vintners. Robert Arnold, who exported 91 sacks entirely of fells, transferred from the haberdashers to the grocers. Richard Merlawe, 713 sacks, had first been a member of the ironmongers mystery but later was admitted to the fishmongers and adopted the practice of wearing the livery of each in alternate years. In consequence of an ordinance of 1415 which prohibited entry into more than one mystery he was obliged to give up membership of the ironmongers and to be formally admitted into the fishmongers, in which craft he was currently engaged.[54]

Apart from Richard Merlawe the leading group of exporters consisted of William Askham, 618 sacks, and William Brampton, 232 sacks, fishmongers, Geoffrey Brook, 880 sacks, and John Olneye, 383 sacks, grocers, Nicholas Wotton, 453 sacks, draper, William Wotton, 348 sacks, woolmonger, William Bedford, 351 sacks, Henry Birton, 222 sacks, Reginald Mytton, 208 sacks, and Richard Wodecote, 215 sacks.

The next London particular of any value is that covering the period Michaelmas 1405 to 28 February 1406, no wool leaving before 4 December.[55] In this time 2344 sacks were exported by 38 men, the leading six, with over 100 sacks each, owning 39 per cent of the total. In view of the brevity of the account too much significance may not be attached to the fact that only eleven of the exporters of 1397–8 are now represented, including five of the former top group. The present leaders were Richard Merlawe, 124 sacks, John Olneye, 106 sacks, Nicholas Wotton, 126 sacks, and three 'newcomers', Thomas Cressy, ironmonger, 299 sacks, Richard Whittington, mercer, 164 sacks and Walter Cotton, mercer, 101 sacks. Taking the newcomers as a whole, six can be identified as mercers, three as grocers, one as an ironmonger and one as a fishmonger, while one transferred from the ironmongers to the grocers.

Towards the end of the fourteenth century the proportion of total denizen exports passing through London declined sharply. In 1362–8

the port handled 42 per cent of the trade, in 1372–6 40 per cent, in
1376–90 48 per cent, in 1391–1401 32 per cent and in 1401–11 32 per
cent. Given that throughout the bulk of the wool dispatched from London belonged to city merchants one is tempted to conclude that
Londoners were losing their commanding position in the wool trade.
However, the conclusion must remain unproven since there is a real
possibility that Londoners may have switched some of their exports to
other ports. In the early fifteenth century Richard Whittington exported
some wool through Chichester,[56] but the real key to the situation lies not
in the ports of the south-east but in Lynn and Ipswich. During the 1380s
Lynn suddenly emerged as an important wool port, but after little more
than a decade this trade was lost to Ipswich. After a few years at Ipswich
the trade returned to Lynn for a while, before finally returning to
Ipswich. In the light of the fact that the initial upsurge of trade at
Lynn did not come at the expense of Boston it appears possible that
Londoners began to patronise the port during the period of the Middelburg staple. Why they should have continued to favour Lynn and
Ipswich in later years, if indeed they did, remains a mystery. In the
absence of good particulars the theory that the upsurge of East Anglian
trade was London inspired is difficult to test, but attention must be
drawn to the fragmentary Ipswich particular for Michaelmas 1397 to
1 March 1398.[57] Given that in 1397–8 Ipswich exports totalled 817
sacks, compared with 350 sacks in the previous year and 307 sacks
in the following year, one must deny coincidence in the fact that at
least ten out of twelve names recoverable from this account are those
of London merchants, including two grocers, a fishmonger and a tailor.
The fact that many of them dispatched wool from London in the
period 17 February 1397 to Michaelmas 1398 clearly indicates that
Londoners were in the habit of using more than one port at this period.

Provincial particulars of the late fourteenth century are disappointing. Although more have survived than for the preceding period the
most important of them are in a very bad state of preservation. Only
for Hull among the major wool ports is it possible to draw a clear
picture of the state of trade. At the end of the century there still existed
a thriving community of Yorkshire wool exporters. Although a few of
them handled a much larger trade than the average the movement
towards monopoly had gone less far than in the case of London. The
relatively large number of merchants still actively engaged in export
probably ensured that the Yorkshiremen enjoyed an important voice
in the counsels of the staple. Accounts for 1379–80 and 1381–2 are too
decayed to yield accurate statistics but they provide a general confirmation of the picture which emerges from the account of 1391–2.[58]

The same merchants were exporting much the same quantities in all three years. The most important was Robert de Howome who exported at least 236 sacks in 1379–80, considerably more than 102 sacks in 1381–2 and 374 sacks in 1391–2. The last account covers the period 8 December 1391, when denizen exports were resumed after the abortive ban on their trade, to the following Michaelmas. A total traffic of 3020 sacks was shared between 80 merchants. Sixty-two with less than 50 sacks each handled just one third of the total, while at the other extreme seven with more than 100 sacks each owned four tenths of the total.

The removal of the staple to Calais undoubtedly discouraged alien participation in the wool trade, although there was no legal impediment to their exporting there. It has already been pointed out that the Hanseatics seem to have withdrawn entirely, and by the late 1360s the northerners most interested in the trade were the Dutch. A large part of the alien trade, however, remained in the hands of Italians. In 1365–6 128 aliens exported 4405 sacks from London, but 60 per cent of this was owned by eight Italian merchants, while a few others owned lesser amounts. At least four of this group were Florentines. John Baldwin of the Strozzi had 782 sacks, Silvester Nicholas of the same company 694 sacks, Reyner Domenik of the Albertini 207 sacks and James Jakemyn 115 sacks. Roger Thomas had 319 sacks, Leone Milache 224 sacks, Alexander Bonefas 149 sacks and Francis Vyncheguerre of Lucca 116 sacks. In the late 1370s the last-named was buying wool from the Bishop of Winchester.

Until 1378 Italians, like other aliens, were legally obliged to ship their wool through the staple. However, they made full use of the opportunity to ship elsewhere when Edward III first suspended the staple and then began to sell licences to avoid it during the late 1360s and 1370s. Some of their greatly increased exports were sent directly to Italy, while the rest were sent to the Low Countries. This course was dictated, no doubt, by the desire to increase sales in Flanders at the expense of the English, as well by a shortage of Mediterranean ships willing to come to England. With the renewal of the war and especially during the Anglo-Flemish dispute of 1370–1, the neutrality of southern European ships was frequently disregarded by English privateers. In 1370 a number of Genoese ships, some of them laden with wool picked up in the Low Countries, were seized and brought into English ports. In 1374 men of the Cinque Ports seized goods from tarets of Genoa, Catalonia and Naples on the pretence that they belonged to the king's enemies. The licences of 1371 and 1372 indicate that the great bulk of Italian export was still handled by Florentines.

In 1372, however, a Venetian, Nicholas Michel, obtained a licence to export 500 sacks in a Venetian taret which he brought to Sandwich. In the following year he was licensed to export 700 sacks.[59]

Even after 1378 Italian merchants continued to send wool to Calais. Out of 1705 sacks which they exported from London between February 1397 and Michaelmas 1398 only 531 sacks were shipped in Venetian galleys in July 1397 and September 1398, while the rest was dispatched to the staple. The leading exporter, Lodewic de Port, had 168 sacks in the galleys and sent 286 sacks to Calais. Aliens exporting to Calais were apparently required, like denizens, to sell their wool in the town, so they should not have direct access to the Flemish market. This obstacle was overcome by means of collusionary sales. An Exchequer enquiry of 1383 revealed that Hugelin Gerard had bought 49 sacks of wool for £552 at the Westminster staple in January 1378 and 120 sarplers for £2035 at other times and places. These he sent to Calais and made a pretended sale with his partner, one de Perle, who then forwarded them to Bruges.[60]

Reviewing the period covered in the preceding chapter it seems clear that the claim of Parliament to enjoy at least a strong voice in the location of the wool staple was firmly established in 1376. On this occasion the staple was returned to Calais, largely, no doubt, at the urging of the London merchants, who had become alarmed at the revival of the alien export trade during the period in which the staple was in abeyance. A compulsory staple at Calais led inevitably to a *de facto*, although not *de jure*, native monopoly of the wool trade in northern Europe. However, vindication of Calais as the permanent home of the staple was not complete until the end of the fourteenth century and until then there seem to have been some Englishmen who doubted that it was in the best interests of the nation as a whole that aliens should be eliminated entirely from the wool trade. It seems impossible to account otherwise for the attempted restoration of home staples and an alien monopoly in the 1390s. The accession of the House of Lancaster greatly strengthened the fellowship of the staple, which was the chief defender of the claims of Calais, although the argument that the town could only be defended and financed through the medium of the wool trade no doubt remained strong. The privileges of the fellowship were renewed as a matter of course at the beginning of each reign and the Crown seems to have been thrown onto the defensive in regard to its prerogative right to license exports to places other than Calais. All in all the merchants of the fellowship were a force to be reckoned with in the fifteenth century.

8

The decline of the wool trade

In 1429 was enacted the parliamentary legislation known as the bullion and partition ordinances. Whatever their intention these measures contributed to a further decline in wool exports. Munro has strongly emphasised that the legislation originated with the Crown, as part of its efforts to obtain bullion at the expense of Burgundy. The partition ordinance he sees as a bribe to obtain the cooperation of the greater wool merchants. He contrasts his position with that of Power who, he claims, credits the initiative to the merchants, the bullion ordinance being a sop to the Crown. In fact her position is not as entrenched as Munro believes. Both writers, however, accept the novelty of the legislation and Power maintains that 'the effect of the ordinance was, in fact, to convert the Fellowship of the Staple from a regulated into something not unlike a joint-stock company'.[1]

It is suggested that the legislation was not as novel as these two writers supposed. The bullion ordinance, if not the partition ordinance, possibly dated back to 1422, while even the latter was not without precedents of a sort. In 1429 Parliament merely confirmed 'the ordinaunce and appointement nowe late made in the said Staple of Caleys'. This ordinance, or a predecessor, may have been made as early as the reopening of the Calais mint in 1422; inability to enforce the regulations on its members probably led the company to request Parliament to give them the full force of English law. The right of the staple organisation to make wide-ranging ordinances for the conduct of the wool trade is beyond dispute. Being of a temporary nature ordinances are never specified in the confirmations of the staple made in the reign of Richard II and at the accession of each Lancastrian king. The accustomed 'liberties' of the staplers are confirmed without definition. Because of this it is only very occasionally that we catch a glimpse of the self-imposed regulations of the staple. In 1343 all English merchants were ordered to sell their wool under the supervision of staple officials in order to maintain the price and to keep the exchange rate under English control. This was the essence of the 1429 ordinances. In 1363 the new Calais company attempted to fix a single price for the wool of each growth. In 1408 the company made an ordinance that no new wool should be brought to Calais until all the old stocks had been sold. Although ordered to abandon this rule because of the loss caused to the king's customs it is clear that they continued to enforce restrictions on sale. In 1410 the merchants of Hull lent the king 1000 marks and in return the staple officials were ordered to let them sell their wool 'any ordinance or composition to the contrary notwithstanding'.[2]

The decisive factor in the reopening of the Calais mint in 1422 was probably the threat of mutiny by the garrison of the town. The staplers' petition in the parliament of December 1421 was accompanied by another from the soldiers calling for payment of arrears of wages. Neither the staplers nor the Crown could treat the prospect of a mutiny lightly. Once before, in 1406 or 1407, the soldiers had seized the wool in Calais and sold it to obtain their wages. On that occasion the merchants were unable to pay their creditors in England and the king was obliged to postpone payment of duty on all wool exported between Whitsun 1406 and Michaelmas 1407. The reopening of the mint in 1422 came too late to prevent another seizure of wool and the staplers were obliged to advance £4000 to recover it. Clearly it was necessary to devise a scheme by which money was always available in Calais if future seizures were to be prevented.[3]

In the reigns of Richard II and Henry IV Parliament had frequently tied its grants of subsidy to the provision that part of the proceeds must be used to meet the expenses of Calais. The life grant to Henry V was free of any restrictions. However, it was inevitable that part of the subsidy would continue to be used to finance Calais since this was the most convenient way to get money to the town. The procedure was for the treasurer of Calais to receive an assignment against the customs collectors of certain English ports. The collectors would then make indentures with individual merchants requiring the latter to pay part of the duty at Calais. It has been estimated that in the early years of Henry V the annual expenses of Calais totalled £16 000–£17 000, while in the period following the Agincourt campaign the total was higher.[4] These sums could easily have been met from the wool still exported to Calais but the government was never in a position to devote the entire proceeds of the subsidy to this purpose.

If the staplers were to become the main providers of funds for the Calais administration two conditions must be satisfied; the merchants must have a sufficiency of money in the town and it must be of the right sort. They had already complained that the treasurer would accept payment only in nobles and that since there was no mint they were obliged to ship these from England, a practice which was frequently condemned. The establishment of a mint enabled them to exchange foreign coin, received in payment for wool, into nobles, but the question of sufficiency remained. Towards the end of the lifetime of the previous mint a remarkably small proportion of the value of the wool sold in Calais was coined there. It has already been explained that this resulted from the fact that a large part of the price was paid on deferred terms in the Low Countries. In June 1396, for example, Richard II wrote to the Duke of Holland and Zeeland on behalf of John de Waghen of Yorkshire. Waghen was owed 850½ nobles 22d for wool delivered at Calais to a citizen of Leyden who subsequently defaulted. Waghen brought a prosecution before the magistrates of Leyden but was unable to produce the bond which had been stolen from him at Delft.[5]

When a large amount of wool was sold at Calais the total expenses of the town might be covered by a proportion of the subsidy due from each sack. As the amount of wool declined a larger proportion of the subsidy, and therefore of the total value of the wool, would be needed to produce the same sum. If the expenses of the town rose the proportion needed would be even greater. In effect this means that any plan to finance Calais entirely out of the proceeds of the subsidy might make it necessary to tighten the credit extended to alien buyers of wool, by calling upon them to pay a larger proportion of the price, although not necessarily the whole amount, in the down payment first made at Calais. It is suggested that such an ordinance may have been made by the staple company when the mint was re-established. How else is one to account for the very large output of the first eighteen months (20 July 1422 – 30 January 1424), which amounted to £60 614 in gold and £10 759 in silver?[6] An alternative explanation, that the staplers had voluntarily changed their methods since the days of the earlier mint, seems less tenable. As to the motive for the ordinance one need look no further than the fact that the staple authorities, having finally persuaded the government to reopen the mint, had to ensure that it received sufficient bullion to justify its existence.

During the next four years (25 February 1424 – 31 January 1428) the Calais mint produced £35 590 in gold and £101 618 in silver.[7] The increase in the ratio of silver to gold probably resulted from a change in the minting policy of the Duke of Burgundy, which from 1426 made it advantageous for his subjects to take gold to his mints and to bring silver to Calais.[8] The altered ratio of gold to silver may have been of less consequence to the Calais authorities than the decline in the combined value of both metals reaching the mint. This fell from £71 373 in eighteen months to £137 208 in almost four years. There are at least two possible explanations for this development. As early as October 1423 the staplers complained that the success of the Calais mint was threatened by the export of nobles from England.[9] They alleged that the coins were becoming so plentiful in Bruges that there was little need for the Flemings to bring bullion to Calais. Although Parliament renewed the ban on the export of nobles it is possible that the flow was not contained and that this accounts for the decline in the output of the Calais mint. The fact that it paid the Burgundians to take gold bullion to their own mints does not mean that they would derive a similar advantage from ready-coined English nobles. It was more profitable to take these to Calais where they could be spent without payment of seignorage. If this was happening it implies that English nobles were employed in a triangle of trade, being exported to the Flemish marts to pay for general imports, taken thence to Calais to pay for wool and finally repatriated by the staplers. On balance, however, it seems unlikely that any very large part of the stock of nobles was engaged in this way.

The alternative explanation of the decline in Calais minting is that the staple authorities failed to enforce the postulated ordinance of 1422 and that merchants began to defer a larger part of the payment. If it be objected that there is no conclusive evidence that this ordinance was ever made it must be pointed that there is little direct evidence about any of the ordinances made solely on the authority of the staple fellowship. If it be objected that there is no evidence of foreign protests against the ordinance, as there were against the ordinance of 1429, it may be said that the relative failure of the ordinance minimised the need for protest. It is not, however, impossible that the bans imposed in 1428 on the import of English cloth into Holland, Zeeland and Brabant were retaliatory as well as protectionist measures.

Whether the staple did or did not make an ordinance about credit, which it found difficult to enforce, it certainly became concerned about breaches of its monopoly in the late 1420s. The merchants of Newcastle, who had obtained a licence to export 1000 sacks outside the staple in 1423, received a licence for a further 2000 sacks in 1427. In the latter year also the Bishop of Winchester was licensed to ship 800 sacks to Normandy. In October 1427 the staplers obtained confirmation of their liberties, although these had been fully confirmed only a few years since. In September 1429 Parliament gave its backing to the bullion and partition ordinances, already made in the staple, and in the following February the liberties of the company were again confirmed by the Crown. The parliament of 1429 also enacted, separately from the above-mentioned ordinances, other regulations about the wool trade, including one which makes it clear that there had been a conspiracy between alien buyers and the permanent residents of Calais to defeat existing regulations of the company. The aliens abjured the town with the result that poor English merchants, who could not afford to tarry there, had to sell their wool cheaply to inhabitants in league with the first party. Because of this, permanent residents were now forbidden to buy staple goods.[10]

The crucial legislation of 1429 clearly originated with the staplers. The parliament rolls enumerate 'v poyntes', the last of which was merely a request to the king and the Lords to accept the Commons' bill about the staple.[11] The bill includes the other matters now enacted besides the five points. Three points deal with credit. They provided that the entire price of the wool must be paid in gold or silver when the bargain was struck at Calais. To prevent fraud the seller was not to hand back any money to the buyer by way of loan. At least one third of the price had to be paid in bullion or foreign coin, since the seller was required to deliver this proportion to the Calais mint. In view of the prominence given to this part of the ordinance it would be rash to conclude that it was merely a sop to the Crown. The staple authorities seem to have had at least an equal interest in it. Only by ensuring full payment at Calais was it possible to enforce the terms of the partition ordinance, since merchants receiving payment in Flanders could ignore it. Because the leaders of the staple still desired the convenience of a mint at Calais they had to guarantee a certain delivery of bullion. The partition regulation, although conceivably the main concern of some of the promoters of the legislation, is the most obscurely worded of the five points. Its full implications only emerge later from the complaints of its opponents. Briefly, however, it meant that each merchant was no longer free to make his own arrangements for payment. His wool was graded and pooled with other wool of a similar quality and only as and when the whole stock was sold did he receive payment for his share. On balance it seems rash to divide the 'v poyntes' into separate, but parallel, bullion and partition ordinances. They seem to be part of the same package, the rationale of which is a matter of debate.

The ordinances emanating from the staple were given parliamentary approval for the period 2 February 1430 to 25 March 1433. The other clauses in the statute relating to the wool trade were apparently not subject to any limitation. In the parliament of 1433 the ordinances were renewed for three years from 25 March 1434, although on this occasion the king reserved the right to modify them at pleasure. The reservation opened the way to the sale of licences permitting individuals to take wool to Calais to be sold outside of the partition. The practice was the subject of protest in the parliament of 1435. Although the king returned a favourable reply to the petition he again reserved his right to modify the ordinances and warranted licences already granted. Almost immediately Parliament dispersed he issued a further licence in return for a loan of 8000 marks. The ordinances should have expired in March 1437 but the king's rejection of a parliamentary request, made the previous January, for a modification of the system seems to have been treated as a warrant for them to continue indefinitely.[12]

In their petition of 1435 the staplers complained about the smuggling of wool to places other than Calais and about the licences to sell outside the partition but claimed that in other respects the 'Statuitz been right streitly observed and kept'. A comparison of denizen wool exports and seignorage receipts at the Calais mint suggests that this statement was correct at least insofar as the mint requirement was concerned. While the former were considerably smaller than in the previous period the latter rose somewhat. Denizen exports in the period 1429–35 averaged about 8300 sacks a year while the mint output (4 February 1429 – 4 February 1436), now entirely in silver, averaged £36 879 a year.[13] Mint receipts comfortably exceeded one third of the value of the wool.

The figures given above indicate that any success enjoyed by the statute was achieved only at the cost of a large fall in wool exports. Alien buyers, under the burden of the new regulations, were unable to purchase as large a quantity of wool as before. Not unnaturally the Duke of Burgundy and his subjects tried to persuade the English government to withdraw the objectionable legislation and a number of fruitless conferences were held with this aim.[14] In 1434 the Burgundians attempted to increase their bargaining strength by organising a ban on English cloth. Initially the boycott failed and cloth exports were little smaller in 1434–5 than in the previous year. It needed a diplomatic revolution and a war to alter the situation radically.[15] Ever since 1420 Duke Philip of Burgundy had been an ally of England in the struggle with the Dauphin, later King Charles VII, of France. By 1435 the duke was ready to make peace with France and if he could not do so in conjunction with England he was willing to do it separately. When the English ambassadors withdrew from the congress of Arras that year Philip did in fact make his own treaty with France. This 'desertion' led directly to a war between England and Burgundy. In July 1436 Philip laid siege to Calais but within a few days was obliged to retreat ignominiously. After a brief English foray into Flanders the war developed into a matter of piracy and protracted economic blockade which damaged both sides. Although English cloth exports did badly for one year they recovered and surged to heights never previously approached. On this side it was the merchants of the staple who bore the brunt of the battle.

The Anglo-Burgundian war gave rise to one of the most serious stoppages in the entire history of the wool trade. In a period of almost 4 years, less than 600 sacks of denizen-owned wool were legally exported from England. It was not, however, the military or naval prowess of the Burgundians which kept the English at home but the fact that the staple authorities would not allow new wool to come to Calais until they had sold the stocks already there. Because of the Burgundian boycott old wool was disposed of only slowly as may be seen from table 16. The ban applied not merely to the duke's own subjects but to those Italians who made a practice of buying wool at Calais. Without his permission they could not forward it either by land or by sea. A comparison of the English enrolled customs accounts and Calais particular accounts of this period enables the effects of the boycott to be studied in detail. Export was halted in the winter of 1435–6 and, with the exception of a single shipload from Hull in the spring of 1437, no more wool was allowed to leave until the summer of 1438, when some 500 or so sacks were sent to Calais. Following this premature revival it is clear that no further export was allowed until after terms for peace were agreed at Michaelmas 1439. By the following February a little over 3000 sacks had been received at Calais.

Duing the period of the boycott the main, or even sole, customers at the Calais staple were the Dutch, who refused to support their ruler in his quarrel with England. As early as 1437 Parliament requested that the bullion laws be relaxed in their favour so as to enable them to buy more wool.[16] It was proposed that they be absolved from the requirement to export English goods equal in value to their imports. Instead they should be allowed to pay the proceeds to the staplers and be credited with this amount at Calais, thereby reducing the amount of bullion they would have to pay. Although this request was refused the Dutch still desired peace with England and in May 1438 opened negotiations for a treaty. Despite the fact that they still demanded the repeal or amendment of the hated staple regulations the talks probably inspired a mood of optimism which led to an increase in wool sales at Calais and a resumption of exports after the clip of 1438. In November 1438 licence was granted to ship corn to the town because of the 'great concourse' of merchants gathered there.[17] Following the Dutch desertion Duke Philip was himself obliged to sue for peace with England. Although the Burgundian talks commenced later than those with the

TABLE 16   *Wool entering and leaving Calais (various dates)*ᵃ

	Entries		Exits	
	Wool (sacks)	Fells	Wool (sacks)	Fells
1 Mar. 1365 – 31 May 1365	1665 sarplers 3 sacks	20 246	—	—
1 June 1365 – 31 May 1366	33 393	407 520	33 917	324 071
1 June 1366 – 19 Mar. 1368	52 095	620 664	3775 Lombard Pokes 56 782 5168 Lombard Pokes	676 249
18 Jan. 1387 – 28 Feb. 1388	10	—	57	6800
29 Sept. 1401 – 30 Mar. 1403	19 748	430 487	22 091	398 913
30 Mar. 1404 – 9 May 1405	6838	157 630	?	?
28 Dec. 1409 – 1 Aug. 1411	17 081	518 497	18 427	451 254
1 Aug. 1411 – 29 Mar. 1412	9152	163 894	7495	73 490
20 Mar. 1413 – 6 Aug. 1413	3097	116 859	5199	55 231
10 Feb. 1437 – 30 May 1437	62	700	776	5692
30 May 1437 – 10 Feb. 1438	—	—	2949	109 658
10 Feb. 1438 – 10 Feb. 1439	117	94 299	4442	114 149
10 Feb. 1439 – 10 Feb. 1440	2892	47 564	2389	55 772
25 Dec. 1442 – 25 Dec. 1443	10 700	281 439	11 006	265 237

ᵃ Sources. Calais Treasurers' and Controllers' Accounts, Enrolled and Particular (E364 and E101). Wool entering is probably by English weight, but exits are by Calais weight. Lombard poke equals half an English sack.

Dutch agreement was reached in the autumn of 1439, while an Anglo-Dutch settlement was not formally achieved until 1445.[18] In neither treaty did the English make any concession in the matter of the Calais regulations and the Duke of Burgundy renewed his effort to prevent bullion from reaching the town.[19]

While the legislation of 1429 was anathema to the subjects of the Duke of Burgundy it by no means promoted harmony among the staplers themselves. It may have been feared that even with parliamentary support the ordinances would be difficult to enforce without a determined effort on the part of the authorities. This is one interpretation which may be put on a royal mandate issued in February 1430. It ordered that the present mayor of the staple, John Reynewell, a London fishmonger, should continue in office until March 1432, any law to the contrary notwithstanding. All that is known about the former method of appointment is that the staplers were empowered to elect the mayor and constables every March, this being done in Calais. The royal action may have been an innovation which led to further abuses of procedure in the struggle to control the mayoralty. In 1444 a Commons petition requested the king to reform the rules of election. It claimed that previously the choice was confined to those owning goods in the staple and being there in person or represented by attorneys. Of recent years, however, the choice had been made by 'multitude of voyces', many of them being persons without goods who had been made free of the fellowship merely to influence the election. The petition requested that in future no one should be allowed a voice unless he had at least ten sacks of his own wool at Calais at the time of the election or during the previous twelve months. It does not state specifically that in former times there had been a minimum qualification of ten sacks.[20]

The fullest account of the consequences of the bullion and partition ordinances is to be found in the case put by the Dutch ambassadors who came to negotiate peace in 1438.[21] They claimed, incidentally, that the new regulations had been enforced at Calais for 14 or 16 years past, which takes us back to the reopening of the mint when, it has been suggested above, the staplers themselves made ordinances which anticipated the legislation of 1429. Although the Dutch were not unbiased observers there seems no reason to reject the substance of their report. Their chief concern was with the harmful effects which the two ordinances had upon their own cloth industry. Not only was their credit restricted but the price of wool was greatly increased and the quality often deteriorated because of the delay in selling it. The price rise was not merely a matter of policy but an inevitable consequence of the delays and monopoly inherent in the new system. The Dutch alleged that the partition law had driven the smaller English merchants out of business. Previously these had been free to dispose of their stocks at discretion. A bargain might be struck quickly, credit extended for a comparatively short period, and payment made in ample time to renew their own credit in England so that they might acquire fresh stocks. Now, however, they were forced into a partition and might have to wait years for full payment even if all of their own wool had been sold. Such delay was fatal to the small men, but those with capital behind them could afford to wait for higher prices, secure in the knowledge that the circle of suppliers was growing smaller.

In 1438 the Dutch claimed that the wool trade was controlled by only twenty to thirty merchants. This was probably an exaggeration, but even if remotely true it suggests a considerable fall in numbers since 1424. A unique document,[22] a register of the cocket letters belonging to each ship, provides full details of all wool delivered to Calais between 19 February and 23 November of that year. The exports of denizens are summarised in table 17, but the 128 sacks belonging to a half-dozen Italian merchants are not included. The total number of exporters was about 217, since there is no doubt that one person is involved in most of the eleven instances of the same names occurring in more than one English port. Because of the limited time-scale it is likely that the table slightly underestimates the number of large exporters and exaggerates the number of small men. Some of the Londoners with small amounts are known to have exported considerably more on other occasions. Despite the limitations of the source it is clear that the chief centres of the trade, London and Hull, represent very different traditions. All of the seven merchants owning more than 200 sacks each were Londoners and any claims on behalf of the large exporters probably came from this quarter. Hull was clearly the stronghold of those of middle stature, men who might well be expected to resist the pretensions of the Londoners. How far they would go to protect the interests of the very small exporters is an open question, for although fairly numerous the latter did not make a very substantial contribution to total trade.

From about 1434, if no earlier, cracks appeared in the partition system as individual merchants obtained royal mandates that they be allowed to sell their wool at Calais without impediment. Nevertheless, partition remained the official policy of the staple. Even in 1437, when the staplers requested that the bullion laws be relaxed in favour of the Dutch, they favoured the retention of partition. They said that merchants should be required to make partition of the moneys re-

TABLE 17 *Denizen wool entering Calais 19 February–23 November 1424 (English sacks)*ᵃ

	Less than 10 sacks		10–30 sacks		30–50 sacks		50–100 sacks		100–200 sacks		Over 200 sacks	
	Exporters	Wool	Exporters	Wool	Exporters	Wool	Exporters	Wool	Exporters	Wool	Exporters	Wool
London	8	54	15	281	7	276	15	894	9	1079	6	1587
Hull	15	126	20	337	12	506	23	1721	5	609	–	–
Boston	7	42	9	172	7	266	6	382	1	111	–	–
Ipswich	2	4	6	111	6	236	10	742	1	122	–	–
Sandwich	1	3	–	–	1	45	–	–	–	–	–	–
Chichester	5	27	2	38	–	–	–	–	–	–	–	–
Southampton	–	–	1	27	–	–	1	83	–	–	–	–
Poole	1	4	–	–	–	–	2	145	–	–	–	–
Melcombe	–	–	2	48	–	–	–	–	–	–	–	–
More than one port	–	–	–	–	3	116	6	497	1	173	1	260
Totals	39	260	55	1014	36	1445	63	4464	17	2094	7	1847

ᵃ Source. E101/189/7.

ceived in England or in Holland. While the Duke of Burgundy maintained his blockade of Calais the debate about partition may have been largely academic. Afterwards, however, when exports were resumed and the king again began to issue licences to sell outside the partition the issue became one of burning importance. In January 1442 a petition to the king in Parliament, reciting the evils which the bullion and partition ordinances had brought upon the staplers and upon the country, requested that they be abolished. It did, however, accept certain limitations upon the freedom of the individual merchant. While he should receive the entire proceeds from the sale of his wool he must abide by any price-fixing ordinance made by the company. Furthermore, he should be required to bring one third of the value of the wool in silver to the Calais mint and afterwards must bring the new coin to England. These rules should be observed for seven years. The king's reply to the petition, which was incorporated in a statute, was that the staplers must set their own house in order according to the tenor of the petition. If they did not do so by 1 August next then the king would take steps to enforce the recommendations.[23]

If the staple authorities had done as they were commanded then the following state of affairs would have resulted. Each merchant would be free to bargain with his own wool, subject to any minimum price fixed by the company. Each would be required to bring one third of its value to the Calais mint, but presumably would be allowed to extend credit for the remainder, which might be paid elsewhere. Whether the staplers had formally implemented these changes before their mayor appeared in person before the king's council in October 1442 is not clear. On this occasion, however, the mayor wished to go further than the terms of the petition. Unfortunately, there appears to be no record of who filled the mayoralty at this time. The situation was complicated by the fact that during August the garrison of Calais had distrained the wool in the town in an attempt to obtain arrears of their wages, although they had not yet sold it. When the mayor appeared before the council on 12 October he made three demands. First, that the government should provide security for all wool sent to Calais; second, that the staplers be assigned one mark out of the subsidy on every sack in repayment of loans already advanced to the king; third, that the provision made in the recent statute that one third of the price of wool be taken to the mint be revoked. The justice of the first request was accepted by the entire council, but they held that payment of the soldiers would be sufficient security for the safety of the wool. The second request was opposed by Cardinal Beaufort and by the Treasurer, on the grounds that the subsidy was already fully assigned. The third was also opposed by Beaufort, who held that the Flemings had been given what they wished for and that if the king dispensed with the bullion requirement on this occasion he would never again be able to enforce it. A week later the mayor once more came before the council and informed them that he had dispensed with the bullion requirement. He seems to have done this on his own initiative, since he claimed that when he asked the advice of his colleagues in England they refused to give it, while it would have taken too long to send to Calais for instructions. He justified his action on the grounds that otherwise the Burgundians would be unable to buy wool and that both the king and the merchants would be the losers. Faced with the *fait acompli* the council gave way and conceded that for this season only the staplers might sell wool free of the bullion requirement.[24] Beaufort's prediction came true, for the inactivity of the Calais mint in subsequent years indicates that the government was unable to re-impose the regulation. The mayor's action, however, provided the re-assurance which the staplers needed. Since some time in the spring or summer of 1441 exports to Calais had either ceased altogether or were reduced to a trickle of a few hundred sacks, but from the late autumn of 1442 to the summer of 1443 at least 12 000 sacks were sent.

The next major exchange between the Crown and the staplers, in February 1444, was probably occasioned by yet another revolt of the garrison because of non-payment of their wages. Any help provided by the staple at this time was made conditional on the king's promise to respect its monopoly, which during the past few years had been widely breached. The evasions may be considered under three headings. Firstly, there was the old problem of Newcastle. In the parliament of 1429 the licence of Newcastle to export outside of the staple had been revoked in return for a guarantee by the staple authorities that if the northerners brought their wool to Calais they would be given the same price that they might expect to receive in the Netherlands. The fact that there was no export from Newcastle during the next three years suggests either that the merchants had no faith in the promise or that the staplers had been correct in their accusation that the licence was used as a cover to export fine wool directly to Low Countries. In the parliament of 1431 a petition requesting the restoration of the New-castle licence was rejected, but towards the end of the following year the merchants were licensed to export to Flanders. Throughout the dispute with Burgundy there was no export from Newcastle, but in July 1441 the northerners were licensed to export to Bruges and dis-patched over 500 sacks in a period when deliveries to the staple were at a virtual standstill.[25]

A second probable cause of concern to the staplers was the question of Italian exports. In 1430–5 alien exports from England averaged 705 sacks a year; in 1435–40 the average was 1181 sacks. Since virtually the whole of this trade was handled by Italians one must assume that merchants denied passage between Calais and Burgundian territories were now exporting direct from England. In May 1438 George Luke was granted a licence to export wool to Antwerp and thence to Italy. Luke was a Florentine who in 1424 had exported to the staple. More serious, however, was the fact that Italians who had previously bought their supplies from the staplers were now buying in England and might be tempted permanently to cut out the middlemen. In June 1439 Milanese merchants were licensed to export to Middelburg and thence to Italy. Thereafter such licences were granted annually. The staplers feared, or professed to fear, that the licensees would not forward the wool to Italy but would sell it in the Low Countries.[26]

Finally from the late 1430s the Crown issued large numbers of licences for Englishmen to export outside of the staple, usually to Normandy or to Holland and Zeeland. Some of the licences permitted pure wool to be taken, but most specified that export must be restricted to lambs' wool, fells or to the inferior fells called morlings and shorlings. In certain circles the latter were coming to be claimed as non-staple ware. There was an acknowledged danger that however restricted the terms of the licence it might be used to cover the shipment of staple goods. From 1436 onwards occasional licences were issued authorising Englishmen to ship wool to Italy, but they were few in number and did not threaten the staplers' monopoly as did the others.

The staplers seem to have used the open discontent among the Calais garrison in 1444 to press their demands on the Crown. In two separate letters issued in February the king confirmed the liberties and ordinances of the staple and promised that he would no longer issue licences which breached its privileges.[27] In guarantee it was agreed that if the king did grant any licences during the next seven years the staplers should export sack for sack entirely free of duty. In fact the promise remained a complete dead letter. The Newcastle exports continued at a higher level than for many years, and licences continued to be issued to both Englishmen and Italians.

The 1440s form such an obscure period in the history of the staple that two commentators have formed diametrically opposite conclusions about it. Power believed that a 'democratic' party, led by Hamo Sutton, emerged victorious from the struggle of 1442 and successfully resisted attempts by an opposing faction to regain control. Munro, however, pictured a partitionist or bullionist group, led by Hamo Sutton, regaining control of the staple at the end of 1443 or early in 1444 and holding on to it until 1452.[28] Sutton was mayor of the staple in May 1433 and May 1434, had been succeeded by Richard Bokeland by July 1435, was mayor again in February 1444 and March 1446 and had been succeeded by Robert White by May 1447. Apart from this so little is known about his career that it is difficult to tell which 'faction' he led or supported, if indeed he consistently belonged to either. He was a citizen of Lincoln and throughout his life his roots remained firmly in that county. In 1424 he exported 64 sacks of wool from Hull and one may suppose that in the early days of his career he saw the staple through the eyes of the middling men of the northern community. In 1435, in association with two London merchants, Sutton lent the king 8000 marks and in return they were allowed to sell wool to this value at Calais outside the partition. The implementation of the licence was opposed by the staple authorities, but the fact that Sutton tried to avoid the partition when out of office says nothing about his attitude towards it while he was mayor.

For Munro the confirmation and grant of February 1444 signified the royal seal of approval of the partitionist victory in the staple, the king's interest being a restoration of the bullion regulation. Although he does not suggest that the partition system was restored Munro does believe that the authorities again required customers to pay for wool in ready cash and bullion.[29] Burgundian discontent with the staple regulations of the 1440s does not necessarily support this contention. Official prices, protected by a restriction of the amount of wool brought to the staple, would in themselves have been a source of grievance. The enormous swings in exports from year to year strongly suggest that the authorities strictly regulated the arrival of wool at Calais. When the fluctuations are eliminated it may be seen that denizen exports during 1439–52 were rather less than two thirds of the pre-1429 level. The annual average, including exports away from the staple, was around 9200 sacks.

The internal difficulties of the staple were brought sharply into focus in 1448 by yet another rising of the garrison, accompanied by the usual seizure of wool. In dealing with the problem the government drew particular attention to disputes about elections to the mayoralty, repeating the allegations which had been made in the petition of 1445.[30] Instead, however, of merely insisting that the staple set its own house in order the Crown imposed the Marquess of Suffolk upon it as governor and *conservator* for a period of five years. Suffolk was empowered to make ordinances for the good government of the staple, but was to do so only by the advice of the more prominent merchants. The office of mayor does not seem to have been suspended as a result of this appointment. Whether or not Suffolk was able to restore a unity of accord among the staplers in February 1449 they sponsored a lengthy petition to the king in Parliament. This recited the evils which had befallen on the wool trade and called for a strict enforcement on the Calais monopoly. With the support of the Commons the petition was accepted and incorporated in a statute which was to be binding for five years from Midsummer. Although the privileges of Berwick were reserved the Newcastle licence was immediately revoked, as were all individual licences with the exception of a handful already issued to specifically named persons. Newcastle merchants were compensated by an adjustment in the rate of the subsidy, which was renewed in the present parliament. The wools of Cumberland and Westmorland, together with those grown between the Tees and Tweed, were to pay only 13s 4d, instead of the usual rate of 33s 4d. This was obviously intended to dispose of the argument that these wools could not compete at Calais. In granting the subsidy the Commons reverted to the earlier practice of providing that 20s on every sack be reserved for the use of the Calais garrison. With these changes Suffolk's powers, if ever exercised, seem to have lapsed.[31]

In 1449 the problems of the staple were overshadowed by the current Burgundian ban on imports of English cloth. Although mooted as early as June 1445 the ban was not formally published until January 1447, part of the interim being taken up with the renewal of the Anglo-Burgundian commercial treaty and discussions of existing grievances alleged by each side.[32] The ban was not simply a sanction to secure changes in the staple regulations. Indeed, during the 1440s English cloth exports had swollen so enormously that in themselves they constituted a threat to Burgundian prosperity, regardless of conditions at the staple. It may, of course, be argued that the increase in cloth exports was not independent of Burgundian difficulties at the staple.

The fact that the Burgundians felt aggrieved at the existing staple regulations meant that this topic had to be included in any talks designed to bring an end to the cloth boycott. In February 1449 the English parliament chose to adopt a strong line and ruled that Burgundian imports into England should cease if the latter did not lift their own ban by Michaelmas next. However, the ambassadors sent to deliver this ultimatum were also instructed to hold out an olive branch in the form of a possibility that the Calais regulations might be amended.

Thay [the ambassadors] shal as colourably as thay can, speke of thutrance of wolles at Calais, remembring the said Duchesse as it were of thaim self, saying if she wolde putte thereto hir hande [to an order relaxing the cloth ban] it might be so purveyyed by meenes that by the saide uttrance good sholde mow growe not oonly to the marchants that uttre theire woll but also to the beyers thereof, the which in gret part be hir subgitts, and thay may say that thay doubte not but that the king wol on his behalf so ordeine that it shal be to the plesir of the said Duchesse and profit to hir people.[33]

At this stage in the negotiations, in March, the offer was to be entirely unofficial.

A second embassy, in the following July, was empowered to make an official offer of talks on the question of Calais and for this reason the mayor and four of his colleagues were included in the delegation. Their presence would also be valuable if, as was considered likely, the Duchess of Burgundy should repeat an earlier claim that the cloth ban had been imposed 'by thavis wille or aggrement' of the staplers. The king admitted that individual staplers, for their selfish profit, might secretly welcome the ban, but, given the impossibility of such thoughts becoming official policy, he deemed it incredible that the duchess should take notice of them. In preparation for the mission the leading ambassadors were instructed to commune with the staplers and to remind them of a promise made by their mayor in the recent parliament. In return for the restoration of their monopoly he had given an undertaking that 'at such tyme as the King wolde send to Calais his comissaries' the fellowship would amend their present regulations. That time had now arrived. The ambassadors were also to instruct the staplers that if the Flemings wished to come to Calais they should 'honestly and frenly comune with thaim and here thaym paciently and wele considre thoffres that thai will make'.[34]

The negotiations of 1449 came to nothing and the Burgundian cloth ban continued until 1452. Although the English Parliament failed to implement their threat to stop imports the merchant adventurers had taken their own retaliatory measures, including a boycott of the Antwerp fairs, and this may have been a major consideration in the Burgundian decision to lift the ban. Munro suggests that they may also have obtained concessions on the question of the Calais regulations and that these were accompanied by the overthrow of the partitionists.[35] One difficulty in the way of accepting the latter idea is the fact that Robert White, mayor in 1449, was again mayor in February 1453. Whatever White's personal stand the anti-partitionists were firmly in command of the staple in 1454, when they successfully resisted an attempt by their opponents to press their own stamp upon it.

The factional strife in the staple was carried into the parliament of

1454 and into the king's council. At first, victory seemed to lie with the partitionists, but the other side marshalled their resources, counted their political allies and finally carried the day. Very soon after Parliament met in February the partitionists secured acceptance of a bill restoring the bullion and partition ordinances. The same bill prohibited the export of wool to any Burgundian territories until the duke should allow silver bullion to be brought to Calais and also should remove a toll imposed on wool at Gravelines. The measures were probably made more palatable to the Commons by a second bill which fixed minimum prices, below which specified growths might not be exported. This was represented as protection both for the growers and the native cloth producers. A third bill which probably emanated from the partitionists called for the continuance of the staple monopoly. This was a necessary precaution, since the statute by which the king had accepted a moratorium on his prerogative to grant licences was due to expire in a few months time. That statute had greatly reduced the issue of licences but had not succeeded in stopping them entirely. As early as March 1452 the merchants of Newcastle were licensed to export for three years to Bruges or Middelburg. Even though they were permitted to trade only in shorlings and lambskins the grant was not in keeping with the spirit of the statute. From 1452, by one device or another, the amount of wool exported outside the staple began to increase.[36]

About the same time that the partitionists introduced their bills, or shortly afterwards, the official establishment of the staple brought in a petition of seven articles. The first article, designed to counter the ban on export to Burgundy, demanded that merchants be allowed to take wool away from Calais without impediment. The second article called for the rejection of the minimum wool prices and the third opposed the partition and bullion ordinances. The fourth article asked that new securities be found for loans amounting to about 12 000 marks still owed by the Crown to individual staplers. The fifth article asked that the staple should have a monopoly of all wool exports, except for that going by sea to Italy. This was more uncompromising than the petition of the other party, which excepted also the licence of Newcastle. The sixth article called for a reduction of 10s in the rate of denizen subsidy. Although not yet put into force the duty had been increased by that amount when Parliament had renewed the subsidy for the term of the king's life the previous year. The seventh article was made conditional upon a favourable response to all those that went before. It offered, subject to sound security, a loan of 10 000 marks, which was to take the form of a levy of 40s on every sarpler leaving Calais.[37]

A favourable answer was given to all but the fifth article in the petition described above. To this it was replied that the king would not grant licences outside the staple without the advice of the council. All the answers were straightforward except that given to the third article, which sought to justify the reversal of the approval just given to the partition ordinance. It is difficult to know whether one should accept the statements at their face value or whether to regard them as merely specious arguments exploiting faulty drafting in the other petition. It was stated that the king had accepted the other in the belief that it desired the reintroduction of the partition system of 1429. However, it had since been pointed out that whereas the earlier system had consisted of a number of partitions between men owning similar qualities of wool the present bill spoke of a single partition between all bringing wool to the staple. Because of the misunderstanding the king's acceptance was declared null and void. Whether the petition really had envisaged a single partition is debatable.

Two factors ensured the reversal of the bills passed in the early part of the 1454 parliament. The first was the appointment in March of the Duke of York as protector of the throne during the king's insanity; the second was the loan, in effect a bribe, offered by the staple company. Since the garrison of Calais was the only standing army at the disposal of the government it was essential to York that he gain control of the town, then under the command of his rival the Duke of Somerset. Although Somerset might easily be replaced as captain, York could only secure the loyalty of the garrison if he could pay their wages. One of the few bodies able to raise a large sum at short notice was the staple company, hence their offer of a loan in return for the reversal of legislation which was detrimental to their interests. Despite the support of the staplers York did not gain control of Calais before the king recovered his sanity in February 1455. Worse still in May 1454 the soldiers seized all the wool in the town as security for their wages. A licence authorising them to sell some of it to realise £4100 arrears of wages was withdrawn in the face of a protest by the staplers. However, between March and December 1455 the soldiers sold all the wool, estimated to be worth £26 050. This money could now be recovered only from the government of the day. In August 1455 the Earl of Warwick was made Captain of Calais in the Yorkist cause, although he did not succeed in gaining control of the town until the following summer. His success was due in large measure to a further loan of £12 000 from the staplers. An agreement of February 1456 shows that the company was owed £39 000, including the value of the confiscated wool, which was to be repaid out of the customs. It has been pointed out that the debts incurred in the winning of Calais 'imposed on (the company) a well nigh inescapable commitment to the Yorkist cause', since the defeat of the latter might mean repudiation of the loans.[38]

Despite the financial assistance which it provided to the government the staple company was quite unable to prevent the distribution of export licences which impinged on its monopoly either directly or indirectly. As early as July 1454 a general licence was granted to Newcastle to trade with Bruges or Middelburg for five years, and shortly afterwards licences began to be given to individuals to trade away from the staple. An attack was mounted against the licence system in the parliament of 1455 and they were apparently included in the act of resumption which was passed that year. A Commons petition alleged that the Crown was impoverished by the fact that many persons licensed to export away from Calais paid less than the full duty or no duty at all. It demanded that in the case of all licences executed since 1 September 1450 the owners should be required to answer for a duty of four marks, though genuine loans to the Crown would be allowed for. This was one mark above the rate paid on denizen wool going to the staple, being equal to the effective alien rate of custom and subsidy. Morlings and shorlings and wool exported in the name of the king were not excepted. A second petition enumerated $1266\frac{1}{2}$ sacks and 11 cloves which had been exported from London in the king's name.[39]

The act of resumption did not put an end to the issue of new licences and in the following year licensed exports threatened to become a flood. Much of the wool was nominally destined for Italy, the warrants specifying land transport, sea transport or either. Some of the land grants, particularly when made out to Englishmen, may have been intended to disguise sales in Burgundy. For a time, however, there was a marked increase in exports by sea to Italy, most of it alien. From Michaelmas 1449 to about the summer of 1455 alien exports had totalled 664 sacks from London, 1325 from Sandwich and 3085 from Southampton. Between March 1455 and November 1457 3359 sacks were sent from London, 1417 sacks from Southampton and 286 sacks from Sandwich. This boom was shattered by the anti-alien riots of 1456 and 1457 and the total alien exports of 1457–60 were only 1168 sacks, although this figure does not include 1137 sacks of royal wool shipped by denizen and alien factors from Southampton to Italy in the summers of 1459 and 1460. There is no reason to suppose that the king had any personal involvement in these shipments, which were merely a variant of the licence system.

Twice in the later years of Henry VI's reign the government gave undertakings that licences would not be issued in breach of the staple monopoly. In 1457 it was agreed that for three years such exports should be restricted to 2000 sacks sent each year to Italy in the king's own name. Thereafter licences generally specified that a grant was part of the king's 2000 sacks. Although the number of licences enrolled appears to exceed the agreed quota it is unlikely that all were executed. On the other hand a few licences were still issued for export to places in northern Europe apart from Calais. More promising was an undertaking given at the end of 1458, when the government was desperately in need of a further loan from the company. It was agreed that talks should be had with the Duke of Burgundy about staple regulations and the method of payment, and that he should be requested to prohibit the import into his dominions of all wool which had not passed through the staple. These talks continued throughout 1459 and at their conclusion the duke gave the guarantee which had been asked of him.[40]

Given their previous relations with the Duke of York the staplers may well have felt that they had little to fear from the accession of his son as Edward IV. This confidence was justified by the fact that Edward did not repudiate debts incurred in the name of Henry VI, although the staplers voluntarily renounced their claims to 3000 marks. At the end of 1462, after several new loans, including payments for the Calais garrison, the Crown debt stood at £40 918, secured on the customs. In some ports the staplers were entitled to only part of the revenues, but in Sandwich they received the whole amount. It was this fact, presumably, which led them to switch some of their exports to this port. In 1439–57 denizen exports from Sandwich averaged 94 sacks a year; in 1457–67 the average was 1216 sacks.

The staplers stood in need of more than the good will of the new king and his recognition of their just claims. During the first two years of the reign total denizen exports of wool failed to reach 8000 sacks. If this record was not improved the loans would never be repaid and the merchants would probably go bankrupt for lack of profits. The problems of the staplers, together with those of other economic groups, were dealt with in the protectionist parliament which assembled in April 1463. Husbandmen were to be protected by a ban on the import of corn while home prices were below specified levels; craftsmen were considered in the ban on the import of a wide variety of manufactured goods; the shipping interest was promoted by a navigation act. As far as the wool trade was concerned the most radical measure was the total ban on alien exports with effect from Midsummer. The monopoly of the staplers was re-enacted, although for the first time statutory recognition was given to the fact that the wools of the northern counties need not go to Calais. To prevent fraud by Newcastle merchants wool from other parts of England was not to be taken into their areas and severe penalties were imposed for breach of the monopoly.[41]

The new legislation also included a bullion law which required the purchaser to deliver coin or bullion to Calais.

> Noo Marchant . . . selle . . . any Wolles . . . but that he afore, or uppon the lyvere of the same, resceyve and take redy payment and contentation for the same . . . in hande; whereof the half part be in lawfull money of Englond, Plate or Bullion of Sylver or Gold; and all the same money duely bring into this Reame, and the Plate and Bullion soo resceyved, duely make to be coyned at the Mynte of Caleis; and all the money thereof made and coyned, duely bring into this same Reame; the same Plate and Bullion to be coyned, and the money thereof brought into the same Reame, within iii monethes next suying the forseid sale.

Two interpretations of this requirement have been suggested and a third will now be proposed. Postan believed that the act allowed un-limited credit for up to one half of the price of the wool and three months credit for the other half. Munro disputed the three months credit, saying that this was merely the time allowed for coining and the return to England.[42] Of the two, Munro's version is to be preferred. However it is suggested that both writers may be mistaken in their belief that unlimited credit was allowed for half of the payment. Unless the construction is at fault the phrase 'redy payment in hande' applies to the entire price of the wool and it is doubtful whether a financial instrument promising payment at a future date can be so described. We have, therefore, to find some other medium for that half which needs not necessarily be paid in English coin, plate or bullion. If one could draw a distinction between bullion and foreign coin, then the latter would provide such a medium and so this is a possibility. However, it is likely that we should also look for a financial instru-ment of some kind, not one promising future payment but one constitut-ing immediate payment. It is suggested, therefore, that the bullion law of 1463 may incorporate the amendment of the 1429 ordinance which had been proposed and rejected in the parliament of 1437. It will be recalled that at the latter date it had been suggested that the Dutch be allowed to dispose of their goods in England in return for notes of credit which might be redeemed at Calais. The same result might be obtained, of course, if the English merchants buying goods in the Low Countries paid not in cash but with notes redeemable at Calais. Support for this interpretation of the statute is provided by the fact that Bur-gundian ambassadors later complained that the staplers would not allow any credit for wool. If this was the case the staplers were not exceeding the legal requirement, as has been suggested, but merely observing it.[43] If the English could persuade the Burgundians to accept notes of credit for goods, whether in England or the Low Countries, they would have turned the tables in a way which would have delighted the author of the *Libelle of Englyshe Polycye*, one of whose complaints was that his countrymen had to sell wool on credit.[44]

Despite the confirmation of their monopoly and the ban on alien trade the staplers again complained, in the parliament of January 1465, that licences were being granted for the shipment of wool away from Calais, both in the king's name and in the names of others. By this time it was not merely commercial competition which concerned the company but fear for the security of its loans, currently estimated to be £32 861. The trouble was that wool exported under licence was frequently exempted from the payment of some or all of the duty, since the licensees satisfied the king in some other manner. This meant, of course, that it would take longer for the staplers to recover their advances. This point was covered in the new provision made for the security of the debt. The staplers were to receive 13s 4d of the subsidy in every port plus the ancient custom of 6s 8d in Boston and Sandwich. This was to be taken from the wool of staplers and non-staplers alike. Although the king did not specifically agree to dispense with licences the point would seem to be covered by the new provisions made for preserving the monopoly. All persons were to give security to the customs officials that they would take wool only to Calais. On arrival they would receive a certificate of delivery which must be presented at the Exchequer within twelve months, on pain of forfeiture of the wool. Exemption was made in favour of northern wools, while the rights of aliens were restored in the traditional exemption given to wool taken by sea to Italy.[45]

Two years later in the parliament of June 1467 it was observed that the staple 'now late was in ruyne and decay, and likely to have been dissolved'. This description, used in the parliamentary confirmation of letters patent of 13 December 1466, was probably not wildly exaggerated.[46] The letters patent recorded an act of retainer made between the Crown and the company of the staple, by which the company took over the entire financial management of the Calais garrison for the period of 8½ years. It was effected by making the mayor of the staple *ex officio* royal treasurer of Calais. The company did not farm the town and was required to render a strict account of its stewardship. Although most of the revenues must necessarily be employed in paying wages and maintaining fortifications the company was to keep £5000 a year to liquidate the king's outstanding obligations to it. As treasurer the mayor received the comparatively small income due to the Crown in Calais itself but his main resource was the trade of his colleagues. The company was to retain the entire custom and subsidy on exported wool, except for that going to Italy by sea. It has been observed, not without justice, that the act of retainer was but a logical extension of the company's involvement in the financing of Calais from the early 1450s onwards.[47] Only by accepting the act of retainer did the company stand much chance of obtaining repayment of earlier loans.

Following the deposition and restoration of Edward IV a new act of retainer was made at the beginning of the parliament of 1473, to run for 16 years from 8 April 1472. The terms were similar to those of the earlier agreement and included provision for repayment of the king's debt, which in December 1473 amounted to £21 000 plus a further £2700 which the staplers were to pay to redeem the Crown jewels. It was agreed that the staple should not be removed from Calais at any time during the next 16 years and thereafter not before outstanding debts had been repaid. Furthermore the king explicitly promised not to license exports away from the staple. This agreement was confirmed at the accessions of Richard III and Henry VII and was renewed for a further term of 16 years when it expired in 1488. In 1503 it was renewed for yet another 16-year term and in 1515 was renewed for 20 years from April 1516. Before the last term expired the staplers were obliged to seek to be released from the agreement on account of their poverty. The staple, however, remained in Calais until the town was lost to France in 1558.[48]

Consideration of the acts of retainer has carried the story of the staple company well ahead of the immediate consequences of the protectionist legislation of 1463, to which return must now be made. The bullion regulation had implied the reopening of the Calais mint but it seems most unlikely that this was done. On the other hand during the late 1460s and 1470s the gold output of the London mint was higher than at any time during the past 40 years. Initially the increase was caused by the recoinage of earlier issues which followed the debasement of 1464–5. However the higher rate of flow into the mint continued for too long for the increase to be attributable solely to the debasement. It appears likely, therefore, that the staplers were importing bullion and that the new legislation was enjoying some degree of success. Following the repeal of the bullion regulation in 1473 the flow of gold was reduced, although remaining higher than the pre-1464 level.

Despite the fact that the ban on many types of imports as well as the new Calais regulations were detrimental to the economic interests of his subjects the Duke of Burgundy took no immediate retaliatory measures. Not until 1464 did he impose, for the third time, a ban on the import of English cloth. In January 1465 Parliament imposed its own ban on the import of all goods from Burgundy, to be effective from 2 February until such time as the duke lifted his boycott. After two conferences had failed to settle the dispute the situation was eased by the death of Duke Philip in June 1467. His son and heir, Charles the Bold, was too anxious to cement a political and military alliance with England against France to continue a commercial quarrel. The treaty made in November 1467 restored *the status quo* and nothing was done about the current Calais regulations, even though during the earlier negotiations the Burgundians had expressed their dissatisfaction with them.[49] The bullion regulation appears to have been abolished by a somewhat obscurely-worded clause about exchanges contained in the act of retainer of 1473.[50] Thereafter individual staplers were free to make their own arrangements for selling wool and the practices amply portrayed in the Cely papers were established or re-established.

Although the first act of retainer may have provided the staplers with hope of recovering their advances to the Crown there seems little reason to suppose that it made any direct contribution to the increase in wool exports which took place in the late 1460s. This probably owed more to the increasing political stability of the country which encouraged a general improvement in all branches of commerce. Denizen wool exports, which had totalled less than 8000 sacks during the first two years of Edward IV's reign, averaged rather less than 7000 sacks a year in 1463–6 and rather more than 8000 sacks a year in 1466–72. The figure for the latter period would have been larger had it not been for trade lost and not recovered during the troubled interlude of Henry VI's restoration. A similar level of trade was maintained over the decade 1472–82, with an average denizen export of 8064 sacks. The temporary decline in exports to less than 1000 sacks in 1476–7 was caused, no doubt, by the combination of two apparently unrelated incidents. In the previous year there had been an exceptionally large export, with 9526 sacks leaving London between June 1475 and Michaelmas 1476 compared with 4367 sacks between May 1474 and June 1475. This wool probably took some time to dispose of. Then in January 1477 Duke Charles of Burgundy died and his territories of Picardy, Artois and the duchy of Burgundy were invaded by Charles XI of France. England, concerned as ever with the state of Franco-Burgundian relations, thereupon reinforced the garrison of Calais and these operations may have placed a temporary stop on trade.

The ability of the staplers to maintain their exports during the 1470s must be seen against the background of the great expansion in cloth exports which took place during this time. At the end of the period (1479–82) the latter averaged 62 500 broadcloths, the highest level yet achieved. By now the home industry was employing considerably more wool than was being exported and the demand from this sector must have been the main determinant of prices. Unfortunately the price data of the late fifteenth century is so sparse that its interpretation is very difficult. It appears likely that the price of wool rose during the 1460s after a prolonged period of depression. The trade recession of 1469–71, as noticeable in cloth exports as in the business of the staplers, can have provided but a temporary check to this rise. At the beginning of the 1480s William Midwinter, agent of the Celys, constantly complains about the scarcity of wool and its great price. At first, in October 1480, he puts the blame on Italians, writing 'I have not bowgyt this yere a loke of woll, for the woll of Cottyswolde is bogwyt be Lombardys.' Although this statement is unacceptable as an explanation of general scarcity it may well be a true expression of his own experience in the Cotswolds that year. The Southampton customs account commencing that Michaelmas records an Italian export considerably higher than for many years past. The following summer, with another large Italian export, Midwinter wrote, 'Woll in Cottyswolld ys at grete pryse, 13s 4d a tode, and gret ryding for woll in Cottyswolld as was anny yere thys vii yere'. A year later prices were higher still, 14s to 14s 6d a todd, and the growers were reluctant to give credit; 'They moste haffe reddy money bey and bey, they that werr wonte to leffe in my honde moste parte of ther money, nowe they moste nedys haffe halle ther money'.[51]

Although the growing export of cloth may have encouraged the staplers to turn increasingly to the Italian market most of their wool was still destined for Burgundian territories. After the death of Edward IV, however, both wool and cloth exports suffered a severe setback. In 1482–5 the former averaged only 5283 sacks a year and the latter not much more than 45 000 broadcloths. Unfortunately the commercial history of Richard III's reign still awaits exposition and no explanation can yet be offered for the decline. For the staplers these years were the first stage in a series of cycles of slump and relative prosperity. In 1485 the staple trade recovered and in the five years to 1490 exports averaged 8742 sacks. The recovery of the cloth trade in the same period was less complete and the five year average was only 50 054 broadcloths. On the other hand the merchant adventurers continued to increase their exports in 1490–3, with an average of 55 344 broadcloths, while wool exports slumped to a derisory average of 3815 sacks.

In September 1493 Henry VII imposed a boycott on trade with all Burgundian territories because of the support which their ruler was providing for the pretender, Perkin Warbeck. The sole exception to this general ban was the provision that the staplers might continue to sell their wool to the Burgundians at Calais.[52] It is surely one of the most pertinent comments on the changed economic circumstances of the late middle ages that the King of England sought to impose his will on the ruler of the Low Countries by refusing to let his subjects sell cloth at Antwerp while continuing to allow them to sell wool. Henry VII's confidence that his merchant adventurers could survive without the Antwerp fairs may have been justified, for broadcloth exports in 1493–4 totalled 59 533. Unfortunately, in the next two years the all-important London cloth customs accounts are missing. Nevertheless, the boycott seems to have provided a temporary stimulus for the looms of the Low Countries, for denizen wool exports increased to 7168 sacks in 1493–4, 10 824 sacks in 1494–5 and 12 626 sacks in 1495–6, an average of 10 206. In February 1496 England and Burgundy agreed to the commercial treaty known as the *Magnus Intercursus*. Wool exports declined to an average of 8822 in 1496–8 and 6493 in 1498–1500, while cloth exports grew steadily and in 1499–1500 stood at an all time record of 70 170. There can be little doubt that by the beginning of the sixteenth century the staplers and their customers were obliged to make do with the leavings of the English cloth industry.

It remains only to give a general picture of the substance of the merchants of the staple at the end of the middle ages. An anonymous treatise written about the 1520s alleges that during the reign of Edward IV there had been a great increase in the numbers of the fellowship of the staple.[53] Although some of the statements made in this work are incorrect this one may well be true. In July 1472 the staple authorities provided Chancery with a certificate listing all the present freemen of the fellowship.[54] Although damaged the document provides a total of about 257 members. In 1505 a pardon was granted to almost 500 named staplers, many of them women, for various alleged offences, including breaches of the obsolete bullion statute of the 1340s.[55] A petition to the Privy Council about 1526 lamented the decay of the staple and alleged that its membership had been reduced from 400 to 140 or 160.[56]

The treatise mentioned above alleges that the staplers 'encreased in nomber oon of a nother by meane of apprentishode'. The certificate of 1472, however, names at least four men styled knight and the pardon of 1505 includes seven of the same rank. Other lists of staplers include many who enjoyed the style of gentleman. It is unlikely that men such as these had served an apprenticeship in the art of merchandising. It is more probable that they were landowners with wool of their own to sell or merely men of substance wishing to make an investment. They can have played little active part in the business. A Chancery action of 1467 or 1471 describes how William Lovelas, gentleman of Merton, had 60 sacks of wool worth £500 at Calais, and how he arranged for John Simond to be his attorney and factor and to sell the wool at discretion.[57] An expansion in the number of the staplers without an increase in the size of the total export implies, of course, that the share of the average merchant declined. Without particular accounts for all wool ports it is impossible at this date to determine the amount of wool exported by known merchants. The reason for this is that all wool was now shipped in convoys organised and paid for by the staple authorities. In consequence exporters had to be more flexible in their own arrangements, so that they might get their wool to whatever port had been designated for a convoy. Notwithstanding this difficulty it is clear from the surviving accounts of Boston that once again there was a not inconsiderable number of small exporters and that monopoly was no longer the hallmark of the wool trade.

Native merchants held a practical monopoly of the sale of English wool in northern Europe throughout the fifteenth century. Alien competition in this area had been discouraged by the creation of the Calais staple and was virtually eliminated when they were required to pay a higher rate of subsidy than denizens towards the end of Richard II's reign. Penalised by higher taxation aliens could no longer compete at Calais. Alien trade passed entirely into the hands of Italians who used the sea route to the Mediterranean and even this declined in the early part of the fifteenth century. Alien exports averaged 1321 sacks in 1399–1412, 946 sacks in 1412–22, 933 sacks in 1422–8 and 703 sacks in 1428–34. The decline in the second of these periods coincided with a protracted breakdown in Anglo-Genoese friendship which followed the arrest of the expedition sent to Italy by London merchants in 1412. During the war between Henry V and France, Genoese ships provided naval assistance to the latter. It is uncertain whether the absence of Genoese merchants or of Genoese ships was the more important factor in the decline in wool exports. However, there was no improvement in exports after Genoese shipping returned in strength to England after 1421. From this time exporters to the Mediterranean seem to have had a distinct preference for galleys to sailing ships, even though the former provided less capacity than the great Genoese carracks. On 30 November 1403 two carracks had left Southampton laden with 449 sacks and 438 sacks respectively, while at the next departure, on 10 March 1405, one carried 480 sacks and a second 1019 sacks.[58] Two Venetian galleys which left London on 2 November 1422 carried only 45 sacks and 76 sacks.[59] However the later Florentine galleys regularly carried more than this.

In the period 1434–45 alien exports increased to an average of at least 1345 sacks and may actually have been somewhat higher. In 1446 a Venetian source records that three years previously their London factory had lent the king £200, which was to have been repaid by allowance of custom on wool exported by its members. Since that time none had exported wool in their own name, but had done so in the names of Englishmen in order to make a personal profit. They were now ordered to liquidate the king's tallies by instalments on their wool.[60] The recovery of alien exports during the late 1430s and early 1440s may have been due in part to the more regular visits to England of the Florentine state galleys. These had appeared here in 1425, 1427, 1428 and 1429, but only from 1436 did the visits become routine.[61] It is probably no coincidence that the regular voyages began during the time when the Duke of Burgundy obstructed the exit of wool from Calais. Since the 1380s Venetian galleys had made regular visits to England but they were not always able to take all the wool which was offered to them. This was because Venetian merchants themselves, unlike the Florentines, were more interested in cloth exports than in wool. In 1414 a dispute about whether the masters of the Venetian galleys were bound to take all the cargo which was offered to them was put to a ballot. It was decided that the Bruges galleys should not be bound to take wool since great inconvenience and delay was caused by stowing it. The London galleys, however, were to load wool before other goods. In 1421 it was ruled that the galleys were not compelled to load wool at Sandwich. The advent of the Florentine galleys probably introduced an element of competition for freight, but the Venetians remained interested in obtaining cargoes of wool. In 1441 it was ruled that no other Venetian vessel was to load cloth or wool in England or Flanders until two months after the departure of the state galleys, unless these had left a surplus.[62]

During the first half of the fifteenth century Florentine merchants probably led the field in Italian wool exports and this commodity made up the greater part of their purchases in England. Venetians, as already pointed out, were more interested in cloth exports. From Easter 1442 to Michaelmas 1443 Federico Cornes and Carlo Contarini spent £4460 16s on English goods, of which only £498 10s was spent on buying 53 sacks of wool from the Abbot of Cirencester and other Cotswold producers.[63] Most of the other Venetians whose transactions are recorded in the London hosting accounts of this period bought no wool. Merchants of Lucca were still involved in the trade and Felix de Fagnano and Alessandro Palestrell paid £1263 for 179 sacks of Cotswold wool between Michaelmas 1441 and Easter 1443.[64] Of exports, if any, by Genoese merchants at this time there is no record.

In the period 1445 to 1455 alien exports declined once more to an average of only 802 sacks a year. During the greater part of this time the Florentine galleys did not come to England, although the decline appears to have begun before their last voyage in 1447. The trend was abruptly reversed in 1455 when Italian merchants became the recipients of royal licences to export wool by way of the Low Countries as well as by the direct sea route. The exact amount of their trade during the next few years cannot be determined, since some of it was exported in the king's name. However, the great volume of trade in 1455–7 must have contributed to the anti-Italian riots of 1456 and 1457.[65]

Soon after the accession of Edward IV the staplers succeeded in getting a total ban on alien participation in the export trade, though this proved to be short lived. From 1464 to 1494 there was little overall change in the level of alien exports with quinquennial averages ranging from about 850 sacks a year to 1000 sacks. Curiously, a considerable fall after 1494 coincided with the frustration of a design to vest a monopoly of the wool trade to Italy in English merchants and English ships. This had become a feasible proposition as a result of an increase in the number of English ships going to the Mediterranean and in the number of English merchants exporting wool to Italy. The two were not necessarily associated, for it is likely that most of the merchants sent their wool in Italian vessels. The English involvement in the Italian wool market cannot be denied, although neither can it be measured accurately. The trade depended in large measure upon Italian factors and, often, upon royal licences which were usually transferable. This means that there is frequently room for doubt about the legal ownership of the goods in question.[66]

Although the English expansion into the Mediterranean may at first have been as unwelcome to Florence as it was to the other naval powers this city was the first to withdraw its opposition and, indeed, sought to turn the development to its advantage. A temporary suspension of the state galleys in 1478 had become permanent and Florence no longer had this vested interest to consider. The city seems to have reasoned that the best way to obtain English wool at the expense of its

Italian rivals was to encourage the English to bring it themselves. All sources agree that it was the Florentines who in 1489 made the suggestion that all English wool coming to the Mediterranean should be directed to a staple at Pisa and that a monopoly of export be vested in English merchants and ships. This was the basis of an Anglo-Florentine commercial treaty made in 1490. The monopoly was not complete, since in the face of Venetian protests and threats it had been agreed that they might continue to export 600 sacks a year outside the staple. Unfortunately, the revolt of Pisa against Florentine rule put an end to the experiment before it really had chance to develop.[67]

During the long period of the decline of the wool trade the determination to maintain the staple at Calais seems to have been more resolute than ever. After 1422 there appears to be no evidence that it was ever proposed to move it elsewhere. Yet although Calais had been a reasonable location for a wool mart in the days when Flanders was the main customer for English wool it became less and less suitable as the Flemish industry declined. Although the Dutch made the journey to Calais they might well have bought greater amounts of English wool had they been able to obtain it directly from England, while during times of peace with France the absence of a staple might have stimulated Normandy's use of English wool. Two facts alone kept the staple at Calais; the English wool merchants saw it as essential to the maintenance of their monopoly, while it was also regarded as a necessary part of the defences of this English bastion in France.

9

Marketing the wool

The familiar picture of the techniques used in the medieval wool trade is drawn to a very large extent from the Cely letters and papers and from other documents belonging to the legal side of the king's Chancery, few of which are earlier than the middle of the fifteenth century. By this date the export trade was but a shadow of its former self and many of its current practices had evolved only since the compulsory staple had finally been located at Calais. Unfortunately it is easier to warn against anachronistic use of late-fifteenth-century evidence than to draw an equally clear picture for the thirteenth and early fourteenth centuries, when the export trade was at its peak. The customs particulars, of which use has already been made, provide little more information than the amount of wool dispatched in the name of each merchant. The supplementary evidence, however, is scattered and when accumulated poses almost as many questions as it answers.

For only one branch of the early medieval trade is there tolerably good evidence about the way in which wool was marketed – that associated with the great monastic producers, particularly the Cistercians. The value of this evidence must not be underrated, for this was the very wool which was most in demand in the export market. It is clear that by the time when the enrolled customs accounts attest the level of exports the monasteries can have been responsible for only a part, almost certainly a minority, of all the wool going overseas. In the early days of the export trade, however, they may have provided the greater part of it. It is perhaps not without significance that as late as 1204 John's assise about overseas trade states that wool shall not be removed from abbeys, but does not mention any other source. The importance of monastic wool output and the ease with which it could be disposed of are attested by the well-known fact that one year's clip of the Cistercians, as well as that of the smaller orders of Gilbert of Sempringham and Prémontré were taken for the ransom of Richard I.[1] Although this event made a profound impression on the chroniclers the seizure may not have been as widespread as it was made out to be. At any rate it appears to have left only two traces in surviving official records. In the pipe roll of 1192–3 the sheriff of Yorkshire was allowed

£8 2s 8d for the carriage of wool from various abbeys to the port of Hulme, while the keeper of the city of Lincoln was allowed 8s for the hire of ships.[2] On one, or even two, occasions Henry III tried unsuccessfully to emulate the government of his late uncle. In October 1242 he demanded a subsidy from the Cistercians and Premonstratensians and let it be known that he would gladly take one year's wool in lieu of cash. A further attempt to extort money from the Cistercians in 1256 may also have led to a similar suggestion. The later demand was particularly unwelcome, since Matthew Paris records that shortly before Cistercian wool sales had suffered because of civil war in Flanders, while at the same time a large part of their flocks had perished in a great murrain.[3]

Although most of the detailed evidence about monastic sales of wool is derived from contracts made in the 1270s and later the conditions they describe are far from new. The most important feature of the transaction, the advance delivery by the buyer of some or all of the purchase price, probably goes back to the early days of the export trade. Although William Cade of St Omer may have been primarily a usurer, he seems also to have been a wool merchant who paid in advance. A list compiled after his death or disgrace about 1166 gives details of debts owed to him, including 70 marks paid to Louth Park for their wool and 22 weys of wool in sacks and 2200 fleeces in sacks owed by Roche. Four similar transactions involve laity.[4] Payment in advance was not without risk and if the sellers failed to deliver the purchaser either became involved in tedious litigation or had to pay the Crown to get a quick verdict. In 1194–5 one Martin son of Edric gave £5 *pro habendo recte* for 6 sacks 4 stones of good wool, 4 sacks of other wool and 10 marks which he claimed from the nunnery of Swine. Three years later William Elyas gave 20 marks to get 7000 fleeces for which he had already paid the abbot of York. William son of Robert who sued Swine for 20 sacks of wool and 10 marks in 1200 was still vainly pursuing the case 4 years later.[5]

So great was the demand for wool of the best quality that the most skilful producers were able to sell their clip many years in advance. As early as 1181 the General Chapter of the Cistercian order ruled that only in case of need might wool be sold one year in advance and must never be anticipated by a longer period. This rule was totally ignored by the mid-thirteenth century. Apart from the fact that concealed interest might be charged on money paid in advance there was a danger that the sheep might be hit by murrain and that insufficient wool would be available to meet the obligation. For many Cistercians nightmare became reality during the scab epidemic of the 1270s and

1280s, when loss of their flocks forced them into bankruptcy. Receivers were appointed and the monks were allowed only sufficient cash to meet their barest needs. Kirkstall was put into receivership in 1276, Flaxley in 1277, 1281 and 1283, Missenden in 1281 and Rievaulx in 1288. In 1285 Kirkstead, which had lost its own flocks, was licensed to buy wool for three years to satisfy its merchants. In 1281–2 Byland lost its flocks and the king intervened with the Frescobaldi to get repayments of its debt reduced from £250 a year to 100 marks. In the same year Dore repaid a large debt to Siennese usurers only by raising a new loan from the merchants of Cahors.[6]

During the first half of the thirteenth century most of the contracts made by monasteries were negotiated with Flemish merchants. In January 1265 the king wrote to ten of the most important Cistercian houses and four others ordering them to honour agreements made with Flemings. The latter had paid in advance between a quarter and a half of the price of the wool but had been unable to take delivery because of the recent disturbances in England. In consequence of these relationships the names of English monasteries became household words in Flanders. The archives of Douai have a manuscript, which is unlikely to be later than the 1260s, listing 102 convents and hospitals of various orders which produced wool for sale.[7] Unlike the later and better-known list of the Italian merchant Pegolotti[8] the Flemish document does not give the amount of wool available and prices are entered for only half the houses. The highest price is £50 (Paris) for the wool of the Cistercian abbey of Neath, but prices between £30 and £40 are more usual. In a couple of instances prices given in the schedule can be compared with those recorded in actual indentures of sales made at Douai. Byland wool, entered at £38, was sold at that price in December 1259, while Holmcultram wool was sold at the same price in the following February. Meaux wool was entered at £36, but in January 1279 was sold at £54.[9] The fact that the Italian contracts of 1294 and Pegolotti's list confirm that Meaux was one of the cheaper Yorkshire wools suggests that Flemish prices rose considerably during the 1270s.

It was shown in an earlier chapter how during the disturbances of the early 1270s Flemish merchants lost most of their contracts to Italians and it is unlikely that many were recovered. When the king ordered Fountains to let a group of Ghent merchants have wool to complete a two-year contract the abbey said that it had already sold the clip to the Riccardi. Eventually the latter repaid at least some of the money which the Flemings had advanced.[10] In the 1290s James Pilate of Douai, one of the biggest Flemish merchants still trading in

England had a contract with Welbeck Priory, which in the late 1270s had been contracted to the Falconieri of Florence. Despite a setback during the war of 1294–7 in 1299 James made a modest contract with Flaxley Abbey for 5 sacks over two years.[11]

The lure of Italian silver seems to have tempted some monasteries to break contracts even without the excuse that the buyers were Flemings. Herbert Weremond was a capitalist of Cambrai who exported large quantities of wool in the early 1270s. In 1275 he sued the abbot of Louth Park for the unjust detention of 14 sacks 20 stones sold by his predecessor. Although Herbert had paid only 4 marks in earnest money he claimed damages of £100. He was awarded 60 marks damages and expenses and was allowed to buy 14 sacks of the wool of 1276 in preference to the existing contractors. It was revealed that the late abbot, who initially caused the trouble, had made a new contract for four years with the Falconieri while the present abbot had made a contract with a Cahorsin company for the ten years following that. While Herbert's attorney was in the king's Chancery on this business he took the opportunity to have enrolled on the dorse of the close roll a contract made by another client, John Weremond of Cambrai, with Darnhall Abbey. This contract, one of the earliest and most detailed that has survived, will be discussed later.[12]

The scab epidemic of the 1270s, which led to a rise in wool prices, was another factor which caused some monks to repent of an earlier bargain. In 1278 the convent of Bordesley petitioned the king in Parliament to have a contract revoked on the grounds that it was in contravention of the usury laws.[13] They alleged that three years previously their abbot had received a loan of 300 marks from the Cerchi, to be repaid over a period of six years at 50 marks a year. Without consulting the convent he gave the merchants his bond for 42 sacks of wool, stating that he had been paid in full, although the monks alleged that he had received nothing at all. Now, having repaid 100 marks of the loan and delivered 12 sacks of wool, the convent sought to have the contract annulled. It is unlikely that any money had actually been repaid, for this was a device to evade the usury laws. What seems to have happened was that the abbot was paid 300 marks in full settlement of the price of 42 sacks of wool, valued in his bond at 9 marks each. This meant that the abbey was paying 78 marks in interest charges. Meanwhile the value of the wool had increased, so the brethren claimed, to 13 marks a sack and they wished to be free of the bargain.

In the late 1270s many monasteries failed to fulfil their contracts either through greed or, more usually, because their flocks were

decimated by scab. This resulted in a flurry of litigation. Suits in which
the cause was given as unjust detention of wool reveal only part of the
story. Failure of the wool clip undoubtedly lay behind some of the
cases where the cause was given as failure to repay a money loan.
Even if only the former cases are taken into consideration we find that
the Exchequer plea rolls of the late 1270s record proceedings against
at least half a dozen monasteries by merchants of Florence, Piacenza,
Cahors and Spain.[14] The Exchequer was a favourite court with merchants because of the comparative speed with which a judgment might
be obtained. Originally the legal jurisdiction of the Exchequer had
extended only to matters which involved the Crown finances but by
this date the right to a hearing in the Exchequer could be claimed by
its own officials and by the king's creditors. This was not always to
the liking of defendants. In 1282 the abbot of Roche was sued for the
unjust detention of 6 sacks of wool by a merchant, probably a Cahorsin,
who claimed to be a 'servant' of the royal official, Walter de Kancia.[15]
The abbot's defence was that he was not bound to answer in this cause
in this place, but only in some other place, and that this was established
by *Magna Carta*. In the absence of the Treasurer the other barons declined to rule on this defence and adjourned the case. It seems later to
have been settled by agreement.

Only a minority of all the prosecutions which were mounted are
recorded in the Exchequer plea rolls. Some cases were heard in other
courts, while it is clear that some of those actually heard in the Exchequer were not written up in the plea rolls. However, another
Exchequer source, its memoranda rolls, records some of the verdicts
reached in other cases, whether heard in or out of the Exchequer. The
verdict took the form of a recognisance of debt made by the losing
party. This means that the loser admitted the debt, accepted terms for
repaying it and agreed that his chattels might be distrained if he
defaulted. The majority of recognisances enrolled in the Exchequer
memoranda rolls are not judgments about disputed debts but simply
a registration of contracts made between two parties. However, there
can be no doubt that some of the recognisances in question were the
outcome of litigation. Others may have been new contracts registered
because of the uncertainty about getting delivery. The earliest recognisance of a debt in wool in the memoranda rolls appears to be in
1230,[16] but they remain a rarity until the late 1270s. In the years
1278–80 there are at least four monastic recognisances in wool to the
Frescobaldi, three to the Falconieri, two to the Bardi, two to the Cerchi
and one to the Riccardi.[17] None of these was the outcome of cases
written up in the Exchequer plea rolls, although the recognisance from

Fountains to the Bardi incorporated a judgment in the *banco* and the prosecution of Meaux by the Riccardi had been handled by the Exchequer.[18]

As with cases described in the plea rolls recognisances in which the defendant agreed to deliver wool may understate the number of confrontations in which wool was involved. If he had no wool but agreed to refund the cash it would be unnecessary to mention the original debt, or it might be mentioned only incidentally. Thus a recognisance from Byland to the Frescobaldi, not counted in those referred to above, states that over a six year period the monks will refund in cash £1000 paid for 120 sacks of wool. Two years later the abbey asked for a respite in payment since it was stricken by murrain and other troubles.

After the panic of the late 1270s there was a decline in the incidence of memoranda roll recognisances specifically acknowledging a debt in wool. Only the Riccardi made regular use of them and between 1283 and 1293 there are at least eighteen from monasteries, besides a large number from lay men. The only other monastic examples in the 1280s appear to be one to the Pulci-Rimbertini in 1282 and three which record the transfer of contracts from the Cerchi to the Mozzi in 1286–8. Although examples of the genus may be found in the memoranda rolls as late as the 1320s it is clear that they did not become as much an institution as they gave promise of becoming about 1280. One is tempted to ascribe the paucity of Exchequer recognisances in wool to the alternative form of debt registration established by the statutes of Acton Burnell (1283) and *de mercatoribus* (1285). However, while the Italians, together with other aliens and English merchants, made abundant use of the new legislation in their dealings with lay wool producers and middlemen there is no evidence that they registered monastic debts in this way. The absence of monasteries among the surviving early certificates of dishonoured debts suggests either that the legislation was not used for this purpose or that no monastery defaulted on a debt so registered in the 1280s.

The statutes referred to above were intended to make life easier for merchants by simplifying the process of debt recovery. Officials were appointed in the main commercial centres throughout the country to keep recognisance rolls, in which A admitted a debt to B and promised to pay at a specified time. If the debt was not paid at the appointed time B obtained from the local officials a certified copy of the recognisance with the aid of which he could obtain an Exchequer writ instructing a sheriff to distrain for the debt. Thousands of these certificates survive in the Public Record Office, some in original Exchequer files, some in bundles reassembled by archivists from disrupted files.

The certificates, then, representing only a fraction of the recognisances enrolled, record dishonoured debts. The great majority of them merely promise payment of a sum of money without entering into any details of the transaction. Although most recognisances probably provided for the payment of goods delivered on credit the same procedure could be used to record a money penalty which would be incurred only if the recognisor did not fulfil some agreement, which is seldom entered in the record. Thus a money recognisance might actually be a sum which was to be repaid if wool, or any other commodity which had already been paid for, was not delivered. However, a proportion of the recognisances actually promised to deliver wool. Out of a total of 2390 certificates in the first thirteen of the existing bundles in the Public Record Office 155 are in this form.[19] The amount of wool promised is generally very small and, as already mentioned, in these early bundles there are no certificates of recognisances made by monasteries.

Monastic contracts were by no means the sole preserve of alien merchants and could be obtained by Englishmen able to command cash to pay in advance. In 1270 William fitz Thomas of Louth sued Thornholm Priory for 900 marks. In the concord made between them William withdrew his claim for 225 marks and it was agreed that the priory should deliver 75 sacks of wool at 9 marks a sack for the remainder of the debt. It was also agreed that no wool should be sold to anyone else until the debt was paid. Four years later William's son returned to the Exchequer and complained that the priory had broken the agreement by selling much of its wool to other merchants. In 1282 Newborough Priory acknowledged a debt of 123 sacks to James de Lissington and his wife, to be delivered over 12 years, although in this case the Lissintons seem not to have paid wholly in advance, and had to pay £508 at the rate of £49 a year. Stephen de Cornhill of London received all the wool of Sheppey Priory for some 16 years before 1288 in settlement of a debt. Another Londoner, Thomas de Basing, was owed wool by Flaxley Abbey when it became bankrupt and for a time he was receiver of the house. Nicholas de Ludlow, one of the greatest English merchants of the 1260s probably had a contract with Bruerne Abbey which may have been disrupted by the scab and was certainly not completed at the time of his death, for in 1286 the abbey admitted debts of 2173 marks and £103 to his heirs. At Easter in this same year it bound itself to Adam de Blakeneye of London for 27 sacks of wool or £500, payable over the next 3 years. In 1289 the debt to the Ludlows was still 2000 marks and 5 sacks of wool, worth 100 marks.[20]

As well as providing a large part of the superior wool which was exported Cistercian monasteries also acted as middlemen in the collection of the lesser grades which were grown by their neighbours. This practice was forbidden by the General Chapter of the order as early as 1157, but to no avail. The statute was renewed in 1206 and in 1214 the abbots of Fountains and Whitland were appointed to conduct a general enquiry into the matter.[21] It also aroused the opposition of lay wool merchants, who periodically during the thirteenth century obtained royal proclamations forbidding the traffic. In the collection of wool as in its production the Cistercians may have provided a model for the Gilbertines, since the historian of Malton Priory believes that its gross income of £5244 from wool sales in the years 1244–57 can only be accounted for on this basis.[22]

The more detailed of the memoranda roll recognisances, together with a number of agreements enrolled on the close rolls, shed considerable light on conditions of sale written into the contracts, apart from the obvious matter of payment. If the contract specified good wool there was invariably a list of certain qualities which might not be included. The more cautious merchants rehearsed a whole gamut of exclusions; *cot* and *gard*, *torch* and *tarch*, *clac* and *loc*, *nigra* and *grisa*, *scabie* and *putrid*, *pellur'*, generally rounded off by 'without any inferior fleece' (*vile vellera*, *vilein tuyson*). These reservations were particularly important in the case of *collecta*, the wool bought by the monasteries from other flocks. *Collecta* contracts frequently laid down the area from which wool would be accepted. A Meaux contract of 1283 said it must come from the region between Holderness and Bridlington and between Kirkham and York. However, a Vaudey contract of 1292 specified that even its own wool must come from pastures within two or three leagues of the house. Contracts sometimes stated that the merchants were to be the sole judge of what was acceptable and that their simple word was to be believed without their being put on oath or required to produce proof that a sack had been below standard.

The vendors were generally required to deliver the wool at their own risk to an appointed *rendezvous*, transport costs usually being reckoned in the price. Since the wool was packed ready for export, cleaning and other preparatory work had to be done before it left the monastery. Places like Rievaulx, Vaudey and Meaux with a sound reputation were entrusted to do this work themselves, probably with the labour of lay brothers. Fountains also did its own packing although one contract stipulated that the wool must be packed as at Rievaulx. Where a house, albeit of the Cistercian order, had no great reputation the merchants sent their own dresser and arrangements were made for his payment. In 1275 Darnhall Abbey made a contract to supply 12 sacks of Herefordshire *collecta* as good as the better *collecta* of Dore Abbey.[23] The wool was to be dressed at Hereford by a man sent, and probably paid, by the merchant, but the abbey was to find his board while he engaged in the work. The price of this wool was only 9 marks a sack, including delivery to London. The next year Fountains received 11¼ marks a sack, for 62 sacks of *collecta* to be delivered to Clifton near York over a four year period. A contract made between Combermere Abbey (Cistercian) and the Frescobaldi in 1298 was another in which the merchants undertook to send a man every year to dress the wool, while the monks were to provide his board. A contract made in 1280 by the Cluniac priory of Pontefract called for the delivery of 10 sacks a year at 10 marks each, 10 marks being paid in advance each year at Stamford fair to provide for the dressing of the wool. If the last illustration is reliable it suggests that dressing was an expensive operation.

Some of the description of the dressing of the wool, such as washing, drying and cleaning, is self-explanatory. However, most contracts stipulate that wool must be well-pressed or well-broken (*bene brusata*). Since *leyne brise* or *lana brusata* was charged a *maltote* of 5 marks in 1294 compared with 3 marks for other wool the operation was clearly one of some importance. Unfortunately no explanation can be given of what was done to the wool, for contracts which expand on the phrase *bene brusata* merely add to the mystery. A Rievaulx contract of 1287 speaks of *lane brisate in rotundis pilotis et pugnatis preparate*. An alternative extension to *rotundis pilotis*, though rather less common, is the phrase four stones, a version from Ford Abbey in 1292 reading that the wool *debent brusari de quolibet sacco quatuor petra*.

The most interesting of all the surviving monastic contracts is that made in November 1288 between Pipewell Abbey and a group of Cahorsin merchants led by Arnold de Soliz and William Servat.[24] The contract specified that in 1289 and the next four years the merchants should receive 9 sacks of good wool at 18 marks, 3 sacks of middle at 12½ marks, 7 sacks of locks at 10 marks and 5 sacks of *tayller* at an unspecified price. The contract was to continue during the ten years from 1294, but the prices were to be increased to 21 marks, 14 marks, 13 marks and 12 marks for *tayller*. Throughout this period the monks were forbidden to sell either their own wool or *collecta* to any other merchants. The merchants had paid £120 in earnest which was to be deducted, at the rate of 10 marks in the first 3 years and £10 in the next 10 years, from the balance owing when the wool was delivered. The monks were to receive two annual payments in advance, £63 6s 8d in November and the same within one month of Easter, these also being deducted from the balance which was to be paid when the wool was delivered in Boston at Midsummer. Delivery was to be at the abbey's expense, but the merchants were to provide a barrel of wine for a celebration of the clip. In addition to the wool already mentioned the merchants were to be given free of charge 1 sack *prout exitus de ouili* for 14 years and 2 sacks in the last year. The contract then continued as a recognisance that the monks had received 733 sheep from the merchants. The monks were to care for the sheep, though apparently the merchants were to pay half of any expenses, and the wool was to be divided equally between the parties. The fleeces of any sheep which died were to be sold and the income shared, while at the end of 15 years the survivors were to be divided equally between the abbey and the merchants. Finally a further recognisance acknowledged that the abbey had received £160 for the wool of the first 8 years, to be allowed at the rate of £20 a year.

From the first this complicated contract was in dispute between the abbey and the merchants and in 1291 it was submitted to arbitration and renegotiated.[25] One cause of conflict was the fact that the *tayller* had been separated from other wools. The arbitrators now ruled that it was to be packed or pressed (*bursetur*) among the 'common wool' of the house, the prices to be 18, 14 and 10 marks for 4 years from 1291 and 21, 14 and 13 marks for the next 10 years. In compensation for past damages and trespasses the merchants were awarded 2 sacks each year of 'wool of the house as it leaves the sheepfold, well washed, dry and cleaned . . . which two sacks shall be received from all the wool of the house before any of it be *bursetur*' [pressed, broken or packed?]. The arbitrators also gave rulings on certain other matters relating to the preparation of the wool, but since these were not mentioned in the original contract it is impossible to tell whether they had been in dispute or not. Now, as previously, the merchants were to send their own dresser to prepare the wool and might have access to him at all times. He was sworn to work indifferently and neither party might challenge his actions nor reject any prepared wool. The expense was to be borne by the monks, who were to provide board and lodging and to give the dresser 5 stones of wool. The arbitration then goes on to make certain specifications about conditions in the wool-shed which are difficult to visualise, but which presumably were necessary to ensure good work. *Lanaria in qua dicte lane preperabuntur et preperarei consueverunt taliter preperata de bordis firmiter attachiatis quod lana iaceat a terra vel pavimento dicte lanaria per altitudimen dimidii pedis et eodem modo de bordis fimiter attachiatis preperabitur dicta lanaria per parietes circa lanam.* This description cannot refer to the construction of the building itself, for monastic wool-sheds were sub-stantial places, that of Meaux being roofed with lead and built of stone.[26]

The arbitration of 1291 also extended to the sheep in which the merchants had invested. Because the abbey had not given a proper account of these 900 of its sheep, half of them ewes, were to be selected by the view of the merchants, marked with the sign of both parties and then returned to the flocks. When they and their issue should reach a total of 2000 the surplus should be divided each year, leaving only 2000 to be divided between the abbey and the merchants at the end of 13 years. During this time they were to share the wool. In the war of 1294–7 the merchants' sheep were confiscated by the Crown and afterwards litigation led to a new contract being made in 1314.[27] The merchants agreed to buy all the abbey's wool for 8 years from 1315 at 15 marks per sack. They also contributed 1000 sheep, beasts which they were owed in settlement of the earlier contract, to which the abbey added only 500, although the wool and the issue were to be divided equally. Direct investment of this kind in sheep farming was distinctly unusual and the only other possible case which has been discovered also involves merchants of Cahors. In 1282 a group sued Dore Abbey for the wool of 800 sheep and £41 4s 8d, a turn of phrase which suggests that the merchants may have had a stake in the sheep themselves.[28]

The prominence which has been given so far to monastic wool sales must not be allowed to obscure the fact that from an early date part of the wool going into the export market came from the estates of the laity, as well as from the lands of the higher secular clergy. The largest amount of wool owed to William Cade was 35 weys (*pensa*, about half a sack) by the Earl of Aumale. The feudal document known as the *rotuli de dominabus et pueris et puellis* provides eloquent testimony of the large numbers of sheep kept on the demesnes of lay manors in 12 counties in 1185. In 1205, 3539 sheep were sold away from the lands of William de Stutevill when they came into the hands of the Crown. In 1225 the Earl of Salisbury bequeathed a total of 2900 sheep to various religious houses. The illustrations could be multiplied.[29]

Although the Exchequer rolls contain a considerable number of recognisances in wool made by the members of the knightly class there are very few made by higher feudal lords. Among the exceptions are the recognisances for 12 sacks of Irish wool made in 1230 by Walter de Lacy and another for 50 sacks of Irish wool made in 1285 by Richard de Burgh, Earl of Ulster. In England Lord Robert de Tateshall of Norfolk agreed in 1260 to supply Cahorsins with 70 sacks of *collecta* of Deeping, Spalding and Holland, and in 1285 promised the same company 19 sacks of his own wool, 13 of them from the earldom of Richmond and 6 from Norfolk.[30] Among the lesser laity it is frequently impossible to differentiate between those contracting to supply wool from their own flocks and those contracting for *collecta*. The best documented of all the English middlemen of the thirteenth century are the Moniwards or Mainwards, one of the leading families of the city of Hereford. They undoubtedly made a regular practice of receiving payment in advance for later delivery of the *collecta* of the marches. In 1262 Reginald Moniward received 80 marks from Peter Beraud of Cahors for 13 sacks 16 stones of lambs wool to be delivered at London in 1263 and the next two years. The price apparently took account of interest payable on the advance, for three years later the sheriff of Hereford was ordered to produce Reginald to answer the charge that he still owed 10 sacks 16 stones worth 7 marks per sack. In 1283 Reginald, still dealing with the Cahorsins undertook to deliver Welsh lambs wool at £6 per sack and 2 sacks of *collecta* at £10 per sack. In June 1287 Reginald, now dealing with the Riccardi, was paid 22 marks for 2 sacks of lambs wool to be delivered at London in August, but about Michaelmas of the same year he was paid only 8½ marks each for 5 sacks of lambs wool of good Herefordshire *collecta* to be delivered at St Giles Fair, Winchester in September 1288. Besides wool the Moniwards dealt in cloth, which they bought on credit at the fairs and probably sold in the marches. At St Giles fair in 1285 Reginald and his son, Hugh, bought Flemish cloth from William de Dunstable of Winchester, agreeing to pay £90 14s in three instalments, the first to be paid in William's house at Christmas and the last at St Ethelbert's fair, Hereford, in May. They defaulted on the last payment and the sheriff was ordered to distrain their goods. Reginald and another son, Roger, also defaulted on money due to merchants of Douai in 1286 and 1287, no doubt for cloth delivered on credit. One of the latter recognisances was made in St Ives fair. There is no evidence that the Moniwards exported wool in their own name in the thirteenth century, but they did so from London in the early fourteenth century.[31]

By the 1270s and 1280s English middlemen are found contracting for *collecta* all over the country. Much of the business seems to have been on a very modest scale for frequently it required a group of men to assemble a comparatively small amount of wool. In 1280 the Riccardi sued 7 burgesses of Banbury for 5 sacks of *bona lana matricia de collecta de Banbury* and 4 Northampton burgesses for 6 sacks worth 84 marks. The latter group in turn sued one Thomas de la Martryn, probably one of their suppliers, for £15 5s.[32] It was not only aliens who used middlemen to collect wool, however, for the larger English merchants did the same.

The vast majority of surviving recognisances and certificates of recognisances relate to money paid in advance by merchants to wool producers and middlemen. Evidence of the extension of credit in the opposite direction is rare in the thirteenth century. One certificate, however, records a recognisance by John Stoke of Winchester of a debt of £17 to William de Overton of Alresford for wool 'sold and lent' to him.[33] It is possible, of course, that money recognisances in this direction might be made without mentioning the fact that wool had already been delivered. This class of evidence, therefore, does not necessarily establish that the extension of credit from merchant to grower was more prevalent than that flowing in the opposite direction.

The dangers inherent in the credit system are illustrated in table 18. This shows some of the certificates sent to the Exchequer in 1287–9 by William fitz Robert de Goldington about recognisances made at Appleby in Westmorland. These are not a complete record of William's business since they relate only to unpaid debts and, moreover, only certificates acknowledging a debt in wool and money owed for cloth sold on credit have been included. One of the points to observe is the comparatively short period of credit, settlement usually being called for at the Whitsun following the date of the recognisance. The period between the default and the issue of a certificate is very short compared with that found in many of the other examples which have survived. William was probably in a good position to obtain certificates, since in one of them he is described as mayor of Appleby. Sometimes, however, it was necessary to obtain a second or third certificate before the debt could be recovered. The William de Stirkeland mentioned in some of the certificates is probably the William de Stirkeland, knight of Westmorland, who also defaulted on wool owed in 1285, 1286 and 1287 to Peter de Appleby, merchant and citizen of York.

The fact that a large part of the business between export merchants, middlemen and wool producers was conducted outside the liberties of towns was a constant source of friction, for townsmen claimed a monopoly of trade in their immediate hinterland. The men of Lincoln repeatedly complained about Cistercian lay brothers buying wool in the county. In 1292 they advanced the extreme claim that strange merchants, both alien and denizen, should not do business anywhere in the county except in the city and procured the sheriff to prevent them from plying their traditional trade in the towns of Grantham and Stamford.[34] Lincoln's concern about maintaining its stake in the wool trade did not stem merely from solicitude for the profits of individual

TABLE 18 *Some transactions of William fitz Robert de Goldington*[a]

Recognisor	Nature of bond		Date of bond	Payment due	Certificates issued
	Wool owed and value	Money owed for cloth			
Robert de Joneby, Cumberland	60 st – 20m.	48s	—	14 Apr. 1287	20 July 1287
Robert Bacoun, Helton, Westmorland	90 st – 33m.		1 June 1286	25 May 1287	5 June 1287
William de Stirkeland and 4 others, Westmorland			2 Sept. 1286	25 May 1287	5 June 1287
Robert de Dereham and another, Cumb.	30 st – £7	43s	9 Dec. 1286	25 May 1287	5 June 1287
William fitz Robert de Stirkeland		16s 6d	19 Dec. 1286	3 Feb. 1287	5 June 1287
Henry de Qwiteby, Northumberland			4 Jan. 1287	25 May 1287	20 July 1287
William Locerd and another, Cumberland	45 st – £10 10s		11 Jan. 1287	25 May 1287	5 June 1287
Will. fitz Robert de Stirkeland	10 sacks – £70		13 Feb. 1287	—	5 June 1287
Thomas fitz Gilbert and 3 others, Appleby	60 st – £14		19 Feb. 1287	25 May 1287	5 June 1287
William de Boynill, Cumberland	60 st – £13 10s	12s	4 and 10 Apr. 1287	25 May 1287	5 June 1287
William de Boynill	60 st – £14	10s	—	25 May 1287	20 July 1287
Eufemia de Askeby, Westmorland		21s	—	25 May 1287	20 July 1287
Joan de Wygenton, Cumberland		£20		25 May and 15 Aug. 1287	24 Aug. 1287
John fitz Thomas of Goldington, sr., Westmorland	30 st – £7		6 Oct. 1287	24 June 1288	11 Oct. 1290, 13 Nov. 1290
Gilbert fitz Guy, Sumerdale	8 st – £1 16s		17 Oct. 1287 and 21 Nov. 1288	29 May 1289	2 June 1289, 10 Mar. 1290
Robert de Joneby	30 st – 10m.		17 Jan. 1288	16 May 1288	26 May 1288, 22 Nov. 1288, 31 Jan. 1289
Robert de Joneby and his brother	15 st – £3 10s	20s	17 Jan. 1288	16 May 1288	26 May 1288
Robert Bacoun			4 Sept. 1288	29 May 1289	27 July 1289, 4 Oct. 1289, 14 Jan. 1290
Robert Bacoun	4 sacks – 40m.		2 Feb. 1289	24 June 1289	4 Oct. 1289, 29 Dec. 1289, 14 Jan. 1290
Eve, widow of Patrick and 2 others, Ulsby	20 st – £4 13s		Mar. 1289	29 May 1289	9 June 1289
Robert de Joneby	15 st – £3 7s 6d	£3 3s 4d	5 Dec. 1289	28 May 1290	6 June 1290

[a] Source. C241 7, 8, 9, 12, 13.

merchants, for tolls on wool made an important contribution to the city's farm. In 1292–3 wool supplied £50 9s 0¼d to the total receipts of £75 1s 11½d at the tollbooths.[35] In 1265 the burgesses of Shrewsbury complained about the decay of the town's trade and supported their plea for help with a reminder of their support of the Crown during the recent troubles and in the Welsh wars.[36] It was immediately proclaimed that wool might not be sold in Shropshire outside of market towns. In 1277 a commission of oyer and terminer was appointed to hear a complaint by the burgesses of Lynn that certain people were taking money from foreign merchants to go into the country to buy for the use of the merchants goods which should first come into the town.[37] In 1301 the merchants of Amiens complained about harassment by the mayor and bailiffs of Newcastle on Tyne. They alleged that for two years and more they had not been permitted to buy less than half a last of hides, half a sack of wool or 100 fells from anyone but burgesses, either in the town itself or for 12 leagues around.[38] Winchester attempted to confine trade to the city by claiming a monopoly of tronage and pessage of wool for a distance of 7 leagues around.[39]

The town which has left most evidence about the desire of its burgesses to dominate the wool trade is Leicester. In the early middle ages Leicester was an important centre of cloth manufacture and the authorities were concerned to safeguard the supply of wool. As late as 1257 non-gildsmen were prosecuted for buying wool in the town. However, by this date the local cloth industry was under pressure. In 1227 the sheriff of Leicestershire had been ordered to ban weavers from all places in the county where they had not been established in the time of the Earl of Leicester. In 1265 it was agreed very reluctantly that Leicester weavers might take work from people outside the borough, but only at such times as gildsmen were unable to provide them with work. With the decay of the local cloth industry the gild merchant was obliged to recognise that the sale of wool had a contribution to make to the town's economy. Therefore instead of opposing the export of wool it endeavoured to bring the local trade under its own control. One of the most controversial issues was whether members of the gild merchant might form partnerships with non-gildsmen. During the 1250s there were a number of prosecutions of members of the gild merchant who sold by wholesale the wool of strangers, including that of men from Coventry and Hinckley. A gild statute made on 11 February 1260 tried to establish a code of conduct in such matters. All members were free to buy wool wherever and in whatever manner they wished and if they borrowed money they might engage to share the profits in any way with the lender. The lender might assist in buying wool outside the borough, but unless he was himself a gild member he was forbidden to meddle within it and was also refused any share of the proceeds of wool sold there. Members of the gild were forbidden to sell merchandise belonging to outsiders until they acquired a title to the property. A fortnight later another statute proclaimed that 'none of the Gild shall sell in Leicester the wool or other merchandise of those who are outside the Gild, to the detriment of the liberties of the Gild, for part-profits'. This was probably intended to clarify the fact that partnerships between gildsmen and non-gildsmen must be restricted to business conducted entirely outside the borough.[40]

The same gild statute of 1260 which authorised partnerships outside the borough between members and non-members declared that 'none of them who should belong to the Gild shall go through the country with strange merchants to teach or help them to buy merchandise to the detriment of the Gild' on penalty of being expelled from the gild, while non-members who did this were barred from entering the town for a year and a day. The gild was apparently able to mark the distinction between a partner and a broker, for prosecutions for leading strangers, in effect broking, were common and continued until the outbreak of the Hundred Years War. Jakemin de Lede, a non-gildsman, convicted of this offence in 1281 was again found guilty of buying at least 40 sacks for strangers in 1289. The role of the wool broker within the borough, apparently unknown in the 1260s and 1270s, had been established by 1290 at the latest. In the early fourteenth century wool brokers had to be accepted and sworn by the town authorities. Prosecutions for betrayal of the oath reveal something of the broker's office. In 1310 Godfrey de Lovan was charged with preventing 'his merchants' from buying wool from certain persons, thereby breaking his oath that he would lead strangers to the houses of rich and poor alike without showing favour to any. A few years before Godfrey had been charged, but pardoned, with keeping in his service a stranger named Robert of Lincoln. If merchants did not like the wool in Leicester Robert took them to Nottingham to make their purchases. In 1311 Robert of Lincoln was himself sworn a public broker and in 1313 and 1315 was convicted of weighing wool too heavily in favour of strange merchants.[41] It was the broker's task to weigh the wool in the house of the vendor. It is not clear whether in Leicester the services of the broker were compulsory or optional. In London, where all freemen enjoyed the right to trade wholesale in any commodity, the services of a broker were only compulsory where neither vendor nor buyer was free of the city.[42] It was an offence to act as a broker without being sworn by the authorities. Sworn brokers were also provided for in Lincoln regulations of the same period.[48]

Until 1274 the gild merchant of Leicester claimed a monopoly of the wool trade throughout the county, but in this year it was obliged to renounce the pretension. A gild statute conceded that

> whereas at one time the merchants from foreign parts went out into the county of Leicester and bought wool in places where they ought not, and caused wool to be carried to Leicester and were convicted thereof that they were very guilty against the community, for which they were heavily amerced and punished, therefore it was provided by assent and consent of all the community and chiefly at the petition of the merchants, that the places should be enrolled and publicly announced where they may buy without hindrance, and the places are written, to wit these, Melton, Loughborough, Breedon, Hinckley, Bosworth, Lutterworth, Lilbourne.

Leicester merchants, however, did not confine themselves to their own county for an enquiry of 1300 indicates they bought wool at Coventry, Warwick, Stratford, Kineton, Alcester, Dassett, Brailes and Henley, all places in Warwickshire. In the fourteenth century this western hinterland was lost to the rising merchants of Coventry and it is clear that by the beginning of the Hundred Years War Leicester men played very little part in the wool trade.[44]

When Leicester first aspired to become a centre of the wool trade it benefited from its earlier role of cloth manufacturer. The skilled labour which had formerly prepared wool for the town's own looms was easily adapted to preparing and packing wool for export. The gild merchant was as anxious to monopolise this skill as the wool itself. Prosecutions of dressers and packers for working outside the town were common. Those presented in 1281 were said to have gone as far afield as Northampton, Hinckley and Tamworth. In 1291, after Walter of Mountsorel had been found guilty of taking women to Derby to dress wool, it was decided to refuse work to all wool-packers attainted of having done anything contrary to the liberty of the town. Following this, if not before, wool-packers had to be sworn by the community and it was an offence to employ anyone not sworn.[45]

Apart from towns such as Lincoln, Leicester and Shrewsbury the focal points of the thirteenth-century wool trade were the great fairs, particularly those of Boston and Winchester. By 1300, however, the fairs were everywhere in decline and they played a minor role in the trade of succeeding centuries. The importance of the two fairs just mentioned was due not merely to their geographical location but to their timing. The first, scheduled to start about St Botulph's day (17 June), varied considerably in duration and sometimes lasted until

Michaelmas. The second ran for sixteen days from St Giles (1 September) but it too was frequently extended for periods of up to a week. Unfortunately the only English fair which has left an adequate record of its business is St Ives, which was held just after Easter and therefore played a minor role in the wool trade.

Although it cannot be doubted that wool was sold in the fairs in the sense in which the word is generally understood much that was taken there had already been bargained for and partly paid for. The fair was merely the delivery point and the time for the settlement of any outstanding balance. It was a convenient place for both buyer and seller, the former having cash in hand from the sale of cloth or other goods and the latter being able to lay out his receipts in items needed for his own use or for purposes of trade. A safe conduct issued to the monks of Chester in 1282 speaks of their taking wool to Boston fair so that they might buy wine and victuals.[46] Wool that had already been bargained for was not exposed for sale and, given the cost of packing, was probably not even opened up at this stage in its journey. This fact may have made Leicester wool merchants reluctant to use the communal facilities which their town provided at the fairs of Stamford and Boston. In both places the gild merchant had a lease of a row of shops, but those in Stamford were surrendered in 1258, apparently because there was no demand for them. In Boston cloth was kept in the shops on the south side of the row and wool in those on the north side. The wool merchants were required to pay seldage whether they used the shops or not.[47] One of the dangers inherent in exporting unexamined goods is revealed by a complaint brought in 1278 by William de Dunstable of Winchester against a fellow citizen, although it is not specifically stated that the transaction was made in the fair. William bought 53 sacks of wool at 8 marks and 50 sacks at 6 marks, all sewn up in 86 sarplers. He examined 4 sarplers of each sort and accepted that the rest were of the same quality. Two and a half sacks were stolen, but when the remainder were opened at St Omer no fewer than 78 sacks were found to be bad and useless.[48]

It may be useful at this stage to summarise the evidence provided so far about ways in which wool came into the possession of export merchants. The chain with the least links was that in which the exporter, whether alien or denizen, contracted in advance to buy wool direct from the grower. This frequently involved payment in advance. Alternatively a similar contract might be made with an English middleman, who made his own arrangements with the growers. He might or might not have a contract with them and might either pay in advance, at the time of purchase or at a later date. Where there was no contract the exporters or their agents might tour the country in the summer buying up wool already shorn. In this case it was advisable to hire the services of a local man to act as a guide, he having already spied out the countryside and determined who would have wool to sell. This practice was resisted by chartered towns which tried to make all strangers buy from their own freemen. The latter bought wool both in the countryside and from peasants who brought wool to the urban market. Finally exporters who intended to spend only a short time in England might buy wool at the fairs, where it was put up for sale by middlemen.

It is unlikely that the bigger exporters, whether denizen or alien, did much travelling themselves. They either employed servants to do the work or had contacts with local men who acted on commission. Many of the latter were of alien descent. The early-fourteenth-century Hull customs accounts record half a dozen or more exporters who were permanently domiciled in England although clearly of German or Picard descent. This is shown by the ambiguity about their nationality when aliens began to be charged a higher rate of duty. There can be little doubt that these men also acted as agents for their former compatriots. Lists of resident Frenchmen compiled in 1295 show that some of them had lived in England for up to 30 years. One of the most interesting families of alien descent is found in Louth. Wlpin John of Louth was probably the son of John Wlpin, a partner or factor of the Frescobaldi in the thirteenth century. The son, who remained in England after the expulsion of the Frescobaldi, was either born here or was able to pass as an Englishman, for more often than not his own wool was exported free of alien duty. Although not himself a major exporter Wlpin John acted as agent for most of the Florentine companies exporting in the early fourteenth century and was responsible for shipping their wool from Hull, Boston and Yarmouth. Later one or more of his own sons were active in the wool trade. In 1338 a Lincoln jury reported that Raland, son of Wlpin of Louth, a common broker, had bought more than 40 sacks of wool for the Bardi, while at Grimsby a Ralph Wlpynsone was said to have bought 2 sacks from the Prior of Ormesby.[49]

When one reaches the point at which wool was exported a veil of obscurity begins to descend on the conditions prevailing in early medieval trade. In particular it is impossible to determine what proportion of the thousands of English exporters named in the customs accounts actually went abroad with their wool. Although it is clear that many merchants still travelled it is equally clear that some others did not. A variety of forms of partnership and commission removed the need for all to go abroad. Just as there were aliens resident in England so there must have been Englishmen resident in Flanders and Picardy willing to act on behalf of their countrymen. In other instances English merchants going abroad for a single season acted on commission or in partnership. There is little or no evidence of permanent partnerships at this date and most were undoubtedly limited to a short period of time or to the duration of a single venture, the proceeds then being divided and the partnership dissolved. The investment of each party and the distribution of risk and profit varied from contract to contract.

In 1282 one William de Pikestock of Stafford entrusted 30 sacks of wool to Thomas Gorbet for the latter to take to Flanders to sell. The clear profit, later said to be £20, was to be divided equally between them.[50] A different arrangement was made in a partnership between John de Redmere of Appleby and a Flemish merchant, James le Roy of Dixmude, about 1277.[51] The latter sent cloth, spices and other wares into England to be sold by John, who was to keep three quarters of the profit or bear a like part of any loss. John sent wool to Flanders to be sold by James, who was to have three quarters of the profit or loss at that end of the operation. The most detailed commercial evidence which has survvied about any partnership relates to that made between two Londoners, John de Chiggewelle and William de Flete, barber, for one year from 1 May 1304.[52] Each contributed a stock of goods valued at £40, to be traded for their common profit or loss. John's share was part of a consignment of woad worth £55 then at St Omer. This was to be brought to London by John's servant, who got as far as St Valery and then disappeared without trace. William's £40 was provided from wine, beans and salt then being sold at Berwick and Stirling by his own men. These goods were initially valued at £68 13s 4d and realised a paper profit of £17 4s, although part of this consisted of a royal bond. John travelled to Scotland and took charge of most of the cash proceeds, which after deducting £5 for his own share of the common profit amounted to £64 15s 8d in William's credit. On 10 June 1304 John was at Stirling and made a deal with a Lombard named W. Persone. He then went to Loch Doron castle where he agreed to pay, with his new partner, £220 for 45 sacks of wool, 1200 fells, 8 lasts of hides and 2 barrels of tallow belonging to Lord John Comyn and others. John took these goods to St Omer and made contact with Cambinus Fulbert, partner of Persone. After deducting the initial purchase price and agreed expenses of £125 there remained a profit of £51 3s 6½d, of which the Italians received half. Of the other half of the profit John claimed half for himself, probably as a return on his own money invested in the Scottish purchase, which left

£12 15s 10½d as the return on William's £64 15s 8d. Since £40 of
the latter sum was William's contribution to their common stock John
then claimed £3 13s 4d as his half share of the profit on this amount
and £2 3s in expenses. He finally claimed £20 as a contribution to
the lost woad. William therupon declared that no man had ever seen
the woad and that he had been cheated, with the result that they
finished up as litigants in the Exchequer.

It is a commonplace of economic history that in the late middle ages
the merchants of the staple confined their business to the export of
wool, neither adventuring in other commodities nor investing their
profits in the import trade. In 1423 it was said in a parliamentary
petition that the staplers '*n' ount illeoques domination ne pouair de
leur or n'argent, jusques a ce qu'ilx passent oultre le Meere en
Engleterre, et ausi ils ne sount commenes acchateurs des Merchantises
en Flaundres*'.[53] Despite this statement it is untrue that by the early
fifteenth century the wool trade was so specialised that its practitioners
had no other investments. In this period members of the London
grocers' company who exported wool also exported cloth and imported
grocery. Even at the end of that century at least one grocer was a
member of both the staple and the merchant adventurers' company.[54]
The popular conception of the staple, therefore, is no more than a
useful generalisation about conditions of the late fifteenth century. In
the thirteenth and fourteenth centuries there may be less reason to
speak of specialist wool merchants. The very fact that England
exported comparatively little apart from wool meant that it was bound
to figure very largely in the consignments of all who traded overseas,
but there was ample scope for variety in the repatriation of profits.
The simplest method, though one which has left virtually no direct
evidence of its existence, was the import of silver, either as bullion or
foreign coin. It is difficult to dispute that in the early fourteenth century England acquired a considerable treasure in this way. Some
merchants, however, preferred to invest their receipts and to take a
further profit from imports. An inquest of 1337 revealed how two
merchants of Durham sent to Flanders 30 sarplers of wool worth
£360. With some of the proceeds their servants bought 39 coloured
cloths worth £104, 14 striped cloths, £32 13s 4d. 1000 canvas, £8,
3 mazers, 6s 3d and a pipe of spices and mercery, £40.[55]

Even in the early fourteenth century, however, the merchant who
did not wish to invest his profits in imports was not bound to run the
risk of carrying money about his person. He could avail himself of the
simple letter of exchange, although not yet of the fully-developed bill
of exchange. In 1305 seven Norfolk merchants sued Lapus Philipi of

the society of Corone of Pistoia for fraud and unjust detention of £564 15s 8d. They had sold wool for gold florins which they paid to Lapus' partner in return for a letter for this amount promising payment in sterling in London. After this case at least six other merchants separately sued Lapus for sums totalling £751 paid to his firm in Antwerp.[56]

The biggest gap in our knowledge about the early medieval wool trade relates to the costs which were incurred and the profit which might be made. There is virtually no hope of remedying the deficiency until some way is discovered of plumbing the depths of the vast bulk of the legal records. Even these, however, are unlikely to shed a great deal of light on this particular topic. In the present state of research the gloom is unrelieved until the Hundred Years War is reached. For this period information can be derived from the accounts relating to the collection and sale of royal wool, some of which have been published *in extenso* or as abstracts.[57] The evidence is most reliable about the costs which were incurred, both in England and abroad. On the other hand the prices at which wool was sold overseas are a poor guide to the normal rate of profit. Although it was the king's intention to create a monopoly which would enhance the price of wool, his interference with the normal flow of trade seems to have had the very opposite effect. While wool may sometimes have been in short supply at others it was in glut. In the early 1340s prices abroad were even lower than those of the late 1330s which have been published by Fryde. The account of William de Cusance,[58] one of the most exemplary of the entire series, shows that in 1342 he sold Oxfordshire wool, one of the best counties, for only £7 9s 3d per sack (English weight), with other prices ranging down to £5 18s 9d for Sussex wool. After the comparative wealth of evidence provided by Edward III's wool levies, costs and profits once more become shrouded in obscurity until we reach the Cely business correspondence and accounts in the late fifteenth century. No attempt can be made to utilise this source in an original manner in the present work since they merit a study to themselves.[59]

One of the darkest periods in the history of the wool trade is the time of contraction in the late fourteenth century. This is particularly unfortunate since one would like to compare the effects of the contraction in different regions of England. Since they were now taking less wool than formerly, the exporters and their customers could be more selective; subject, of course, to the *caveat* that they were in greater competition with English cloth manufacturers than they had been a century before. It is in this period that the supremacy of Cotswold wool was firmly established, although there had been indications of its growing popularity earlier in the century. The converse was a decline in overseas demand for the wools of eastern and north-eastern England. An interesting illustration of the latter tendency may be provided from the reign of Richard II. In March 1393 a commission was appointed to deal with a complaint that the merchants of Yorkshire and Northumberland had made a conspiracy not to buy wool and so to force down the price. It was authorised to buy up sufficient wool to clear these parts before the new season. Although this appears to be a most unusual form of action for a medieval government the order was carried out and the customers of Newcastle accounted for 482 sacks of wool bought for £800 0s 6¾d. In fact the king made a comfortable profit. Apart from the purchase price the only cost recorded was £87 16s 11½d for canvas, freight being provided by ships forfeited by one Robert Oliver. The customers dispatched 442 sacks to Calais, where they were sold by the treasurer for £2100. The king, of course, did not pay custom and subsidy, which in private trade would have taken a large part of the difference between the buying price and selling price. The low selling price, £4 15s per sack, provides some support for the complaint of northern merchants that they could not trade profitably at Calais.[60]

As well as the geographical shift from the north and east to the Cotswolds the composition of wool exports in the late middle ages was altered by an increase in the proportion of fells to shorn fleeces. Although much of this change was delayed until the late fifteenth century the trend can clearly be observed in the earlier period of contraction. The switch to fells might well have occurred more quickly had it not been for a tax change instituted in 1368. Before this date 300 fells paid the same duty as 364 lb of fleece wool. Although there is little doubt that 300 carefully selected fells might easily yield more than 364 lb of wool, the saving in duty at the rate which was charged prior to 1336 may have been swallowed up in increased handling costs. With the introduction of the subsidy, however, there was a greater incentive to export fells. The saving in tax was reduced, although perhaps not entirely eliminated, when the number of fells equivalent to a sack of wool was reduced to 240 in 1368. A further incentive to export fells, at least to the dishonest, may have been the fact that fells, declared by number not weight, were more easily smuggled through the English customs than wool. Most of the cases of smuggling detected upon arrival at Calais in the 1360s concerned fells. Neither tax change nor smuggling can account for the big increase in the number and proportion of fells exported during the 1470s. The most likely cause was the continuing growth of the cloth industry around Leyden in Holland which, even before 1470, was the main customer for fells.[61]

The fall in the demand for wool in the early fifteenth century meant that large producers frequently had stocks left on their hands for many years. Illustrations have been given elsewhere of marketing difficulties experienced by the Duchy of Lancaster,[62] while even more significant examples may be quoted from the estates of the Bishop of Winchester.

TABLE 19   *Woolfells as a proportion of total exports*[a]

	Annual average export of fells	Equivalence[b] in sacks of wool	Total export (sacks)	% of fells in total
1355–8	309 492	1290	33 306	3.9
1365–8	364 540	1519	28 864	5.3
1399–1402	235 280	980	15 125	6.5
1425–8	278 959	1162	15 897	7.3
1445–8	318 720	1328	10 772	12.4
1465–8	327 600	1365	9121	15.0
1479–82	626 239	2609	9706	26.9

[a] Source. Beardwood, *Alien Merchants in England*, pp. 142–60. Power and Postan, *Studies in English Trade*, pp. 330–60.
[b] Converted at 240 fells to the sack.

Since the beginning of the fourteenth century all wool had usually been delivered each year to the bishop's palace at Wolvesey in Hampshire. From 1370 the wool of the manors of Berkshire, Buckinghamshire and Oxfordshire was held at Wargrave and Witney until it was collected by purchasers. Since all these manors were ravaged by a highly contagious sheep disease this year it is possible that the change was intended as a hygiene measure. Alternatively it may have been made necessary by a shortage of storage space at Wolvesey for the total production of the bishopric at this date was about 150 sacks a year and any delay in selling must have raised problems for the officials at Wolvesey. In 1373 the wool of the Wiltshire manors began to be stored at Downton.

Whatever the reason for the change the accounts of these three bailiwicks, which produced the bishop's best wool, suggest marketing problems which may safely be taken as representative of the estate as a whole. In the thirteenth century wool was normally sold by the Michaelmas which followed the clip. In the last three decades of the fourteenth century it was rare for wool to be disposed of within less than eighteen months or so and two, or more frequently three, clips were accumulated before being sold. In the crisis of the early 1380s

four years' wool accumulated at Witney and Wargrave, while in the
former manor it again piled up for four years from 1399 to 1402. In
the fifteenth century the situation became even worse. Wool remained
unsold at Wargrave, and probably also at Witney, for eight years
between 1410 and 1417, for five years from 1418 to 1423 at Wargrave
and again for eight years at both manors from 1423 to 1430. On this
last occasion the bishop could only dispose of his wool by exporting it
himself to Normandy.

The fall in the demand for wool meant that even when a buyer
came forward he was likely to be much more selective than in former
times. He might agree to take only the best wool in a clip, leaving the
unfortunate grower to dispose of the rest as he might. There are
some indications that this happened in the Winchester manors mentioned above. Immediately after shearing, the worst wool was sold
locally while the rest was stored in the wool-house of the head manor of
each bailiwick until a bargain was struck. When the wool was packed
a not inconsiderable proportion was cast aside as refuse. This too was
sold locally for whatever price it could command. In 1390 Parliament
legislated against this growing abuse.[63] It was enacted that no wool
should be made refuse except for that traditionally classed as such,
namely *cot, gare* and *vilein.* Furthermore no-one was to buy wool by
the words 'good packing' or any similar phrase. It is not clear what
this meant. In the thirteenth century Italians and other exporters
had generally stipulated that the wool supplied by middlemen and
small producers must be *bone pacabile,* but it is not clear how this
phrase relates to the later English term 'goodpakkying'. Power
states that good packing meant winding good fleeces in with inferior
wool and she represents it as fraud of the customs. However, this
definition does not fit the context of the statute, which makes it clear
that it was not the king who was harmed by the practice but his
subjects.

The desire of the exporters to reject all but the best wool placed
even greater responsibility on the packers, who were charged with the
duty of casting aside inferior fleeces as they packed them. It was essential that woolpackers be accepted as indifferent by both buyer and
seller. By the fifteenth century the craft was a highly influential one and
its members were used as valuers of wool and called upon to arbitrate
in disputes between merchants. Not unnaturally the woolpackers
were sometimes asked to abuse their skills, as in the illegal practice of
clacking and bearding. This meant clipping away all the inferior parts
of fleeces intended for export, so that only the very best wool remained.
Wool so treated had a much higher value than untreated wool and

customs duty, which depended on weight, was correspondingly less burdensome.

By the late fifteenth century, and no doubt earlier, wool was frequently bought on approval, with the understanding that the buyer might repudiate the bargain if he did not like the wool or if it was not of the sort described by the seller. In the 1470s Thomas Wysman of London paid £20 to Thomas White, husbandman of Broadway, in earnest of 12 sacks of good Cotswold with the proviso that he should be repaid if he did not like the wool when he came to Broadway to view it.[64] Wysman did in fact like it but he delayed so long in collecting it that the price fell by 4 marks a sack. He then wrote to White instructing him to sell the wool locally for whatever he could get for it. White did this, but he lost £8, above the £20 already paid, for which he sued Wysman in Chancery. Another informative case, reported in detail by Power, concerns Buckinghamshire wool falsely described as as good young Cotswold.[65]

Because of the glut of wool there was clearly no necessity for exporters to contract ahead or to pay in advance of delivery as they had done in the thirteenth century. Although credit was widespread in the trade it is likely that it was now directed almost exclusively from growers to merchants. The decline in the total number of exporters in the late fourteenth century, coupled with the increase in their average volume of business, poses questions about their relationship with middlemen and growers. Unfortunately these are more easily asked than answered. Some exporters still bought directly from the growers. In the 1370s and 1380s the Bishop of Winchester sold to Italians and in the 1390s and later years to London exporters. In 1374 a group of Salisbury merchants was made to give security in Chancery that they would not hinder Italians from gathering and buying wool in Wiltshire.[66] On the other hand it seems likely that the middleman, although not a new figure in the trade, now secured a very firm place for himself. William Midwinter of Northleach, who sold wool to the Celys, and the other fifteenth-century woolmen identified by Power,[67] had their precursors a century before. It is clear that very many of the 155 or so wool-buyers, wool-merchants, wool-brokers, woolmen and the like, who were pardoned in 1395 for weighing offences, were occupied largely or exclusively in the middle reaches of the trade.[68] These men were not mere pedlars of wool and included William and John of the famous Grevell family of Chipping Camden. It is possible that the Grevells thrived more as middlemen than as exporters, for although they appear in one of the surviving London customs particulars they are conspicuous by their absence from the remainder. In the corresponding area of the trade of the late fifteenth century Power distinguishes two distinct groups of middlemen. On the one hand there were still the substantial local families of the main wool-producing regions, who sometimes combined the business of wool gatherer with that of grazier and clothier. On the other hand were London merchants, for whom wool was one speculation among several. These middlemen, of course, enjoyed the prospect of supplying the home cloth industry as well as the export trade. Unfortunately the passage of wool from sheep to the looms of the English weaver is the one almost totally obscure area of the medieval wool trade.

Successive changes in the scale of enterprise by the export merchants have been considered at some length in each of the earlier chapters. Unfortunately, for the greater part of the middle ages our knowledge of their business is almost non-existent once the wool had left an English port. Only in the late fifteenth century is the gloom somewhat relieved by evidence of the Celys' transactions at Calais and in the Low Countries. For reasons which have already been given, and which it is hoped will be accepted as valid, it is not possible to deal with that evidence in the present work. It only remains, therefore, to summarise briefly the picture which has been offered of the rise and decline of the overseas trade in wool and to speculate on the relationship between that enterprise and the fortunes of the native cloth industry. Unfortunately the continued lack of an authoritative history of the cloth industry makes it impossible to do more than speculate about the latter connection.

Although the absolute beginning of the wool export trade must for ever remain unknown it appears unlikely that wool was regularly sent abroad, if indeed ever, before the Norman Conquest. The basis of the English wool trade was the 'great industry' – the urban cloth industry – of Flanders which grew up in the twelfth century. During this period the English and Flemish cloth industries may have competed on terms which were not too unequal, but in the thirteenth century the Flemish industry must have pulled ahead and made considerable inroads into the markets of its rivals. At the beginning of the fourteenth century unless England possessed truly remarkable numbers of sheep the bulk of its wool production was being sent abroad, which inevitably meant a shortage of raw material for what remained of the home industry. It must be admitted, however, that this situation lasted for only a few years, after which exports fell to a much lower level. A revival in the 1330s was frustrated by the outbreak of the Hundred Years War, interference with the free flow of trade and the imposition of a heavy tax on wool exports.

In the 1360s, following a post-plague boom, exports commenced a long secular decline. Despite the possibility of an element of supply shortage in its initial stages, the decline overwhelmingly reflects falling overseas demand. This indicates that continental cloth industries were either contracting their production or turning elsewhere for supplies of wool. Unless there was an overall expansion of the international cloth market in the late fourteenth century, a thesis which can be supported only with difficulty, the growth of English cloth exports in the same period appears to indicate some contraction in one or more continental centres. Whether these increasing cloth exports were the cause or the effect of continental contraction must for the moment remain an open question. Historians have tended to judge the competitiveness of the rising English industry and its rivals largely on the basis of what each had to pay for wool. The fact that from the middle of the fourteenth century exported wool carried a heavy duty, while English cloth paid only a light duty, is believed to have given the latter a considerable advantage. The growth of the Dutch industry, using English wool, in the late fourteenth century suggests that one should not make too much of the alleged advantage. Clearly the price of the finished product was determined by many factors besides the cost of wool. Furthermore, one has to consider the highly contentious question of who it was carried the true incident of the wool export tax – wool grower, wool exporter, cloth manufacturer or cloth wearer. In theory unless the second and third parties were willing and able to absorb the tax the English manufacturer should have enjoyed an advantage either in buying wool or in selling cloth. In the early years of the heavy wool tax English cloth exports were but a small fraction of the amount of cloth made abroad from English wool. This means that foreign manufacturers, although unable to sell in England, could not have been deterred by English competition from passing on the tax to foreign consumers of their cloth. In fact it may not even have been necessary for them to do this, for it has been suggested earlier that in the 1350s and early 1360s the exporters may have been able to make the English wool growers bear the burden of the tax in the form of low prices. If this was so it indicates a monopsony situation in which the demand from home industry was as yet too small to exert much influence on the general level of wool prices. Provided that English cloth manufacturers were able to buy wool at the same price as the exporters, which depends on market perfectibility, they would, of course, benefit from the prevailing low prices and would still enjoy a cheaper raw material than the foreign manufacturer. Unless this differential was swallowed up by higher costs in other directions it would have made English cloth cheaper than foreign cloth made from English wool. Nevertheless while exports of English cloth were relatively small this is likely to have provided excess profits for the cloth exporters rather than resulted in any serious undercutting of the selling price of foreign cloth.

During the 1360s there may have been some reduction, albeit temporary, in the supply of wool, which, coupled with a gradual increase in demand from home industry, made it less easy for wool exporters to pass on the tax to the sheep farmers. It is difficult otherwise to account for the coincidence of rising prices and falling exports of wool. When the exporters deferred the incidence of the tax they increased the price charged to the foreign manufacturer and thereby encouraged him to seek cheaper supplies either at home or in other foreign countries, such as Spain. Nevertheless although this substitution factor may have helped to dampen overseas demand for English wool in the late fourteenth century it was probably less influential at this stage than the damage inflicted on continental industries by wars and civil wars.

The general increase in wool prices in the 1360s increased the costs of the English manufacturer as well as those of the foreigner, but did not, of course, dispense with the differential enjoyed by the former. In the 1380s, however, prices paid to growers collapsed and remained depressed for most of the fifteenth century. Although it is impossible to dissociate wool prices from the generally low price levels of the late middle ages sheep farmers undoubtedly had their own difficulties. The increasing demand of the home cloth industry was insufficient to compensate for the declining demand of the export market and for much of the time there was a surplus of wool, in which the poorer qualities no doubt predominated. The character of the international cloth market had the effect of depressing the demand for mediocre English wools while sustaining competition between export merchants and home manufacturers for the better qualities. Since the export duty was not an *ad valorem* tax but a fixed levy on each sack mediocre wools no longer commanded the attention of the foreign manufacturer, who could buy Spanish or other wools of a similar quality for a lower price. This was probably the greatest disservice which the export tax did to the sheep farmer. The home manufacturer could make only limited use of these mediocre wools since in the international market cloth of this quality enjoyed little or no price advantage over that made from foreign wools. It was only with superior cloth, for which English wool was still needed even by foreign industries, that the home producer could hope to exploit his cheaper raw material. However, in this field expertise in production must also have been an important consideration and it may have taken the English some time to acquire skills to match those of the old-established Flemish industries.

Although the revival of the English cloth industry deprived the Low Countries of their island market there is little reason to suppose that the expansion of English exports in the late fourteenth century was directly responsible for other major losses of markets. It seems more likely that English growth was the consequence of autonomous decline in European industrial centres. During the first two decades of the fifteenth century the rate of decline of wool exports slowed down significantly while English cloth exports suffered a major setback. This perhaps reflects a slowing down in the decline of the older industries coupled with the rise of Dutch industry. Later phases of expansion in English cloth exports probably owed less to purely internal difficulties of European industries, for well before the middle of the fifteenth century English industry must have been sufficiently developed to pose its own threat to its rivals. Many openings were created for English industry, however, not by economic but by political factors and interference with the wool trade still counted among the latter. Disputes about the Calais regulations in the reign of Henry VI showed that Burgundian industry was still dependent in large measure upon English wool and suffered when prevented from buying it on strictly commercial terms. Nevertheless it took England a very long time to establish complete ascendancy in international markets and until that was achieved the cost of inflicting high wool prices on continental producers was low prices and unsold stocks for English sheep farmers.

Notes

1 THE GROWTH OF THE FLEMISH CONNECTION

1 J. G. Edwards, '*Confirmatio Cartarum* and Baronial Grievances in 1297,' *EHR*, 48 (1943), p. 171.

2 E. Sabbe, 'Les relations économiques entre l'Angleterre et le Continent au Haut Moyen Age', *Le Moyen Age*, ser. 4, 5 (1950), pp. 181–4. *Cambridge Economic History of Europe*, ed. M. M. Postan and E. E. Rich (Cambridge, 1952), pp. 363–6.

3 The Laws of Ine (688–94) state that every household or, alternatively, hide of land (*hiwisce*) shall render a blanket (*gafolhwitel*) worth sixpence. F. Liebermann, '*Die Gesetze der Angelsachsen*', 1, (Halle, 1903), p. 108.

4 One version reads *undeoror* while the others read *deoror*. *Gesetze der Angelsachsen*, 1, p. 204.

5 P. H. Sawyer has constructed an elaborate picture of a society in the early eleventh century whose wealth was based on the export of wool. Many of his arguments are tautological and his contention that there were large exports of wool apparently rests upon nothing more tangible than the fact that there was, allegedly, a great deal of silver in England at that time. 'The Wealth of England in the Eleventh Century', *TRHS*, ser. 5, 15 (1965), p. 163.

6 *The Laws of the Kings of England from Edmund to Henry I*, ed. A. J. Robertson (Cambridge, 1925), p. 73.

7 The earliest extant version appears to be that found in the Textus Roffensis, a twelfth-century manuscript written well over a hundred years later than the compilation of the tolls.

8 G. Espinas, *La Draperie dans la Flandre Française au Moyen-Age*, 1 (Paris, 1923), pp. 25–6.

9 A. Verhulst, 'La laine indigène dans les anciens Pays-Bas entre le XIIe et le XVIIe siècle', *Revue Historique*, 248 (1972). A. Derville, 'Le Draperies flamandes et artésiennes vers 1250–1350', *Revue du Nord*, 54 (1972).

10 H. van Werveke, 'Industrial Growth in the Middle Ages: The Cloth Industry in Flanders', *EcHR*, ser. 2, 6 (1954), p. 240.

11 J. Dhondt, 'Devéloppement Urbain et Initiative Comtale en Flandre au XIe Siècle, *Revue du Nord*, 30 (1948).

12 Ch. Verlinden, 'Marchands ou Tisserands? A propos des Origines Urbaines', *Annales*, 27 (1972), p. 406.

13 E. Sabbe, 'Les relations économiques'. P. Grierson, 'Relations between England and Flanders before the Norman Conquest', *TRHS*, ser. 4, 23 (1941). G. C. Dunning, 'Trade Relations between England and the Continent in the Late Anglo-Saxon Period', *Studies Presented to E. T. Leeds*, ed. D. B. Harden (London, 1956).

14 R. H. George, 'The Contribution of Flanders to the Conquest of England 1065–1086,' *Rev. Belge*, 5 (1926).

15 H. Laurent, *Un grand commerce d'exportation au moyen-age. La draperie des Pays-Bas en France et dans les Pays Mediterranéens, XIIe–XVe siècle*,

(Paris, 1935). R. L. Reynolds, 'The market for northern textiles in Genoa, 1179–1200', *Rev. Belge*, 5 (1926). 'Merchants of Arras and the overland trade with Genoa', *ibid.* 9 (1930). 'Some English settlers in Genoa in the late twelfth century', *EcHR*, 4 (1932–4). H. Amman, 'Die Anfänge des Aktivhandels und der Tucheinfuhr aus Nordwesteuropa nach dem Mittelmeergebiet', *Studi in Onore di Amando Sapori* (Milan, 1957). This last work gives in tabular form all known early references to the sale of 'named' northern cloths in the Mediterranean.

16 R. Patterson, 'Spinning and Weaving', *A History of Technology*, II, ed. C. Singer (Oxford, 1956). P. Váczy, *La transformation de la technique et de l'organisation de l'industrie textile en Flandre aux XIe–XIIIe siècles*, Studia Historica Academiae Scientiarum Hungaricae, 48 (Budapest, 1960). G. de Poerk, *La Draperie Medievale en Flandre et en Artois* (Bruges, 1951).

17 J. S. P. Tatlock, 'The English Journey of the Laon Canons', *Speculum*, 8 (1933).

18 G. Dept, 'Les marchands flamands et le roi d'Angleterre', *Revue du Nord*, 12 (1926) and *Les Influences Anglaise et Française dans le Comte de Flandre au debut du XIIIme siècle* (Paris–Ghent, 1928).

19 'The Metrical Chronicle of Jordan Fantosme', *Chronicles of the Reigns of Stephen, Henry II and Richard I*, ed. R. Howlett, III (London, 1886), pp. 289, 293.

20 *PR* 6 Ric. I, p. 118.

21 *PR* 7 Ric. I, p. 79; 8 Ric. I, p. 295; 10 Ric. I, p. 182.

22 *PR* 6 Ric. I, pp. 66–7; 8 Ric. I, p. 296; 9 Ric. I, p. 226; 10 Ric. I, p. 182.

23 *PR* 7 Ric, I, p. 166. *Rotuli de Oblatis et Finibus*, p. 37. *Rotuli de Chartarum* 1199–1216, pp. 60, 64.

24 *Rot. Litt. Pat.*, pp. 14, 30.

25 *PR* 6 John, p. xliii. These are the dates adopted by W. R. Powell, 'The Administration of the Navy and the Stannaries', *EHR*, 71 (1956), p. 182.

26 N. S. B. Gras, *The Early English Customs System* (Cambridge, Mass., 1926), p. 221.

27 A. L. Poole, *From Domesday Book to Magna Carta* (Oxford, 1951), p. 93.

28 *PR* 5 John, pp. 11–12.

29 F. W. Brooks, 'William de Wrotham and the Office of Keeper of the King's Ports and Galleys', *EHR*, 40 (1925). W. R. Powell, 'The Administration of the Navy'.

30 *Rot. Litt. Pat.*, pp. 42–3. *PR* 6 John, pp. 48, 50, 56; 13 John, pp. 105, 186–7; 14 John, pp. 16, 42, 46.

31 *Rot. Litt. Pat.*, p. 43. *Rot. Litt. Claus.* I, p. 21.

32 *Rot. Litt. Pat.*, pp. 83, 85.

33 Dept, *Les Influences Anglaise*, p. 73, *Rot. Litt. Pat.*, p. 91.

34 *Rot. Litt. Pat.*, pp. 90, 98, 100, 155, 173. *Rot. Litt. Claus.* I, pp. 120, 209, 211, 222. Hants Co. Record Office, Pipe Roll, 159273.

35 For biographical notes on his earlier career see Dept, 'Les marchands flamands', pp. 319–33.

36 *CPR*, 1216–25, p. 114, 160. *Rot. Litt. Claus.* I, pp. 349, 351, 360, 369, 383, 388.

37 *CPR*, 1216–25, p. 435. *Rot. Litt. Claus.* I, pp. 605, 631, 646–7, 665; II, p. 38.

38 *CPR*, 1216–25, pp. 449, 451–4, 457, 459, 461, 463, 471–2, 474, 492, 509, 519–20, 522, 538. *Rot. Litt. Claus.* I, p. 634; II, pp. 7, 14, 16.

39 *CPR*, 1216–25, p. 546. *Rot. Litt. Claus.* II, pp. 106, 130, 136, 155, 159, 204, 207.

40 *Rot. Litt. Claus.*, p. 183. *CCR*, 1227–31, p. 247. *CPR*, 1225–32, pp. 334, 432.
41 *CPR*, 1232–47, pp. 56, 62, 96. *CCR*, 1231–4, pp. 455, 474, 476; 1234–7, pp. 24, 41, 48, 54.
42 *CCR*, 1234–7, pp. 89, 90, 192, 205.
43 *CCR*, 1231–4, pp. 13, 14, 18, 53; *CPR*, 1232–47, pp. 27, 29, 36, 98, 122.
44 *Rot. de Oblatis*, p. 520. *Rot. Litt. Claus.* I, pp. 182, 189, 501. *Rot. Litt. Pat.*, pp. 122–3, 133, 142, 155, 184. *CPR*, 1216–25, pp. 22, 193, 277. *CCR*, 1227–31, pp. 49, 55, 57.
45 *CPR*, 1232–47, pp. 150, 168, 170. *CCR*, 1234–7, p. 513.
46 *CCR*, 1242–7, pp. 300, 456, 472.
47 *CCR*, 1237–42, p. 508; 1242–7, p. 8. *CPR*, 1232–47, p. 356.
48 *CPR*, 1232–47, p. 170.
49 *CPR*, 1225–32, p. 460; 1258–66, p. 110, *CChR*. I, p. 441; II, pp. 22, 32.
50 H. Pirenne, 'La Hanse Flamande de Londres', *Les Villes et les Institutions Urbaines* (Paris–Brussels, 1939), II, pp. 157–84. H. van Werveke, 'Les Statuts Latins et les Statuts Française de la Hanse Flamande de Londres', *Bulletin de la Commission Royale d'Histoire*, 118 (1953). E. Perroy, 'Le Commerce Anglo-Flamande au XIIIe siècle: la Hanse Flamande de Londres', *Revue Historique*, 252 (1974).

2 THE END OF THE FLEMISH ASCENDANCY

1 *The Chronicle of Walter of Guisborough*, ed. H. Rothwell, Camden Society, 89 (1957), p. 186.
2 R. F. Treharne, *The Baronial Plan of Reform* (Manchester, 1932), p. 80. *Annales Monastici*, IV, ed. H. R. Luard (London, 1869), pp. 158–9.
3 *CCR*, 1261–4, p. 329. *CPR*, 1258–66, pp. 320, 350, 372, 398. *Diplomatic Documents*, 1101–1272, 392, 395.
4 *CCR*, 1264–8, pp. 84, 90, 97–8. *CPR*, 1258–66, pp. 477, 480.
5 *CCR*, 1264–8, pp. 46, 75, 126, 137. *CPR*, 1258–66, pp. 420, 446, 454, 459–60, 465–6, 509, 514, 650–1.
6 £532 5s 8d from Londoners' goods was paid by the countess to Roger de Morteyn in settlement of a Crown debt. This sum was eventually allowed against the 20 000 marks which the city paid to have the king's peace. *Letter Book C*, p. 231.
7 A. Schaube, 'Die Wollausfuhr Englands vom Jahre 1273, *VJSSWG*, 8 (1908). H. Berben, 'Une Guerre Économique au Moyen Age. L'Embargo sur l'Exportation des Laines Anglaises (1270–74)', *Études d'Histoire Dédiées a la Mémoire de Henri Pirenne* (Brussels, 1937). 'Het Verdrag van Montreuil, 1274. De Englesch-Vlaamsche Handelspolitick, 1266–87', *Rev. Belge*, 23 (1944). C. Wyffels, 'De Vlaamse Handel Op Engeland Vóór Het Engels-Vlaams Konflikt Van 1270–1274', *Bijdragen Voor De Geschiedenis Der Nederlanden*, 17 (1962–3), E. von Roon-Bassermann, 'Die Handelssperre Englands gegen Flandern, 1270–74, und die lizenzierte englische Wollausfuhr', *VJSSWG*, 50 (1963).
8 M. Powicke, *The Thirteenth Century*, p. 621.
9 *CCR*, 1259–61, p. 487. *CPR*, 1247–58, pp. 9, 38. *Diplomatic Documents*, 290, 442.
10 *CPR*, 1266–72, pp. 195, 231, 290, 320, 420, 702. *Diplomatic Documents*, 422, 441, 443–4.
11 *CPR*, 1266–72, pp. 462, 512, 520, 575, 578, 626, 646.
12 *CPR*, 1266–72, pp. 462, 489, 524, 526, 548–9, 557–8, 571–2, 658–9, 663.

13 *CPR*, 1266–72, p. 625. *Rotuli Hundredorum*, I, pp. 1–12 passim, II, p. 171, 259–402 passim.

14 *CPR*, 1266–72, pp. 526, 593–5.

15 *CPR*, 1266–72, pp. 553–6.

16 *CPR*, 1266–72, pp. 685–93, 698–704, 712–13; 1272–81, pp. 13–15.

17 *CPR*, 1272–81, pp. 15–27, 33–9, 64.

18 The first to point this out was E. von Roon-Bassermann, 'Die Handelssperre Englands gegen Flandern', pp. 75–6.

19 *CPR*, 1266–72, pp. 486, 599, 687, 695, 700.

20 *CCR*, 1272–9, pp. 70, 119. *CPR*, 1272–81, pp. 46, 48 *Foedera*, I, ii, p. 513. SC1/22/28.

21 *CPR*, 1272–81, p. 60. E163/5/17. E101/127/3.

22 The Flemish document is printed and commented on in G. Espinas, *Sire Jehan Boinebroke* (Lille, 1933), pp. 7–10, 104–7. Espinas seems to have counted some wool twice. The English document is E163/5/17.

23 *CPR*, 1272–81, pp. 54–5, 122, 124, 127.

24 *CPR*, 1272–81, pp. 85, 101, 163, 187, 307–8.

25 *Calendar of Chancery Rolls (Various)*, *1277–1326*, pp. 1, 16. *CPR*, 1272–81, p. 248.

26 *CCR*, 1272–9, p. 459. *CPR*, 1272–81, pp. 330, 400; 1281–92, pp. 36, 178. *Foedera*, I, ii, p. 555. E159/59 m 20; 61 m 2.

27 *Rotuli Hundredorum*, II, pp. 105, 176, *CPR*, 1272–8, pp. 86, 95. *CCR*, 1272–9, p. 354. SC1/19/113, 153; SC1/20/177; SC1/21/62.

28 *CPR*, 1247–58, p. 90.

29 *Chronicle*, p. 293.

30 *Rot. Litt. Claus.*, I, p. 654.

31 *CPR*, 1232–47, p. 74. E. von Roon-Bassermann, 'Die ersten Florentiner Gesellschaften in England', *VJSSWG*, 39 (1952).

32 *CChR*, I, p. 407. *Liberate*, v, p. 249.

33 W. E. Lunt, *Financial Relations of the Papacy with England to 1327* (Cambridge, Mass. 1939), p. 600.

34 *CPR*, 1247–58, p. 485. 'Die ersten Florentiner Handels-Gesellschaften', p. 118.

35 *CPR*, 1247–58, p. 629; 1258–66, pp. 218, 279, 413. *CCR*, 1261–4, p. 131. *Calendar of Papal Registers, Papal Letters*, 1198–1304, p. 409.

36 E159/42. *CPR*, 1266–72, p. 554; 1272–81, pp. 91–2.

37 'Die Handelssperre Englands gegen Flandern', p. 81. *CCR*, 1272–9, p. 354. *CPR*, 1266–72, pp. 554, 561, 594, 699; 1272–81, pp. 20–1, 24, 91. E13/4 m. 6.

38 *CPR*, 1247–58, p. 481.

39 E. Re, 'La Compagnia dei Riccardi in Inghilterra e il suo fallimento alla fine del secolo XIII', *Archivio della Societa Romana di Storia Patria*, 37 (1914), p. 89.

40 Including the merchants of small towns around Cahors. The Geraudon brothers, who are usually described as 'of Cahors' or 'of Tolouse', are once pin-pointed as burgesses of Castel Sarrasin, a town 60 kilometres south-west of Cahors. Stephen Reymundi was from Agen, 80 kilometres west of Cahors.

41 N. Denholm-Young, *Collected Papers* (Cardiff, 1969), p. 297. E. Albe, 'Les marchands de Cahors à Londres au XIIIᵉ siècle', *Bulletin de la Société des Etudes du départment du Lot* (1908), p. 32. Y. Renouard, 'Les Cahorsins, Hommes d'Affaires Française du XIIIᵉ siècle', *TRHS*, ser. 5, 11 (1961), p. 48.

42 *CPR*, 1216–25, pp. 533, 538; 1232–47, p. 46; 1258–66, p. 263; 1266–72, p. 24. *CCR*, 1242–7, p. 143.

43 *Rot. Litt. Pat.*, p. 191.
44 'Les Cahorsins', p. 44. F. Pegolotti, *La Pratica della Mercatura*, ed. A. Evans (Cambridge, Mass., 1936), p. 257.
45 I have included only one of the 4 licences, each for 400 sacks, issued to John Donedeu. Similarly I have counted only one of the 2 licences, each for 163 sacks, issued to a group of merchants described firstly as 'of Cahors' and later 'of Provence'. These are obvious duplicates. On the other hand I have assigned to Montpellier all licences issued to the members of the society of Chapdemaill, even where the patent rolls state Paris or Rouen.
46 *CPR*, 1272–81, pp. 124, 185. E159/32 m 17. For Servat's career, see F. Arens, 'Wilhelm Servat von Cahors als Kaufmann zu London (1273–1320)', *VJSSWG*, 11 (1913).
47 Including Cambrai, which was actually in the empire. It was within the French sphere of influence and I have left it in the French totals.
48 'Die Handelssperre Englands gegen Flandern', p. 77.
49 J. de Sturler gives 1422 sacks, but this includes exports in March 1271 which properly belong to the previous season. *Les Relations Politiques et les Echanges Commerciaux entre le Duche de Brabant et L'Angleterre au Moyen Age* (Paris, 1936), p. 129.
50 A short list of Englishmen whose wool was seized at Bruges and Dammes in 1265. Published by E. Varenbergh, *Histoire des Relations Diplomatiques entre le Comté de Flandre et L'Angleterre au Moyen Age* (Brussels, 1874), p. 208. The list of English goods seized in Flanders in 1270, E163/5/17.
51 E. Miller, 'The Fortunes of the English Textile Industry in the Thirteenth Century', *EcHR* ser. 2, 18 (1965).
52 G. A. Williams, *Medieval London* (London, 1963), especially Chapter 5.
53 *CPR*, 1272–81, p. 68.
54 C47/29/File 1, 5.
55 C145/211, 7.
56 C47/29/File 1, 4.

3 THE ITALIAN HEGEMONY

1 Gras, *Early English Customs System*, p. 64. B. Wilkinson, *Studies in the Constitutional History of the Thirteenth and Fourteenth Centuries* (Manchester, 1937), p. 59.
2 *CPR*, 1258–66, pp. 551, 575–6, 580; 1266–72, pp. 1, 141.
3 For the fullest discussion of the new aid see R. W. Kaeuper, *Bankers to the Crown* (Princeton, NJ, 1973), pp. 136–41. In addition to the references he cites see *CPR*, 1272–81, pp. 286–7, for evidence that after taking over the farm from the consortium of Willelmi-del Papa the Beraud brothers handed it back to Hugh Pape.
4 Kaeuper, p. 141, shows that they had probably been collecting it for the preceding twelve months.
5 E101/126/1. *CPR*, 1272–81, pp. 90–1; *CCR*, 1272–9, p. 534. *Calendar of Documents Relating to Ireland*, 1251–84, p. 194.
6 For the fullest discussion of customs administration in this period see Kaeuper, pp. 148–68.
7 For details see E. M. Carus-Wilson and O. Coleman, *England's Export Trade, 1275–1547* (Oxford, 1963).
8 T. H. Lloyd, *The Movement of Wool Prices in Medieval England* (Cambridge, 1973), pp. 14–16.

9 E122/55/1. Printed in Gras, *Early English Customs System*, pp. 225–44.
10 E122/55/2.
11 E122/5/1.
12 E122/5/2.
13 E122/93/1.
14 The accountant's total is 27 962. His wool total of 1406 sacks 6 stones is virtually identical with my count of 1406 sacks 27 stones.
15 E122/105/1, 2; E122/148/4. My totals for the last 2 years amount to 824 sacks and 7602 fells and 560 sacks and 4574 fells respectively compared with accountants' totals of 841 sacks 10 stones and 8042 fells, 572 sacks 2 stones and 5230 fells. There are no ship totals in these accounts.
16 E122/50/2.
17 E122/213/1.
18 E122/148/1–3.
19 E122/136/1–3.
20 E122/32/1–4. See also R. A. Pelham, 'The Exportation of Wool from Sussex in the late Thirteenth Century', *Sussex Archaelogical Collections*, 74 (1933).
21 E122/135/2–4.
22 E122/135/2A–4A.
23 E122/124/1, 1A.
24 For full particulars see Lloyd, *Wool Prices*, pp. 52–61.
25 *Della Decima e delle altre gravezze imposte dal Comune di Firenze, della moneta, e della mercatura dei Fiorentini fino al secolo XVI*, ed. G. F. Pagnini, III (Lisbonne–Lucques, 1766), pp. 324–7.
26 *Rot. Parl.*, I, p. 61. *CCR*, 1288–96, p. 186.
27 *CPR*, 1281–92, pp. 423, 430, 482, 489. *CCR*, 1288–96, p. 261.
28 *Foedera*, I, ii, p. 801.
29 E159/68 m 82.
30 E101/126/7.
31 E122/47/1. The return is fragmentary and does not allow statistical treatment.
32 For further evidence of domestic cloth manufacture in this area see R. H. Hilton, *A Medieval Society* (London, 1966), pp. 208–13.
33 *Rôles Gascons*, III, ed. Ch. Bemont (Paris, 1906), 2676, 2683–4. Bartholomaei Cotton, *Historia Anglicana*, ed. H. R. Luard (London, 1852), pp. 245–7.
34 It is possible that it was an extension of a plan to seize only the wool of the bishops and the monasteries. This is suggested by C49/File 1, No. 17. Dated in the PRO lists as c1280, internal evidence shows that it belongs to the year 1294. Unfortunately, it is so badly damaged that it is not possible to be certain of its exact meaning.
35 *Annales Prioratus de Dunstaplia*, ed. H. R. Luard (London, 1866), p. 389.
36 C. V. Langlois, 'Project for Taxation Presented to Edward I', *EHR*, 4 (1891).
37 E159/68 m 82.
38 E159/68 m 86.
39 From the text of the *monstraunces* established by J. G. Edwards in 'Confirmatio Cartarum and Baronial Grievances in 1297', *EHR*, 58 (1943), p. 171. D. Beddoe, 'Some Financial and Political Aspects of the Constitutional Crisis of 1297', unpublished PhD thesis (Aberystwyth, 1960), p. 132, dismisses the statement as 'curious rhetoric', but she seems to have overlooked the writs of September 1295.
40 For a list of those engaged in the enterprise, together with notes on many

of them, see J. de Sturler, 'Deux comptes enrôlés de Robert de Segre, receveur et agent payeur d'Édouard Ier, roi d'Angleterre, aux Pays-Bas (1294–1296)', *Bulletin de la Commission Royale D'Histoire*, 215 (1959), pp. 586–593.

41 E372/145 m 30. *Rôles Gascons*, III, 3299.

42 *CPR*, 1292–1301 p. 99. *Annales Prioratus de Wigornia*, ed. H. R. Luard (London, 1869), p. 510. E159/68 m 78.

43 Made up of £2560 customs paid to Segre, £1046 from the sale of Riccardi wool and £1386 loans from merchants; the last figure including £639 from the sale of Laurence de Ludlow's wool. Sturler, 'Deux Comptes'.

44 Because of the absence of accounts from Southampton it is not possible to reckon precisely the total exports in this period. The lower figure includes 460 sacks exported from Southampton after the Easter prise of 1297, while the higher figure presumes that other exports from this port did not reach 1000 sacks a year. Exports were banned from the port in the autumn of 1296.

45 During the period of the war the yield of the customs exceeded the yield of taxes on lay moveables, M. Prestwich, *War, Politics and Finance under Edward I* (London, 1972), p. 197.

46 In July Walter Langton sent word from the continent that a force of Flemings, at least 1000 strong and disguised as fishermen, were preparing to raid Yarmouth. E368/67 m 41.

47 E159/69 m 83, 70 m 99. E122/5/5,5A. E101/457/2.

48 E159/70 m 110.

49 For the failure of Flemish merchants to collect their wool and the subsequent legal disputes see, *Select Cases Concerning the Law Merchant, 1239–1633*, II, ed. H. Hall, Selden Society, 45 (1930), pp. 64, 69.

50 E. Re, 'La Compagnia dei Ricciardi in Inghilterra'. Kaeuper, *Bankers to the Crown*, pp. 209–27.

51 E159/68 m 82–4. The total amount of wool exported was slightly larger than that licensed. See table 7.

52 G. Bigwood, 'Un Marche de Matières Premières: Laines D'Angleterre et Marchands Italiens vers la Fin du XIIIᵉ Siècle', *Annales D'Histoire Économique et Sociale*, 2 (1930), p. 205.

53 E159/68 m 82.

54 Wartime customs particulars. Boston, E122/5/4,5,5A; Hull, E122/55/3; Newcastle, E122/105/3; Sandwich, E122/124/2–4; Ipswich, E122/50/4.

55 Beddoe, 'The Constitutional Crisis of 1297', p. 123.

56 Sturler 'Deux Comptes', p. 594, where Segre receives £196 from Cosyn and Thunderly from the sale of salvaged wool.

57 E159/68–70.

58 For details of the organisation see Sturler, *Les Relations Politiques*, pp. 196–206.

59 E159/70 m 98.

60 E101/457/3.

61 There is no existing text of this ordinance, hereafter called the first ordinance, which must apparently be distinguished from the proclamation made by the sheriffs as well as from a later ordinance. The first ordinance was probably directed against reluctant sellers and, possibly, alien merchants.

62 *CCR*, 1296–1302, p. 111. The calendar fails to make the point that the wealthy merchants are denizens, but see note 67.

63 E159/70 m 98.

64 For these arrests see below p. 89.

65 *CCR*, 1296–1302, pp. 33, 102–4, 107–8, 110, 112. Other release orders are to be found in the Exchequer Memoranda Rolls.
66 *CCR*, 1296–1302, pp. 30, 109–111. The Sandwich wool, 204 sacks, was exported 10–22 June. E122/124/3.
67 The text of the letter is printed by G. O. Sayles, 'The Seizure of Wool at Easter 1297', *EHR*, 67 (1952), pp. 546–7.
68 *CCR*, 1296–1302, pp. 35, 112.
69 *CCR*, 1296–1302, pp. 104, 107, 109. E101/457/2. SC1/48/105.
70 E372/146 m 54.
71 E159/70 m 101. E368/68 m 44.
72 This was the total amount exported. It excludes wool restored in England, but includes the small amount restored on the continent and 70 sacks of Newcastle wool lost at sea. Table 11 gives full details of the Easter and July prices. For most counties there are three or four sources which record the wool taken and minor discrepancies must be explained by reweighing at each stage of delivery.
73 *Parliamentary Writs*, I, pp. 394–5.
74 E159/71 m 14. E101/457/2. The sale of wool on the continent realised something in excess of £15 000.
75 E101/457/3,21.
76 E368/68 m 43–4.
77 *CPR*, 1292–1301, pp. 310–11, 321–3, 332, 335. E159/80 m 35. E101/457/21.
78 E122/156/19.
79 E368/68 m 52. E159/72 m 99, 73 m 35, 80 m 35.
80 *Rot. Parl.*, I, p. 165.
81 E159/80 m. 14, 18.
82 *CCR*, 1302–7, pp. 504–5. The pardon petition is Ancient Petition (SC 8) No. 3808. It has been printed by G. L. Haskins in 'Three Early Petitions of the Commonalty', *Speculum*, 12 (1937), p. 316. Haskins, however, dates it to 1297. Setting it in its correct context probably invalidates his view that it is a sectional petition from wool merchants rather than one from the whole community.
83 For a full discussion of the crisis see Edwards, *Confirmatio Cartarum*. Wilkinson, *Constitutional History of the Thirteenth and Fourteenth Centuries*, pp. 62–6. H. Rothwell, 'The Confirmation of the Charters, 1297', *EHR*, 60 (1945). G. L. Harriss, *King, Parliament and Public Finance in Medieval England to 1369* (Oxford, 1975), pp. 48–74, 423–5.
84 *CCR*, 1296–1302, pp. 254, 266–7, 269, 315. *CPR*, 1291–1301, p. 432. M. Prestwich, 'Edward I's Monetary Policies and their Consequences', *EcHR*, ser. 2, 22 (1969), p. 412.

4 THE ENGLISH TRIUMPHANT

1 *CCR*, 1296–1302, p. 555. *CPR*, 1301–7, pp. 130, 158. E30/51A.
2 *Cal. of Chancery Warrants*, 1230–1326, p. 214. *CCR*, 1302–7, p. 209.
3 G. P. Cuttino, *English Diplomatic Administration* (2nd edn Oxford, 1971), pp. 63–87, 212–20.
4 *CCR*, 1318–23, p. 234.
5 T. F. Tout, *The Place of the Reign of Edward II in English History* (Manchester, 1914), pp. 236–66.
6 Sturler, *Relations Politiques*, pp. 172–227.
7 *CCR*, 1307–13, p. 293.

8 *CPR*, 1307–13, p. 591.
9 R. L. Baker, 'The Establishment of the English wool staple in 1313', *Speculum*, 31 (1956). W. S. Reid, 'The Scots and the staple ordinance of 1313', *Speculum*, 34 (1959).
10 *CCR*, 1307–13, p. 154. *Foedera*, II, i, p. 70.
11 *CCR*, 1307–13, pp. 223, 229, 238, 278, 335.
12 *CCR*, 1307–13, p. 337.
13 The incident is the subject of much unpublished correspondence in Chancery Diplomatic Documents (C47).
14 *CCR*, 1307–13, p. 341.
15 *CCR*, 1307–13, pp. 347, 438.
16 *CCR*, 1307–13, pp. 451, 454, 473, 558. *Rot. Parl.* I, p. 357.
17 *CCR*, 1307–13, p. 570. SC1/33/171.
18 *CPR*, 1313–17, p. 260. *CCR*, 1313–18, p. 218. *Rot. Parl.* I, p. 358. *Foedera*, II, i, p. 252.
19 *Cal. of Chancery Warrants*, 1230–1326, p. 422. *Foedera*, II, i, pp. 252, 277–278.
20 *CCR*, 1313–18, pp. 258, 449, 486. *CPR*, 1313–17, p. 663. *Cal. of Chancery Warrants*, 1230–1326, p. 455.
21 *CCR*, 1313–18, pp. 517, 526, 528, 567, 571, 582. *Foedera*, II, i, p. 338. C47/29/8 (12–14).
22 *CCR*, 1313–18, p. 616. *CPR*, 1317–21, pp. 55, 93, 145, 190. *Foedera*, II, i, pp. 367–8.
23 *CCR*, 1318–23, p. 164. *Foedera*, II, i, p. 394.
24 A. E. Bland, 'The Establishment of Home Staples, 1319', *EHR*, 29 (1914).
25 *CFR*, III, pp. 12, 14. E159/94 m 34d.
26 *CCR*, 1318–23, p. 234.
27 *CCR*, 1318–23, pp. 243–4, 252–4, 261, 318, *CPR*, 1317–21, pp. 500, 539.
28 *CCR*, 1318–23, pp. 186, 391.
29 *CCR*, 1318–23, pp. 221, 224, 233, 238, 324. *Cal. of Chancery Warrants*, 1230–1326, p. 509.
30 *CCR*, 1318–23, pp. 347, 349. *CPR*, 1317–21, p. 602.
31 *CCR*, 1318–23, pp. 400, 540.
32 *CCR*, 1318–23, pp. 401, 414, 549. *CPR*, 1321–4, p. 102. J. C. Davies, 'An Assembly of Wool Merchants in 1322', *EHR*, 31 (1916).
33 *CCR*, 1318–23, pp. 644, 690, 698, 703, 706. *CPR*, 1321–4, pp. 248, 269, 276.
34 For the 1330s see H. S. Lucas, 'Diplomatic Relations between England and Flanders from 1329 to 1336', *Speculum*, 11 (1936).
35 *CPR*, 1321–4, p. 334. *CCR*, 1323–7, pp. 9, 134, 308, 378.
36 *CPR*, 1324–7, pp. 269, 274.
37 *CCR*, 1323–7, p. 565. *CPR*, 1327–30, pp. 98–9. *CPMR*, 1323–64, p. 64.
38 *CPR*, 1327–30, p. 155.
39 *CCR*, 1323–7, p. 564. *CPR*, 1324–7, p. 301. *CPMR*, 1323–64, pp. 16–18.
40 *CPR*, 1324–7, p. 319. *CCR*, 1323–7, p. 585; 1327–30, p. 41.
41 *CCR*, 1327–30, pp. 78, 116, 134. *CPR*, 1327–30, p. 98.
42 *CPR*, 1327–30, pp. 129, 169.
43 *CPR*, 1327–30, pp. 138, 140. *CFR*, IV, p. 54. *CPMR*, 1323–64, p. 32.
44 *CPMR*, 1323–64, pp. 52–60. *CPR*, 1327–30, p. 237.
45 *CPR*, 1330–4, pp. 283, 466–7, 498, 519.
46 *CPR*, 1330–4, p. 362. *CCR*, 1333–7, pp. 302, 503.
47 *CFR*, III, p. 342.
48 *CCR*, 1333–7, pp. 60, 256, 277, 326, 433. *CFR*, III, pp. 353–5, 404.

49 For a general defence of the statistics see Carus-Wilson and Coleman, *England's Export Trade*, pp. 201–7.

50 R. L. Baker, *The English Customs Service, 1307–1343* (Philadelphia, 1961), pp. 12–23.

51 Gras, *English Customs System*, pp. 259–64.

52 *CCR*, 1307–13, pp. 170, 275, 380. *Cal of Chancery Warrants, 1230–1326*, p. 475. *Letter Book C*, p. 122.

53 For a full list of accounts see, *Exchequer K. R. Customs Accounts*, I, pp. 164–71, List and Index Society, 43 (1969).

54 Two earlier accounts are in a very poor condition. For the full list see *Exchequer K. R. Customs Accounts*, I, pp. 14–17.

55 Williams, *Medieval London*, pp. 149–151. For alien customs accounts see *Exchequer K. R. Customs Accounts*, I, pp. 206–8.

56 *Exchequer K. R. Customs Accounts*, II, pp. 126–8, List and Index Society, 60 (1970).

57 *Exchequer K. R. Customs Accounts*, II, pp. 161–4.

58 *CCR*, 1333–7, p. 102.

59 Davies, 'An Assembly of Wool Merchants', p. 605.

60 The figure of 2706 sacks shown in *England's Export Trade* for the year 1308–9 is a misprint for 706 sacks.

61 *Exchequer K. R. Customs Accounts*, II, pp. 5–7.

62 *Hansisches Urkundenbuch*, II, ed. K. Höhlbaum (Halle, 1879), pp. 19–22.

63 E122/105/4,9.

64 *CCR*, 1296–1302, p. 461; 1302–7, pp. 87, 175, 426.

65 *CPR*, 1307–13, p. 399; 1313–17, p. 169. *CCR*, 1313–18, p. 427. E159/84 m 62d; 88 m 39; 91 m 111.

66 R. W. Kaeuper, 'The Frescobaldi of Florence and the English Crown', *Studies in Medieval and Renaissance History*, 10 (1973).

67 C47/13/1 No. 28.

68 *CPR*, 1317–21, p. 518. E365/5.

69 *CCR*, 1318–21, p. 303.

70 *CCR*, 1313–18, p. 452. E159/88 m 135.

71 A. A. Ruddock, *Italian Merchants and Shipping in Southampton, 1270–1600* (Southampton, 1951), pp. 9–36.

5 EDWARD III – WOOLMONGER EXTRAORDINARY

1 For earlier studies of this period see D. Hughes, *A Study of Social and Constitutional Tendencies in the Early Years of Edward III* (London, 1915). S. B. Terry, *The Financing of the Hundred Years War* (London, 1914). F. R. Barnes, 'The Taxation of Wool, 1327–1348' and G. Unwin, 'The Estate of Merchants, 1336–1365', in *Finance and Trade under Edward III*, ed. G. Unwin (Manchester, 1918). E. B. Fryde, 'Edward III's War Finance, 1337–1341', unpublished PhD Thesis (Oxford, 1947); 'Edward III's Wool Monopoly of 1337: A Fourteenth-Century Royal Trading Venture', *History*, NS 38 (1952). Sources for the narrative of events are generally documented in these works and are not repeated here. However, I have re-examined most of the sources and my conclusions do not always agree with those of earlier writers.

2 Fryde quotes evidence which suggests that the Gloucestershire surveyors were commissioned on 26 April 1337, 'Edward III's War Finance', p. 56. I am not convinced that this date was not a clerical error.

3 Hughes, *Social and Constitutional Tendencies*, p. 35.
4 He converts the total into about 10 300 sacks by English weight. 'Edward III's Wool Monopoly', p. 21.
5 'Edward III's War Finance', chapter 2, note 94a.
6 Both sets are enrolled in E358/10.
7 Extracts from the enrolled account of Pole and Conduit have been printed in E. B. Fryde, *The Wool Accounts of William de la Pole*, St Anthony's Hall Publications, No. 25 (York, 1964), pp. 21–4.
8 In January 1338 the government was aware that more than 10 000 sacks had been dispatched in the first wool fleet, while a warning against smuggling had been issued in October 1337, *CCR*, 1337–9 pp. 188, 228.
9 It was revealed at the trial of Pole and Conduit E159/117, mm 178, 186.
10 *CCR*, 1337–9, pp. 400, 412.
11 These figures are given in Fryde, 'Edward III's War Finance', Table II.
12 *Treaty Rolls*, II, pp. 193–200, 205–13.
13 'Edward III's War Finance', p. 163.
14 'Edward III's War Finance', p. 198.
15 'Edward III's War Finance', p. 200.
16 The lower figure is from 'Edward III's War Finance', Tables III and VI. The higher is my own calculation.
17 For a full discussion of this question compare Wilkinson, *Constitutional History of the Thirteenth and Fourteenth Centuries*, pp. 70–8, and Harriss, *King, Parliament and Public Finance*, pp. 426–49. *Statutes*, I, pp. 291–4.
18 *Rot. Parl.* II, pp. 118–22.
19 'Edward III's War Finance', Table VII.
20 *CCR*, 1339–41, pp. 54, 71, 100. *Rot. Parl.*, II, pp. 131–4.
21 *CPR*, 1340–3, p. 247.
22 *CPR*, 1340–3, p. 187.
23 C76/16 mm 22, 25. *CCR*, 1343–6, p. 191. *CFR*, v, p. 353.
24 *CPR*, 1340–3, p. 314.
25 *CPR*, 1340–3, pp. 284, 326, 386. *CCR*, 1341–3, pp. 220, 493, 495. C76/16 m 3.
26 Statements about the wool levies of 1341 and 1342 for which no printed source is cited are based on incidental information noted in the enrolled accounts of the collectors and receivers in E358/10.
27 *CCR*, 1341–3, p. 352.
28 C76/16 m 15.
29 *CPR*, 1340–3, p. 255.
30 *CCR*, 1341–3, pp. 260, 451.
31 The officials were not charged increment on this wool, presumably because it was not packed in sarplers. E101/507/22 records that it was packed at the king's expense.
32 E179/242/1.
33 E179/73/23–5.
34 *CCR*, 1341–3, pp. 399, 414, 472.
35 The figure of 18 350 sacks includes wool bought by officials and merchants with money provided by taxpayers, but it excludes instances where assignees of arrears probably received cash.
36 *CPR*, 1340–3, p. 290.
37 *CCR*, 1341–3, p. 258.
38 *CPR*, 1340–3, p. 303.
39 *CCR*, 1341–3, pp. 255–60.

40 'The Estate of Merchants', p. 208.
41 C76/16 m 4.
42 *CCR*, 1341–3, pp. 225, 415. E358/10 m 25.
43 *CCR*. 1341–3, p. 272.
44 *CCR*. 1341–3, p. 430.
45 *CCR*, 1341–3, pp. 542–4.
46 *CPR*, 1341–3, p. 553.
47 E358/10. The total number of indentures is said to be 317, but there appear to be only 316. Possibly this helps to explain why my total of wool delivered, shown in table 14, is some 80 sacks lower than the total given in the account.
48 On smuggling in this period see Baker, *English Customs Service*, pp. 36–43.
49 *CCR*, 1339–41, pp. 134, 414.
50 For the Yorkshire loans see E. B. Fryde, *Some Business Transactions of York Merchants*, Borthwick Papers, No. 29 (York, 1966), appendix.
51 E101/457/29.
52 *Rot. Parl.*, II, p. 105.
53 Writ quoted in subsidy account for Hull.
54 *CCR*, 1341–3, p. 411. The writ, in its calendered form at least, merely refers to payment and makes no mention of bonds. However, the distinction between 6 sacks and larger amounts does not seem to make sense if the payments in question were in cash.
55 *CCR*, 1341–3, p. 553.
56 *CCR*, 1341–3, p. 595.
57 Statements about the effects of the bullion deposit are based on figures of exports given in the enrolled accounts of the subsidy, which are broken down into shorter periods than those found in the accounts of the ancient custom.
58 *CCR*, 1341–3, p. 685.
59 *CFR*, v, pp. 37, 39, 142–3, 205, 307. *CPR*, 1338–40, p. 307.
60 *CFR*, v, p. 25. *CCR*, 1337–9, pp. 177, 181, 208, 210. *CPR*, 1334–8, p. 337.
61 *CCR*, 1339–41, pp. 180, 184.
62 *CCR*, 1337–9, p. 228. E101/127/23. E101/642/28.
63 *CPR*, 1343–5, pp. 467–9.
64 *CCR*, 1339–41, pp. 189, 198, 305, 323, 353. E372/187 m 45.
65 *CCR*, 1341–3, pp. 193, 395, 402, 425, 475. *CPR*, 1340–3, p. 398.
66 *CPR*, 1340–3, pp. 275, 336. *CCR*, 1341–3, pp. 229, 418.
67 *CCR*, 1339–41, 13, 32, 38, 43, 79, 273, 599, 622, 660.
68 *Treaty Rolls*, II, pp. 16–27.
69 *CCR*, 1337–9, pp. 303, 306, 315, 318, 364, 417. *CFR*, v, p. 73.
70 *CPR*, 1338–40, p. 191. *CCR*, 1339–41, pp. 284, 506, 659.

6 QUEST FOR A STAPLE POLICY

1 *Rot. Parl.*, II, p. 143.
2 *CCR*, 1343–6, pp. 190, 217. *CPR*, 1343–5, p. 43.
3 *Rot. Parl.*, II, pp. 138, 140.
4 *CCR*, 1343–6, p. 226.
5 G. Sayles, 'The "English Company" of 1343 and a Merchant's Oath', *Speculum*, 6(1931), p. 184.
6 Unwin, 'Estate of Merchants', p. 215.
7 E. B. Fryde, 'The English Farmers of the Customs, 1343–51', *TRHS*, ser. 5, 9(1959), p. 9.
8 *Rot. Parl.* II, pp. 148–50, 156.

9 *CCR*, 1343–6, p. 428.
10 *Rot. Parl.*, ii, p. 202. *CCR*, 1346–9, p. 430.
11 The figures for silver coined are based on J. Craig, *The Mint* (Cambridge, 1953), p. 411. For a general discussion of monetary problems in the years 1335–48 see pp. 61–8. See also R. Ruding, *Annals of the Coinage of Great Britain* (London, 1817), i, pp. 405–34. A. Feaveryear, *The Pound Sterling*, 2nd edn (Oxford, 1963), pp. 15–18, 27–32. T. F. Reddaway, 'The King's Mint and Exchange in London, 1343–1543', *EHR*, 82(1967).
12 In 1314 the minimum market rate of the florin had been 3s 1d sterling.
13 Sayles, 'The English Company', p. 178.
14 A writ sent to the Exchequer in October 1344 described the members of the rump as 'newly associated', *CCR*, 1343–6, 427.
15 *CCR*, 1343–6, p. 573.
16 *Rot. Parl.*, ii, p. 191.
17 A large number of merchants was summoned to confer with the king's council in July 1345, but many were reluctant to attend. Unwin, in *Finance and Trade*, p. 216.
18 *CCR*, 1343–6, pp. 601–2, 611, 648–9. *CPR*, 1343–5, p. 19.
19 *CCR*, 1346–9, pp. 72–4, 557; 1349–54, pp. 30, 99–100. *CPR*, 1348–50, p. 145.
20 For a description of how the loans were raised see Fryde, 'Farmers of the Customs', pp. 11–16; *Business Transactions of York Merchants*, pp. 10–20.
21 *CFR*, v, pp. 1–2.
22 *CCR*, 1346–9, pp. 290–1.
23 *Rot. Parl.*, ii, p. 170. *CFR*, pp. 1–15. E358/10. E179/180/20.
24 *Rot. Parl.*, ii, pp. 161, 165–71, 201.
25 *Rot. Parl.*, ii, pp. 171, 175. *CCR*, 1343–6, p. 632; 1346–9, p. 173. *CPR*, 1348–1350, pp. 76–7.
26 *Rot. Parl.* ii, pp. 200–2. *CPR*, 1345–8, p. 453.
27 *CCR*, 1346–9, p. 494. *CPR*, 1345–8, p. 569.
28 *CCR*, 1346–9, pp. 568, 597, 599; 1349–54, pp. 6–9, 34, 59. *Rot. Parl.*, ii, p. 229.
29 *CFR*, vi, p. 223. *CCR*, 1349–54, p. 213.
30 *CCR*, 1349–54, pp. 196, 199, 267, 297, 310, 361, 393, 496. *CPR*, 1350–54, pp. 142–6.
31 Export under the new staple regulations began on 2 August 1353, but some licences had been issued to Italians since the previous April.
32 *CCR*, 1349–54, p. 506.
33 *Finance and Trade under Edward III*, ed. Unwin, pp. xxiii–xxiv. Unwin's theses about the establishment of home staples in 1353 and the wool policies adopted in the later years of Edward III have never been subjected to critical appraisal. Since my interpretation is radically different from his I have thought it right to show his position by direct quotation. I hope, and believe, that the extracts chosen do no injustice to his case.
34 Unwin, 'Estate of Merchants', pp. 225–32.
35 *Rot. Parl.*, ii, p. 246.
36 *Rot. Parl.*, ii, p. 253.
37 Chichester had been added by 12 November. The fact that both Canterbury and Chichester are named in the version of the ordinance copied in the staple and ordinance rolls merely indicates that these were written up later than the events now under consideration. The staple roll copy, used in *Statutes of the Realm*, seems to have been written in January 1354. *Statutes*, i, pp. 332–43. C67/22.

38 C67/22.
39 *Rot. Parl.*, II, pp. 262, 265.
40 For other aspects of the legislation see E. E. Rich, 'The Mayors of the Staples', *Cambridge Historical Journal*, 4(1932–4).
41 In a writ of 10 June 1353 Shrewsbury was named as a second staple for Wales, but it had been dropped by the time that the ordinance was issued.
42 Unwin, 'Estate of Merchants', p. 242. A. Beardwood, *Alien Merchants in England, 1350 to 1377* (Cambridge, Mass., 1931), p. 26.
43 *CPR*, 1354–8, p. 433.
44 *Letter Book G*, p. 87.
45 *Statutes*, I, p. 351.
46 'Estate of Merchants', p. 50.
47 The price schedule was enrolled in the staple roll, C67/22. The only printed version is in a writ sent to the sheriffs of London. *Letter Book G*, p. 87.
48 *CPR*, 1358–61, p. 564. *CCR*, 1360–4, p. 14.
49 *Statutes*, I, p. 374.
50 'Estate of Merchants', p. 244.
51 *Foedera*, III, ii, p. 617.
52 Letters dated 20 July ordering the surrender of the town to the merchants were cancelled because the king wished first to hear the accounts of the present officials. C67/22.
53 *Rot. Parl.*, II, p. 269.
54 *Foedera*, III, ii, pp. 688–93.
55 E101/173/7. E101/174/7.
56 The term 'new company' does not appear in the letters of appointment, but it is used by Parliament at a later date. For biographies of the merchants see A. M. Oakley, 'The Establishment of the Calais Staple (1363)', unpublished MA thesis (Leeds, 1959), Appendix 2. This work must be used with caution since it contains a number of inaccuracies.
57 E101/178/2.
58 *Rot. Parl.*, II, p. 276.
59 E101/178/2,3.
60 'Estate of Merchants', p. 247.
61 *Rot. Parl.*, II, pp. 285–7. *Statutes*, I, p. 384.
62 *CFR*, VII, pp. 302, 306. *CCR*, 1364–8, p. 479.
63 *Foedera*, III, ii, pp. 745–6, 767.
64 G. A. Holmes, 'Florentine Merchants in England, 1340–1436', *EcHR* ser. 2, 13(1960), p. 201.
65 Ruddock, *Italian Merchants and Shipping*, p. 39.
66 Beardwood, *Alien Merchants*, p. 57. *CPR*, 1354–8, p. 225.
67 *CPR*, 1364–8, p. 46. *CFR*, VII, p. 180.
68 See below p. 220.
69 *Foedera*, III, ii, p. 616.
70 H. van Werveke, 'Currency Manipulation in the Middle Ages: the Case of Louis de Mâle, Count of Flanders', *TRHS*, ser. 4, 31 (1949).
71 G. A. Brucker, *Florentine Politics and Society, 1343–78* (Princeton, 1962), p. 11.
72 Lloyd, *Wool Prices*, p. 19.
73 *Rot. Parl.*, II, p. 301. *Statutes*, I, p. 390.
74 Beardwood, *Alien Merchants*, p. 25.
75 *England's Export Trade*, pp. 76–7.

76 *CCR*, 1369–74, p. 192. *CFR*, VIII, p. 170.
77 SC1/41/20. *CCR*, 1369–74, p. 170.
78 T. Walsingham, *Historia Anglicana*, I, ed. H. T. Riley (London, 1863), p. 313.
  Rot. Parl., II, p. 308. *Foedera*, III, ii, p. 918.
79 *CCR*, 1369–74, pp. 301–2, 307, 224–6. *CFR*, VIII, pp. 145, 149, 151. *Foedera*,
  III, ii, pp. 898–9, 921, 938–9, 953. Walsingham, *Historia Anglicana*, I, p. 313.
80 *CCR*, 1369–74, pp. 434, 467. *CFR*, VIII, p. 185.
81 *CCR*, 1369–74, p. 409. *CFR*, VIII, p. 194.
82 It was next renewed, well in advance of expiry, in November 1373. It was to
  last until Michaelmas 1376, but the last year was conditional upon the continuance of the war.
83 *Rot. Parl.*, II, p. 310. *CFR*, VIII, pp. 196–7.
84 *Rot. Parl.*, II, p. 315.
85 *Rot. Parl.*, II, p. 318.
86 For the background to the Good Parliament see A. Steel, *Richard II* (Cambridge, 1941), pp. 23–8. M. McKisack, *The Fourteenth Century* (Oxford,
  1959), pp. 387–92 J. S. Roskell, *The Commons and their Speakers in English
  Parliaments*, 1376–1523 (Manchester, 1963), pp. 16–22. G. Holmes, *The
  Good Parliament* (Oxford, 1975).
87 *The Anonimalle Chronicle*, ed. V. H. Galbraith (Manchester, 1927), pp. 81,
  85–6, 183.
88 *Statutes*, I, p. 390. *Rot. Parl.*, II, p. 301.

7 THE EVOLUTION OF THE CALAIS STAPLE

1 D. Nicholas, *Town and Countryside: Social, Economic and Political Tensions
  in Fourteenth-Century Flanders* (Bruges, 1971), p. 340.
2 *CCR*, 1377–81, pp. 11, 30–3, 113, 133. *CFR*, IX, pp. 59–60. *Rot. Parl.*, III,
  p. 22.
3 *CCR*, 1377–81, p. 82, *Rot. Parl.*, III, pp. 48, 67.
4 *Rot. Parl.*, III, p. 63; IV, p. 250. *CPR*, 1377–81, p. 378.
5 *Rot. Parl.*, IV, p. 309. *CCR*, 1389–92, p. 465. *CPR*, 1408–13, p. 194.
6 *Rot. Parl.*, III, pp. 73, 88, 114, 122. *Statutes*, II, p. 24. *CCR*, 1378–81, pp. 138,
  328.
7 *Rot. Parl.*, III, p. 136. *CCR*, 1381–5, pp. 185, 187–8. Walsingham, *Historia
  Anglicana*, II, pp. 61, 81.
8 *CCR*, 1381–5, pp. 202, 265, 330.
9 *Rot. Parl.*, III, p. 159.
10 *Rot. Parl.*, III, pp. 204–5, 214. *CCR*, 1385–9, pp. 68, 167, 293. *CPR*, 1385–9,
  p. 253. For amounts of wool exported to Middelburg and Calais respectively
  see F. Miller, 'The Middelburg Staple, 1383–88', *Cambridge Historical
  Journal*, 2 (1926–8), p. 65.
11 *Rot. Parl.*, III, p. 250. *CCR*, 1385–9, pp. 536, 541, 618, 673.
12 *Rot. Parl.*, III, pp. 268, 273.
13 *Rot. Parl.*, III, pp. 278–9, *Statutes*, II, pp. 76–7. *CCR*, 1389–92, pp. 237–8.
14 *Rot. Parl.*, III, p. 284. *CCR*, 1389–92, pp. 447–8, 560.
15 *Rot. Parl.*, III, p. 322. *CCR*, 1389–92, p. 237; 1392–6, pp. 25, 46, 69–70, 74;
  1396–9, p. 158. *CPR*, 1391–6, pp. 291, 512, 514.
16 *Rot. Parl.*, III, pp. 370, 429. *CCR*, 1396–9, p. 51; 1399–1402, p. 180.
17 *Rot. Parl.*, III, pp. 465, 500, 530, 538, 661. *CCR*, 1405–9, pp. 169, 196. *CPR*,
  1405–8, p. 456; 1408–13, p. 216.
18 E101/185/10. C76/95 mm 12, 21. *Rot. Parl.*, III, p. 662. *CPR*, 1413–16, p. 90.

19 *Rot. Parl.*, IV, pp. 127, 146.
20 *Rot. Parl.*, IV, pp. 118, 250–1. C76/106 m 12; 109, m 12.
21 *Rot. Parl.*, III, pp. 7, 38, 57, 74, 90.
22 *Rot. Parl.*, III, pp. 104, 114, 204.
23 *Rot. Parl.*, III, p. 220. *CCR*, 1385–9, pp. 198–9.
24 *Rot. Parl.*, III, p. 245. *CCR*, 1385–9, pp. 366, 380, 414.
25 *Rot. Parl.*, III, pp. 263, 268, 273.
26 *Rot. Parl.*, III, pp. 340, 368.
27 *Rot. Parl.*, III, pp. 425, 457, 533.
28 *Rot. Parl.*, III, pp. 425, 491, 546, 556; IV, pp. 63, 173. *CFR*, XII, p. 287.
29 *CCR*, 1402–5, p. 107. *Rot. Parl.*, IV, p. 173.
30 Craig, *The Mint*, p. 411.
31 E101/176/16–18; 177/2.
32 *Rot. Parl.*, III, p. 64. *CCR*, 1377–81, p. 193. E364/20.
33 *Rot. Parl.*, III, pp. 120, 126–7, 138.
34 *Statutes*, II, pp. 76–7.
35 *Rot. Parl.*, III, p. 285. *CCR*, 1389–92, pp. 422, 527–8.
36 Figures for coinage at Calais, 1387 to 1404, are based on seignorage received by the treasurer. An account of 29 September 1401–30 March 1403 (E101/184/10) shows that only gold was coined and this has been assumed to have been the case throughout the period.
37 J. H. A. Munro, *Wool, Cloth, and Gold: The Struggle for Bullion in Anglo-Burgundian Trade, 1340–1478* (Toronto, 1973), p. 47.
38 *Rot. Parl.*, III, pp. 340, 369, 429. *CCR*, 1396–9, pp. 37–8, 88.
39 *Rot. Parl.*, III, pp. 468, 470.
40 *Wool, Cloth and Gold*, pp. 43–63, 187.
41 C76/95 mm 5, 13.
42 Munro, *Wool, Cloth and Gold*, p. 62.
43 *Rot. Parl.*, IV, pp. 125–6.
44 *Rot. Parl.*, IV, pp. 139, 146, 154, 159.
45 *CCR*, 1374–7, p. 422.
46 C76/87 m 11. *Rot. Parl.*, III, p. 553.
47 *CPR*, 1405–8, p. 425. *CCR*, 1413–19, p. 434. C76/88 m 5; 91 m 5; 93 m 20.
48 E122/70/18.
49 R. Bird, *The Turbulent London of Richard II* (London, 1949), does not trace Brembre's career this far back but states that his first appearance in the London hustings records is dated 1369.
50 *Calendar of Letters from the Mayor and Corporation of the City of London*, ed. R. R. Sharpe (London, 1885), p. 84.
51 *CFR*, VIII, pp. 145–6, 149, 150–1, 161, 163–7, 170–1, 180, 182–5, 189, 193–8, 233–7, 276–9, 329, 378–9.
52 E122/71/9.
53 E122/71/20, 23, 25.
54 *Letter Book*, I, pp. 8, 149.
55 E122/71/6.
56 C. M. Baron, 'Richard Whittington: the Man behind the Myth', *Studies in London History*, ed. R. E. J. Hollaender and W. Kellaway (London, 1969), p. 246.
57 E122/50/40.
58 E122/59/5, 7, 24.
59 *CCR*, 1369–74, pp. 209, 216–17, 277, 485. *CFR*, VIII, p. 182.
60 E101/128/18.

8 THE DECLINE OF THE WOOL TRADE

1 Munro, *Wool, Cloth and Gold*, p. 85. E. Power, 'The Wool Trade in the Fifteenth Century', in E. Power and M. M. Postan, *Studies in English Trade in the Fifteenth Century* (London, 1933), pp. 82–3.

2 *CCR*, 1405–9, pp. 359, 406; 1409–13, p. 53.

3 C76/90 m 8. *POPC*, III, p. 67.

4 J. L. Kirby, 'The Financing of Calais under Henry V', *Bulletin of the Institute of Historical Research*, 23 (1950), p. 167.

5 C76/80 m 2.

6 *CPR*, 1422–9, pp. 337–8.

7 *CPR*, 1429–36, pp. 256–7.

8 Munro, *Wool, Cloth and Gold*, p. 82. P. Spufford, *Monetary Problems and Policies in the Burgundian Netherlands, 1433–1496* (Leiden, 1970), p. 97.

9 *Rot. Parl.*, IV, p. 252.

10 *POPC*, III, pp. 43, 253, 356. *Rot. Parl.*, IV, pp. 358–60.

11 The published statute naturally omitted the fifth point, which contains no legislation. *Statutes*, II, pp. 254–6.

12 *Rot. Parl.*, IV, pp. 454, 490, 508–9.

13 E364/65, 66, 69, 72.

14 Power, 'Wool Trade in the Fifteenth Century', pp. 84–5. Munro, *Wool, Cloth and Gold*, pp. 93, 103–10.

15 For details see R. Vaughan, *Philip the Good: The Apogee of Burgundy* (London, 1970), pp. 98–126. J. G. Dickinson, *The Congress of Arras, 1435: a Study in Medieval Diplomacy* (Oxford, 1955). G. A. Holmes, 'The "Libel of English Policy" ', *EHR*, 76 (1961).

16 *Rot. Parl.*, IV, p. 508.

17 C76/121 m 18.

18 For details of both negotiations see M. Thielemanns, *Bourgogne et Angleterre: Relations Politiques et Economiques entre les Pays-Bas Bourguingnons et L'Angleterre, 1435–1467* (Brussels, 1966), pp. 116–45.

19 Spufford, *Monetary Problems*, p. 103.

20 C76/115 m 12. *Rot. Parl.*, V, p. 105.

21 Power, 'Wool Trade in the Fifteenth Century', pp. 83–5.

22 E101/189/7.

23 *Rot. Parl.*, V, p. 64. *Statutes*, II, pp. 324–5.

24 *POPC*, V, pp. 203, 215–17, 219–21.

25 *Rot. Parl.*, IV, pp. 360, 379. C76/115 m 17, 123 m 4.

26 C76/120 m 6, 121 m 1.

27 C76/126 m 13. Printed in G. Daumet, *Calais sous la Domination Anglaise* (Arras, 1902), pp. 170–1.

28 Power, 'Wool Trade in the Fifteenth Century', p. 89. Munro, *Wool, Cloth and Gold*, pp. 127, 146–7.

29 Munro, *Wool, Cloth and Gold*, p. 132.

30 C76/130 m 11. Printed in Daumet, *Calais sous la Domination Anglaise*, pp. 176–9.

31 *Rot. Parl.*, V, pp. 144–50. *Statutes*, II, pp. 346–9.

32 Munro, *Wool, Cloth and Gold*, pp. 132–4.

33 *POPC*, VI, p. 72.

34 *POPC*, VI, pp. 79, 84.

35 Munro, *Wool, Cloth and Gold*, pp. 146–7.

36 *Rot. Parl.*, V, pp. 273–7. *POPC*, VI, pp. 117–18.

37 *Rot. Parl.*, v, pp. 256–7.
38 G. L. Harriss, 'The Struggle for Calais: An Aspect of the Rivalry between Lancaster and York', *EHR*, 75 (1960), p. 53. An opposite view, that the staplers were largely neutral in the struggle, was put by W. I. Hayward, 'The Financial Transactions between the Lancastrian Government and the Merchants of the Staple from 1449 to 1461', *Studies in English Trade in the Fifteenth Century*, pp. 318–20. Hayward's statement that the government paid no interest on loans, p. 300, is disproved by Harriss, p. 50.
39 *Rot. Parl.*, v, pp. 330–1, 335–6.
40 Hayward, 'The Lancastrian Government and the Merchants of the Staple', pp. 308, 313.
41 *Rot. Parl.*, v, pp. 503–8. *Statutes*, II, pp. 392–4.
42 M. M. Postan, *Medieval Trade and Finance* (Cambridge, 1973), p. 9, Munro, *Wool, Cloth and Gold*, p. 159.
43 Munro, *Wool, Cloth and Gold*, p. 163. Thielemans, *Bourgogne et Angleterre*, p. 471.
44 *The Libelle of Englyshe Polycye*, ed. G. Warner (Oxford 1926), p. 23.
45 *Rot. Parl.*, v, pp. 563–4. *Statutes*, II, pp. 407–10.
46 *Rot. Parl.*, v, pp. 613–16.
47 Harriss, 'The Struggle for Calais', pp. 51–2.
48 *Rot. Parl.*, VI, pp. 55–61, 239, 269, 395–7, 523–5. *Statutes*, III, pp. 199–202. *The Ordinance Book of the Merchants of the Staple*, ed. E. E. Rich (Cambridge, 1937), p. 10.
49 *Rot. Parl.*, v, p. 565. Munro, *Wool, Cloth and Gold*, pp. 163–73. Thielemans, *Bourgogne et Angleterre*, pp. 403–24.
50 *Rot. Parl.*, VI, p. 60.
51 *The Cely Papers: Correspondence and Memoranda of the Cely family of Merchants of the Staple in London and Calais*, ed. H. E. Malden, Camden Society, ser. 3, I (1900), pp. 45, 64, 121.
52 *CPR*, 1485–94, p. 475.
53 *Tudor Economic Documents*, ed. R. H. Tawney and E. Power, III (London, 1924), p. 91.
54 SC1/57/80.
55 *CPR*, 1494–1509, pp. 447–50.
56 *Tudor Economic Documents*, III, p. 27.
57 C1/43/50.
58 E122/139/4, 11.
59 E122/76/2.
60 *State Papers, Venice, 1202–1509*, p. 72.
61 W. B. Watson, 'The Florentine Galley Trade with Flanders and England', *Rev. Belge*, 39 (1961), pp. 1090–1. M. E. Mallett, *The Florentine Galleys in the Fifteenth Century* (Oxford, 1967), p. 138.
62 *State Papers, Venice, 1202–1509*, pp. 54, 62, 65.
63 E101/128/30 m 10.
64 E101/128/31 mm 1, 2, 24.
65 Ruddock, *Italian Merchants and Shipping*, pp. 163–73. R. Flenley, 'London and Foreign Merchants in the reign of Henry VI', *EHR*, 25 (1910).
66 Ruddock, *Italian Merchants and Shipping*, pp. 194–8.
67 M. E. Mallett, 'Anglo-Florentine Commercial Relations, 1465–91', *EcHR*, ser. 2, 15 (1962), pp. 260–4. His contention that Milan accepted the scheme is contradicted by *State Papers, Milan, 1385–1618*, p. 252, where the city lodges a formal protest because of the harm which will be done to Genoa.

9 MARKETING THE WOOL

1 R. J. Whitwell, 'English Monasteries and the Wool Trade in the 13th Century', p. 4.
2 *PR*, 5 Ric. i, pp. 44, 69
3 *CPR*, 1232–47, p. 330. Matthew Paris, *Chronica Majora*, ed. H. R. Luard, v (London, 1880), pp. 427, 439.
4 H. Jenkinson, 'William Cade, a Financier of the Twelfth Century', *EHR*, 28 (1913), pp. 221–2, 224–5.
5 *PR*, 7 Ric. i, p. 166. *PR*, 13 John, p. 38. *Curia Regis*, i, p. 144.
6 *CPR*, 1272–81, pp. 17, 200; 1281–92, pp. 2, 4, 77, 160, 294. E159/55 mm 1, 3.
7 E. Varenbergh, *Relations Diplomatiques entre le Comte de Flandre et l'Angleterre*, pp. 214–17.
8 F. B. Pegolotti, *La Practica della Mercatura*, pp. 258–69.
9 *Recueil de Documents relatifs a l'Histoire de l'Industrie Drapière en Flandre*, ed. G. Espinas and H. Pirenne, ii (Brussels, 1909), pp. 100, 111, 138.
10 *CPR*, 1272–81, p. 95, E159/64 m 21.
11 *Select Cases Concerning the Law Merchant, 1239–1633*, ed. H. Hall, ii, Selden Society, 45 (1930), p. 64. E159/73 m 35.
12 *CCR*, 1272–9, pp. 254–5, 321–2.
13 *Rot. Parl.*, i, p. 1.
14 E13/5–8.
15 E13/10 m 7.
16 *Calendar of Documents relating to Ireland, 1171–1251*, p. 279.
17 E159/52, 53. E368/53.
18 For the Riccardi v Meaux see Whitwell, *Monasteries and the Wool Trade*, pp. 25–9.
19 C241/1–13.
20 E13/1E, 3, 10. E159/55 m 6, 59 m 8, 62 m 4. *CCR*, 1279–88, p. 424; 1288–96, p. 42.
21 *Statuta Capitulorum Generalium Ordinis Cisterciensis*, ed. D. J. M. Canivez, i (Louvain, 1933), pp. 61, 334, 426.
22 R. Graham, *English Ecclesiastical Studies* (London, 1929), p. 264.
23 *CCR*, 1288–96, pp. 192–5.
24 E159/62 m 4.
25 *CCR*, 1288–96, pp. 192–5.
26 Whitwell, *Monasteries and the Wool Trade*, p. 24.
27 E159/87 m 20.
28 E13/10 m 8.
29 *Rotuli de Dominabus et Pueris et Puellis*, ed. J. H. Round, Pipe Roll Society, 35 (London, 1913). *PR*, 5 John, p. 222. *Rot. Litt. Claus.*, i, p. 71.
30 *Calendar of Documents relating to Ireland, 1171–1251*, p. 27. E159/32, m 17; 58 m 14; 60 m 20.
31 E159/37 m 8; 40 m 14; 53 m 16; 57 m 13; 60 m 20; 61 m 20. C241/7, mm 75, 259; 8 mm 10–11.
32 E13/8 mm 3, 9.
33 C241/7 m 307.
34 *Select Cases in the Court of the King's Bench*, ed. G. O. Sayles, ii, Selden Society, 57 (1938), pp. 123–4.
35 E101/505/24.
36 *Royal and other Historical Letters of the Reign of Henry III*, ed. W. W. Shirley, ii (London, 1866), pp. 310–11.

37 *CPR*, 1272–8, p. 239.
38 *CPR*, 1292–1301, p. 630.
39 E159/94.
40 *Records of the Borough of Leicester*, ed. M. Bateson, I (London, 1899), pp. 72, 69, 80, 91–3. *Rot. Litt. Claus.*, II, p. 171.
41 *Leicester Records*, I, pp. 205, 253, 268, 273, 279, 292.
42 *Letter Book D*, p. 238. *CPMR*, 1323–64, p. 212.
43 *Royal Commission on Historical Manuscripts, 14th Report, Appendix, part 8* (1895), pp. 14–15.
44 *Leicester Records*, I, pp. 123, 234–5.
45 *Leicester Records*, I, pp. 185, 216, 230.
46 *CPR*, 1281–92, p. 25.
47 *Leicester Records*, I, pp. 82, 84–5.
48 *CPR*, 1272–8, p. 284 *Select Cases concerning the Law Merchant*, II, pp. 28–30.
49 *Calendar of Inquisitions Miscellaneous (Chancery)*, II, p. 399.
50 *Select Bills in Eyre*, ed. W. C. Bolland, Selden Society, 30 (1914), pp. 77–8.
51 *Law Merchant*, II, pp. 18–25.
52 E101/506/1.
53 *Rot. Parl.*, IV, p. 252.
54 S. Thrupp, 'The Grocers of London, A Study of the Distributive Trade', *Studies in English Overseas Trade in the Fifteenth Century*, pp. 263–4.
55 *Calendar of Inquisitions Miscellaneous (Chancery)*, II, p. 390.
56 E159/79 m 28.
57 E. B. Fryde, *Wool Accounts of William de la Pole*. N. J. M. Kerling, 'Abrekening van de Engelse Koopman Reginald de Conducto Bettreffende de Onkosten Gemaakt voor Vervoer en Berging van Engelse Wol Naar en in Dordrecht (1335–1338)', *Bijdragen en Medeleelingen van het Historisch Genootschap*, 68 (1953). See also J. F. Willard, 'Inland Transportation in England during the Fourteenth Century', *Speculum*, I (1926).
58 E358/10 m 20.
59 For the most recent work on the Celys see A. Hanham, 'Foreign Exchange and the English Wool Merchant in the Late Fifteenth Century', *BIHR*, 46 (1973); ' "Make a Careful Examination": Some Fraudulent Accounts in the Cely Papers', *Speculum*, 48 (1973).
60 *CPR*, 1391–6, p. 290. E364/27 m F.
61 N. J. M. Kerling, *Commercial Relations of Holland and Zeeland with England from the late Thirteenth Century to the close of the Middle Ages* (Leyden, 1954), pp. 65–6.
62 Lloyd, *Wool Prices*, p. 26.
63 *Statutes*, II, p. 64.
64 C1/66/462.
65 E. Power, 'The English Wool Trade in the reign of Edward IV', *Cambridge Historical Journal*, 2 (1926–8), pp. 26–7.
66 *CCR*, 1374–7, p. 88.
67 'Wool Trade in the Fifteenth Century', pp. 52–3.
68 *CPR*, 1391–6, pp. 626–9.

Bibliography

I MANUSCRIPT SOURCES

a. Public Record Office

C1   Early Chancery Proceedings.
C47   Chancery Miscellanea.
C49   Parliamentary and Council Proceedings.
C67   Staple Rolls.
C76   Treaty Rolls.
C145 Miscellaneous Inquisitions.
C241 Certificates of Recognisances.
E13   Exchequer Plea Rolls.
E30   Exchequer Diplomatic Documents.
E101 Exchequer Accounts Various.
E122 Particulars of Customs Accounts.
E159 King's Remembrancer's Memoranda Rolls.
E163 Exchequer Miscellanea.
E179 Lay Subsidy Accounts.
E356 Enrolled Accounts of Customs and Subsidy.
E358 Enrolled Miscellaneous Accounts.
E364 Enrolled Foreign Accounts.
E368 Lord Treasurer's Remembrancer's Memoranda Rolls.
E372 Pipe Rolls.
SC1   Ancient Correspondence.
SC8   Ancient Petitions.

b. Hampshire Record Office
Bishopric of Winchester Pipe Rolls. For details see W. H. Beveridge,
'The Winchester Rolls and their Dating', *EcHR*, 2 (1929).

II PRINTED SOURCES

Annales Monastici, iv, ed. H. R. Luard (London, 1869).
Annales Prioratus de Dunstaplia, ed. H. R. Luard (London, 1866).
Annales Prioratus de Wigornia, ed. H. R. Luard (London, 1869).
The Anonimalle Chronicle, ed. V. H. Galbraith (Manchester, 1927).
Calendar of Chancery Rolls (Various), 1277–1326 (London, 1912).
Calendar of Chancery Warrants, 1230–1326 (London, 1927).
Calendar of Charter Rolls, 1226–1300, 2 vols. (London, 1903–6).
Calendar of Close Rolls, 1272–1509, 47 vols. (London, 1892–1963).
Calendar of Documents Relating to Ireland, 1171–1284, 2 vols. (London, 1875–
    1877).

Calendar of Fine Rolls, 1272–1509, 22 vols. (London, 1911–49).
Calendar of Inquisitions Miscellaneous (Chancery), II (London, 1916).
Calendar of Liberate Rolls, v (London, 1961).
Calendar of Letters from the Mayor and Corporation of the City of London, ed. R. R. Sharpe (London, 1885).
Calendar of Papal Registers, Papal Letters, 1198–1304 (London, 1893).
Calendar of Patent Rolls, 1232–1509, 53 vols. (London, 1906–16).
Calendars of Plea and Memoranda Rolls of the City of London, 1323–1482, ed. A. H. Thomas and P. E. Jones, 6 vols. (Cambridge, 1926–61).
Calendar of State Papers, Milan, 1385–1618 (London, 1912).
Calendar of State Papers, Venice, 1202–1509 (London, 1864).
The Cely Papers; Correspondence and Memoranda of the Cely Family of Merchants of the Staple in London and Calais, ed. H. E. Malden, Camden Society, ser. 3, I (1900).
A Century of Agricultural Statistics (London, 1968).
Cotton, B. *Historia Anglicana*, ed. H. R. Luard (London, 1852).
Chronicles of the Reigns of Stephen, Henry II and Richard I, III, ed. R. Howlett (London, 1886).
Chronicon Domini Walter de Heminburgh, II, ed. E. C. Hamilton (London, 1848).
Close Rolls, 1227–72, 14 vols. (London, 1902–38).
Curia Regis Rolls, I (London, 1922).
Della Decima e delle altre gravezze imposte dal Comune di Firrenze, della moneta, e della mercatura dei Fiorentini fino al secolo XVI, ed. G. F. Pagnini, III (Lisbonne–Lucques, 1766).
Diplomatic Documents, 1101–1272 (London, 1964).
Exchequer King's Remembrancer's Customs Accounts, List and Index Society, 43 and 60 (1969–70).
Foedera, Conventiones, Litterae, ed. T. Rymer, enlarged edition (London, 1816–1869).
Die Gesetze der Angelsachsen, I, ed. F. Liebermann (Halle, 1903).
Hansisches Urkundenbuch, II, ed. K. Höhlbaum (Halle, 1879).
The Laws of the Kings of England from Edmund to Henry I, ed. A. J. Robertson (Cambridge, 1925).
Letter Books of the City of London, ed. R. R. Sharpe, 12 vols. (London, 1899–1911).
The Libelle of Englysche Polycye, ed. G. Warner (Oxford, 1926).
Nonarum Inquisitiones (London, 1807).
Paris, M. *Chronica Majora*, ed. H. R. Luard, v (London, 1880).
The Ordinance Book of the Merchants of the Staple, ed. E. E. Rich (Cambridge, 1937).
Parliamentary Writs, I (London, 1827).
Patent Rolls, 1216–32, 2 vols. (London, 1901 and 1903).
Pegolotti, F. B. *La Pratica della Mercatura*, ed. A. Evans (Cambridge, Mass., 1936).
Pipe Rolls, Pipe Roll Society, old series, 1–38 (1884–1925) and new series, 1–34 (1925–72).
Pipe Roll, 1 Ric. I, ed. J. Hunter (London, 1844).
Proceedings and Ordinances of the Privy Council of England, 6 vols. (London, 1834–7).
Records of the Borough of Leicester, ed. M. Bateson, I (London, 1899).
Recueil de Documents relatifs a l'Histoire de l'Industrie Drapière en Flandre, ed. G. Espinas and H. Pirenne, II (Brussels), 1909).

Rôles Gascons, III, ed. Ch. Bemont (Paris, 1906).
Rotuli de Dominabus et Pueris et Puellis, ed. J. H. Round, P. R. Society, 35 (London, 1913).
Rotuli Chartarum, 1199–1216 (London, 1844).
Rotuli Hundredorum, 2 vols. (London, 1812–18).
Rotuli Litterarum Clausarum, 1204–26, 2 vols. (London 1833 and 1844).
Rotuli Litterarum Patentium, 1201–16 (London, 1835).
Rotuli de Oblatis et Finibus (London, 1835).
Rotuli Parliamentorum, 6 vols. and index.
Royal and other Historical Letters of the Reign of Henry III, ed. W. W. Shirley (London, 1862–6).
Royal Commission on Historical Manuscripts, 14th Report (1895).
Select Bills in Eyre, ed. W. C. Bolland, Selden Society, 30 (1914).
Select Cases in the Court of the King's Bench, ed. G. O. Sayles, II, Selden Society, 57 (1938).
Select Cases Concerning the Law Merchant, 1239–1633, ed. H. Hall, II, Selden Society, 45 (1930).
Statuta Capitulorum Generalium Ordinis Cisterciensis ed. D. J. M. Canivez, I (Louvain, 1933).
Statutes of the Realm, I–III (London, 1810–17).
Treaty Rolls, II (London, 1972).
Tudor Economic Documents, ed. R. H. Tawney and E. Power (London, 1924).
Walsingham, T. *Historia Anglicana*, I, ed. H. T. Riley, (London, 1863).
'Walter of Henley' and Other Treatises on Estate Management and Accounting, ed. D. Oschinsky (Oxford, 1971).

III SECONDARY WORKS

Albe, E. 'Les marchands de Cahors à Londres au XIII⁰ siècle', *Bulletin de la Société des Etudes du départment du Lot* (1908).
Arens, F. 'Wilhelm Servat von Cahors als Kaufmann zu London (1273–1320)', *VJSSWG*, 11 (1913).
Baker, R. L. *The English Customs Service, 1307–1343* (Philadelphia, 1961).
'The Establishment of the English Wool Staple in 1313', *Speculum*, 31 (1956).
Beardwood, A. *Alien Merchants in England, 1350 to 1377* (Cambridge, Mass., 1931).
Beddoe, D. 'Some Financial and Political Aspects of the Constitutional Crisis of 1297', unpublished PhD Thesis (Aberystwyth, 1960).
Berben, H. 'Het Verdrag van Montreuil, 1274. De Englesch-Vlaamsche Handelspolitick, 1266–87', *Rev. Belge*, 23 (1944).
Bigwood, G. 'Un Marche de Matières Premieres: Laines D'Angleterre et Marchands Italiens vers la Fin du XIII⁰ siècle, *Annales D'Histoire Économique et Sociale*, 2 (1930).
Bird, R. *The Turbulent London of Richard II* (London, 1949).
Bland, A. E. 'The Establishment of Home Staples, 1319', *EHR*, 29 (1914).
'Extracts relative to loans supplied by Italian Merchants to the Kings of England in the 13th and 14th Centuries', *Archaeologia*, 28 (1840).
Brooks, F. W. 'William de Wrotham and the Office of Keeper of the King's Ports and Galleys', *EHR*, 40 (1925).
Brucker, G. A. *Florentine Politics and Society, 1343–78* (Princeton, 1962).
Cambridge Economic History of Europe, II, ed. M. M. Postan and E. E. Rich (Cambridge, 1952).

Carus-Wilson, E. and Coleman, O. *England's Export Trade, 1275–1547* (Oxford, 1963).

Craig, J. *The Mint* (Cambridge, 1953).

Cuttino, G. P. *English Diplomatic Administration* (2nd edn Oxford, 1971).

Davies, J. C. 'An Assembly of Wool Merchants in 1322', *EHR*, 31 (1916).

Daumet, G. *Calais sous la Domination Anglaise* (Arras, 1902).

Denholm-Young, N. *Collected Papers* (Cardiff, 1969).

de Poerck, G. *La Draperie Médiévale en Flandre et en Artois* (Bruges, 1951).

Dept, G. *Les Influences Anglaise et Française dans le Comte de Flandre au debut du XIIIe siècle* (Paris–Ghent, 1928).

'Les marchands flamands et le roi d'Angleterre', *Revue du Nord*, 12 (1926).

Derville, A. 'Le Draperies flamandes et artésiennes vers 1250–1350', *Revue du Nord*, 54 (1972).

de Sturler, J. 'Deux comptes enrôlés de Robert de Segre, receveur et agent payeur d'Édouard Ier, roi d'Angleterre, aux Pays-Bas (1294–1296)', *Bulletin de la Commission Royale D'Histoire*, 125 (1959).

Les Relations Politiques et les Echanges Commerciaux entre le Duche de Brabant et L'Angleterre au Moyen Age (Paris, 1936).

Dhondt, J. 'Devéloppement Urbain et Initiative Comtale en Flandre au XIe Siècle', *Revue du Nord*, 30 (1948).

Dickinson, J. *The Congress of Arras, 1435: a Study in Medieval Diplomacy* (Oxford, 1955).

Edwards, J. G. '*Confirmatio Cartarum* and Baronial Grievances in 1297', *EHR*, 58 (1943).

Espinas, G. *La Draperie dans la Flandre Française au Moyen-Age*, 1 (Paris, 1923).

Sire Jehan Boinebroke (Lille, 1933).

Études d'Histoire Dédiées a la Mémoire de Henry Pirenne (Brussels, 1937).

Farmer, D. L. 'Some Livestock Price Movements in Thirteenth Century England', *EcHR*, ser. 2, 22 (1969).

Feaveryear, A. *The Pound Sterling*, 2nd edn (Oxford, 1963).

Finance and Trade under Edward III, ed. G. Unwin (Manchester, 1918).

Flenley, R. 'London and Foreign Merchants in the Reign of Henry VI', *EHR*, 25 (1910).

Fryde, E. B. 'Edward III's War Finance, 1337–1341', unpublished PhD Thesis (Oxford, 1947).

'Edward III's Wool Monopoly of 1337: A Fourteenth-Century Royal Trading Venture', *History*, NS 38 (1952).

'The English Farmers of the Customs, 1343–51', *TRHS*, ser. 5, 9 (1959).

Some Business Transactions of York Merchants, Borthwick Papers, No. 29 (York, 1966).

The Wool Accounts of William de la Pole, St Anthony's Hall Publications, No. 25 (York, 1964).

George, R. H. 'The Contribution of Flanders to the Conquest of England 1065–1086', *Rev. Belge*, 5 (1926).

Graham, R. *English Ecclesiastical Studies* (London, 1929).

Gras, N. S. B. *The Early English Customs System* (Cambridge, Mass., 1926).

Grierson, P. 'Relations between England and Flanders before the Norman Conquest', *TRHS*, ser. 4, 23 (1941).

Hanham, A. 'Foreign Exchange and the English Wool Merchant in the late Fifteenth Century', *Bulletin of the Institute of Historical Research*, 46 (1973).

Hanham, A. '"Make a Careful Examination": Some Fraudulent Accounts in the Cely Papers', *Speculum*, 48 (1973).

Harriss, G. L. 'The Struggle for Calais: An Aspect of the Rivalry between Lancaster and York', *EHR*, 75 (1960).

King, Parliament and Public Finance in Medieval England to 1369 (Oxford, 1975).

Haskins, G. L. 'Three Early Petitions of the Commonalty', *Speculum*, 12 (1937), p. 316.

Hilton, R. H. *The English Peasantry in the Later Middle Ages* (Oxford, 1975).

A Medieval Society (London, 1966).

A History of Technology, II, ed. C. Singer (Oxford, 1956).

Holmes, G. A. 'Florentine Merchants in England, 1340–1436', *EcHR*, ser. 2, 13 (1960).

The Good Parliament (Oxford, 1975).

'The "Libel of English Policy"', *EHR*, 76 (1961).

Hughes, D. *A Study of Social and Constitutional Tendencies in the Early Years of Edward III* (London, 1915).

Jenkinson, H. 'William Cade, a Financier of the Twelfth Century', *EHR*, 28 (1913).

Kaeuper, R. W. *Bankers to the Crown* (Princeton, N. J., 1973).

'The Frescobaldi of Florence and the English Crown', *Studies in Medieval and Renaissance History*, 10 (1973).

Kerling, N. J. M. 'Abrekening van de Engelse Koopman Reginald de Conducto Bettreffende de Onkosten Gemaakt voor Veroer en Berging van Engelse Wol Naar in Dordrecht (1335–1338)', *Bijdragen en Medellingen van het Historisch Genootschap*, 68 (1953).

Commercial Relations of Holland and Zeeland with England from the late Thirteenth Century to the Close of the Middle Ages (Leyden, 1954).

Kirby, J. L. 'The Financing of Calais under Henry V', *Bulletin of the Institute of Historical Research*, 23 (1950).

Langlois, C. V. 'Project for Taxation Presented to Edward I', *EHR* 4 (1891).

Laurent, H. *Un grand commerce d'exportation au moyen-âge. La draperie des Pays-Bas en France et dans les Pays Mediterranéens, XII*ᵉ–XV*ᵉ siècle* (Paris, 1935).

Lloyd, T. H. *The Movement of Wool Prices in Medieval England*, Economic History Review, Supplement 6 (Cambridge 1973).

Lucas, H. C. 'Diplomatic Relations between England and Flanders from 1329 to 1336', *Speculum*, 11 (1936).

Lunt, W. E. *Financial Relations of the Papacy with England to 1327* (Cambridge, Mass., 1939).

Mallett, M. E. 'Anglo-Florentine Commercial Relations, 1465–91', *EcHR*, ser. 2, 15 (1962).

The Florentine Galleys in the Fifteenth Century (Oxford, 1967).

Mate, M. 'High Prices in Early Fourteenth-Century England: Causes and Consequences', *EcHR*, ser. 2, 28 (1975).

McKisack, M. *The Fourteenth Century* (Oxford, 1959).

Miller, E. 'The Fortunes of the English Textile Industry in the Thirteenth Century', *EcHR*, ser. 2, 18 (1965).

Miller, F, 'The Middelburg Staple, 1383–88', *Cambridge Historical Journal*, 2 (1926–8).

Munro, J. H. A. *Wool, Cloth and Gold: The Struggle for Bullion in Anglo-Burgundian Trade, 1340–1478* (Toronto, 1973).

Nicholas, D. *Town and Countryside: Social and Political Tensions in Fourteenth-Century Flanders* (Bruges, 1971).

Oakley, A. M. 'The Establishment of the Calais Staple (1363)', unpublished MA thesis (Leeds, 1959).

Pelham, R. A. 'The exportation of Wool from Sussex in the late Thirteenth Century', *Sussex Archaeological Collections*, 74 (1933).

Pirenne, H. *Les Villes et les Institutions Urbaines* (Paris–Brussels, 1939).

Poole, A. L. *From Domesday Book to Magna Carta* (Oxford, 1951).

Postan, M. M. *Medieval Trade and Finance* (Cambridge, 1973).

'Village Livestock in the Thirteenth Century', *EcHR*, ser. 2, 15 (1962).

Powell, W. R. 'The Administration of the Navy and the Stannaries', *EHR*, 71 (1956).

Power, E. 'The English Wool Trade in the Reign of Edward IV', *Cambridge Historical Journal*, 2 (1926–8).

The Wool Trade in English Medieval History (Oxford, 1941).

Powicke, M. *The Thirteenth Century* (Oxford, 1953).

Prestwich, M. 'Edward I's Monetary Policies and their Consequences', *EcHR*, ser. 2, 22 (1969).

War, Politics and Finance under Edward I (London 1972).

Re, E. 'La Compagnia dei Ricciardi in Inghilterra e il suo fallimento alla fine del secolo XIII', *Archivio della Societa Romana di Storia Patria*, 37 (1914).

Reddaway, T. F. 'The King's Mint and Exchange in London, 1343–1543', *EHR*, 82 (1967).

Reid, W. A. 'The Scots and the staple ordinance of 1313', *Speculum*, 34 (1959).

Renouard, Y. 'Les Cahorsins, Hommes D'affaires Française du XIIIᵉ siècle', *TRHS*, ser. 5, 11 (1961).

Reynolds, R. L. 'Merchants of Arras and the overland trade with Genoa', *Rev. Belge*, 9 (1930.

'Some English settlers in Genoa in the late twelfth century', *EcHR*, 4 (1932–4).

'The market for northern textiles in Genoa, 1179–1200', *Rev. Belge*, 5 (1926).

Rich, E. E. 'The Mayors of the Staples', *Cambridge Historical Journal*, 4 (1932–4).

Rothwell, H. 'The Confirmation of the Charters, 1297', *EHR*, 60 (1945).

Roskell, J. S. *The Commons and their Speakers in the English Parliaments, 1376–1523* (Manchester, 1963).

Ruddock, A. A. *Italian Merchants and Shipping in Southampton, 1270–1600* (Southampton, 1951).

Ruding, R. *Annals of the Coinage of Great Britain*, 1 (London, 1817).

Sabbe, E. 'Les relations économique entre l'Angleterre et le Continent au Haut Moyen Age', *Le Moyen Age*, ser. 4, 5 (1950).

Sawyer, P. H. 'The Wealth of England in the Eleventh Century', *TRHS*, ser. 5, 15 (1965).

Sayles, G. O. 'The "English Company" of 1343 and a Merchant's Oath', *Speculum*, 6 (1931).

'The Seizure of Wool at Easter 1297', *EHR*, 67 (1952).

Schaube, A. 'Die Wollausfuhr Englands vom Jahre 1273', *VJSSWG*, 8 (1908).

Spufford, P. *Monetary Problems and Policies in the Burgundian Netherlands, 1433–1496* (Leiden, 1970).

Steel, A. *Richard II* (Cambridge, 1941).

Studi in Onore di Amando Sapori (Milan, 1957).

Studies in English Trade in the Fifteenth Century, ed. E. Power and M. M. Postan (London, 1933).

Studies in London History, ed. R. E. J. Hollaender and W. Kellaway (London, 1969).

Studies Presented to E. T. Leeds, ed. D. B. Harden (London, 1956).

Tatlock, J. S. P. 'The English Journey of the Laon Canons', *Speculum*, 8 (1933).

Terry, S. B. *The Financing of the Hundred Years War* (London, 1914).

Thielemanns, M. *Bourgogne et Angleterre: Relations Politiques et Économiques entre les Pays-Bas Bourguignons et L'Angleterre, 1435–67* (Brussels, 1966).

Thrupp, S. 'The Grocers of London, a Study of the Distributive Trade', *Studies in English Overseas Trade in the Fifteenth Century*.

Tout, T. F. *The Place of the Reign of Edward II in English History* (Manchester, 1914).

Treharne, R. F. *The Baronial Plan of Reform* (Manchester, 1932).

Váczy, P. *La transformation de la technique et de l'organisation de l'industrie textile en Flandre aux XIᵉ–XIIIᵉ siècles*, Studia Historica Academiae Scientiarum Hungaricae, 48 (Budapest, 1960).

Varenbergh, E. *Histoire des Relations Diplomatiques entre le Comté de Flandre et L'Angleterre au Moyen Age* (Brussels, 1874).

van Werveke, H. 'Currency Manipulation in the Middle Ages: the Case of Louis de Mâle, Count of Flanders', *TRHS*, ser. 4, 31 (1949).

'Industrial Growth in the Middle Ages: The Cloth Industry in Flanders', *EcHR*, ser. 2, 6 (1954).

'Les Statuts Latins et les Statuts Française de la Hanse Flamande de Londres', *Bulletin de la Commission Royale d'Histoire*, 118 (1953).

Vaughan, R. *Philip the Good: the Apogee of Burgundy* (London, 1970).

Verhulst, A. 'La laine indigène dans les anciens Pays-Bas entre le XIIᵉ et le XVIIᵉ siècle', *Revue Historique*, 248 (1972).

Verlinden, Ch. 'Marchands ou Tisserands? A propos des Origines Urbaines', *Annales*, 27 (1972).

von Roon-Bassermann, E. 'Die ersten Florentiner Gesellschaften in England', *VJSSWG*, 39 (1952).

'Die Handelssperre Englands gegen Flandern, 1270–74, und die lizenzierte englische Wollausfuhr', *VJSSWG*, 50 (1963).

Watson, W. B. 'The Florentine Galley Trade with Flanders and England', *Rev. Belge*, 39 (1961).

Whitwell, R. J. 'Italian Bankers and the English Crown', *TRHS*, N.S. 17 (1903).

'English Monasteries and the Wool Trade in the 13th Century', *VJSSWG*, 2 (1904).

Wilkinson, B. *Studies in the Constitutional History of the Thirteenth and Fourteenth Centuries* (Manchester, 1937).

Willard, J. F. 'Inland Transportation in England during the Fourteenth Century', *Speculum*, 1 (1926).

Williams, G. A. *Medieval London* (London, 1963).

Wyffels, C. 'De Vlaamse Handel Op Engeland Voor Het Engels-Vlaams Konflict Van 1270–1274', *Bijdragen Voor De Geschiedenis Der Nederlanden*, 17 (1962–3).

Index

Printed in the United States
34388LVS00007B/40